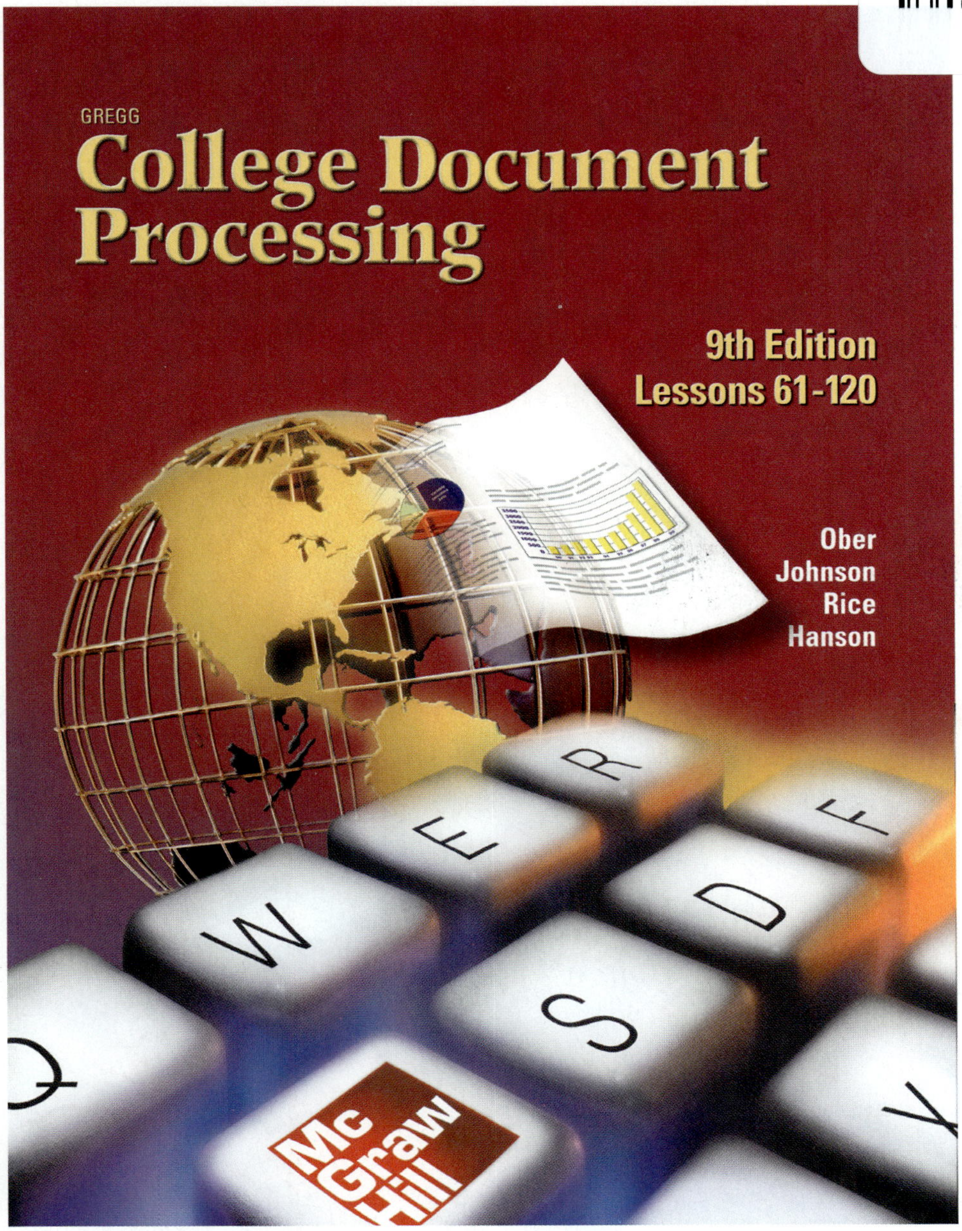

Scot Ober
Ball State University

Jack E. Johnson
State University of West Georgia

Arlene Rice
Los Angeles City College

Robert N. Hanson
Northern Michigan University

Visit the *College Keyboarding* Web site at **www.gdp.glencoe.com**

Glencoe McGraw-Hill

New York, New York   Columbus, Ohio   Woodland Hills, California   Peoria, Illinois

Glencoe/McGraw-Hill

A Division of The ***McGraw-Hill*** *Companies*

Gregg College Document Processing Lessons 61–120, 9th Edition

Send all inquiries to:
Glencoe/McGraw-Hill
21600 Oxnard Street, Suite 500
Woodland Hills, CA 91367

ISBN 0-07-825757-3

Printed in the United States of America.

3 4 5 6 7 8 9 027 06 05 04 03 02

REVIEWERS

Peggy Burrus
Red Rocks Community College
Lakewood, CO

Judy Ehresman
Mercer County Community College
Trenton, NJ

Mary Hanson
Northwest Technical College
East Grand Forks, MN

Rebecca Jones
Bladen Community College
Dublin, NC

Patricia King
Blackhawk Technical College
Janesville, WI

Barb Muchnok
Westmoreland County Community College
Youngwood, PA

Carolyn Seefer
Diablo Valley College
Pleasant Hill, CA

Pam Strong
Shelton State Community College
Tuscaloosa, AL

CONTENTS

About Keyboarding . . . xi
Preface . . . xii
Introduction . . . xiv
Before You Begin . . . xvi
About Your Book . . . xvii
Reference Manual . . . R1–R22

PART FOUR: Advanced Formatting

Unit 13 SKILL REFINEMENT . . . 214

61 Skillbuilding and Report Review . . . 215
Report 61-36: Business Report
Report 61-37: Multipage Academic Report With Footnotes
Report 61-38: Multipage Business Report With Footnote

62 Skillbuilding and Letter Review . . . 219
Correspondence 62-55: Personal-Business Letter in Block Style
Correspondence 62-56: Business Letter in Modified-Block Style
Correspondence 62-57: Business Letter in Block Style

63 Skillbuilding, Memo, and Email Review . . . 222
Correspondence 63-58: Memo With Attachment
Correspondence 63-59: Email Message
Correspondence 63-60: Memo With Attachment and Copy Notation
Correspondence 63-61: Memo

64 Skillbuilding and Table Review . . . 225
Table 64-23: Three-Column Boxed Table
Table 64-24: Three-Column Open Table
Table 64-25: Three-Column Ruled Table

65 Skillbuilding and Employment Document Review . . . 228
Report 65-39: Traditional Resume
Correspondence 65-62: Application Letter in Block Style With Enclosure Notation
Correspondence 65-63: Follow-Up Letter in Block Style

Unit 14 REPORTS . . . 231

66 Itineraries . . . 232
Report 66-40: Itinerary
Report 66-41: Itinerary
Report 66-42: Itinerary

67 Agendas and Minutes of Meetings . . . 236
Report 67-43: Agenda
Report 67-44: Agenda
Report 67-45: Minutes of a Meeting
Report 67-46: Minutes of a Meeting

68 Procedures Manual . . . 242
Report 68-47: Procedures Manual
Report 68-48: Procedures Manual
Report 68-49: Procedures Manual

69 Reports Formatted in Columns 246
Report 69-50: Magazine Article in Two Columns
Report 69-51: Magazine Article in Two Columns
Report 69-52: Magazine Article in Two Columns
70 Report Review 252
Report 70-53: Agenda
Report 70-54: Minutes of a Meeting
Report 70-55: Magazine Article in Two Columns

Unit 15 CORRESPONDENCE 256
71 Multipage Letters 257
Correspondence 71-64: Multipage Business Letter in Modified-Block Style With Enclosure Notation
Correspondence 71-65: Multipage Business Letter in Block Style With Copy Notation
Correspondence 71-66: Multipage Business Letter in Modified-Block Style With Enclosure Notation
72 Special Letter Features 261
Correspondence 72-67: Business Letter in Block Style With Subject Line and Copy Notation
Correspondence 72-68: Multipage Business Letter in Block Style With Multiple Addresses
Correspondence 72-69: Personal-Business Letter in Block Style With Subject Line
73 More Special Letter Features 267
Correspondence 73-70: Business Letter in Block Style With Open Table and Delivery and Blind Copy Notations
Correspondence 73-71: Business Letter in Block Style With Boxed Table and Delivery and Blind Copy Notations
Correspondence 73-72: Multipage Business Letter in Modified-Block Style With Enclosure, Delivery, and Postscript Notations
74 Multipage Memos With Tables 272
Correspondence 74-73: Multipage Memo With Open Table and Postscript Notation
Correspondence 74-74: Multipage Memo With Open Table and Postscript Notation
Correspondence 74-75: Memo With Boxed Table
75 Memo Reports 276
Report 75-56: Memo Report
Report 75-57: Memo Report
Report 75-58: Memo Report

Unit 16 TABLES 280
76 Tables With Footnotes or Source Notes 281
Table 76-26: Seven-Column Boxed Table With Table Note
Table 76-27: Seven-Column Boxed Table
Table 76-28: Six-Column Boxed Table With Source Note
77 Tables With Braced Column Headings 284
Table 77-29: Six-Column Boxed Table With Braced Column Headings
Table 77-30: Four-Column Boxed Table With Braced Column Headings
Table 77-31: Four-Column Boxed Table With Braced Column Headings

78 Tables Formatted Sideways 287
Table 78-32: Seven-Column Boxed Table in Landscape
Table 78-33: Seven-Column Boxed Table in Landscape
Table 78-34: Seven-Column Boxed Table in Landscape
79 Multipage Tables 291
Table 79-35: Multipage Four-Column Boxed Table
Table 79-36: Multipage Four-Column Boxed Table
Table 79-37: Five-Column Boxed Table in Landscape
80 Using Predesigned Table Formats 295
Table 80-38: Three-Column Table
Table 80-39: Three-Column Table With Table Note
Table 80-40: Four-Column Table

Test 4 SKILLS ASSESSMENT ON PART 4 299
Correspondence Test 4-76: Memo Report With Boxed Table
Correspondence Test 4-77: Business Letter in Block Style With Blind Copy and Postscript Notations
Table Test 4-41: Four-Column Boxed Table

PART FIVE: Specialized Applications

Unit 17 FORMAL REPORT PROJECT 304
81 Formal Report Project 305
Report 81-59: Report
82 Formal Report Project 309
Report 81-59: Report (continued)
83 Formal Report Project 313
Report 81-59: Report (continued)
84 Formal Report Project 316
Table 84-42: Three-Column Boxed Table
Report 81-59: Report (continued)
85 Formal Report Project 320
Report 85-60: Title Page
Report 85-61: Table of Contents
Report 85-62: Bibliography

Unit 18 INTERNATIONAL FORMATTING 323
86 International Formatting (Canada) 324
Correspondence 86-78: Business Letter in Modified-Block With Copy and Postscript Notations
Table 86-43: Five-Column Boxed Table in Landscape
Table 86-44: Five-Column Boxed Table in Landscape
87 International Formatting (Mexico) 330
Correspondence 87-79: Email Message
Report 87-63: Business Report With Four-Column Boxed Table
88 International Formatting (France) 335
Correspondence 88-80: Business Letter in Block Style With Enclosure and Copy Notations
Table 88-45: Three-Column Boxed Table
Correspondence 88-81: Email Message
89 International Formatting (Germany) 339
Correspondence 89-82: Email Message
Correspondence 89-83: Business Letter in Block Style
Report 89-64: Multipage Report in Business Style

90 International Formatting (Japan) 344
Correspondence 90-84: Business Letter in Block Style With Copy Notations
Correspondence 90-85: Email Message
Correspondence 90-86: Business Letter in Block Style With Illustration and Copy Notation
Table 90-46: Two-Column Boxed Table
Correspondence 90-87: Business Letter in Block Style With Enclosure Notation

Unit 19 MEDICAL OFFICE APPLICATIONS 348

91 Medical Office Applications 349
Correspondence 91-88: Business Letter in Block Style With Enclosure Notation
Table 91-47: Three-Column Boxed Table With Shaded Cells
Correspondence 91-89: Memo With Copy Notation

92 Medical Office Applications 353
Report 92-65: Multipage Business Report
Table 92-48: Five-Column Boxed Table

93 Medical Office Applications 357
Correspondence 93-90: Business Letter in Modified-Block Style With Enclosure and Postscript Notations
Report 93-66: Multipage Business Report With Side and Paragraph Headings

94 Medical Office Applications 361
Table 94-49: Two-Column Open Table
Correspondence 94-91: Business Letter in Block Style With Subject Line
Table 94-50: Two-Column Boxed Table

95 Medical Office Applications 364
Table 95-51: Two-Column Boxed Table
Report 95-67: Business Report With Numbered and Bulleted Lists
Correspondence 95-92: Email Message
Correspondence 95-93: Memo With Copy Notations

Unit 20 LEGAL OFFICE APPLICATIONS 368

96 Legal Office Applications 369
Report 96-68: Affadavit of Possession
Correspondence 96-94: Business Letter in Block Style With Enclosure and Copy Notations

97 Legal Office Applications 373
Report 97-69: Warranty Deed
Table 97-52: Two-Column Boxed Table
Correspondence 97-95: Email Message

98 Legal Office Applications 377
Report 98-70: Summons
Correspondence 98-96: Memo With Enclosure and Copy Notations
Table 98-53: Four-Column Boxed Table

99 Legal Office Applications 382
Report 99-71: Last Will and Testament
Correspondence 99-97: Business Letter in Block Style With Subject Line, Bulleted List, Enclosure, and Copy Notations

100 Legal Office Applications 386
Report 100-72: Complaint
Report 100-73: Judgment
Report 100-74: Affadavit

Test 5 Skills Assessment on Part 5 392
Correspondence Test 5-98: Business Letter in Block Style With Copy Notations
Table Test 5-54: Two-Column Boxed Table
Report Test 5-75: Summons

PART SIX: Using and Designing Business Documents

Unit 21 USING AND DESIGNING OFFICE FORMS 398
101 Using Correspondence Templates 399
Form 101-1: Memo Template
Form 101-2: Letter Template With Enclosure Notation
Form 101-3: Memo Template With Attachment Notation
102 Using Report Templates 403
Form 102-4: Report Template
Form 102-5: Report Template
103 Designing Letterheads 408
Form 103-6: Letterhead Form
Form 103-7: Letterhead Form
Form 103-8: Letterhead Form
104 Designing Notepads 412
Form 104-9: Notepad Form
Form 104-10: Notepad Form
Form 104-11: Notepad Form
105 Designing Miscellaneous Office Forms 417
Form 105-12: Directory Form
Form 105-13: Sign-In Form
Form 105-14: Memo Template With Attachment Notation

Unit 22 DESIGNING OFFICE PUBLICATIONS 421
106 Designing Cover Pages 422
Report 106-76: Cover Page
Report 106-77: Cover Page
Report 106-78: Cover Page
107 Designing Announcements and Flyers 426
Report 107-79: Announcement
Report 107-80: Flyer
Report 107-81: Announcement or Flyer
108 Designing Newsletters: A 431
Report 108-82: Newsletter
Report 108-83: Newsletter
109 Designing Newsletters: B 434
Report 109-84: Newsletter (continued)
Report 109-85: Newsletter
110 Designing Newsletters: C 439
Report 110-86: Newsletter (continued)
Report 110-87: Flyer

Unit 23 Designing Web Pages 444
111 Creating, Saving, and Viewing Web pages 445
Report 111-88: Web Site
Report 111-89: Your Web Site
112 Creating Frames 449
Report 112-90: Web Site (continued)
Report 112-91: Your Web Site (continued)

113 Creating and Saving More Web Pages 453
Report 113-92: Web Site (continued)
Report 113-93: Web Site (continued)
Report 113-94: Your Web Site (continued)
Report 113-95: Your Web Site (continued)
114 Creating Web Pages With Hyperlinks 457
Report 114-96: Web Site (continued)
Report 114-97: Web Site (continued)
Report 114-98: Your Web Site (continued)
Report 114-99: Your Web Site (continued)
115 Formatting Web Pages 462
Report 115-100: Web Site (continued)
Report 115-101: Web Site

Unit 24 Skillbuilding and In-Basket Review 468
116 In-Basket Review 469
Form 116-15: Letter Template With Enclosure Notation
Table 116-55: Three-Column Boxed Table
Form 116-16: Letterhead Form
117 In-Basket Review (Hospitality) 473
Report 117-102: Web Site
Report 107-103: Web Site
118 In-Basket Review (Retail) 477
Form 118-17: Memo Template
Report 118-104: Agenda
Report 118-105: Cover Page
119 In-Basket Review (Government) 481
Correspondence 119-99: Business Letter in Block Style With Postscript Notation
Correspondence 119-100: Business Letter in Block Style With Postscript Notation
Correspondence 119-101: Email Message
120 In-Basket Review (Manufacturing) 485
Report 120-106: Multipage Business Report
Correspondence 120-102: Multipage Business Letter in Block Style With Three-Column Boxed Table

Test 6 SKILLS ASSESSMENT ON PART 6 490
Form Test 6-18: Memo Template With Attachment Notation
Report Test 6-107: Web Page
Report Test 6-108: Flyer

SKILLBUILDING
Diagnostic Practice: Alphabet SB2–SB4
Diagnostic Practice: Numbers SB5–SB6
Progressive Practice: Alphabet SB7–SB10
Progressive Practice: Numbers SB11–SB13
Paced Practice SB14–SB27
Supplementary Timings SB28–SB36

APPENDIX
Ten-Key Numeric Keypad A1–A3

INDEX I1–I8

About Keyboarding

Each day the world becomes more and more technologically advanced. As a result, learning new skills for the world of work is even more important.

One such skill that can prepare you for virtually any job in the world is keyboarding. From accountants to zoologists and every occupation in between, the ability to quickly and accurately type information is an essential skill that can increase your chances of being hired (or getting your dream job).

Formerly referred to as "typing," keyboarding is the act of entering data by means of designated computer keys. Today, as we rely more and more on computers to handle everyday work and leisure activities, the art of accurately conveying information is a necessity. So whether you are emailing a relative, developing a class presentation, or downloading map directions, keyboarding knowledge can make the job easier.

Preface

Gregg College Keyboarding & Document Processing Lessons 1–120, 9th Edition, is a multi-component instructional program designed to give the student and the instructor a high degree of flexibility and a high degree of success in meeting their respective goals. For student and instructor convenience, the core components of this instructional system are available in either a kit format or a book format. *Gregg College Keyboarding Lessons 1–20, 5th Edition*, is also available for the development of touch-typing skills for use in shorter computer keyboarding classes.

THE KIT FORMAT

Gregg College Keyboarding & Document Processing Lessons 1–120, 9th Edition, provides a complete kit of materials for both courses in the keyboarding curriculum generally offered by colleges. Each kit, which is briefly described below, contains a softcover textbook and a student word processing manual.

Kit 1: Lessons 1–60. This kit provides the text and word processing manual for the first course. Since this kit is designed for the beginning student, its major objectives are to develop touch control of the keyboard and proper typing techniques, to build basic speed and accuracy, and to provide practice in applying those basic skills to the formatting of letters, reports, tables, memos, and other kinds of personal and business communications.

Kit 2: Lessons 61–120. This kit provides the text and word processing manual for the second course. This course continues the development of basic typing skills and emphasizes the formatting of various kinds of business correspondence, reports, tables, electronic forms, and desktop publishing projects from unarranged and rough-draft sources.

THE BOOK FORMAT

For the convenience of those who wish to obtain the core instructional materials in separate volumes, *Gregg College Keyboarding & Document Processing Lessons 1–120, 9th Edition*, offers textbooks for the first course: *Gregg College Keyboarding & Document Processing Lessons 1–60, 9th Edition,* or *Gregg College Keyboarding Lessons 1–20, 5th Edition*. For the second course, *Gregg College Document Processing Lessons 61–120* is offered, and for the two-semester course, *Gregg College Keyboarding & Document Processing Lessons 1–120* is available. In each instance, the content of the textbooks is identical to that of the corresponding textbooks in kit format. Third semester instruction is available in *Gregg College Document Processing Lessons 121–180.*

SUPPORTING MATERIALS

Gregg College Keyboarding & Document Processing Lessons 1–120, 9th Edition, includes the following additional components:

Instructional Materials. Supporting materials are provided for instructor use with either the kits or the textbooks. The special Instructor Wraparound Edition offers lesson plans and reduced-size student pages to enhance classroom instruction. Distance learning tips, instructional methodology, adult learner strategies, and special needs features are also included in this wraparound edition. Solution keys for all of the formatting exercises in Lessons 1–180 are contained in separate booklets used with this program. Finally, test booklets are available with the objective test formats and alternative document processing tests for each part.

Computer Software. IBM-compatible computer software is available for the entire program. The computer software provides a complete instructional system.

STRUCTURE

Gregg College Keyboarding & Document Processing, 9th Edition, opens with a two-page part opener that introduces students to the focus of the instruction. Objectives are presented, and opportunities within career clusters are highlighted. The unit opener familiarizes students with the lesson content to be presented in the five lessons for the unit.

Every lesson begins with a *Warmup* that should be typed as soon as students are settled at the keyboard. Drill lines in this section provide the practice necessary to achieve keyboarding skills.

An easily identifiable *Skillbuilding* section can be found in every lesson. Each drill presents to the student a variety of different activities designed to improve speed and accuracy. Skillbuilding exercises include Technique Timings, Diagnostic Practices, Paced Practices, MAP (Misstroke Analysis and Prescription), and Timings that progress from 1 to 5 minutes in length.

Many of the skillbuilding sections also include a *Pretest, Practice,* and *Posttest* routine. This routine is designed to build speed and accuracy skills as well as confidence. The Pretest helps identify speed and accuracy needs. The Practice activities consist of a variety of intensive enrichment drills. Finally, the Posttest measures improvement.

Introduction

GOALS

- Type at least 28wpm/2′/5e
- Format simple reports

STARTING A LESSON

Each lesson begins with the goals for that lesson. Read the goals carefully so that you understand the purpose of your practice. In the example at the left, the goals for the lesson are to type 28wpm (words per minute) on a 2-minute timing with no more than 5 errors and to format simple reports.

BUILDING STRAIGHT-COPY SKILL

Warmups. Each lesson begins with a warmup that reinforces learned alphabet, number, and/or symbol keys.

Skillbuilding. The skillbuilding portion of each lesson includes a variety of drills to individualize your keyboarding speed and accuracy development. Instructions for completing the drills are always provided beside each activity.

Additional skillbuilding drills are included in the back of the textbook. These drills are used to help you meet your individual goals.

MEASURING STRAIGHT-COPY SKILL

Straight-copy skill is measured in wpm (words per minute). All timings are the exact length needed to meet the speed goal for the lesson. If you finish a timing before time is up, you have automatically reached your speed goal for the lesson.

Counting Errors. Specific criteria are used for counting errors. Count an error when:

1. Any stroke is incorrect.
2. Any punctuation after a word is incorrect or omitted. Count the word before the punctuation as incorrect.
3. The spacing after a word or after its punctuation is incorrect. Count the word as incorrect.
4. A letter or word is omitted.
5. A letter or word is repeated.
6. A direction about spacing, indenting, and so on, is violated.
7. Words are transposed.

(**Note:** Only one error is counted for each word, no matter how many errors it may contain.)

Determining Speed. Typing speed is measured in words per minute (wpm). To compute wpm, count every 5 strokes, including spaces, as 1 "word." Horizontal word scales below an activity divide lines into 5-stroke words. Vertical word scales beside an activity show the number of words in each line cumulatively totaled. For example, in the illustration shown, if you complete a line, you have typed 8 words. If you complete 2 lines, you have typed 16 words. Use the bottom word scale to determine the word count of a partial line. Add that number to the cumulative total for the last complete line.

```
23 Ada lost her letter; Dee lost her card.        8
24 Dave sold some of the food to a market.       16
25 Alva asked Walt for three more matches.       24
26 Dale asked Seth to watch the last show.       32
   | 1 | 2 | 3 | 4 | 5 | 6 | 7 | 8 |
```

CORRECTING ERRORS

As you learn to type, you will probably make some errors. To correct an error, press **Backspace** (shown as ← on some keyboards) to delete the incorrect character. Then type the correct character.

If you notice an error on a different line, use the up, down, left, or right arrows to move the insertion point immediately to the left or right of the error. Press **Backspace** to delete a character to the left of the insertion point or **Delete** to delete a character to the right of the insertion point.

TYPING TECHNIQUE

Correct position at the keyboard enables you to type with greater speed and accuracy and with less fatigue. When typing for a long period, rest your eyes occasionally by looking away from the screen. Change position, walk around, or stretch when your muscles feel tired. Making such movements and adjustments may help prevent your body from becoming too tired. Additionally, long-term bodily damage, such as carpal tunnel syndrome, can be prevented.

If possible, adjust your workstation as follows:

Chair. Adjust the height so that your upper and lower legs form a 90-degree angle and your lower back is supported by the back of the chair.

Keyboard. Center your body opposite the J key, and lean forward slightly. Keep your forearms horizontal to the keyboard.

Screen. Position the monitor so that the top of the screen is just below eye level and about 18 to 26 inches away.

Text. Position your textbook or other copy on either side of the monitor as close to it as vertically and horizontally possible to minimize head and eye movement and to avoid neck strain.

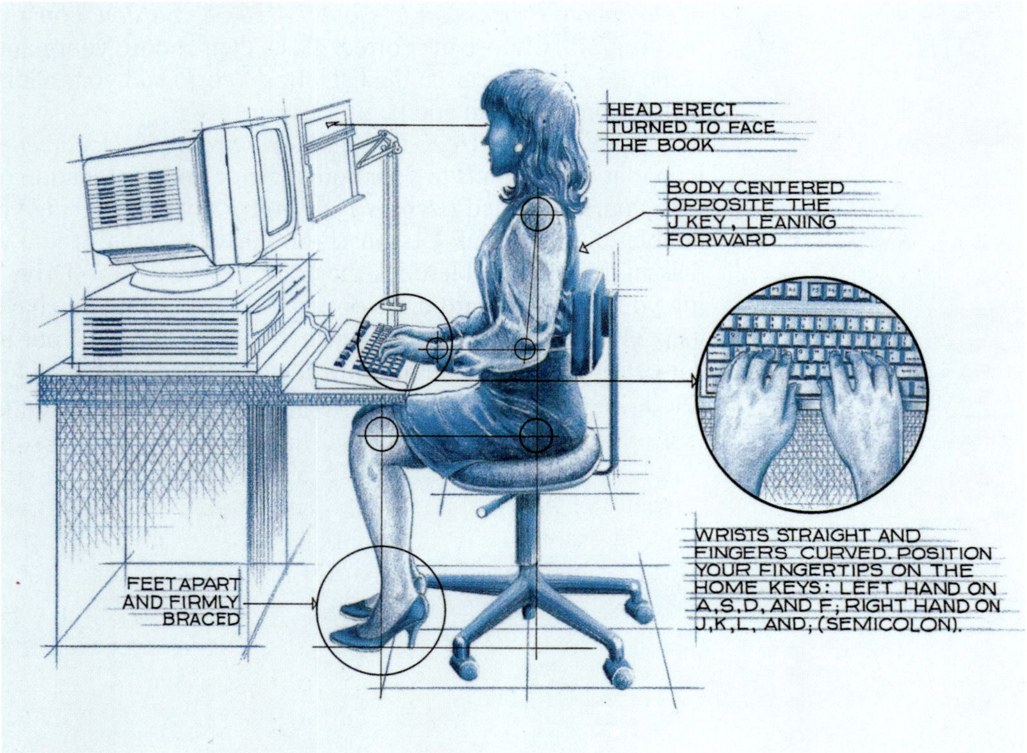

Before You Begin

USING MICROSOFT WINDOWS

If you are using *Gregg College Keyboarding & Document Processing Lessons 1–120, 9th Edition*, you must know how to use a mouse, and you must know some basic information about Microsoft Windows.

Before you begin Lesson 1, turn to the Introduction section in your word processing manual and read the information presented there. Note: If you are using the book with Lessons 1–20, then use Windows Help to familiarize yourself with Windows. You will learn how to navigate within a program and learn the skills you will need to use Windows.

Moving around, or navigating, within a program with a mouse involves pointing, clicking, double-clicking, and dragging.

Through Windows Help, you will learn the names and functions of the different parts of a window. You will want to pay close attention to the menu bar and command names as well as how to select options in a dialog box.

STARTING YOUR PROGRAM

Once you have completed the Introduction, you are ready to begin Lesson 1. If you are using the *Gregg College Keyboarding & Document Processing Lessons 1–120, 9th Edition,* software that is correlated with this textbook, you must first start Windows. To start the *Gregg College Keyboarding & Document Processing Lessons 1–120* software, in the Program Manager, locate the Glencoe Keyboarding group icon. Double-click the icon to open the group window. If you will be saving your data to a disk, insert your data disk into the correct drive before you continue.

In the Glencoe Keyboarding group window, if there is a *Gregg College Keyboarding & Document Processing Lessons 1–120, 9th Edition* icon, double-click that icon to start the program. Choose the correct class; then choose your name from the class list. If your name does not appear on the list, click *New* to add your name to the list. Then follow the instructions to log in and begin Lesson 1.

If there is no *Gregg College Keyboarding & Document Processing* icon, select the icon that corresponds to your course name and the location of your data. For example, if your course is called *Lessons 1–60* and you will be saving your data to a disk in drive A, double-click the GDP Lessons 1–60 (Drive A) icon. If you will be saving your data to a disk in drive B, double-click the GDP Lessons 1–60 (Drive B) icon. If you will be saving your data to a hard drive or network drive, you may have an icon specified for your use only. (If you are unsure of which icon to use, ask your instructor.) Double-click the correct program icon, and follow the on-screen directions to log in and begin Lesson 1.

About Your Book

Each **Part Opener** is a two-page spread that provides a list of the part objectives and a special feature that focuses on the use of your keyboarding skills in various career clusters.

PART 4

Advanced Formatting

OBJECTIVES

KEYBOARDING

- Type at least 43 words per minute on a 5-minute timing with no more than 5 errors.

LANGUAGE ARTS

- Refine proofreading skills and correctly use proofreaders' marks.
- Use capitals, punctuation, and grammar correctly.
- Improve composing and spelling skills.
- Recognize subject/verb agreement.

WORD PROCESSING

- Use the word processing commands necessary to complete the document processing activities.

DOCUMENT PROCESSING

- Format reports, multipage letters, multipage memos, and tables.

TECHNICAL

- Answer at least 90 percent of the questions correctly on an objective test.

212

KEYBOARDING IN ARTS, AUDIO, VIDEO TECHNOLOGY, AND COMMUNICATIONS SERVICES

Occupations in this cluster deal with organizing and communicating information to the public in various forms and media. This cluster includes jobs in radio and television broadcasting, journalism, motion pictures, the recording industry, the performing arts, multimedia publishing, and the entertainment services. Work as a book editor, computer artist, technical writer, radio announcer, news correspondent, and camera operator are just a few jobs within this cluster.

Qualifications and Skills

Strong oral and written communication skills and technical skills are necessary for anyone in communications and media. Without a doubt, enhancing keyboarding skill is extremely advantageous.

Working in the media requires creativity, talent, and accurate use of language. In journalism, being observant, thinking clearly, and seeing the significance of events are all of utmost importance. Announcers must have exceptional voices, excellent speaking skills, and a unique style. The ability to work under pressure is important in all areas of media.

213

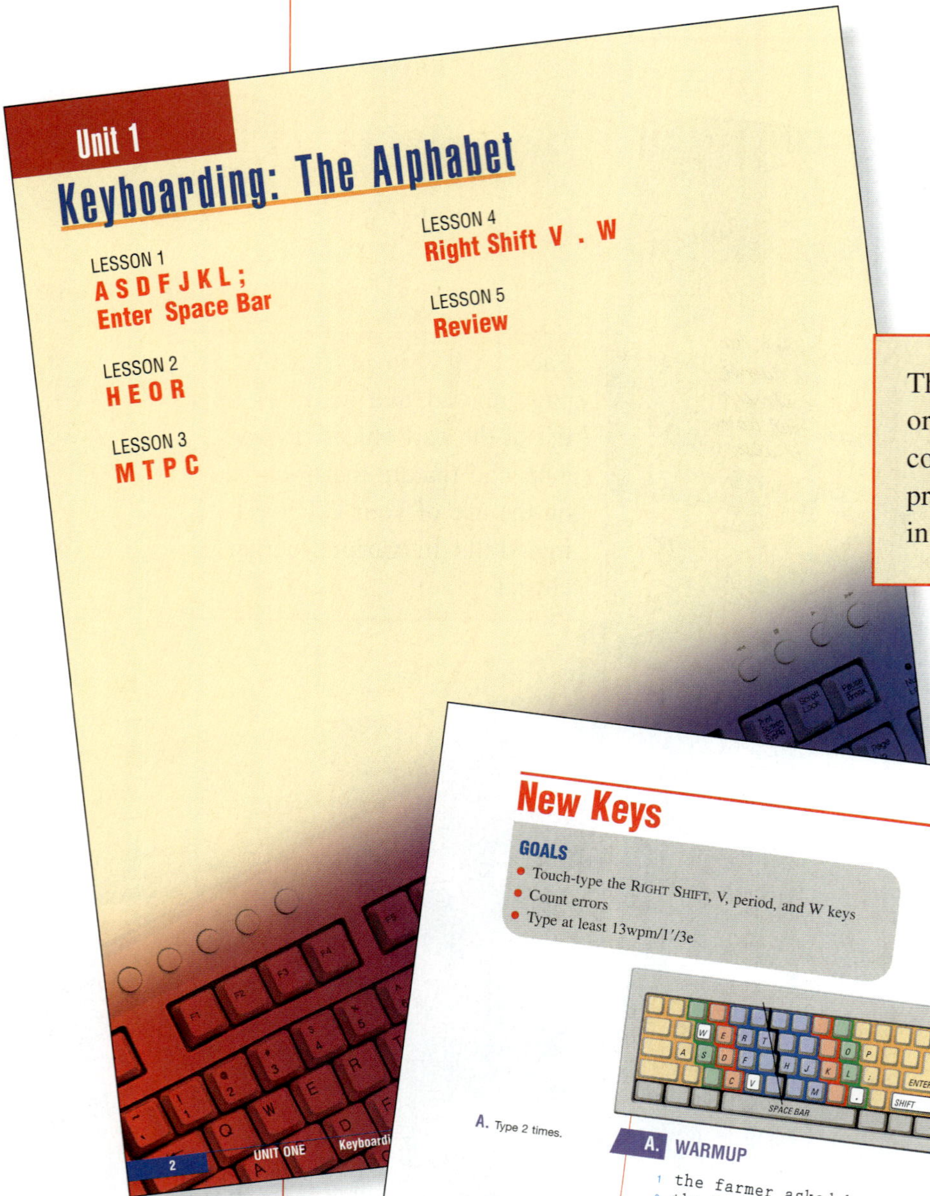

The **Unit Opener** helps you organize your study of unit concepts. The visual listing previews what will be taught in the unit.

Color Coding is used in the early lessons to let you easily differentiate which finger is used. On the keyboard chart shown at the beginning of each new-key lesson, new keys are highlighted, previously learned keys are labeled but not highlighted, and unlearned keys are blank. You will have a sense of progress as you move through the 20 new-key lessons.

Handwritten examples are used to make lessons more realistic since many letters, reports, etc., are originally conceived with pen and paper. Incorporating handwritten manuscript also enhances your ability to accurately read and type at the same time.

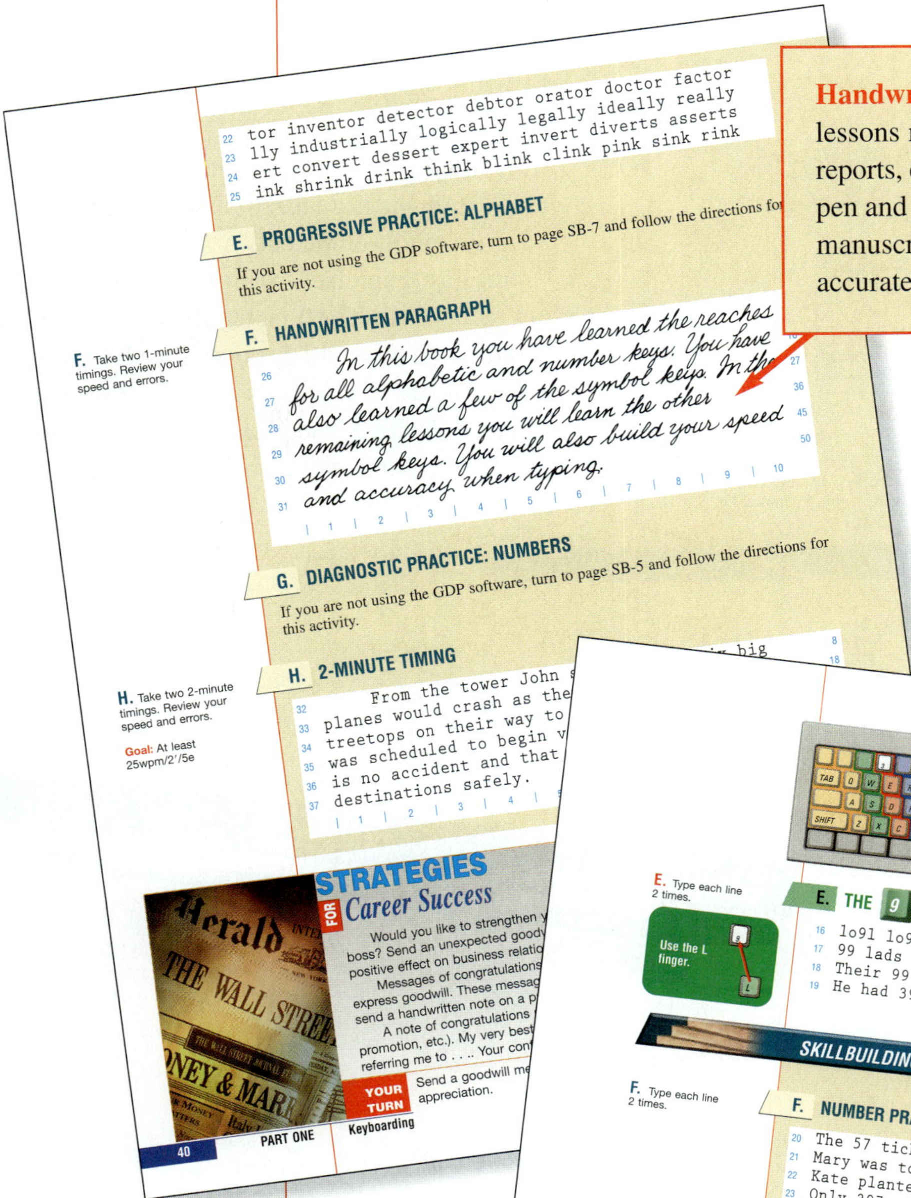

```
tor inventor detector debtor orator doctor factor
lly industrially logically legally ideally really
ert convert dessert expert invert diverts asserts
ink shrink drink think blink clink pink sink rink
```

E. PROGRESSIVE PRACTICE: ALPHABET

If you are not using the GDP software, turn to page SB-7 and follow the directions for this activity.

F. HANDWRITTEN PARAGRAPH

F. Take two 1-minute timings. Review your speed and errors.

In this book you have learned the reaches for all alphabetic and number keys. You have also learned a few of the symbol keys. In the remaining lessons you will learn the other symbol keys. You will also build your speed and accuracy when typing.

G. DIAGNOSTIC PRACTICE: NUMBERS

If you are not using the GDP software, turn to page SB-5 and follow the directions for this activity.

H. 2-MINUTE TIMING

H. Take two 2-minute timings. Review your speed and errors.

Goal: At least 25wpm/2'/5e

```
From the tower John s... big
planes would crash as the...
treetops on their way to...
was scheduled to begin v...
is no accident and that...
destinations safely.
```

STRATEGIES FOR Career Success

Would you like to strengthen y... boss? Send an unexpected good... positive effect on business relatio...

Messages of congratulations... express goodwill. These messag... send a handwritten note on a p...

A note of congratulations... promotion, etc.). My very best... referring me to . . .. Your con...

YOUR TURN Send a goodwill me... appreciation.

40 PART ONE Keyboarding

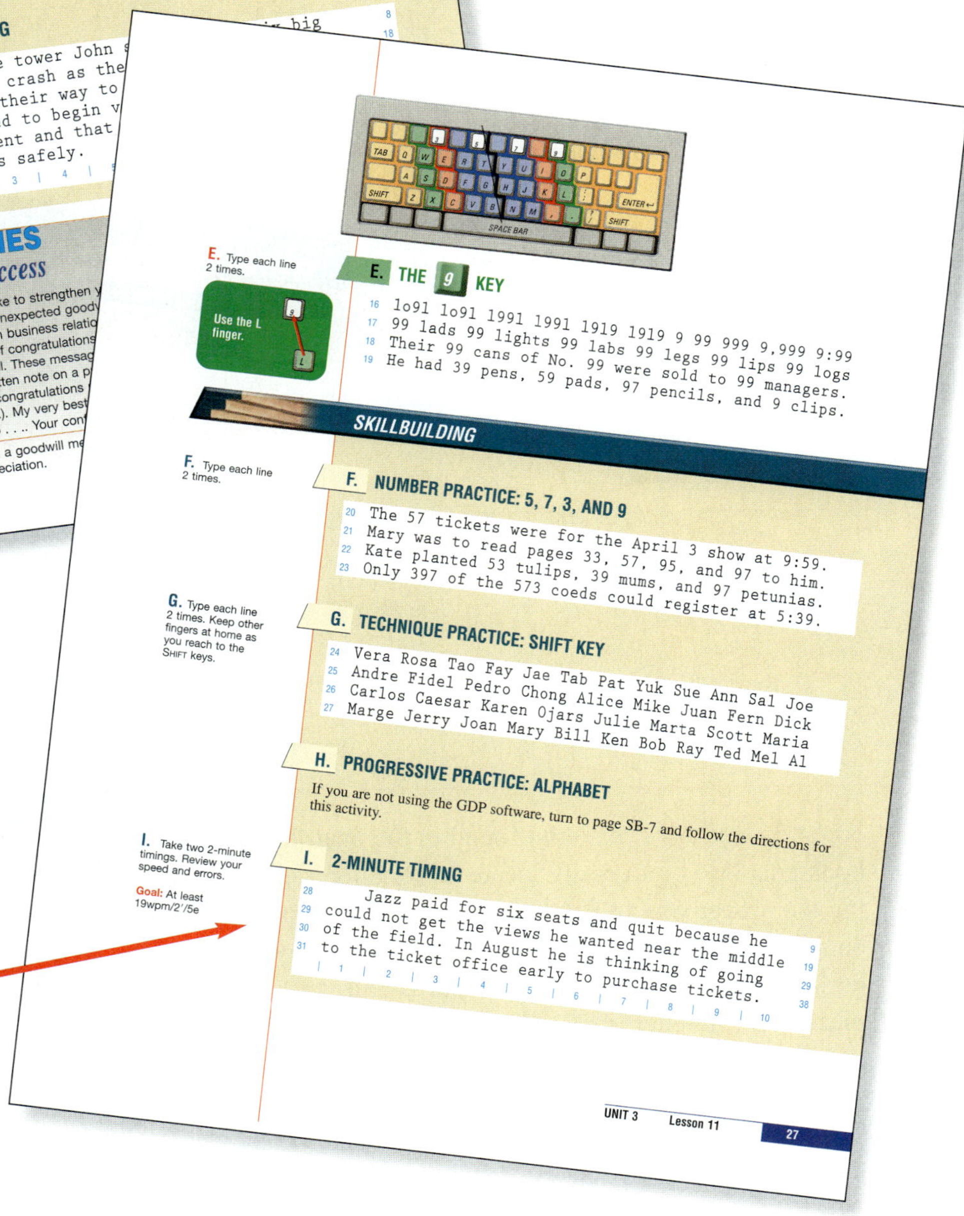

E. THE g KEY

E. Type each line 2 times.

Use the L finger.

```
lo91 lo91 1991 1991 1919 1919 9 99 999 9,999 9:99
99 lads 99 lights 99 labs 99 legs 99 lips 99 logs
Their 99 cans of No. 99 were sold to 99 managers.
He had 39 pens, 59 pads, 97 pencils, and 9 clips.
```

SKILLBUILDING

F. NUMBER PRACTICE: 5, 7, 3, AND 9

F. Type each line 2 times.

```
The 57 tickets were for the April 3 show at 9:59.
Mary was to read pages 33, 57, 95, and 97 to him.
Kate planted 53 tulips, 39 mums, and 97 petunias.
Only 397 of the 573 coeds could register at 5:39.
```

G. TECHNIQUE PRACTICE: SHIFT KEY

G. Type each line 2 times. Keep other fingers at home as you reach to the SHIFT keys.

```
Vera Rosa Tao Fay Jae Tab Pat Yuk Sue Ann Sal Joe
Andre Fidel Pedro Chong Alice Mike Juan Fern Dick
Carlos Caesar Karen Ojars Julie Marta Scott Maria
Marge Jerry Joan Mary Bill Ken Bob Ray Ted Mel Al
```

H. PROGRESSIVE PRACTICE: ALPHABET

If you are not using the GDP software, turn to page SB-7 and follow the directions for this activity.

I. 2-MINUTE TIMING

I. Take two 2-minute timings. Review your speed and errors.

Goal: At least 19wpm/2'/5e

```
Jazz paid for six seats and quit because he
could not get the views he wanted near the middle
of the field. In August he is thinking of going
to the ticket office early to purchase tickets.
```

UNIT 3 Lesson 11 27

Timings are used to improve both accuracy and speed. Timings measure how well you are progressing in keyboarding skill development. Additionally, timings bolster your self-confidence and ability.

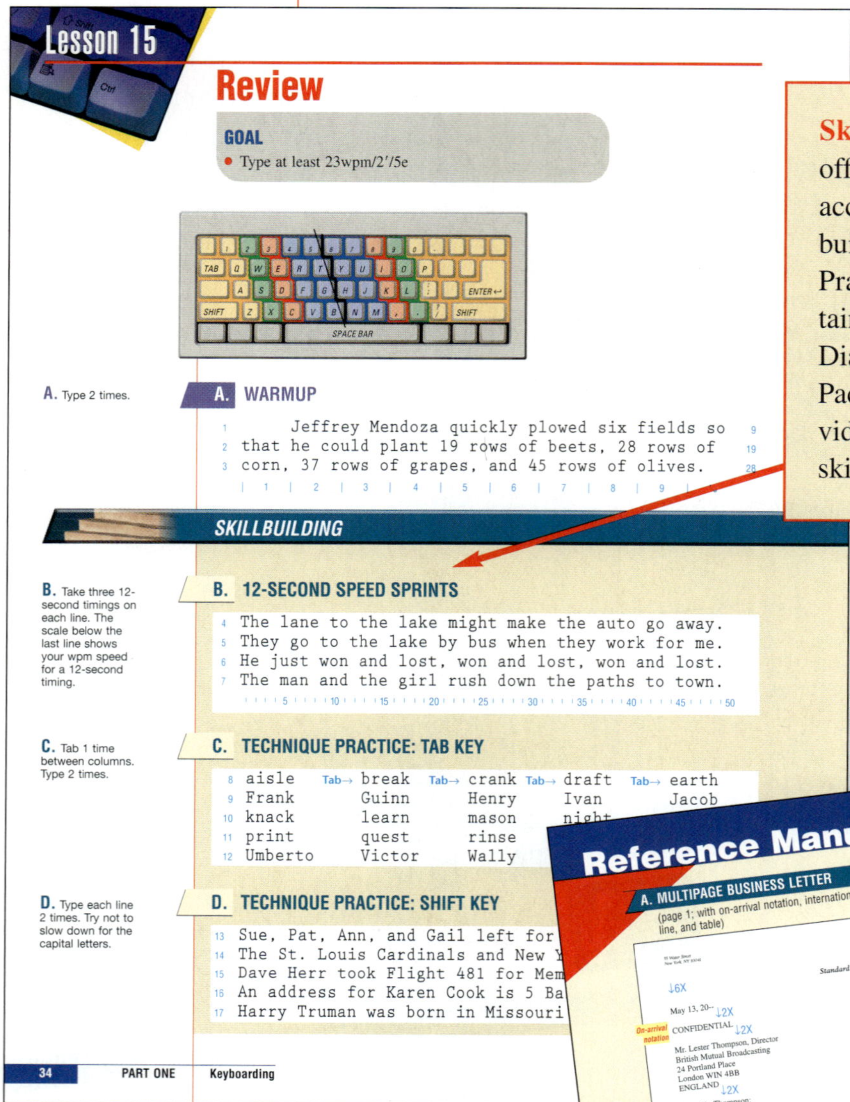
Lesson 15

Review

GOAL

- Type at least 23wpm/2′/5e

A. Type 2 times.

A. WARMUP

1 Jeffrey Mendoza quickly plowed six fields so 9
2 that he could plant 19 rows of beets, 28 rows of 19
3 corn, 37 rows of grapes, and 45 rows of olives. 28

SKILLBUILDING

B. Take three 12-second timings on each line. The scale below the last line shows your wpm speed for a 12-second timing.

B. 12-SECOND SPEED SPRINTS

4 The lane to the lake might make the auto go away.
5 They go to the lake by bus when they work for me.
6 He just won and lost, won and lost, won and lost.
7 The man and the girl rush down the paths to town.

C. Tab 1 time between columns. Type 2 times.

C. TECHNIQUE PRACTICE: TAB KEY

8 aisle Tab→ break Tab→ crank Tab→ draft Tab→ earth
9 Frank Guinn Henry Ivan Jacob
10 knack learn mason night
11 print quest rinse
12 Umberto Victor Wally

D. Type each line 2 times. Try not to slow down for the capital letters.

D. TECHNIQUE PRACTICE: SHIFT KEY

13 Sue, Pat, Ann, and Gail left for
14 The St. Louis Cardinals and New Y
15 Dave Herr took Flight 481 for Mem
16 An address for Karen Cook is 5 Ba
17 Harry Truman was born in Missouri

34 PART ONE Keyboarding

Skillbuilding practice in every lesson offers an individualized plan for speed and accuracy development. A variety of skill-building exercises, including Technique Practice, Pretest/Practice/Posttest, Sustained Practice, 12-Second Speed Sprints, Diagnostic Practice, Progressive Practice, Paced Practice, and Number Practice, provides the foundation for progress in your skill development.

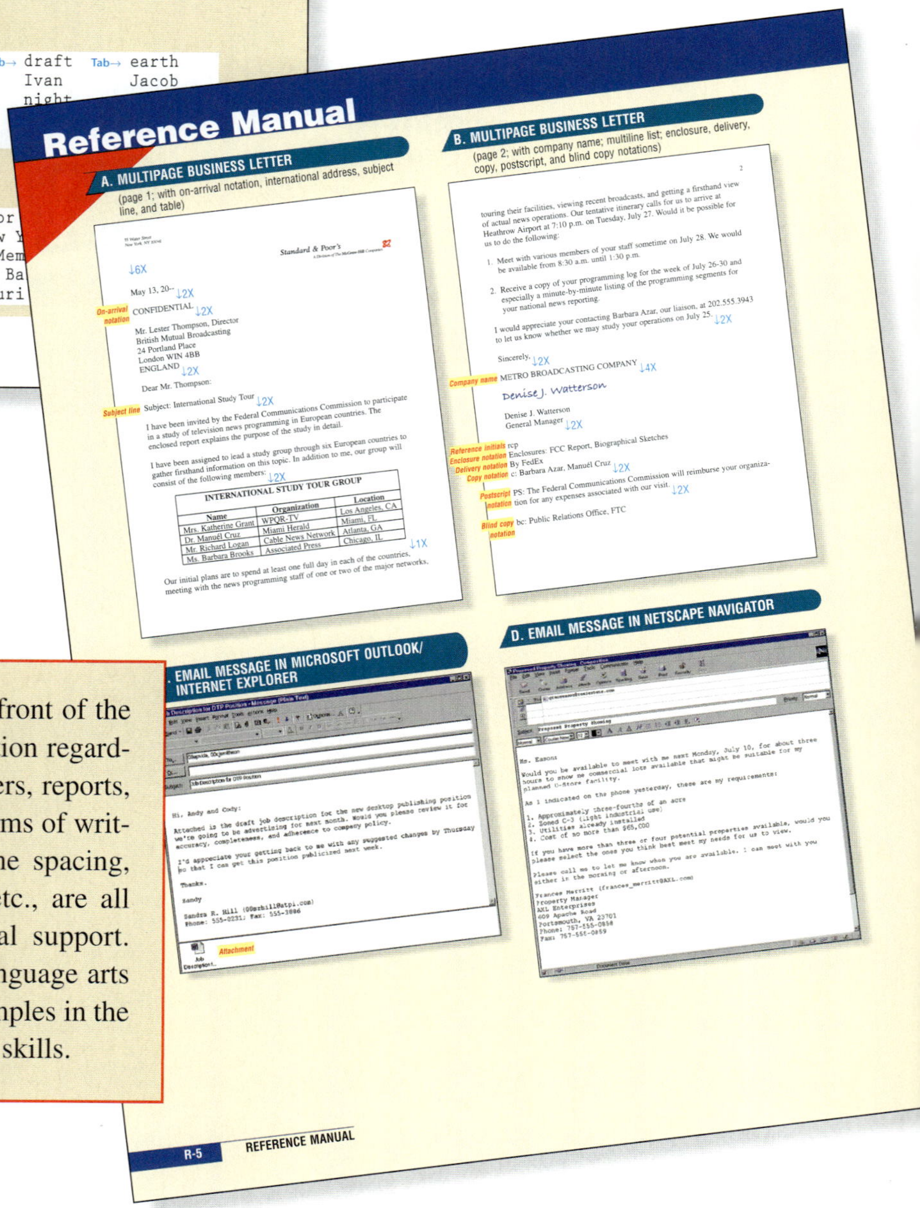
Reference Manual

A. MULTIPAGE BUSINESS LETTER (page 1; with on-arrival notation, international address, subject line, and table)

B. MULTIPAGE BUSINESS LETTER (page 2; with company name; multiline list; enclosure, delivery, copy, postscript, and blind copy notations)

C. EMAIL MESSAGE IN MICROSOFT OUTLOOK/INTERNET EXPLORER

D. EMAIL MESSAGE IN NETSCAPE NAVIGATOR

R-5 REFERENCE MANUAL

Reference Manual material found in the front of the book enables you to easily locate information regarding the proper way to format business letters, reports, email messages, memoranda, and other forms of written communication. Elements such as line spacing, placement of letterhead and body text, etc., are all illustrated in detail for your instructional support. Additionally, 50 "must-know" rules for language arts in business contexts are included with examples in the Reference Manual to help improve writing skills.

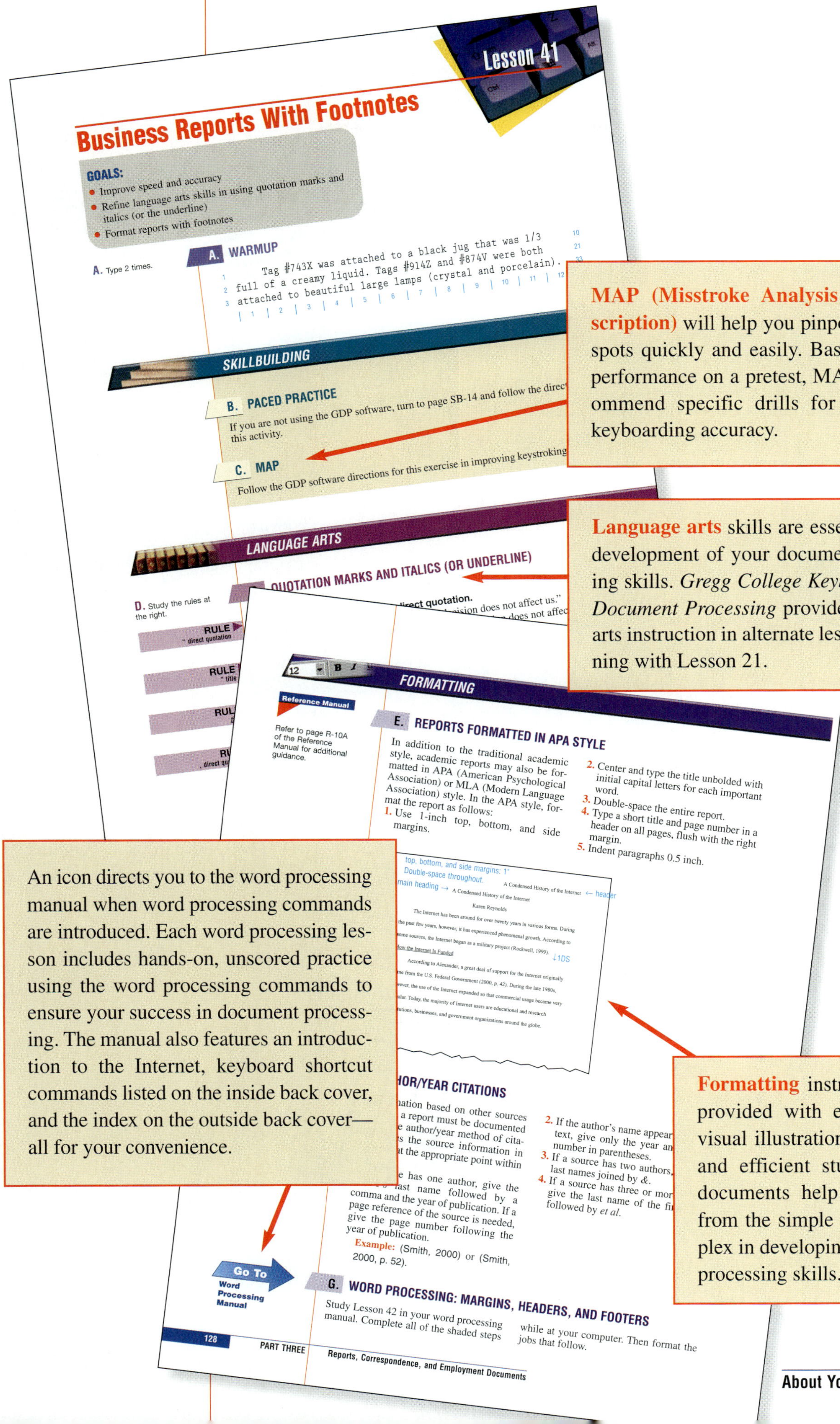
Lesson 41

Business Reports With Footnotes

GOALS:
- Improve speed and accuracy
- Refine language arts skills in using quotation marks and italics (or the underline)
- Format reports with footnotes

A. Type 2 times.

A. WARMUP

1 Tag #743X was attached to a black jug that was 1/3
2 full of a creamy liquid. Tags #914Z and #874V were both
3 attached to beautiful large lamps (crystal and porcelain).

SKILLBUILDING

B. PACED PRACTICE

If you are not using the GDP software, turn to page SB-14 and follow the directions for this activity.

C. MAP

Follow the GDP software directions for this exercise in improving keystroking

LANGUAGE ARTS

D. Study the rules at the right.

QUOTATION MARKS AND ITALICS (OR UNDERLINE)

FORMATTING

Reference Manual

Refer to page R-10A of the Reference Manual for additional guidance.

E. REPORTS FORMATTED IN APA STYLE

In addition to the traditional academic style, academic reports may also be formatted in APA (American Psychological Association) or MLA (Modern Language Association) style. In the APA style, format the report as follows:
1. Use 1-inch top, bottom, and side margins.
2. Center and type the title unbolded with initial capital letters for each important word.
3. Double-space the entire report.
4. Type a short title and page number in a header on all pages, flush with the right margin.
5. Indent paragraphs 0.5 inch.

Example: (Smith, 2000) or (Smith, 2000, p. 52).

Go To Word Processing Manual

G. WORD PROCESSING: MARGINS, HEADERS, AND FOOTERS

Study Lesson 42 in your word processing manual. Complete all of the shaded steps while at your computer. Then format the jobs that follow.

128 PART THREE Reports, Correspondence, and Employment Documents

MAP (Misstroke Analysis and Prescription) will help you pinpoint trouble spots quickly and easily. Based on your performance on a pretest, MAP will recommend specific drills for improving keyboarding accuracy.

Language arts skills are essential in the development of your document processing skills. *Gregg College Keyboarding & Document Processing* provides language arts instruction in alternate lessons beginning with Lesson 21.

An icon directs you to the word processing manual when word processing commands are introduced. Each word processing lesson includes hands-on, unscored practice using the word processing commands to ensure your success in document processing. The manual also features an introduction to the Internet, keyboard shortcut commands listed on the inside back cover, and the index on the outside back cover—all for your convenience.

Formatting instructions are provided with easy-to-read visual illustrations for quick and efficient study. Model documents help you move from the simple to the complex in developing document processing skills.

The last document processing exercise in most units is designated as a Progress Check/Proofreading Check. Make it your goal to have zero typographical errors when the GDP software first scores the document.

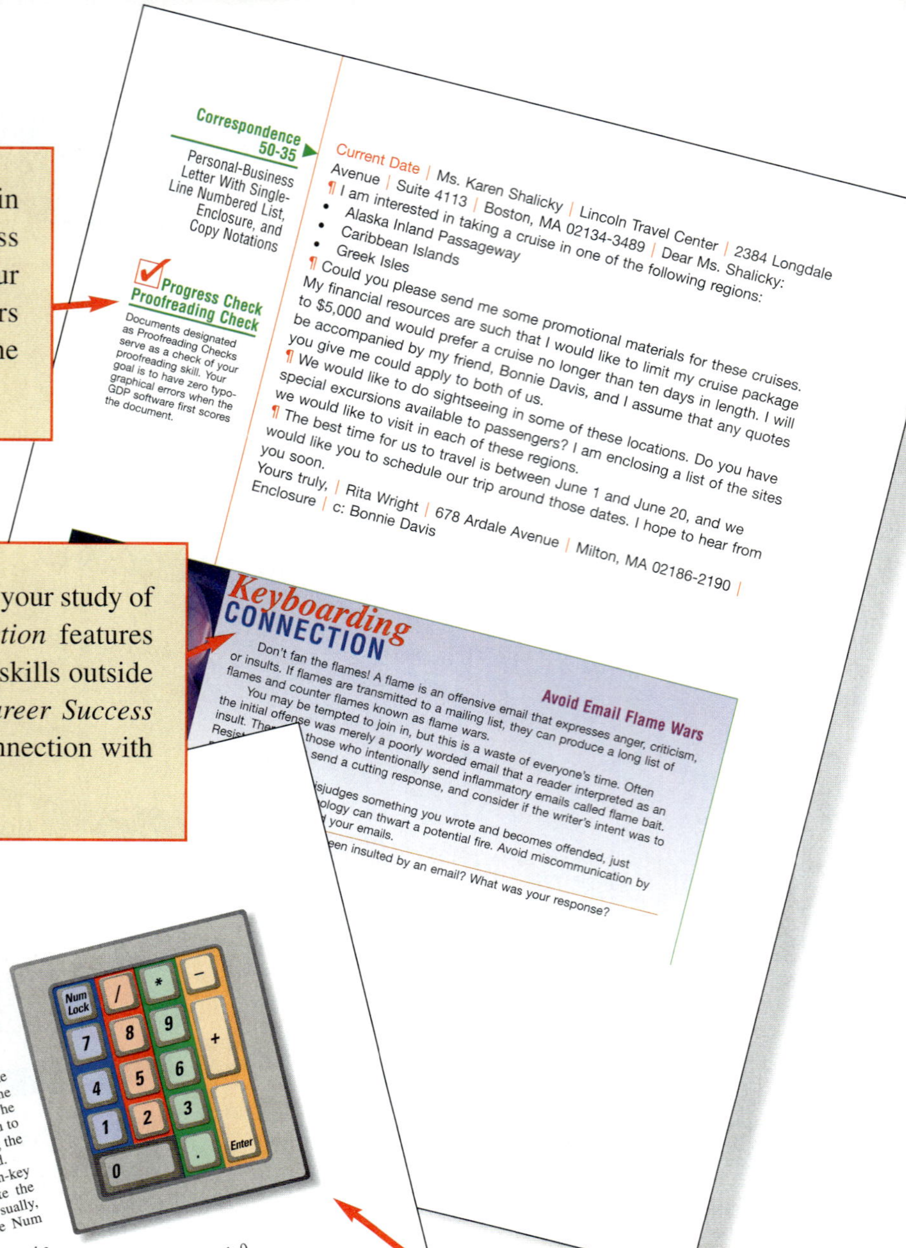
Correspondence 50-35

Personal-Business Letter With Single-Line Numbered List, Enclosure, and Copy Notations

Current Date | Ms. Karen Shalicky | Lincoln Travel Center | 2384 Longdale Avenue | Suite 4113 | Boston, MA 02134-3489 | Dear Ms. Shalicky:

¶ I am interested in taking a cruise in one of the following regions:

- Alaska Inland Passageway
- Caribbean Islands
- Greek Isles

¶ Could you please send me some promotional materials for these cruises. My financial resources are such that I would like to limit my cruise package to $5,000 and would prefer a cruise no longer than ten days in length. I will be accompanied by my friend, Bonnie Davis, and I assume that any quotes you give me could apply to both of us.

¶ We would like to do sightseeing in some of these locations. Do you have special excursions available to passengers? I am enclosing a list of the sites we would like to visit in each of these regions.

¶ The best time for us to travel is between June 1 and June 20, and we would like you to schedule our trip around those dates. I hope to hear from you soon.

Yours truly, | Rita Wright | 678 Ardale Avenue | Milton, MA 02186-2190 | Enclosure | c: Bonnie Davis

Progress Check / Proofreading Check

Documents designated as Proofreading Checks serve as a check of your proofreading skill. Your goal is to have zero typographical errors when the GDP software first scores the document.

Keyboarding CONNECTION

Avoid Email Flame Wars

Don't fan the flames! A flame is an offensive email that expresses anger, criticism, or insults. If flames are transmitted to a mailing list, they can produce a long list of flames and counter flames known as flame wars.

You may be tempted to join in, but this is a waste of everyone's time. Often the initial offense was merely a poorly worded email that a reader interpreted as an insult. There ... those who intentionally send inflammatory emails called flame bait. Resist ... send a cutting response, and consider if the writer's intent was to ...

... misjudges something you wrote and becomes offended, just ... apology can thwart a potential fire. Avoid miscommunication by ... your emails.

... been insulted by an email? What was your response?

Special features are designed to enhance your study of keyboarding. The *Keyboarding Connection* features illustrate the importance of keyboarding skills outside of the classroom. The *Strategies for Career Success* features offer an employment-related connection with useful hints for succeeding in any career.

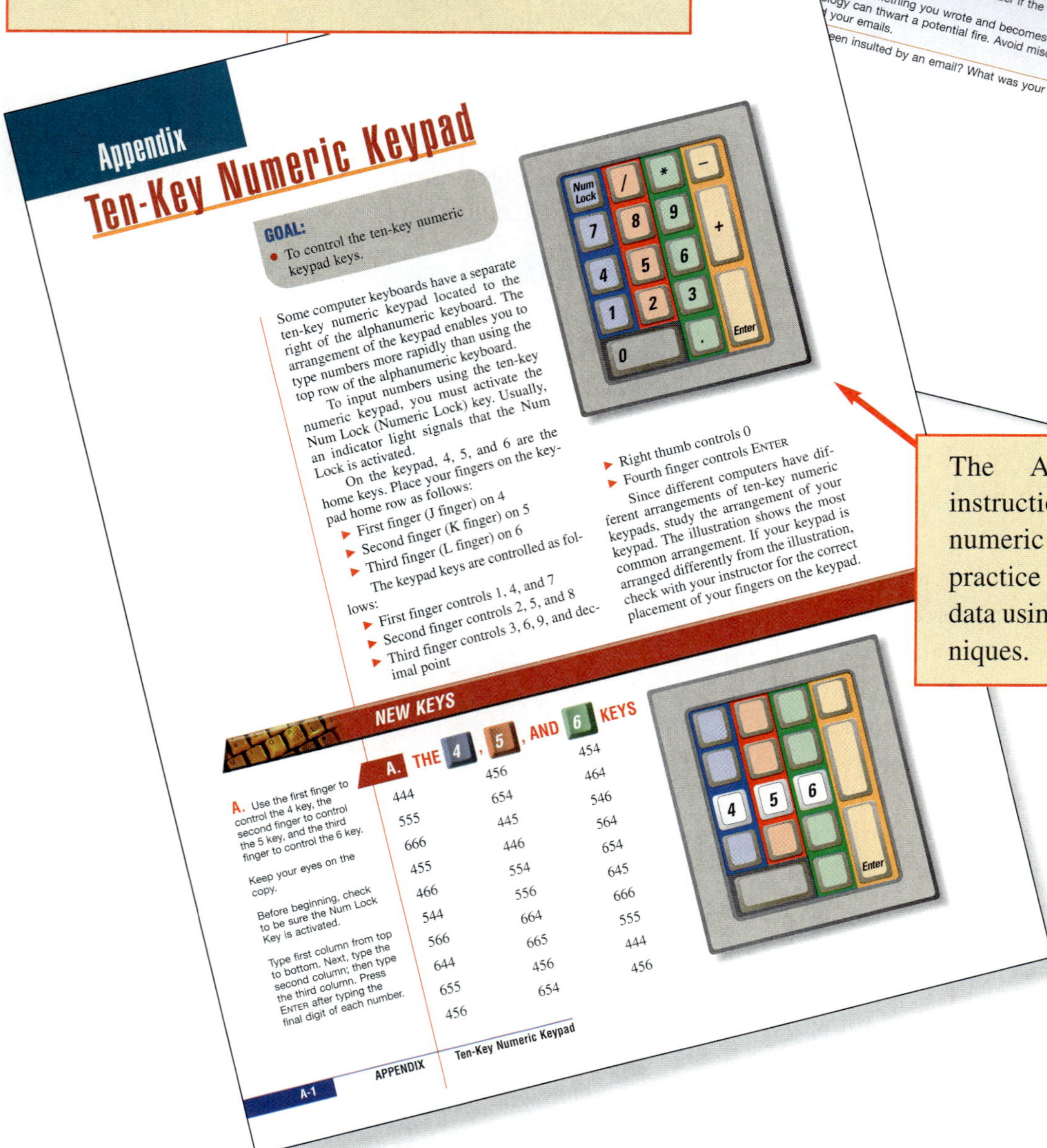
Appendix

Ten-Key Numeric Keypad

GOAL:
- To control the ten-key numeric keypad keys.

Some computer keyboards have a separate ten-key numeric keypad located to the right of the alphanumeric keyboard. The arrangement of the keypad enables you to type numbers more rapidly than using the top row of the alphanumeric keyboard.

To input numbers using the ten-key numeric keypad, you must activate the Num Lock (Numeric Lock) key. Usually, an indicator light signals that the Num Lock is activated.

On the keypad, 4, 5, and 6 are the home keys. Place your fingers on the keypad home row as follows:

- First finger (J finger) on 4
- Second finger (K finger) on 5
- Third finger (L finger) on 6

The keypad keys are controlled as follows:

- First finger controls 1, 4, and 7
- Second finger controls 2, 5, and 8
- Third finger controls 3, 6, 9, and decimal point
- Right thumb controls 0
- Fourth finger controls ENTER

Since different computers have different arrangements of ten-key numeric keypads, study the arrangement of your keypad. The illustration shows the most common arrangement. If your keypad is arranged differently from the illustration, check with your instructor for the correct placement of your fingers on the keypad.

NEW KEYS

A. THE 4, 5, AND 6 KEYS

A. Use the first finger to control the 4 key, the second finger to control the 5 key, and the third finger to control the 6 key.

Keep your eyes on the copy.

Before beginning, check to be sure the Num Lock Key is activated.

Type first column from top to bottom. Next, type the second column; then type the third column. Press ENTER after typing the final digit of each number.

444	456	454
555	654	464
666	445	546
455	446	564
466	554	654
544	556	645
566	664	666
644	665	555
655	456	444
456	654	456

A-1 APPENDIX Ten-Key Numeric Keypad

The Appendix contains instructions for the ten-key numeric keypad. Students practice entering numerical data using touch-typing techniques.

SKILLBUILDING

22wpm

What is the difference between a job and a career? Think carefully. A job is work that people do for money. A career is a sequence of related jobs built on a foundation of interests, knowledge, training, and experiences.

24wpm

Learn more about the world of work by looking at the sixteen career clusters. Most jobs are included in one of the clusters that have been organized by the government. During your exploration of careers, list the clusters that interest you.

26wpm

Once you identify your career clusters of interest, look at the jobs within each cluster. Find out what skills and aptitudes are needed, what education and training are required, what the work environment is like, and what is the possibility for advancements.

28wpm

Use your career center and school or public libraries to research career choices. Search the Internet. Consult with professionals for another perspective of a specific career. As you gather information about career options, you may discover other i... career possibilities.

30wpm

Gain insights int... participating in an i... temporary job within... familiar with a spec... You'll gain valuabl... career or not.

32wpm

Whichever pa... pride in yoursel... what you believ... how you view y... in yourself. I... your self-con...

The back-of-the book skillbuilding routines are designed with YOU in mind. The Paced Practice skillbuilding paragraphs use an upbeat, motivational storyline with guidance in career choices. The Supplementary Timings relate critical thinking skills to careers.

SKILLBUILDING

Supplementary Timing 9

One of the most important decisions we all have to 10
face is choosing a career. The possibilities can appear 21
overwhelming. Fear not! Your critical thinking skills will 33
save you! Start your career planning today. Begin with 44
self-assessment. What are your interests? Do you enjoy 55
working indoors or outdoors? Do you prefer working with 66
numbers or with words? Are you the independent type or 77
would you rather work with a group? What are your favorite 89
academic studies? Think about these questions and then 100
create a list of your interests, skills, aptitudes, and 111
values. What you discover about yourself will help you in 123
finding the career that is right for you. 131
After you have explored your personal interests, look 142
at the sixteen career clusters for a wide range of job 153
prospects. Most jobs are included in one of these clusters 165
that have been organized by the government. During your 176
exploration, make a note of the clusters that interest you 188
and investigate these clusters. 194
Gather as much information as possible by using all 205
available resources. Scan the Help Wanted section in the 216
major Sunday newspapers for job descriptions and salaries. 228
Search the Net. The Internet provides electronic access to 240
worldwide job listings. If you want to know more about a 251
specific company, access its home page. Go to your college 263
placement office. Sign up for interviews with companies 274
that visit your campus. Visit your local school or county 286
library and ask the reference librarian for occupational 297
handbooks. Talk with people in your field of interest to 308
ask questions and get advice. Attend chapter meetings of 319
professional organizations to network with people working 331
in your chosen profession. Volunteer, intern, or work a 342
part-time or temporary job within your career choice for 353
valuable, first-hand insight. Taking an initiative in your 365
job search will pay off. 370
A career search requires the use of critical thinking 381
skills. These skills will help you to choose the career 392
that will match your skills and talents. 400

| 1 | 2 | 3 | 4 | 5 | 6 | 7 | 8 | 9 | 10 | 11 | 12 |

Reference Manual

COMPUTER SYSTEM

keyboard, R-2B
parts of, R-2A

CORRESPONDENCE

application letter, R-12B
attachment notation, R-4D, R-7C
blind-copy notation, R-5B
block style, R-3A
body, R-3A
company name, R-5B
complimentary closing, R-3A
copy notation, R-3C, R-5B
date line, R-3A
delivery notation, R-4A, R-5B
email, R-5C, R-5D
enclosure notation, R-3B, R-5B
envelope formatting, R-6A
executive stationery, R-4A
half-page stationery, R-4B
inside address, R-3A
international address, R-3D
letter folding, R-6B
letterhead, R-3A
list, bulleted, R-3C
list, multiline, R-3B, R-5B
list, numbered, R-3B
list, single-line, R-3C, R-8A
memo, R-4D, R-7C
modified-block style, R-3B
multipage, R-5A, R-5B
on-arrival notation, R-5A
open punctuation, R-3B
personal-business, R-3D
postscript notation, R-5B
reference initials, R-3A, R-5B
return address, R-3D
salutation, R-3A
simplified style, R-3C
standard punctuation, R-3A, R-3D
subject line, R-5A, R-7C
table, R-4D
window envelope, folding for, R-6B
window envelope, formatted for, R-4C
window envelope, formatting, R-6A
writer's identification, R-3A

EMPLOYMENT DOCUMENTS

application letter, R-12B
job-application form, R-12D
resume, R-12A

FORMS

business forms, R-14A
job-application form, R-12D
placing information on printed lines, R-12C

LANGUAGE ARTS

abbreviations, R-22
adjectives and adverbs, R-20
agreement, R-19
apostrophes, R-17
capitalization, R-21
colons, R-18
commas, R-15
grammar, R-19
hyphens, R-17
italics, R-18
mechanics, R-21
number expression, R-21
periods, R-18
pronouns, R-20
punctuation, R-15
quotation marks, R-18
semicolons, R-16
sentences, R-19
underline, R-18
word usage, R-20

PROOFREADERS' MARKS

R-14C

REPORTS

academic style, R-8C, R-8D
agenda, R-11A
APA style, R-10A, R-10B
author/year citations, R-10A
bibliography, R-9B
business style, R-8A, R-8B, R-9A
byline, R-8A
citations, R-9D
date, R-7A, R-8A
endnotes, R-8D
footnotes, R-8A
headings, R-9D
headings, main, R-10A
headings, paragraph, R-8A
headings, side, R-8A
itinerary, R-11C
left-bound, R-9A
legal document, R-11D
lists, R-8A, R-8C, R-9A, R-9C
margins, R-9D
memo, R-9C
minutes of a meeting, R-11B
MLA style, R-10C, R-10D
outline, R-7A
quotation, long, R-8B, R-8D
references page, R-10B
resume, R-12A
spacing, R-9D
subheadings, R-10A
subtitle, R-8A
table, R-8B
table of contents, R-7D
title, R-8A
title page, R-7B
transmittal memo, R-7C
works-cited page, R-10D

TABLES

2-line column heading, R-13B
body, R-13A
boxed, R-13A
braced headings, R-13A
capitalization in columns, R-13D
column headings, R-13A, R-13D
column headings, blocked, R-13B
in correspondence, R-4D, R-5A, R-13C
dollar signs, R-13D
note, R-13A
open, R-13B
percent signs, R-13D
in reports, R-8B
ruled, R-13C
subtitle, R-13A, R-13B
table number, R-13C
title, R-13A
title block, R-13D
total line, R-13A, R-13D
vertical placement, R-13D

U.S. POSTAL SERVICE STATE ABBREVIATIONS

R-14B

A. MAJOR PARTS OF A MICROCOMPUTER SYSTEM

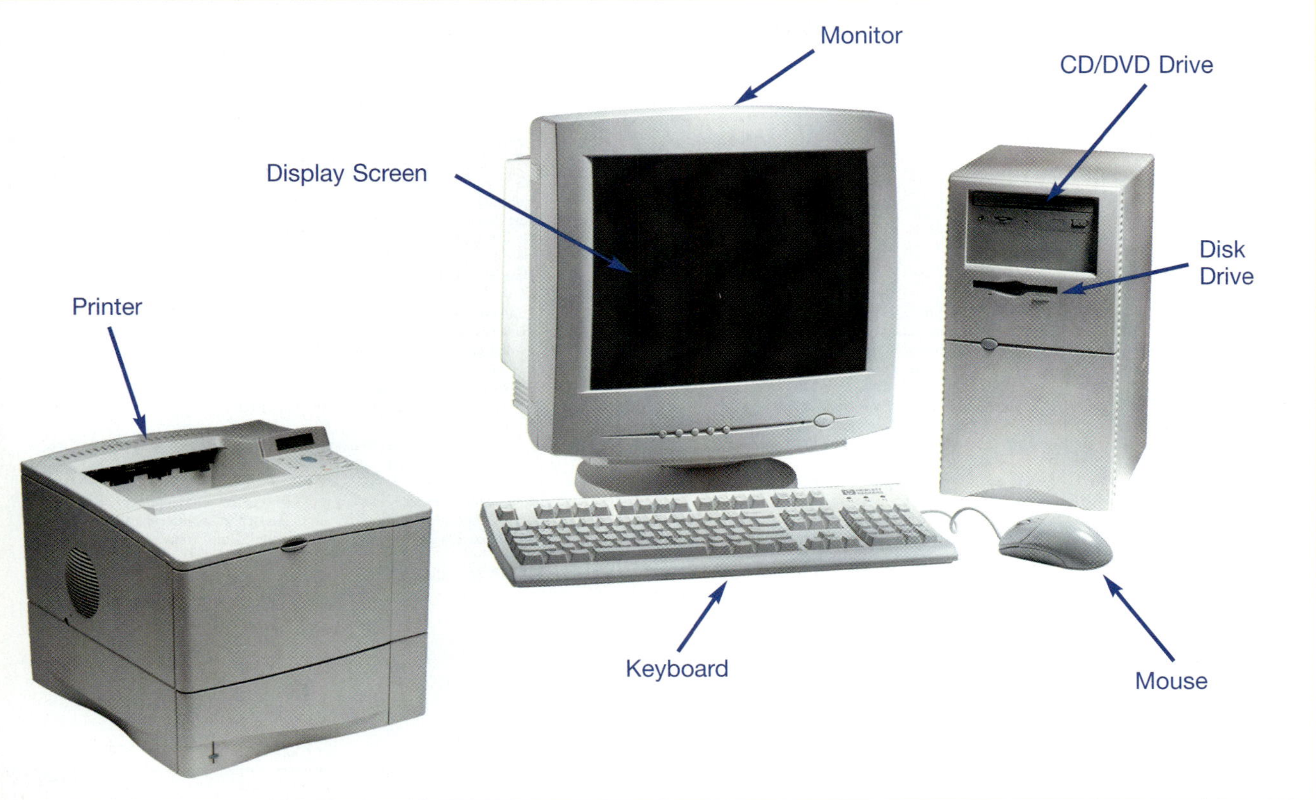

B. THE COMPUTER KEYBOARD

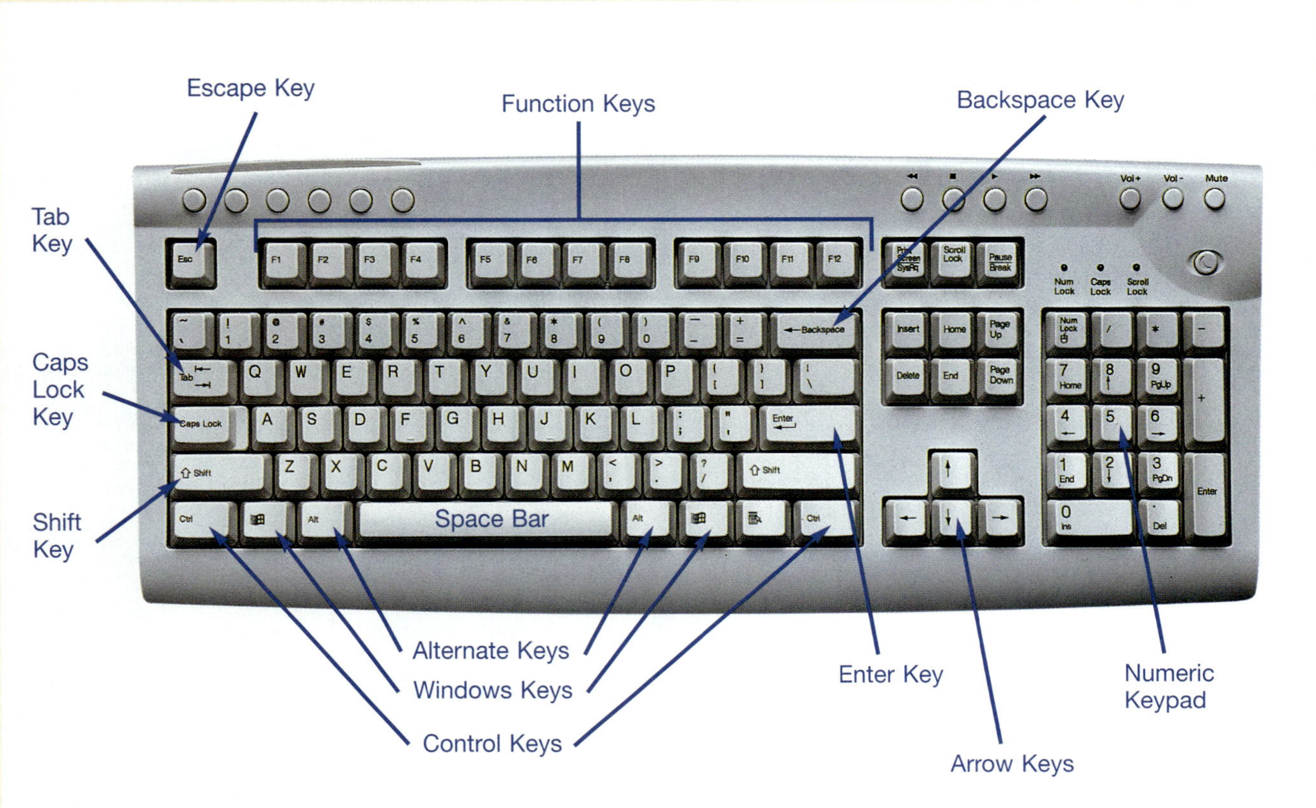

Reference Manual

A. BUSINESS LETTER

(in block style with standard punctuation)

Letterhead NATIONAL
GEOGRAPHIC
SOCIETY

↓6X

Date line September 5, 20-- ↓4X

Inside address Ms. Joan R. Hunter
Bolwater Associates
One Parklands Drive
Darien, CT 06820 ↓2X

Salutation Dear Ms. Hunter: ↓2X

Body

You will soon receive the signed contract to have your organization conduct a one-day workshop for our employees on eliminating repetitive-motion injuries in the workplace. As we agreed, this workshop will apply to both our office and factory workers and you will conduct separate sessions for each group.

We revised Paragraph 4b to require the instructor of this workshop to be a full-time employee of Bolwater Associates. In addition, we made changes to Paragraph 10-c to require our prior approval of the agenda for the workshop.

If these revisions are satisfactory, please sign and return one copy of the contract for our files. We look forward to this opportunity to enhance the health of our employees. I know that all of us will enjoy this workshop. ↓2X

Complimentary closing Sincerely, ↓4X

John L. Merritt

Writer's identification John L. Merritt, Director ↓2X

Reference initials fej

1145 17th Street N.W., Washington, D.C. 20036-4688, U.S.A. Telephone: (202) 857-7537 Fax: (202) 429-5776
Recycled-content paper

B. BUSINESS LETTER IN MODIFIED-BLOCK STYLE

(with open punctuation, multiline list, and enclosure notation)

8787 Orion Place
Columbus, OH 43240-4027
Tel 614 430 6000
Fax 614 430 6621

SRA/McGraw-Hill
A Division of The McGraw-Hill Companies

↓6X
→tab to centerpoint May 15, 20-- ↓4X

Ms. Joan R. Hunter
Bolwater Associates
One Parklands Drive
Darien, CT 06820 ↓2X

Dear Ms. Hunter ↓2X

I am returning a signed contract to have your organization conduct a one-day workshop for our employees on eliminating repetitive-motion injuries in the workplace. We have made the following changes to the contract:

Multiline list

1. We revised Paragraph 4b to require the instructor of this workshop to be a full-time employee of Bolwater Associates.

2. We made changes to Paragraph 10-c to require our prior approval of the agenda for the workshop.

If these revisions are satisfactory, please sign and return one copy of the contract for our files. We look forward to this opportunity to enhance the health of our employees. I know that all of us will enjoy this workshop. ↓2X

→tab to centerpoint Sincerely ↓4X

John L. Merritt

John L. Merritt, Director ↓2X

pec
Enclosure notation Enclosure

C. BUSINESS LETTER IN SIMPLIFIED STYLE

(with single-line list, enclosure notation, and copy notation)

20 Ryan Ranch Road
Monterey, CA 93940
Tel 831 393 7910
800 538 9547 ext. 7910
Fax 831 393 7211

CTB/McGraw-Hill
A Division of The McGraw-Hill Companies

↓6X

October 5, 20-- ↓4X

Ms. Joan R. Hunter
Bolwater Associates
One Parklands Drive
Darien, CT 06820 ↓3X

WORKSHOP CONTRACT ↓3X

I am returning the signed contract, Ms. Hunter, to have your organization conduct a one-day workshop for our employees on eliminating repetitive-motion injuries in the workplace. We have amended the following sections of the contract:

Single-line list

- Paragraph 4b
- Table 3
- Attachment 2

If these revisions are satisfactory, please sign and return one copy of the contract for our files. We look forward to this opportunity to enhance the health of our employees. I know that all of us will enjoy this workshop. ↓4X

John L. Merritt

JOHN L. MERRITT, DIRECTOR ↓2X

iww
Enclosure
Copy notation c: Legal Department

D. PERSONAL-BUSINESS LETTER

(in modified-block style and with international address and standard punctuation)

↓6X
→tab to centerpoint July 15, 20-- ↓4X

Mr. Luis Fernandez, President
Arvon Industries, Inc.
21 St. Claire Avenue East
Toronto, Ontario M4T IL9
CANADA ↓2X

Dear Mr. Fernandez: ↓2X

As a former employee and present stockholder of Arvon Industries, I wish to protest the planned sale of the Consumer Products Division.

According to published reports, consumer products accounted for 19 percent of last year's corporate profits, and they are expected to account for even more this year. In addition, Dun & Bradstreet predicts that consumer products nationwide will outpace the general economy for the next five years.

I am concerned about the effect that this planned sale will have on overall corporate profits, on cash dividends for investors, and on the economy of Melbourne, where the two consumer-products plants are located.

Please ask your board of directors to reconsider this matter. ↓2X

→tab to centerpoint Sincerely, ↓4X

Roger J. Michaelson

Return address Roger J. Michaelson
901 East Benson, Apt. 3
Ft. Lauderdale, FL 33301

A. BUSINESS LETTER ON EXECUTIVE STATIONERY

(7¼″ × 10½″; 1-inch side margins; with delivery notation)

Two Penn Plaza
10th Floor
New York, NY 10121-2298
Tel 212 904 2500
Fax 212 904 6630

Sweet's Group
McGraw-Hill Construction Information Group
A Division of The ***McGraw-Hill*** *Companies*

↓6X
July 18, 20-- ↓4X

Mr. Rodney Eastwood
BBL Resources
52A Northern Ridge
Fayetteville, PA 17222 ↓2X

Dear Rodney: ↓2X

I see no reason that we should continue to consider the locality around Geraldton for our new plant. Even though the desirability of this site from an economic view is undeniable, there is insufficient housing readily available for our workers.

In trying to control urban growth, the city has been turning down the building permits for new housing or placing so many restrictions on foreign investment as to make it too expensive.

Please continue to seek out other areas of exploration where we might form a joint partnership. ↓2X

Sincerely, ↓4X

Arlyn J. Bunch

Arlyn J. Bunch
Vice President for Operations ↓2X

mme
Delivery notation By Fax

B. BUSINESS LETTER ON HALF-PAGE STATIONERY

(5½″ × 8½″; 0.75-inch side margins)

1221 Avenue of the Americas
New York, NY 10020-1095

Business Week
A Division of The ***McGraw-Hill*** *Companies*

↓4X
July 18, 20-- ↓4X

Mr. Rodney Eastwood
BBL Resources
52A Northern Ridge
Fayetteville, PA 17222 ↓2X

Dear Rodney: ↓2X

We should continue considering Geraldton for our new plant. Even though the desirability of this site from an economic view is undeniable, there is insufficient housing readily available.

Please continue to seek out other areas of exploration where we might form a joint partnership. ↓2X

Sincerely, ↓4X

Arlyn J. Bunch

Arlyn J. Bunch
Vice President for Operations ↓2X

adk

C. BUSINESS LETTER FORMATTED FOR A WINDOW ENVELOPE

APH
AMERICAN PRINTING HOUSE FOR THE BLIND, INC.

↓6X
July 18, 20-- ↓3X

Mr. Rodney Eastwood
BBL Resources
52A Northern Ridge
Fayetteville, PA 17222 ↓3X

Dear Rodney: ↓2X

I see no reason that we should continue to consider the locality around Geraldton for our new plant. Even though the desirability of this site from an economic view is undeniable, there is insufficient housing readily available for our workers.

In trying to control urban growth, the city has been turning down the building permits for new housing or placing so many restrictions on foreign investment as to make it too expensive.

Please continue to seek out other areas of exploration where we might form a joint partnership. ↓2X

Sincerely, ↓4X

Arlyn J. Bunch

Arlyn J. Bunch
Vice President for Operations ↓2X

woc

D. MEMO

(with table and attachment notation)

↓6X
→tab
MEMO TO: Nancy Price, Executive Vice President ↓2X

FROM: Arlyn J. Bunch, Operations *ajb* ↓2X

DATE: July 18, 20-- ↓2X

SUBJECT: New Plant Site ↓2X

As you can see from the attached letter, I've informed BBL Resources that I see no reason why we should continue to consider the locality around Geraldton for our new plant. Even though the desirability of this site from an economic standpoint is undeniable, there is insufficient housing available. In fact, as of June 25, the number of appropriate single-family houses listed for sale within a 25-mile radius of Geraldton was as follows: ↓2X

Agent	Units
Belle Real Estate	123
Castleton Homes	11
Red Carpet	9
Geraldton Homes	5

↓1X

In addition, in trying to control urban growth, Geraldton has been either turning down building permits for new housing or placing excessive restrictions on them.

Because of this deficiency of housing for our employees, we have no choice but to look elsewhere. ↓2X

llw
Attachment notation Attachment

A. MULTIPAGE BUSINESS LETTER

(page 1; with on-arrival notation, international address, subject line, and table)

55 Water Street
New York, NY 10041

↓6X

Standard & Poor's
A Division of The McGraw-Hill Companies

May 13, 20-- ↓2X

On-arrival notation: CONFIDENTIAL ↓2X

Mr. Lester Thompson, Director
British Mutual Broadcasting
24 Portland Place
London WIN 4BB
ENGLAND ↓2X

Dear Mr. Thompson:

Subject line: Subject: International Study Tour ↓2X

I have been invited by the Federal Communications Commission to participate in a study of television news programming in European countries. The enclosed report explains the purpose of the study in detail.

I have been assigned to lead a study group through six European countries to gather firsthand information on this topic. In addition to me, our group will consist of the following members: ↓2X

INTERNATIONAL STUDY TOUR GROUP		
Name	**Organization**	**Location**
Mrs. Katherine Grant	WPQR-TV	Los Angeles, CA
Dr. Manuél Cruz	Miami Herald	Miami, FL
Mr. Richard Logan	Cable News Network	Atlanta, GA
Ms. Barbara Brooks	Associated Press	Chicago, IL

↓1X

Our initial plans are to spend at least one full day in each of the countries, meeting with the news programming staff of one or two of the major networks,

B. MULTIPAGE BUSINESS LETTER

(page 2; with company name; multiline list; enclosure, delivery, copy, postscript, and blind copy notations)

2

touring their facilities, viewing recent broadcasts, and getting a firsthand view of actual news operations. Our tentative itinerary calls for us to arrive at Heathrow Airport at 7:10 p.m. on Tuesday, July 27. Would it be possible for us to do the following:

1. Meet with various members of your staff sometime on July 28. We would be available from 8:30 a.m. until 1:30 p.m.

2. Receive a copy of your programming log for the week of July 26-30 and especially a minute-by-minute listing of the programming segments for your national news reporting.

I would appreciate your contacting Barbara Azar, our liaison, at 202.555.3943 to let us know whether we may study your operations on July 25. ↓2X

Sincerely, ↓2X

Company name: METRO BROADCASTING COMPANY ↓4X

Denise J. Watterson

Denise J. Watterson
General Manager ↓2X

Reference initials: rcp
Enclosure notation: Enclosures: FCC Report, Biographical Sketches
Delivery notation: By FedEx
Copy notation: c: Barbara Azar, Manuél Cruz ↓2X

Postscript notation: PS: The Federal Communications Commission will reimburse your organization for any expenses associated with our visit. ↓2X

Blind copy notation: bc: Public Relations Office, FTC

C. EMAIL MESSAGE IN MICROSOFT OUTLOOK/ INTERNET EXPLORER

Job Description for DTP Position - Message (Plain Text)

File Edit View Insert Format Tools Actions Help

To... 00apvida, 00cjsmithson
Cc...
Subject: Job Description for DTP Position

```
Hi, Andy and Cody:

Attached is the draft job description for the new desktop publishing position
we're going to be advertising for next month. Would you please review it for
accuracy, completeness, and adherence to company policy.

I'd appreciate your getting back to me with any suggested changes by Thursday
so that I can get this position publicized next week.

Thanks.

Sandy

Sandra R. Hill (00srhill@atpi.com)
Phone: 555-0231; Fax: 555-3886
```

Job Description f...

Attachment

D. EMAIL MESSAGE IN NETSCAPE NAVIGATOR

Proposed Property Showing - Composition

File Edit View Insert Format Tools Communicator Help

To: graceeason@realestate.com
Subject: Proposed Property Showing   Priority: Normal

```
Ms. Eason:

Would you be available to meet with me next Monday, July 10, for about three
hours to show me commercial lots available that might be suitable for my
planned U-Store facility.

As I indicated on the phone yesterday, these are my requirements:

1. Approximately three-fourths of an acre
2. Zoned C-3 (light industrial use)
3. Utilities already installed
4. Cost of no more than $65,000

If you have more than three or four potential properties available, would you
please select the ones you think best meet my needs for us to view.

Please call me to let me know when you are available. I can meet with you
either in the morning or afternoon.

Frances Merritt (frances_merritt@AXL.com)
Property Manager
AXL Enterprises
609 Apache Road
Portsmouth, VA 23701
Phone: 757-555-0858
Fax: 757-555-0859
```

Document: Done

A. FORMATTING ENVELOPES

A standard large (No. 10) envelope is 9½ by 4⅛ inches. A standard small (No. 6¾) envelope is 6½ by 3⅝ inches. Although either address format shown below is acceptable, the format shown for the large envelope (all capital letters and no punctuation) is recommended by the U.S. Postal Service for mail that will be sorted by an electronic scanning device.

Window envelopes are often used in a word processing environment because of the difficulty of aligning envelopes correctly in some printers. A window envelope requires no formatting, since the letter is formatted and folded so that the inside address is visible through the window.

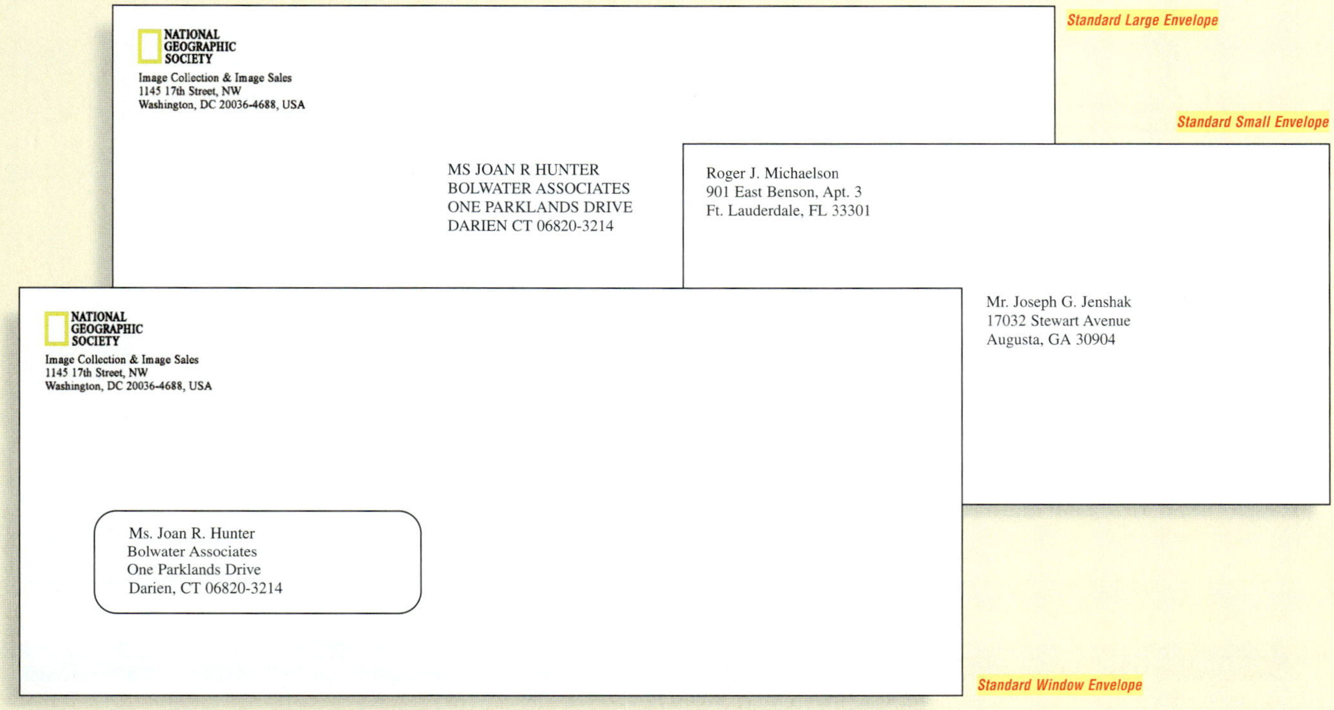

Standard Large Envelope

Standard Small Envelope

Standard Window Envelope

B. FOLDING LETTERS

To fold a letter for a large envelope:

1. Place the letter *face up* and fold up the bottom third.
2. Fold the top third down to 0.5 inch from the bottom edge.
3. Insert the last crease into the envelope first, with the flap facing up.

To fold a letter for a small envelope:

1. Place the letter *face up* and fold up the bottom half to 0.5 inch from the top.
2. Fold the right third over to the left.
3. Fold the left third over to 0.5 inch from the right edge.
4. Insert the last crease into the envelope first, with the flap facing up.

To fold a letter for a window envelope:

1. Place the letter *face down* with the letterhead at the top and fold the bottom third of the letter up.
2. Fold the top third down so that the address shows.
3. Insert the letter into the envelope so that the address shows through the window.

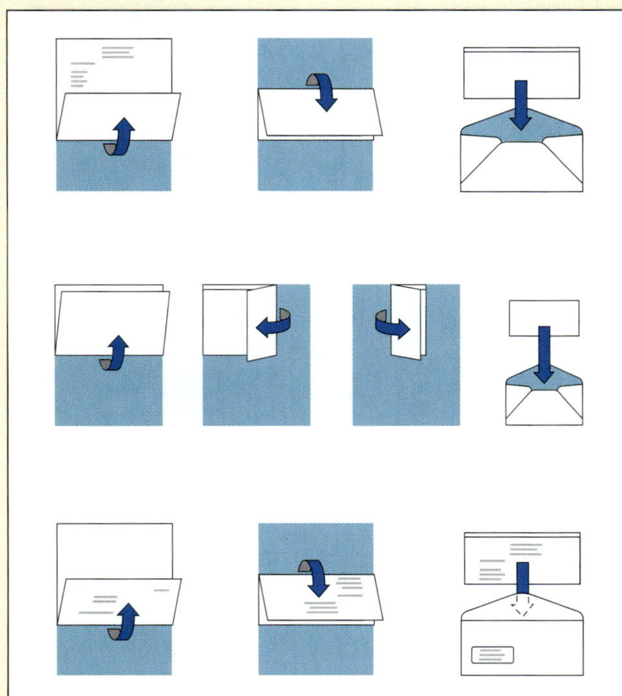

Reference Manual

A. OUTLINE

Set right tab at 0.3; left tabs at 0.4 and 0.7.

↓6X

14 pt **AN ANALYSIS OF THE SCOPE AND EFFECTIVENESS OF ONLINE ADVERTISING** ↓2X

12 pt↓ **The Status of Point-and-Click Selling** ↓2X

Jonathan R. Evans ↓2X

January 19, 20-- ↓2X

tab

I. INTRODUCTION ↓2X

II. SCOPE AND TRENDS IN INTERNET ADVERTISING
A. Internet Advertising
B. Major Online Advertisers
C. Positioning and Pricing
D. Types of Advertising ↓2X

III. ADVERTISING EFFECTIVENESS
A. The Banner Debate
B. Increasing Advertising Effectiveness
C. Measuring ROI ↓2X

IV. CONCLUSION

B. TITLE PAGE

center page↓

14 pt **AN ANALYSIS OF THE SCOPE AND EFFECTIVENESS OF ONLINE ADVERTISING** ↓2X

12 pt↓ **The Status of Point-and-Click Selling** ↓12X

Submitted to
↓2X
Luis Torres
General Manager
ViaWorld, International ↓12X

Prepared by ↓2X

Jonathan R. Evans
Assistant Marketing Manager
ViaWorld, International ↓2X

January 19, 20--

C. TRANSMITTAL MEMO

(with 2-line subject line and attachment notation)

↓6X

→ tab

MEMO TO: Luis Torres, General Manager ↓2X

FROM: Jonathan R. Evans, Assistant Marketing Manager jre ↓2X

DATE: January 19, 20-- ↓2X

SUBJECT: An Analysis of the Scope and Effectiveness of Online Advertising ↓2X

Here is the report analyzing the scope and effectiveness of Internet Advertising that you requested on January 5, 20--.

The report predicts that the total value of business-to-business e-commerce market will reach $1.3 trillion by 2003, up from $190 billion in 1999. New technologies aimed at increasing Internet ad interactivity and the adoption of standards for advertising response measurement and tracking will contribute to this increase. Unfortunately, as discussed in this report, the use of "rich media" and interactivity in Web advertising will create its own set of problems.

I enjoyed working on this assignment, Luis, and learned quite a bit from my analysis of the situation. Please let me know if you have any questions about the report. ↓2X

urs
Attachment

D. TABLE OF CONTENTS

Set left tab at 0.5; right dot-leader tab at 6.

↓6X

14 pt **CONTENTS** ↓2X

12 pt↓ INTRODUCTION . . . . 1 ↓2X

SCOPE AND TRENDS IN ONLINE ADVERTISING . . . . 3 ↓2X

→tab Internet Advertising Spending 4
Major Online Advertisers 5
Positioning and Pricing 7
Types of Advertising . . . . 8 ↓2X

ADVERTISING EFFECTIVENESS . . . . 9 ↓2X

The Banner Debate 9
Increasing Advertising Effectiveness 11
Measuring ROI . . . . 12 ↓2X

CONCLUSION . . . . 13 ↓2X

APPENDIX . . . . 15 ↓2X

Sample Internet Advertising 15
Proposed WEFA Standards . . . . 18 ↓2X

BIBLIOGRAPHY 19

A. REPORT IN BUSINESS STYLE

(page 1; with footnotes and single-line list)

↓6X

Title 14 pt **AN ANALYSIS OF THE SCOPE AND EFFECTIVENESS OF ONLINE ADVERTISING** ↓2X

Subtitle 12 pt↓ **The Status of Point-and-Click Selling** ↓2X

Byline **Jonathan R. Evans** ↓2X

Date **January 19, 20--** ↓2X

Side hd **INTRODUCTION** ↓2X

Over the past three years, the number of American households online has tripled, from an estimated 15 million in 1996 to 45 million in 1999. Jupiter Communications, predicts that by the year 2003, 70 million households, representing about 62% of all U.S. households, will be online. Online business has grown in tandem with the expanding number of Internet users. Forrester Research Inc. predicts that the total value of business-to-business e-commerce will reach $109 billion in 1999 and is likely to reach $1.3 trillion by 2003.[1] ↓2X

Para hd **Uncertainty**. The uncertainties surrounding advertising on the Internet remain one of the major impediments to the expansion. Dating from just 1994 when the first banner ads appeared on the Hotwired home page, the young Internet advertising industry is today in a state of flux. ↓2X

Some analysts argue that advertising on the Internet can and should follow the same principles as advertising on television and other visual media. Others contend that advertising on the Internet should reflect the unique characteristics of this new medium. ↓2X

Reasons for Not Advertising Online. A recent Association of National Advertisers survey found two main reasons cited for not advertising online:[2] ↓2X

1. The difficulty of determining return on investment
2. The lack of reliable tracking and measurement data

Footnotes

[1] George Anders, "Buying Frenzy," *Wall Street Journal*, July 12, 1999, p. R6.
[2] "eStats: Advertising Revenues and Trends," *eMarketer Home Page*, August 11, 1999, http:www.emarketer.com/estats/ad (January 7, 2000).

B. REPORT IN BUSINESS STYLE

(page 3; with long quotation and table)

3

who argue that banners have a strong potential for advertising effectiveness point out that it is not the banner format itself which presents a problem to advertising effectiveness, but rather the quality of the banner and the attention to its placement. According to Mike Windsor, president of Ogilvy Interactive: ↓2X

indent 0.5″→ ←indent 0.5″

Long quotation

> It's more a case of bad banner ads, just like there are bad television ads. The space itself has huge potential. As important as using the space within the banner creatively is to aim it effectively. Unlike broadcast media, the Web offers advertisers the opportunity to reach a specific audience based on data gathered about who is surfing at a particular site and what their interests are.[1]

Thus, while some analysts continue to argue that the banner advertisement is passé, there is little evidence of its abandonment. Instead ad agencies are focusing on increasing the banner's effectiveness. ↓2X

SCOPE AND TRENDS IN ONLINE ADVERTISING ↓2X

Starting from zero in 1994, analysts agree that the volume of Internet advertising spending has risen rapidly. However, as indicated in Table 3, analysts provide a wide range of the exact amount of such advertising. ↓2X

TABLE 3. INTERNET ADVERTISING
1998 Estimates ↓1X

Source	Estimate
Internet Advertising Board	$1.92 billion
Forester	1.30 billion
IDC	1.20 billion
Burst! Media	560 million

Source: "Advertising Age Teams with eMarketer for Research Report," *Advertising Age*, May 3, 1999, p. 24. ↓1X

The differences in estimates of total Web advertising spending is generally attributed to the different methodologies used by the research agencies to

[1] Lisa Napoli, "Banner Ads Are Under the Gun—And On the Move," *New York Times*, June 17, 1999, p. D1.

C. REPORT IN ACADEMIC STYLE

(page 1; with endnotes and multiline list)

↓3DS

14 pt **AN ANALYSIS OF THE SCOPE AND EFFECTIVENESS** ↓1DS

OF ONLINE ADVERTISING ↓1DS

12 pt↓ **The Status of Point-and-Click Selling** ↓1DS

Jonathan R. Evans ↓1DS

January 19, 20-- ↓1DS

INTRODUCTION

Over the past three years, the number of American households online has tripled, from an estimated 15 million in 1996 to 45 million in 1999. Jupiter Communications, predicts that by the year 2003, 70 million households, representing about 62% of all U.S. households, will be online. Online business has grown in tandem with the expanding number of Internet users. Forrester Research Inc. predicts that the total value of business-to-business e-commerce will reach $109 billion in 1999 and is likely to reach $1.3 trillion by 2003.[i]

Reasons for Not Advertising Online. A recent Association of National Advertisers survey found two main reasons cited for not advertising online:[ii]

1. The difficulty of determining return on investment, especially in terms of repeat business.
2. The lack of reliable tracking and measurement data

Some analysts argue that advertising on the Internet can and should follow the same principles as advertising on television.[iii] Other visual media

D. REPORT IN ACADEMIC STYLE

(last page; with long quotation and endnotes)

14

advertising effectiveness, but rather the quality of the banner and the attention to its placement. According to Mike Windsor, president of Ogilvy Interactive:

indent 0.5″→ ←indent 0.5″

Long quotation

> It's more a case of bad banner ads, just like there are bad television ads. The space itself has huge potential. As important as using the space within the banner creatively is to aim it effectively. Unlike broadcast media, the Web offers advertisers the opportunity to reach a specific audience based on data gathered about who is surfing at a particular site and what their interests are.[vii]

From the advertiser's perspective, the most effective Internet ads do more than just deliver information to the consumer and grab the consumer's attention—they also gather information about consumers (e.g., through "cookies" and other methodologies). From the consumer's perspective, this type of interactivity may represent an intrusion and an invasion of privacy. There appears to be a shift away from the ad-supported model and toward the transaction model, wherein users pay for the content they want and the specific transactions they perform.

Endnotes

i George Anders, "Buying Frenzy," *Wall Street Journal*, July 12, 1999, p. R6.
ii "eStats: Advertising Revenues and Trends," *eMarketer Home Page*, August 11, 1999, http:www.emarketer.com/estats/ad (January 7, 2000).
iii Bradley Johnson, "Nielsen/NetRatings Index Shows 4% Rise in Web Ads," *Advertising Age*, July 19, 1999, p. 18.
iv Tom Hyland, "Web Advertising: A Year of Growth," *Internet Advertising Board Home Page*, November 13, 1999, http:www.iab.net/advertise (January 8, 2000).
v Adrian Mand, "Click Here: Free Ride Doles Out Freebies to Ad Surfers," *Brandweek*, March 8, 1999, p. 30.
vi Andrea Petersen, "High Price of Internet Banner Ads Slips Amid Increase in Web Sites," *Wall Street Journal*, March 2, 1999, p. B20.
vii Lisa Napoli, "Banner Ads Are Under the Gun—And On the Move," *New York Times*, June 17, 1999, p. D1.

A. LEFT-BOUND REPORT IN BUSINESS STYLE

(page 1; with endnotes and single-line list)

left margin: 1.75″ right margin: *default* (1.25″)

↓6X

14 pt **AN ANALYSIS OF THE SCOPE AND EFFECTIVENESS OF ONLINE ADVERTISING** ↓2X

12 pt↓ **The Status of Point-and-Click Selling** ↓2X

Jonathan R. Evans ↓2X

January 19, 20-- ↓2X

INTRODUCTION ↓2X

Over the past three years, the number of American households online has tripled, from an estimated 15 million in 1996 to 45 million in 1999. Jupiter Communications, predicts that by the year 2003, 70 million households, representing about 62% of all U.S. households, will be online. Online business has grown in tandem with the expanding number of Internet users. Forrester Research Inc. predicts that the total value of business-to-business e-commerce will reach $109 billion in 1999 and is likely to reach $1.3 trillion by 2003.[i] ↓2X

Uncertainty. The uncertainties surrounding advertising on the Internet remain one of the major impediments to the expansion. Dating from just 1994 when the first banner ads appeared on the Hotwired home page, the young Internet advertising industry is today in a state of flux. ↓2X

Some analysts argue that advertising on the Internet can and should follow the same principles as advertising on television and other visual media. Others contend that advertising on the Internet should reflect the unique characteristics of this new medium. ↓2X

Reasons for Not Advertising Online. A recent Association of National Advertisers survey found two main reasons cited for not advertising online:[ii] ↓2X

1. The difficulty of determining return on investment
2. The lack of reliable tracking and measurement data

B. BIBLIOGRAPHY

(For business or academic style using either endnotes or footnotes)

↓6X

hanging indent

12 pt↓ 14 pt **BIBLIOGRAPHY** ↓2X

Book—one author: Adams, Jeffrey B., *Internet Advertising,* Brunswick Press, Boston, 2000.

Annual report: AdCom Industries, *2001 Annual Report,* ACI, Inc., San Francisco, 2002.

Newspaper article: Anders, George, "Buying Frenzy," *Wall Street Journal,* July 12, 1999, p. R6.

Book—two authors: Arlens, Ramon, and Seymour Stevens, *E-Tailing,* All-State, Cambridge, Mass., 1999.

Book—organization as author: *Directory of Business and Financial Services,* Corporate Libraries Assoc., New York, 1998.

WWW page: "eStats: Advertising Revenues and Trends," *eMarketer Home Page,* August 11, 1999, http:www.emarketer.com/estats/ad (January 7, 2000).

Journal article—paged continuously: Ivans, Edward, "Typical ROIs in Online Advertising," *Personnel Quarterly,* Vol. 20, September 2001, pp. 804-816.

Journal article—pages each issue: Johnson, Bradley, "Nielsen/NetRatings Index Shows 4% Rise in Web Ads," *Advertising Age,* July 19, 1999, p. 18.

Online database: "Modern Advertising Techniques," *Advertising Encyclopedia,* N.D., http://www.advency.com/modern_advertising_techniques.html (January 7, 2000).

Gov. document: National Institute of Mental Health, *Who clicks? Four Years of Internet Advertising,* DHHS Publication No. ADM 82-1195, U.S. Government Printing Office, Washington, 1998.

Email: Waerov, Denis V. dvwaerov@aol.com, "Reaction to Management's Offer," August 18, 2001, personal email (August 19, 2001).

C. MEMO REPORT

(page 1, with single-line list)

↓6X

→tab

MEMO TO: Luis Torres, General Manager ↓2X

FROM: Jonathan R. Evans, Assistant Marketing Manager jre ↓2X

DATE: January 19, 20-- ↓2X

SUBJECT: An Analysis of the Scope and Effectiveness of Online Advertising ↓2X

According to a July 12, 1999, *Wall Street* Journal article, over the past three years, the number of American households online has tripled, from an estimated 15 million in 1996 to 45 million in 1999. Jupiter Communications, predicts that by the year 2003, 70 million households, representing about 62% of all U.S. households, will be online. Online business has grown in tandem with the expanding number of Internet users. Forrester Research Inc. predicts that the total value of business-to-business e-commerce will reach $109 billion in 1999 and is likely to reach $1.3 trillion by 2003.

UNCERTAINTY

The uncertainties surrounding advertising on the Internet remain one of the major impediments to the expansion. Dating from just 1994 when the first banner ads appeared on the Hotwired home page, the young Internet advertising industry is today in a state of flux.

Some analysts argue that advertising on the Internet can and should follow the same principles as advertising on television and other visual media. Others contend that advertising on the Internet should reflect the unique characteristics of this new medium.

A recent Association of National Advertisers survey found two main reasons cited for not advertising online:

1. The difficulty of determining return on investment
2. The lack of reliable tracking and measurement data

D. REPORTS: SPECIAL FEATURES

MARGINS AND SPACING. Use a 2″ top margin for the first page of each section of a report (for example, the table of contents, first page of the body, and bibliography page) and a 1″ top margin for other pages. Use default side margins (1.25″) and bottom margins (1″) for all pages. If the report is going to be bound on the left, add 0.5″ to the left margin. Single-space business reports and double-space academic reports.

HEADINGS. Center the report title in 14-point font (press **Enter** to space down before switching to 12-point font). Single-space multiline report titles in a single-spaced report and double-space multiline titles in a double-spaced report. Leave 1 blank line before and after all parts of a heading block (consisting of the title, subtitle, author, and/or date) and format all lines in bold.

Leave 1 blank line before and after side headings and format in bold, beginning at the left margin. Format paragraph headings in bold; begin at the left margin for single-spaced reports and indent for double-spaced reports. The text follows on the same line, preceded by a period and 1 space.

CITATIONS. For business and academic reports, format citations using your word processor's footnote (or endnote) feature. For reports formatted in APA or MLA style, use the format shown on page R-10.

A. REPORT IN APA STYLE

(page 3; with author/year citations)

top, bottom, and side margins: 1″
Double-space throughout.

Online Advertising 3 header

An Analysis of the Scope and Effectiveness

of Online Advertising

Jonathan R. Evans

main hd. Introduction

Over the past three years, the number of American households online has tripled, from an estimated 15 million in 1996 to 45 million in 1999. Jupiter Communications, predicts that by the year 2003, 70 million households, representing about 62% of all U.S. households, will be online (Napoli, 1999). Online business has grown in tandem with the expanding number of Internet users. Forrester Research Inc. predicts that the total value of business-to-business e-commerce will reach $109 billion in 1999 and is likely to reach $1.3 trillion by 2003 (Arlens & Stevens, 1999). ↓1DS

subhd. Uncertainty

The uncertainties surrounding advertising on the Internet remain one of the major impediments to the expansion. Dating from just 1994 when the first banner ads appeared on the Hotwired home page, the young Internet advertising industry is today in a state of flux.

Some analysts argue that advertising on the Internet can and should follow the same principles as advertising on television and other visual media ("eStats," 1999). Others contend that advertising on the Internet should reflect

B. REFERENCES IN APA STYLE

top, bottom, and side margins: 1″
Double-space throughout.

Online Advertising 14 header

References

→tab Adams, J. B. (2000). *Internet advertising.* Boston: Brunswick Press.

AdCom Industries. (2002). *2001 annual report.* San Francisco: ACI, Inc.

Anders, G. (1999, July 12). Buying frenzy. *Wall Street Journal,* p. R6.

Arlens, R., & Stevens, S. (1999). *E-tailing.* Cambridge, MA: All-State.

Directory of business and financial services. (1998). New York: Corporate Libraries Association.

eStats: Advertising revenues and trends. (n.d.). New York: eMarketer. Retrieved August 11, 1999 from the World Wide Web: http:www.emarketer.com/estats/ad.

Ivans, E. (2001). Typical ROIs in online advertising. *Personnel Quarterly, 20,* 804-816.

Johnson, B. (1999, July 19). Nielsen/NetRatings Index shows 4% rise in Web ads. *Advertising Age, 39,* 18.

Napoli, L, (1999, June 17). Banner ads are under the gun—And on the move. *New York Times,* p. D1.

National Institute of Mental Health. (1998). *Who clicks? Four years of Internet advertising* (DHHS Publication No. ADM 82-1195). Washington,

C. REPORT IN MLA STYLE

(page 1; with author/page citations)

top, bottom, and side margins: 1″
Double-space throughout.

Evans 1 header

Jonathan R. Evans

Professor Inman

Management 302

19 January 20--

An Analysis of the Scope and Effectiveness

of Online Advertising

Over the past three years, the number of American households online has tripled, from an estimated 15 million in 1996 to 45 million in 1999. Jupiter Communications, predicts that by the year 2003, 70 million households, representing about 62% of all U.S. households, will be online (Napoli D1). Online business has grown in tandem with the expanding number of Internet users. Forrester Research Inc. predicts that the total value of business-to-business e-commerce will reach $109 billion in 1999 and is likely to reach $1.3 trillion by 2003 (Arlens & Stevens 376-379).

The uncertainties surrounding advertising on the Internet remain one of the major impediments to the expansion. Dating from just 1994 when the first banner ads appeared on the Hotwired home page, the young Internet advertising industry is today in a state of flux.

Some analysts argue that advertising on the Internet can and should follow the same principles as advertising on television and other visual media ("eStats"). Others contend that advertising on the Internet should reflect the

D. WORKS CITED IN MLA STYLE

top, bottom, and side margins: 1″
Double-space throughout.

Evans 13 header

Works Cited

Adams, Jeffrey B. *Internet Advertising.* Boston: Brunswick Press, 2000.

AdCom Industries. *2001 Annual Report.* San Francisco: ACI, Inc., 2002.

Anders, George. "Buying Frenzy," *Wall Street Journal,* July 12, 1999, p. R6.

Arlens, Ramon, and Seymour Stevens. *E-Tailing.* Cambridge, MA: All-State, 1999. (hanging indent)

Corporate Libraries Association. *Directory of Business and Financial Services.* New York: Corporate Libraries Association, 1998.

"eStats: Advertising Revenues and Trends." *eMarketer Home Page.* 11 Aug. 1999. 7 Jan. 2000. http:www.emarketer.com/estats/ad.

Ivans, Edward. "Typical ROIs in Online Advertising." *Personnel Quarterly* Sep. 2001: 804-816.

Johnson, Bradley. "Nielsen/NetRatings Index Shows 4% Rise in Web Ads." *Advertising Age* 19 Jul. 1999: 18.

Napoli, Lisa. "Banner Ads Are Under the Gun—And On the Move." *New York Times* 17 Jun. 1999: D1.

National Institute of Mental Health. *Who Clicks? Four Years of Internet Advertising.* DHHS Publication No. ADM 82-1195. Washington, DC: GPO, 1998.

A. MEETING AGENDA

First type list unformatted; then apply numbering feature.

↓6X

14 pt **MILES HARDWARE EXECUTIVE COMMITTEE** ↓2X

12 pt↓ **Meeting Agenda** ↓2X

June 7, 20--, 3 p.m. ↓2X

1. Call to order ↓2X
2. Approval of minutes of May 5 meeting
3. Progress report on building addition and parking lot restrictions (Norman Hodges and Anthony Pascarelli)
4. May 15 draft of five-Year Plan
5. Review of National Hardware Association annual convention
6. Employee grievance filed by Ellen Burrows (John Landstrom)
7. New expense-report forms (Anne Richards)
8. Announcements
9. Adjournment

B. MINUTES OF A MEETING

Format body as a two-column open table; manually adjust column widths as needed.

↓6X

14 pt **RESOURCE COMMITTEE** ↓2X

12 pt↓ **Minutes of the Meeting** ↓2X

March 13, 20-- ↓2X

ATTENDANCE	The Resource Committee met on March 13, 20--, at the Airport Sheraton in Portland, Oregon, with all members were present. Michael Davis, chairperson, called the meeting to order at 2:30 p.m. ↓2X
APPROVAL OF MINUTES	The minutes of the January 27 meeting were read and approved.
OLD BUSINESS	The members of the committee reviewed the sales brochure on electronic copyboards and agreed to purchase one for the conference room. Cynthia Giovanni will secure quotations from at least two suppliers.
NEW BUSINESS	The committee reviewed a request from the Purchasing Department for three new computers. After extensive discussion regarding the appropriate use of the computers and software to be purchased, the committee approved the request.
ADJOURNMENT	The meeting was adjourned at 4:45 p.m. ↓2X
	Respectfully submitted, ↓4X
	D. S. Madsen
	D. S. Madsen, Secretary

C. ITINERARY

Format body as a two-column open table; manually adjust column widths as needed.

↓6X

14 pt **ITINERARY** ↓2X

12 pt↓ **For Arlene Gilsdorf** ↓2X

March 12-15, 20-- ↓2X

THURSDAY, MARCH 12 ↓2X	
5:10 p.m.-7:06 p.m.	Flight from Detroit to Portland; Northwest 83 (Phone: 800-555-1212); e-ticket; Seat 8D; nonstop; dinner ↓2X
	Jack Weatherford (Home: 503-555-8029; Office: 503-555-7631) will meet your flight on Thursday, provide transportation during your visit, and return you to the airport on Saturday morning. ↓2X
	Airport Sheraton (503-555-4032) King-sized bed, nonsmoking room; late arrival guaranteed (Reservation No. 30ZM6-02) ↓2X
FRIDAY, MARCH 13	
9 a.m.-5:30 p.m.	Portland Sales Meeting 1931 Executive Way, Suite 10 Portland (503-555-7631)
Evening	On your own
SATURDAY, MARCH 14	
7:30 a.m.-2:47 p.m.	Flight from Portland to Detroit; Northwest 360; e-ticket; Seat 9a; nonstop; breakfast

D. LEGAL DOCUMENT

Set left tabs at 1″ and 3″.

↓3DS

14 pt **POWER OF ATTORNEY** ↓1DS

12 pt↓ KNOW ALL MEN BY THESE PRESENTS that I, ATTORNEY LEE FERNANDEZ, of the City of Tulia, County of Swisher, State of Texas, do hereby appoint my son, Robert Fernandez, of this City, County, and State as my attorney-in-fact to act in my name, place, and stead as my agent in the management of my business operating transactions.

I give and grant unto my said attorney full power and authority to do and perform every act and thing requisite and necessary to be done in the said management as fully, to all intents and purposes, as I might or could do if personally present, with full power of revocation, hereby ratifying all that my said attorney shall lawfully do.

IN WITNESS WHEREOF, I have hereunto set my hand and seal this thirteenth day of April, 20--. ↓2DS

→tab to centerpoint ______________________ (L.S.) ↓1DS

SIGNED and affirmed in the presence of: ↓2DS

______________________ ↓2DS

____

footer Page 1 of 1

A. RESUME

Format body as a two-column open table; manually adjust column widths as needed.

↓6X

14 pt **TERRY M. MARTINA** ↓2X

12 pt ↓ **250 Maxwell Avenue, Boulder, CO 80305**
Phone: 303-555-9311; email: tmartina@ecc.edu ↓1X

↓1X

OBJECTIVE	Position in resort management anywhere in Colorado ↓2X
EDUCATION	A. A. in hotel management to be awarded May 2001 Edgewood Community College, Boulder, CO
EXPERIENCE	*Assistant Manager, Burger King Restaurant* Boulder, CO: 1999-Present • Achieved grade point average of 3.1 (on 4.0 scale). • Received Board of Regent tuition scholarship. • Financed all college expenses through savings, scholarships, and part-time work. *Student Intern, Ski Valley Haven* Aspen, CO: September-December 2000 • Worked as an assistant to the night manager of 200-room ski resort. • Gained practical experience in operating First-Guest management system. • Was in charge of producing daily occupancy reports.
PERSONAL	• Speak and write fluent Spanish • Competent in Microsoft Office 2000 • Secretary of ECC Hospitality Services Association • Special Olympics volunteer: Summer 2000
REFERENCES	Available upon request

B. APPLICATION LETTER

↓6X

March 1, 20-- ↓4X

Mr. Lou Mansfield, Director
Human Resources Department
Rocky Resorts International
P.O. Box 1412
Denver, CO 80214 ↓2X

Dear Mr. Mansfield: ↓2X

Please consider me an applicant for the position of concierge for Suite Retreat, as advertised in last Sunday's *Denver Times*.

I will receive my A.A. degree in hotel administration from Edgewood Community College in May and will be available for full-time employment immediately. In addition to my extensive coursework in hospitality services and business, I've had experience in working for a ski lodge similar to Suite Retreats in Aspen. As a lifelong resident of Colorado and an avid skier, I would be able to provide your guests with any information they request.

After you've reviewed my enclosed resume, I would appreciate having an opportunity to discuss with you why I believe I have the right qualifications and personality to serve as your concierge. I can be reached at 303-555-9311. ↓2X

Sincerely, ↓4X

Terry M. Martina

Terry M. Martina
250 Maxwell Avenue, Apt. 8
Boulder, CO 80305 ↓2X

Enclosure

C. PLACING INFORMATION ON PRINTED LINES

Because of the difficulty of aligning copy on a printed line with a computer and printer, lined forms such as job-application forms are most efficiently completed on a typewriter.

When typing on a lined form, use the typewriter's variable line spacer to adjust the paper so that the line is in the position that a row of underlines would occupy. (On many machines, this is accomplished by pressing in the left platen knob.)

Do not leave any lines for requested information blank; use *N/A* ("not applicable") if necessary. Because of space limitations, it may be necessary to abbreviate some words.

Because first impressions are important, ensure that all your employment documents are in correct format, are neat in appearance, and are free from errors.

D. JOB-APPLICATION FORM

(first page)

ROCKY RESORTS INTERNATIONAL
P.O. Box 1412 Denver, CO 80218

Employment Application

POSITION APPLIED FOR Concierge DATE OF APPLICATION 3/18/02

TYPE OF EMPLOYMENT DESIRED [X] Full-time [ ] Part-time [ ] Temporary [ ] Co-op/Internship

NAME Martina (LAST) Terry (FIRST) M (MI)

ADDRESS 250 Maxwell Avenue, Apt. B (STREET) Boulder (CITY) CO (STATE) 80305 (ZIP)

TELEPHONE 303-555-9331 SOCIAL SECURITY NO. 247-72-8431

If you are under 18, can you furnish a work permit? .... N/A .... [ ] Yes ... [ ] No

Have you ever worked here before? .... [X] Yes ... [ ] No

Are you legally eligible for employment in this country? .... [X] Yes ... [ ] No

Have you been convicted of a felony within the past seven years? .... [ ] Yes ... [X] No

If yes, please explain N/A

EDUCATION (most recent first)

Institution	City/State	Degree/Major	Dates
Edgewood Community College, Boulder, CO		A.A.—Hotel Admin.	2000-02
Durango High School, Durango, CO		Diploma	1997-2000

WORK EXPERIENCE (most recent first)

Organization	City/State	Position	Dates (inclusive)
Burger King Restaurant	Boulder, CO	Asst. Mgr.	1999-present
Ski Valley Haven	Aspen, CO	Intern	Sep-Dec 1999

AN EQUAL OPPORTUNITY EMPLOYER

A. BOXED TABLE *(Default Style)*

(with subtitle, braced headings, total line, and table note.)

center page ↓

Title / Subtitle: 12 pt ↓

AUSTIN-REEVES PRINTER DEPOT
Sales Through September 2001
(000s omitted) ↓1X

Column hds ↓1X — Braced column hd

Product	**Year-to-Date Sales**		**Prior-Year Sales**	
	2002	**2001**	**2000**	**1999**
Dot matrix	$ 5	$ 14	$ 19	$ 28
Ink-jet: color	188	423	569	841
Ink-jet: color portable	4	7	6	24
Ink-jet: black and white	146	200	273	588
Printer and copier combination	1,000	1,184	1,622	2,054
Black-and-white laser: standard	144	316	389	507
Black-and-white laser: premium	2,591	1,636	2368	87
Color laser	6	0	0	0
Totals	$4,084	$3,780	$5,246	$4,129
Note: Year-to-date sales have increased 7.4%.				

Body — Total line — Table note

B. OPEN TABLE

(with subtitle, blocked column headings, and 2-line heading)

First, format the table in default (boxed) style. Then delete all borders.

center page ↓

12 pt ↓ **SUITE RETREAT**
New Lodging Rates ↓1X

↓1X

Location	**Rack Rate**	**Discount Rate**	**Saving**
Bozeman, Montana	$ 95.75	$ 91.50	4.4%
Chicago, Illinois	159.00	139.50	12.3%
Dallas, Texas	249.50	219.00	12.2%
Las Vegas, Nevada	98.50	89.95	8.7%
Los Angeles, California	179.00	139.00	22.3%
Minneapolis, Minnesota	115.00	95.00	17.4%
New York City, New York	227.50	175.00	23.1%
Orlando, Florida	105.75	98.50	6.3%
Portland, Maine	93.50	93.50	0.0%
Seattle, Washington	143.75	125.75	12.5%

C. RULED TABLE

(with table number and centered column headings)

2

an effort to reduce errors and provide increased customer support, we have recently added numerous additional telephone support services, some of which are available 24 hours a day and others available during the work day. These are shown in Table 2. ↓2X

12 pt↓ **Table 2. COMPUTER SUPPLIES SUPPORT SERVICES** ↓1X

Support Service	**Telephone**	**Hours**
Product literature	800-555-3867	6 a.m. to 5 p.m.
Replacement parts	303-555-3388	24 hours a day
Technical documentation	408-555-3309	24 hours a day
Troubleshooting	800-555-8277	10 a.m. to 5 p.m.
Printer drivers	800-555-2377	6 a.m. to 5 p.m.
Software notes	800-555-3496	24 hours a day
Technical support	800-555-1205	24 hours a day
Hardware information	303-555-4289	6 a.m. to 5 p.m.

↓1X

We hope you will take advantages of these additional services to ensure that the computer hardware and software you purchase from Computer Supplies continues to provide you the quality and service you have come to expect from our company.

Sincerely,

Douglas Pullis

Douglas Pullis
General Manager

cds

First, format the table in default (boxed) style. Then delete all borders. Finally, add borders to the top and bottom of the column-heading row and to the bottom of the last row of the body of the table.

D. TABLES: SPECIAL FEATURES

VERTICAL PLACEMENT. Vertically center a table that appears on a page by itself. Leave 1 blank line before and after a table appearing with other text.

TITLE BLOCK. Center and bold all lines of the title block, typing the title in all caps and the subtitle in upper- and lowercase. If a table has a number, type the word *Table* in upper- and lowercase. Follow the table number with a period and 1 space.

COLUMN HEADINGS. Center column headings if *all* columns consist of text (e.g., words, phone numbers, or years). Block column headings if columns consist of text (left-aligned) and quantities (right-aligned). Regardless of the type of column, center braced headings. If the column headings do not take the same number of lines, align the headings at the bottom (by choosing the *bottom alignment* option). Use bold upper- and lowercase.

COLUMN CAPITALIZATION. Capitalize only the first word and proper nouns in column entries.

PERCENTAGES AND DOLLARS. Repeat the % sign for each number in a column (unless the heading identifies the data as percentages). Insert the $ sign only before the first amount and before a total amount. Align the $ sign with the longest amount in the column, inserting spaces after the $ sign as needed (leaving 2 spaces for each digit and 1 space for each comma).

TOTAL LINE. Add a border above a total line. Use the word *Total* or *Totals* as appropriate.

A. FORMATTING BUSINESS FORMS

Many business forms can be created and filled in by using templates that are provided within commercial word processing software. Template forms can be used "as is" or they can be edited. Templates can also be used to create customized forms for any business.

When a template is opened, the form is displayed on screen. The user can then fill in the necessary information, including personalized company information. Data is entered into cells or fields and you can move quickly from field to field with a single keystroke—usually by pressing TAB or ENTER.

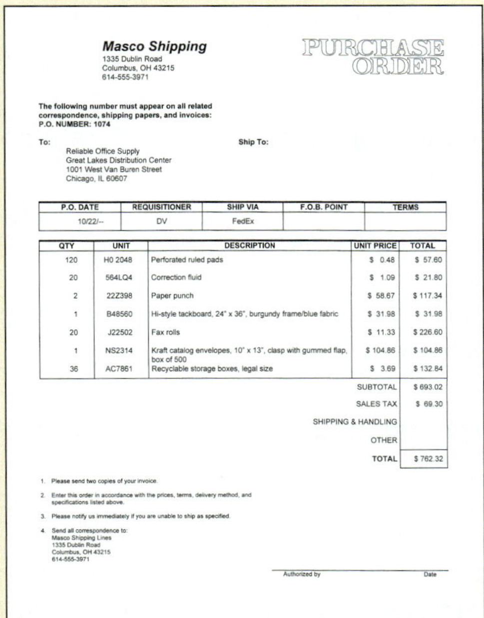

Masco Shipping
1335 Dublin Road
Columbus, OH 43215
614-555-3971

PURCHASE ORDER

The following number must appear on all related correspondence, shipping papers, and invoices:
P.O. NUMBER: 1074

To:
Reliable Office Supply
Great Lakes Distribution Center
1001 West Van Buren Street
Chicago, IL 60607

Ship To:

P.O. DATE	REQUISITIONER	SHIP VIA	F.O.B. POINT	TERMS
10/22/--	DV	FedEx		

QTY	UNIT	DESCRIPTION	UNIT PRICE	TOTAL
120	H0 2048	Perforated ruled pads	$ 0.48	$ 57.60
20	564LQ4	Correction fluid	$ 1.09	$ 21.80
2	22Z398	Paper punch	$ 58.67	$ 117.34
1	B48560	Hi-style tackboard, 24" x 36", burgundy frame/blue fabric	$ 31.98	$ 31.98
20	J22502	Fax rolls	$ 11.33	$ 226.60
1	NS2314	Kraft catalog envelopes, 10" x 13", clasp with gummed flap, box of 500	$ 104.86	$ 104.86
36	AC7861	Recyclable storage boxes, legal size	$ 3.69	$ 132.84
			SUBTOTAL	$ 693.02
			SALES TAX	$ 69.30
			SHIPPING & HANDLING	
			OTHER	
			TOTAL	$ 762.32

1. Please send two copies of your invoice.
2. Enter this order in accordance with the prices, terms, delivery method, and specifications listed above.
3. Please notify us immediately if you are unable to ship as specified.
4. Send all correspondence to:
   Masco Shipping Lines
   1335 Dublin Road
   Columbus, OH 43215
   614-555-3971

Authorized by   Date

B. U.S. POSTAL SERVICE ABBREVIATIONS

(for States, Territories, and Canadian Provinces)

States and Territories

Alabama	AL
Alaska	AK
Arizona	AZ
Arkansas	AR
California	CA
Colorado	CO
Connecticut	CT
Delaware	DE
District of Columbia	DC
Florida	FL
Georgia	GA
Guam	GU
Hawaii	HI
Idaho	ID
Illinois	IL
Indiana	IN
Iowa	IA
Kansas	KS
Kentucky	KY
Louisiana	LA
Maine	ME
Maryland	MD
Massachusetts	MA
Michigan	MI
Minnesota	MN
Mississippi	MS
Missouri	MO
Montana	MT
Nebraska	NE
Nevada	NV
New Hampshire	NH
New Jersey	NJ
New Mexico	NM
New York	NY
North Carolina	NC
North Dakota	ND
Ohio	OH
Oklahoma	OK
Oregon	OR
Pennsylvania	PA
Puerto Rico	PR
Rhode Island	RI
South Carolina	SC
South Dakota	SD
Tennessee	TN
Texas	TX
Utah	UT
Vermont	VT
Virgin Islands	VI
Virginia	VA
Washington	WA
West Virginia	WV
Wisconsin	WI
Wyoming	WY

Canadian Provinces

Alberta	AB
British Columbia	BC
Labrador	LB
Manitoba	MB
New Brunswick	NB
Newfoundland	NF
Northwest Territories	NT
Nova Scotia	NS
Ontario	ON
Prince Edward Island	PE
Quebec	PQ
Saskatchewan	SK
Yukon Territory	YT

C. PROOFREADERS' MARKS

Proofreaders' Marks		Draft	Final Copy
⌣	Omit space	data base	database
v or ^	Insert	if he's going (not)	if he's not going,
≡	Capitalize	Maple street	Maple Street
	Delete	a final draft	a draft
#	Insert space	allready to	all ready to
when	Change word	and if you	and when you
/	Use lowercase letter	our President	our president
¶	Paragraph	¶ Most of the	Most of the
•••	Don't delete	a true story	a true story
○	Spell out	the only 1	the only one
∽	Transpose	they all see	they see all
SS	Single-space	SS first line second line	first line second line
ds	Double-space	ds first line second line	first line second line
	Move right	Please send	Please send
	Move left	May I	May I
~~	Bold	Column Heading	**Column Heading**
ital	Italic	ital Time magazine	*Time* magazine
u/l	Underline	u/l Time magazine readers	Time magazine readers
	Move as shown	readers will see	will see

Language Arts for Business

(50 "must-know" rules)

PUNCTUATION

COMMAS

RULE 1 , direct address (L. 21)

Use commas before and after a name used in direct address.

Thank you, John, for responding to my email so quickly.

Ladies and gentlemen, the program has been canceled.

RULE 2 , independent clause (L. 27)

Use a comma between independent clauses joined by a coordinate conjunction (unless both clauses are short).

Ellen left her job with IBM, and she and her sister went to Paris.

But: Ellen left her job with IBM_ and went to Paris with her sister.

But: John drove_ and I navigated.

Note: An independent clause is one that can stand alone as a complete sentence. The most common coordinate conjunctions are *and, but, or,* and *nor.*

RULE 3 , introductory expression (L. 27)

Use a comma after an introductory expression (unless it is a short prepositional phrase).

Before we can make a decision, we must have all the facts.

But: In 2000_ our nation elected a new president.

Note: An introductory expression is a group of words that come before the subject and verb of the independent clause. Common prepositions are *to, in, on, of, at, by, for,* and *with.*

RULE 4 , direct quotation (L. 41)

Use a comma before and after a direct quotation.

James said, "I shall return," and then left.

RULE 5 , date (L. 57)

Use a comma before and after the year in a complete date.

We will arrive on June 2, 2001, for the conference.

But: We will arrive on June 2_ for the conference.

RULE 6 , place (L. 57)

Use a comma before and after a state or country that follows a city (but not before a ZIP Code).

Joan moved to Vancouver, British Columbia, in May.

Send the package to Douglasville, GA_ 30135, by Express Mail.

But: Send the package to Georgia_ by Express Mail.

RULE 7 , series (L. 61)

Use a comma between each item in a series of three or more.

We need to order paper, toner, and font cartridges for the printer.

They saved their work, exited their program, and turned off their computers when they finished.

Note: Do not use a comma after the last item in a series.

RULE 8 , transitional expression (L. 61)

Use a comma before and after a transitional expression or independent comment.

It is critical, therefore, that we finish the project on time.

Our present projections, you must admit, are inadequate.

But: You must admit our present projections are inadequate.

Note: Examples of transitional expressions and independent comments are *in addition to, therefore, however, on the other hand, as a matter of fact,* and *unfortunately.*

RULE 9 , nonessential expression (L. 71)

Use a comma before and after a nonessential expression.

Andre, who was there, can verify the statement.

But: Anyone who was there can verify the statement.

Van's first book, *Crisis of Management,* was not discussed.

Van's book *Crisis of Management* was not discussed.

Note: A nonessential expression is a group of words that may be omitted without changing the basic meaning of the sentence. Always examine the noun or pronoun that comes before the expression to determine whether the noun needs the expression to complete its meaning. If it does, the expression is *essential* and does *not* take a comma.

RULE 10 , adjacent adjectives (L. 71)

Use a comma between two adjacent adjectives that modify the same noun.

We need an intelligent, enthusiastic individual for this job.

But: Please order a new bulletin board for our main conference room.

Note: Do not use a comma after the second adjective. Also, do not use a comma if the first adjective modifies the combined idea of the second adjective and the noun (for example, *bulletin board* and *conference room* in the second example above).

SEMICOLONS

RULE 11 ; no conjunction (L. 97)

Use a semicolon to separate two closely related independent clauses that are *not* joined by a conjunction (such as *and, but, or,* or *nor).*

Management favored the vote; stockholders did not.

But: Management favored the vote, but stockholders did not.

RULE 12 ; series (L. 97)

Use a semicolon to separate three or more items in a series if any of the items already contain commas.

Staff meetings were held on Thursday, May 7; Monday, June 7; and Friday, June 12.

Note: Be sure to insert the semicolon *between* (not within) the items in a series.

HYPHENS

RULE 13 - number (L. 57)

Hyphenate compound numbers between twenty-one and ninety-nine and fractions that are expressed as words.

Twenty-nine recommendations were approved by at least three-fourths of the members.

RULE 14 - compound adjective (L. 67)

Hyphenate compound adjectives that come before a noun (unless the first word is an adverb ending in *–ly*).

We reviewed an up-to-date report on Wednesday.

But: The report was up to date.

But: We reviewed the highly rated report.

Note: A compound adjective is two or more words that function as a unit to describe a noun.

APOSTROPHES

RULE 15 ' singular noun (L. 37)

Use *'s* to form the possessive of singular nouns.

The hurricane's force caused major damage to North Carolina's coastline.

RULE 16 ' plural noun (L. 37)

Use only an apostrophe to form the possessive of plural nouns that end in *s*.

The investors' goals were outlined in the stockholders' report.

But: The investors outlined their goals in the report to the stockholders.

But: The women's and children's clothing was on sale.

RULE 17 ' pronoun (L. 37)

Use *'s* to form the possessive of indefinite pronouns (such as *someone's* or *anybody's*); do not use an apostrophe with personal pronouns (such as *hers, his, its, ours, theirs,* and *yours*).

She could select anybody's paper for a sample.

It's time to put the file back into its cabinet.

COLONS

RULE 18 : explanatory material (L. 91)

Use a colon to introduce explanatory material that follows an independent clause.

The computer satisfies three criteria: speed, cost, and power.

But: The computer satisfies the three criteria of speed, cost, and power.

Remember this: only one coupon is allowed per customer.

Note: An independent clause can stand alone as a complete sentence. Do not capitalize the word following the colon.

PERIODS

RULE 19 . polite request (L. 91)

Use a period to end a sentence that is a polite request.

Will you please call me if I can be of further assistance.

Note: Consider a sentence a polite request if you expect the reader to respond by doing as you ask rather than by giving a yes-or-no answer.

QUOTATION MARKS

RULE 20 " quotation (L. 41)

Use quotation marks around a direct quotation.

Harrison responded by saying, "Their decision does not affect us."

But: Harrison responded by saying that their decision does not affect us.

RULE 21 " title (L. 41)

Use quotation marks around the title of a newspaper or magazine article, chapter in a book, report, and similar terms.

The most helpful article I found was "Multimedia for All."

ITALICS (OR UNDERLINE)

RULE 22 *title* (L. 41)

Italicize (or underline) the titles of books, magazines, newspapers, and other complete published works.

Grisham's *The Brethren* was reviewed in a recent *USA Today* article.

GRAMMAR

SENTENCES

RULE 23 fragment (L. 21)

Avoid sentence fragments.

Not: She had always wanted to be a financial manager. But had not had the needed education.

But: She had always wanted to be a financial manager but had not had the needed education.

Note: A fragment is a part of a sentence that is incorrectly punctuated as a complete sentence. In the first sentence above, "but had not had the needed education" is not a complete sentence because it does not contain a subject.

RULE 24 run-on (L. 21)

Avoid run-on sentences.

Not: Mohamed is a competent worker he has even passed the MOUS exam.

Not: Mohamed is a competent worker, he has even passed the MOUS exam.

But: Mohamed is a competent worker; he has even passed the MOUS exam.

Or: Mohamed is a competent worker. He has even passed the MOUS exam.

Note: A run-on sentence is two independent clauses that run together without any punctuation between them or with only a comma between them.

AGREEMENT

RULE 25 agreement singular agreement plural (L. 67)

Use singular verbs and pronouns with singular subjects; use plural verbs and pronouns with plural subjects.

I was happy with my performance.

Janet and Phoenix were happy with their performance.

Among the items discussed were our raises and benefits.

RULE 26 agreement pronoun (L. 81)

Some pronouns *(anybody, each, either, everybody, everyone, much, neither, no one, nobody,* and *one)* are always singular and take a singular verb. Other pronouns *(all, any, more, most, none,* and *some)* may be singular or plural, depending on the noun to which they refer.

Each of the employees has finished his or her task.

Much remains to be done.

Most of the pie was eaten, but most of the cookies were left.

RULE 27 agreement intervening words (L. 81)

Disregard any intervening words that come between the subject and verb when establishing agreement.

The box containing the books and pencils has not been found.

Alex, accompanied by Tricia, is attending the conference and taking his computer.

RULE 28 agreement nearer noun (L. 101)

If two subjects are joined by *or, either/or, neither/nor,* or *not only/but also,* make the verb agree with the subject nearer to the verb.

Neither the coach nor the players are at home.

Not only the coach but also the referee is at home.

But: Both the coach and the referee are at home.

PRONOUNS

RULE 29 nominative pronoun (L. 107)

Use nominative pronouns (such as *I, he, she, we, they,* and *who)* as subjects of a sentence or clause.

The programmer and he are reviewing the code.

Barb is a person who can do the job.

RULE 30 objective pronoun (L. 107)

Use objective pronouns (such as *me, him, her, us, them,* and *whom)* as objects of a sentence, clause, or phrase.

The code was reviewed by the programmer and him.

Barb is the type of person whom we can trust.

ADJECTIVES AND ADVERBS

RULE 31 adjective/adverb (L. 101)

Use comparative adjectives and adverbs (*-er, more,* and *less)* when referring to two nouns or pronouns; use superlative adjectives and adverbs *(-est, most,* and *least)* when referring to more than two.

The shorter of the two training sessions is the more helpful one.

The longest of the three training sessions is the least helpful one.

WORD USAGE

RULE 32 accept/except (L. 117)

***Accept* means "to agree to"; *except* means "to leave out."**

All employees except the maintenance staff should accept the agreement.

RULE 33 affect/effect (L. 117)

***Affect* is most often used as a verb meaning "to influence"; *effect* is most often used as a noun meaning "result."**

The ruling will affect our domestic operations but will have no effect on our Asian operations.

RULE 34 farther/further (L. 117)

***Farther* refers to distance; *further* refers to extent or degree.**

The farther we drove, the further agitated he became.

RULE 35 personal/personnel (L. 117)

***Personal* means "private"; *personnel* means "employees."**

All personnel agreed not to use email for personal business.

RULE 36 principal/ principle (L. 117)

***Principal* means "primary"; *principle* means "rule."**

The principle of fairness is our principal means of dealing with customers.

MECHANICS

CAPITALIZATION

RULE 37 ≡ sentence (L. 31)

Capitalize the first word of a sentence.

Please prepare a summary of your activities.

RULE 38 ≡ proper noun (L. 31)

Capitalize proper nouns and adjectives derived from proper nouns.

Judy Hendrix drove to Albuquerque in her new Pontiac convertible.

Note: A proper noun is the official name of a particular person, place, or thing.

RULE 39 ≡ time (L. 31)

Capitalize the names of the days of the week, months, holidays, and religious days (but do not capitalize the names of the seasons).

On Thursday, November 25, we will celebrate Thanksgiving, the most popular holiday in the fall.

RULE 40 ≡ noun # (L. 77)

Capitalize nouns followed by a number or letter (except for the nouns *line, note, page, paragraph,* and *size).*

Please read Chapter 5, which begins on page 94.

RULE 41 ≡ compass point (L. 77)

Capitalize compass points (such as *north, south,* or *northeast)* only when they designate definite regions.

From Montana we drove south to reach the Southwest.

RULE 42 ≡ organization (L. 111)

Capitalize common organizational terms (such as *advertising department* and *finance committee)* only when they are the actual names of the units in the writer's own organization and when they are preceded by the word *the*.

The report from the Advertising Department is due today.

But: Our advertising department will submit its report today.

RULE 43 ≡ course (L. 111)

Capitalize the names of specific course titles but not the names of subjects or areas of study.

I have enrolled in Accounting 201 and will also take a marketing course.

NUMBER EXPRESSION

RULE 44 # general (L. 41)

In general, spell out numbers zero through ten, and use figures for numbers above ten.

We rented two movies for tonight.

The decision was reached after 27 precincts sent in their results.

RULE 45 ▶
figure
(L. 41)

Use figures for

- **Dates. (Use *st, d,* or *th* only if the day comes before the month.)**
  The tax report is due on April 15 (*not* April 15th)
  We will drive to the camp on the 23d (or *23rd* or *23rd*) of May.
- **All numbers if two or more *related* numbers both above and below ten are used in the same sentence.**
  Mr. Carter sent in 7 receipts, and Ms. Cantrell sent in 22.
  But: The 13 accountants owned three computers each.
- **Measurements (time, money, distance, weight, and percent).**
  The $500 statue we delivered at 7 a.m. weighed 6 pounds.
- **Mixed numbers.**
  Our sales are up 9½ (or *9 1/2)* percent over last year.

RULE 46 ▶
word
(L. 57)

Spell out

- **A number used as the first word of a sentence.**
  Seventy-five people attended the conference in San Diego.
- **The shorter of two adjacent numbers.**
  We have ordered 3 two-pound cakes and one 5-pound cake for the reception.
- **The words *million* and *billion* in even amounts (do not use decimals with even amounts).**
  A $5 ticket can win $28 million in this month's lottery.
- **Fractions.**
  Almost one-half of the audience responded to the question.

Note: When fractions and the numbers twenty-one through ninety-nine are spelled out, they should be hyphenated.

ABBREVIATIONS

RULE 47 ▶
abbreviate none
(L. 67)

In general business writing, do not abbreviate common words (such as *dept.* or *pkg.),* compass points, units of measure, or the names of months, days of the week, cities, or states (except in addresses).

Almost one-half of the audience indicated they were at least 5 feet_8 inches tall.

Note: Do not insert a comma between the parts of a single measurement.

RULE 48 ▶
abbreviate measure
(L. 87)

In technical writing, on forms, and in tables, abbreviate units of measure when they occur frequently. Do not use periods.

14 oz   5 ft 10 in   50 mph   2 yrs 10 mo

RULE 49 ▶
abbreviate lowercase
(L. 87)

In most lowercase abbreviations made up of single initials, use a period after each initial but no internal spaces.

a.m.   p.m.   i.e.   e.g.   e.o.m.

Exceptions: mph   mpg   wpm

RULE 50 ▶
abbreviate ≡
(L. 87)

In most all-capital abbreviations made up of single initials, do not use periods or internal spaces.

OSHA   PBS   NBEA   WWW   VCR   MBA

Exceptions: U.S.A.   A.A.   B.S.   Ph.D.   P.O.   B.C.   A.D.

PART 4

Advanced Formatting

OBJECTIVES

KEYBOARDING

- Type at least 43 words per minute on a 5-minute timing with no more than 5 errors.

LANGUAGE ARTS

- Refine proofreading skills and correctly use proofreaders' marks.
- Use capitals, punctuation, and grammar correctly.
- Improve composing and spelling skills.
- Recognize subject/verb agreement.

WORD PROCESSING

- Use the word processing commands necessary to complete the document processing activities.

DOCUMENT PROCESSING

- Format reports, multipage letters, multipage memos, and tables.

TECHNICAL

- Answer at least 90 percent of the questions correctly on an objective test.

KEYBOARDING IN ARTS, AUDIO, VIDEO TECHNOLOGY, AND COMMUNICATIONS SERVICES

Occupations in this cluster deal with organizing and communicating information to the public in various forms and media. This cluster includes jobs in radio and television broadcasting, journalism, motion pictures, the recording industry, the performing arts, multimedia publishing, and the entertainment services. Work as a book editor, computer artist, technical writer, radio announcer, news correspondent, and camera operator are just a few jobs within this cluster.

Qualifications and Skills

Strong oral and written communication skills and technical skills are necessary for anyone in communications and media. Without a doubt, enhancing keyboarding skill is extremely advantageous.

Working in the media requires creativity, talent, and accurate use of language. In journalism, being observant, thinking clearly, and seeing the significance of events are all of utmost importance. Announcers must have exceptional voices, excellent speaking skills, and a unique style. The ability to work under pressure is important in all areas of media.

Unit 13

Skill Refinement

LESSON 61
Skillbuilding and Report Review

LESSON 62
Skillbuilding and Letter Review

LESSON 63
Skillbuilding, Memo, and Email Review

LESSON 64
Skillbuilding and Table Review

LESSON 65
Skillbuilding and Employment Document Review

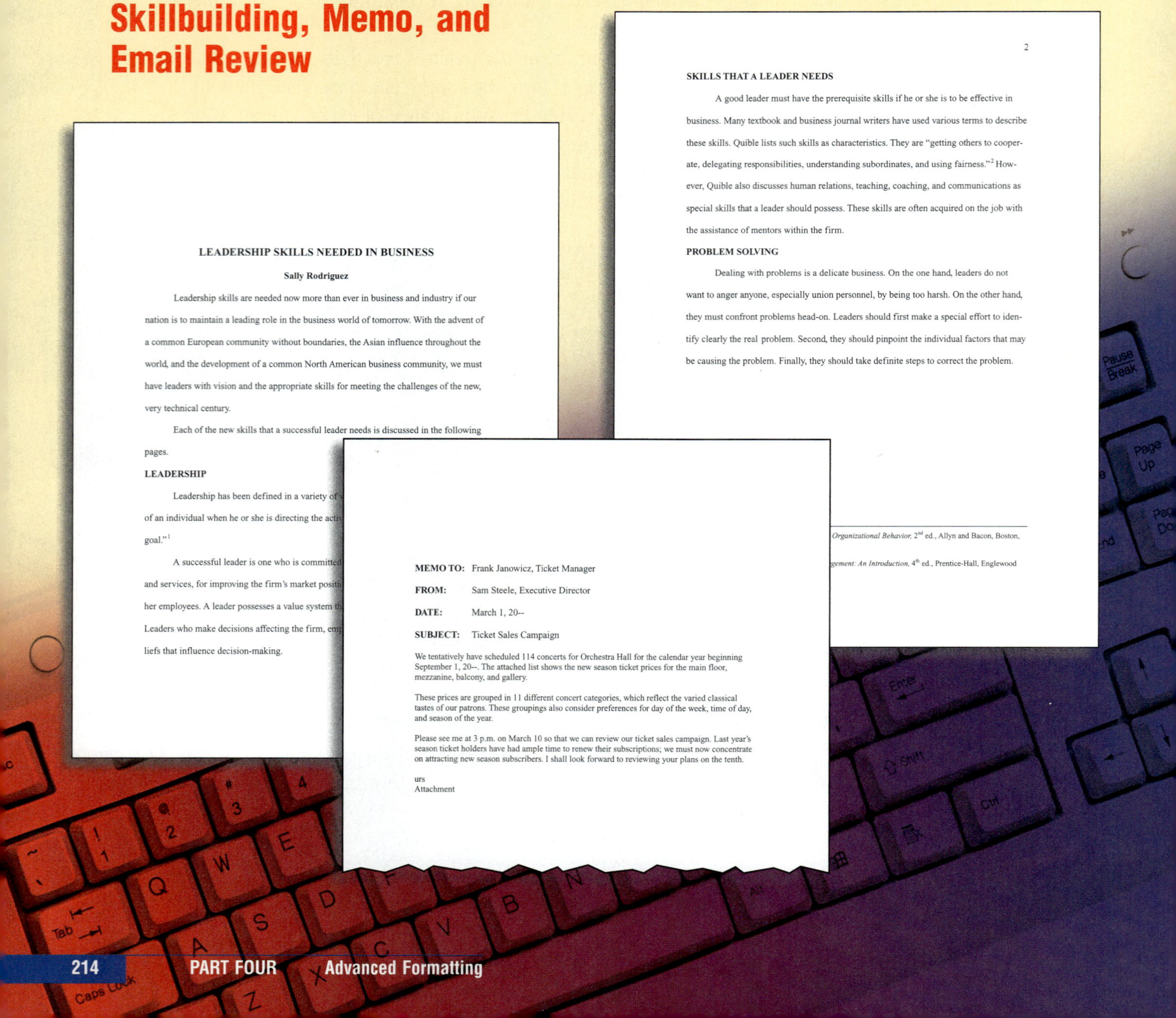

Lesson 61

Skillbuilding and Report Review

GOALS

- Improve speed and accuracy
- Refine language arts skills in the use of commas
- Format reports

A. Type 2 times.

A. WARMUP

```
     A queen quickly adjusted 12 blinds as the bright sun    11
blazed down from the sky; she then paced through the 19      22
rooms (all very large) next to the castle for 38 minutes.    33
| 1 | 2 | 3 | 4 | 5 | 6 | 7 | 8 | 9 | 10 | 11 | 12
```

SKILLBUILDING

B. Take three 12-second timings on each line. The scale below the last line shows your wpm speed for a 12-second timing.

B. 12-SECOND SPEED SPRINTS

```
Most of those autos on the road had only one or two people.
Those boys and girls did the right thing by doing the work.
Some of the men ran to the gym to work out with their kids.
All of the new male workers were given a tour of the plant.
| | | | 5 | | | | 10 | | | | 15 | | | | 20 | | | | 25 | | | | 30 | | | | 35 | | | | 40 | | | | 45 | | | | 50 | | | | 55 | | | | 60
```

C. DIAGNOSTIC PRACTICE: ALPHABET

If you are not using the GDP software, turn to page SB-2 and follow the directions for this activity.

LANGUAGE ARTS

D. Study the rules at the right.

D. COMMAS

RULE ▶ , series

Use a comma between each item in a series of three or more.

We need to order paper, toner, and font cartridges for the printer.

They saved their work, exited their program, and turned off their computers when they finished.

Note: Do not use a comma after the last item in a series.

RULE ▶ ,transitional expression

Use a comma before and after a transitional expression or independent comment.

It is critical, therefore, that we finish the project on time.

Our present projections, you must admit, are inadequate.

But: You must admit our present projections are inadequate.

Note: Examples of transitional expressions and independent comments are *in addition to, therefore, however, on the other hand, as a matter of fact,* and *unfortunately.*

Edit the sentences to correct any errors in the use of the comma.

8 The lawyer the bank and the courthouse received copies.
9 The closing was delayed therefore for more than an hour.
10 The abstract deed and contract were all three in order.
11 Ms. Sperry's flight was delayed however for two hours.
12 Happily the drinks snacks and napkins arrived on time.
13 This offer I think will be unacceptable to the board.

DOCUMENT PROCESSING

Report 61-36

Business Report

UTI EMPLOYEE TRAINING PROGRAMS

Your Name, Training Coordinator

¶ Various training techniques are used in business and industry to ~~update~~ *help* employees *acquire new* skills ~~and to assist them in acquiring new skills. It should be no surprise, therefore, that conscientious employees are eager to participate in training programs.~~ Some ~~of the various~~ *effective* techniques that United Transportation Inc. *(UTI)* uses in its training programs are ~~described below~~ *discussed in this report*.

,transitional expression

Go To

Word Processing Manual Review:
L. 21–24: *All*
L. 23: Bold
L. 26: Alignment and Font Size

Reference Manual Review:
R-8A: Report in Business Style

ON-THE-JOB TRAINING AND LECTURES

¶ Two of the most frequently used and *highly effective* training methods are on-th*e*-job training and lectures.

¶ **On-the-Job Training.** on the job training saves time and money by ~~permitting~~ *enabling* individuals *to* train at the workplace. ~~This method lets~~ the trainer use*s* the workstation in place of a classroom. ~~While there are many benefits from this type of experience,~~ on-the-job training does require careful coordination to *e*nsure that learning objectives are achieved.

¶ **Lectures.** Lectures are often used because they are a low-cost method of ~~training.~~ *instruction.* Lectures, which require little action on the part of the trainer, may not be effective when introducing employees to new techniques and work program*s*.

CONFERENCES

¶ In ~~the~~ *a* conference ~~method of instruction,~~ small groups of employees are taught by a ~~conference~~ director, manager, or outside consultant. ~~This method of instruction results in~~ *Conferences provide* considerable give-and-take ~~between the director and the employees~~. For learning to occur, the ~~director~~ *trainer* must be *skilled* in the use of interactive tech*n*iques.

, series

(Continued on next page)

DISTANCE EDUCATION

¶ A growing segment of UTI's training is now delivered on-line via the internet. Some of these courses, called distance education, are designed and managed by UTI, but an increasing number are designed and managed form independent vendors, such as educational institutions and management-consulting firms. These on-line courses are not only cost-effective, but also permit the trainee to complete the course at a time that is convenient for them.

The UTI Training Department estimates that within five years, 80% or more of its training modules will be delivered on-line, at a projected annual cost savings of at least 575,000 dollars.

Report 61-37

Multipage Academic Report With Footnotes

Go To

Word Processing Manual Review:
L. 27: Page Numbering and Page Break
L. 29: Line Spacing
L. 35: Italics
L.41: Footnotes

Reference Manual

Review:
R-8C and **R-8D:** Report in Academic Style

LEADERSHIP SKILLS NEEDED IN BUSINESS

Sally Rodriguez

Leadership skills are needed now more than ever in business and industry if our nation is to maintain a leading role in the business world of tomorrow. With the advent of a common European community without boundaries, the Asian influence throughout the world, and the development of a common North American business community, we must have leaders with vision and the appropriate skills for meeting the challenges of the new, very technical century.

Each of the new skills that a successful leader needs is discussed in the following pages.

LEADERSHIP

Leadership has been defined in a variety of ways. One definition is "the behavior of an individual when he or she is directing the activities of a group toward a shared goal."[1]

A successful leader is one who is committed to ideas—ideas for future products and services, for improving the firm's market position, and for the well-being of his or her employees. A leader possesses a value system that is ethically and morally sound. Leaders who make decisions affecting the firm, employees, and society have a set of beliefs that influence decision-making.

SKILLS THAT A LEADER NEEDS

A good leader must have the prerequisite skills if he or she is to be effective in business. Many textbook and business journal writers have used various terms to describe these skills. Quible lists such skills as characteristics. They are "getting others to cooperate, delegating responsibilities, understanding subordinates, and using fairness."[2] However, Quible also

,series

,transitional expression

(Continued on next page)

,series

discusses human relations, teaching, coaching, and communications as special skills that a leader *should* possess. These skills are often acquired on the job with the assistance of mentors within the firm.

PROBLEM SOLVING

,transitional expression

,transitional expression

,transitional expression

Dealing with problems is a delicate business. On the one hand, leaders do not want to anger anyone, especially union personnel, by being too harsh. On the other hand, they must confront problems head-on. Leaders should first make a special effort to identify clearly the *real* problem. Second, they should pinpoint the individual factors that may be causing the problem. Finally, they should take definite steps to correct the problem.

[1]Judith R. Gordon, *A Diagnostic Approach to Organizational Behavior,* 2nd ed., Allyn and Bacon, Boston, 1997, p. 393.
[2]Zane K. Quible, *Administrative Office Management: An Introduction,* 4th ed., Prentice-Hall, Englewood Cliffs, N.J., 1996, pp. 212-216.

Report 61-38

Multipage Business Report With Footnote

Open the file for Report 61-37 and make the following changes.

1. Change the report from academic style to business style.
2. Assume that you wrote the report, and change the byline accordingly.
3. Delete the third paragraph. Note that this results in the elimination of the first footnote.
4. Add a fourth side heading, THE LEADER AS TEACHER. Then add the following paragraph:

   Those who are in leadership positions often assume that workers learn how to perform a job simply by doing it without guidance. The real leader plans well-structured orientation sessions for new workers and does the same for all workers whenever there is new technology to be learned or when there is a change in policy or procedure.

   (**Note:** If necessary, force a page break to prevent the new side heading from appearing at the bottom of the first page.)
5. Finally, add a footnote at the end of the paragraph you inserted in Step 4:

   Ahmed Bazarak, "The Leader as Teacher," *The Manager's Newsletter,* July 18, 2001, pp. 14-17.

Lesson 62

Skillbuilding and Letter Review

GOALS

- Type at least 40wpm/5′/5e
- Format business letters and personal-business letters

A. Type 2 times.

A. WARMUP

```
     Quist & Zenk's sales were exactly $247,650; but the      10
cost of goods sold was $174,280 (70.37%). The profit made     22
was small after other, extensive expenses were subtracted.    34
| 1 | 2 | 3 | 4 | 5 | 6 | 7 | 8 | 9 | 10 | 11 | 12
```

SKILLBUILDING

B. MAP

Follow the GDP software directions for this exercise in improving keystroking accuracy.

C. PACED PRACTICE

If you are not using the GDP software, turn to page SB-14 and follow the directions for this activity.

STRATEGIES FOR *Career Success*

Corrective Feedback

Sometime in your career, you will give someone corrective feedback. You can use positive communication to do this and not appear to criticize the person.

Here are some things you should not do. Do not correct the person in front of others. Avoid giving feedback when you are angry. Stay away from personal comments (e.g., "That idea will get us nowhere!"). Do not diminish a person's enthusiasm (e.g., "We've never done that before, and we're not starting now.").

Here are some things you should do. Listen to the person's side of the situation. Express yourself in a positive way (e.g., "You're getting much closer."). Be specific about what the person can do to correct the situation. Follow up within a short time and identify all progress.

YOUR TURN Think about the last time you received corrective feedback. Did the person giving you feedback use techniques to create a positive outcome?

D. Take two 5-minute timings. Review your speed and errors.

Goal: At least 40wpm/5'/5e

D. 5-MINUTE TIMING

Many computer users are quite familiar with software 11
commands. However, many users do not know the importance 22
of system software. System software controls the operation 34
of computer hardware. 38
The operating system is one type of system software. 49
It manages the operations of a computer and functions as 60
the interface between the user, application software, and 72
computer hardware. Application software includes the word 84
processing, spreadsheet, and database software. Computer 95
hardware includes the mouse, keyboard, printer, and disk 106
drives. A computer must have an operating system to work. 118
Windows is a popular operating system. It allows the user 130
to click icons and issue commands to move within screens 141
called windows. 144
Another type of system software is utility software. 155
Utility programs perform specific tasks. Utilities manage 167
resources. File conversion, file compression, backup, and 179
virus protection are examples of utility programs. These 190
programs are analyzed in many computer magazines. 200

| 1 | 2 | 3 | 4 | 5 | 6 | 7 | 8 | 9 | 10 | 11 | 12

DOCUMENT PROCESSING

Correspondence 62-55

Personal-Business Letter in Block Style

Reference Manual

Review:
R-3D: Personal-Business Letter

October 1, 20-- | Dr. Anthony L. Robbins | 2345 South Main Street | Bowling Green, OH 43402 | Dear Anthony:

¶ Thank you for your letter of September 25 in which you inquired about my trip to New York City. Your letter brought back a lot of memories of those days when I was one of your students.

¶ I plan to leave on October 15 for a two-week business and vacation trip to the city. While at Columbia University, I will be conducting a workshop on the utilization of voice-activated equipment.

¶ My work at Columbia will be completed on October 22, after which I plan to attend a number of plays, visit the Metropolitan Museum of Art, and take one of the sightseeing tours of the city.

¶ If you and your wife would care to join me on October 22, please let me know. I would be most happy to make reservations at the hotel for you and to purchase theater tickets. Why don't you consider joining me in the "Big Apple."

Sincerely, | Bryan Goldberg | 320 South Summit Street | Toledo, OH 43604

Correspondence 62-56

Business Letter in Modified-Block Style

Go To
Word Processing Manual Review:
L. 50: Ruler Tabs and Tab Sets

Reference Manual
Review:
R-3B: Business Letter in Modified-Block Style

June 3, 20--

Director of Product Development
Hampton Associates, Inc.
830 Market St.
San Francisco, Ca 94103-1925

Dear Director of Product Development:

¶ I recently read an article in Business Week concerning how computer buyers can make standards happen. It was a very interesting article. ¶ The article indicated that if customers demand standard products ~~standard~~ when they purchase computers, participate in standard-setting groups, and band together with other customers, they will do better in the long run. Have you had customer groups ~~help~~ assist you or provide you with information on the adoption of more computer standards? ~~such as in the areas of~~ These standards include industry-wide interfaces, a mix and match of computer gear and programs, and building the best system for each application utilized.

¶ I would appreciate any data that you might furnish for me with ~~relationship~~ regard to customers and your firm working together to set past or future standards.

Sincerely yours,

Alice Karns
Vice President

urs

Correspondence 62-57

Business Letter in Block Style

Go To
Word Processing Manual Review:
L. 33: Envelopes

Reference Manual
Review pages **R-3A** and **R-6A** of the Reference Manual.

Revise Correspondence 62-56, making the following changes:

1. Change the letter to block style.
2. Change the date to `June 5, 20--`.
3. Send the letter to Ms. Heidi M. Fischer at Gramstad Brothers, Inc., located at 5417 Harbord Drive in Oakland, CA 94618.
4. Change the salutation.
5. Combine the second and third paragraphs into one paragraph.
6. Add the following text as a new third paragraph:

    ```
    Some of my colleagues and I
    would like to get involved
    with others in an effort to
    make desired changes. I am
    confident that there are
    others around the Bay area
    that feel the same way.
    ```
7. Prepare an envelope for the letter.

Lesson 63

Skillbuilding, Memo, and Email Review

GOALS
- Improve speed and accuracy
- Refine language arts skills in composing paragraphs
- Format memos and an email message

A. WARMUP

A. Type 2 times.

```
     "When is the quarterly jury report due?" asked Glenn.   11
He had faxed forms* to 64 of the 135 prospective jurors.     22
Only about one dozen of 596 citizens could not be located.   34
| 1 | 2 | 3 | 4 | 5 | 6 | 7 | 8 | 9 | 10 | 11 | 12
```

SKILLBUILDING

PPP

PRETEST → PRACTICE → POSTTEST

B. PRETEST: Discrimination Practice

PRETEST
Take a 1-minute timing. Review your speed and errors.

```
     The entire trip on a large train was better than we     11
had hoped. Polite police looked out for both the young and   23
old. One unit was outnumbered by herds of frolicking deer.   35
| 1 | 2 | 3 | 4 | 5 | 6 | 7 | 8 | 9 | 10 | 11 | 12
```

C. PRACTICE: Left Hand

PRACTICE
Speed Emphasis:
If you made no more than 1 error on the Pretest, type each *individual* line 2 times.
Accuracy Emphasis:
If you made 2 or more errors, type each *group* of lines (as though it were a paragraph) 2 times.

```
rtr trip trot sport train alert courts assert tragic truest
asa mass salt usage cased cease astute dashed masked castle
rer rear rest overt rerun older before entire surest better
```

D. PRACTICE: Right Hand

```
mnm menu numb hymns unmet manly mental namely manner number
pop post coop opera pools opens polite proper police oppose
iui unit quit fruit suits built medium guided helium podium
```

E. POSTTEST: Discrimination Practice

POSTTEST
Repeat the Pretest timing and compare performance.

F. PROGRESSIVE PRACTICE: ALPHABET

If you are not using the GDP software, turn to page SB-7 and follow the directions for this activity.

LANGUAGE ARTS

G. COMPOSING: PARAGRAPH

Read through the paragraphs in the 5-minute timing in Lesson 62. Compose a paragraph to include the type of operating system, application software, and utility programs loaded on the computers used in your keyboarding class.

DOCUMENT PROCESSING

Correspondence 63-58

Memo With Attachment

Reference Manual

Review:
R-4D: Memo

Do not indent paragraphs in a memo.

Remember to type your reference initials.

MEMO TO: Frank Janowicz, Ticket Manager | **FROM**: Sam Steele, Executive Director | **DATE**: March 1, 20-- | **SUBJECT**: Ticket Sales Campaign

¶ We tentatively have scheduled 114 concerts for Orchestra Hall for the calendar year beginning September 1, 20--. The attached list shows the new season ticket prices for the main floor, mezzanine, balcony, and gallery.

¶ These prices are grouped in 11 different concert categories, which reflect the varied classical tastes of our patrons. These groupings also consider preferences for day of the week, time of day, and season of the year.

¶ Please see me at 3 p.m. on March 10 so that we can review our ticket sales campaign. Last year's season ticket holders have had ample time to renew their subscriptions; we must now concentrate on attracting new season subscribers. I shall look forward to reviewing your plans on the tenth.

urs | Attachment

Correspondence 63-59

Email Message

Go To

Word Processing Manual Review:
L. 25: Email a Document

Reference Manual

Review:
R-5C: Email Message in Internet Explorer, or
R-5D: Email Message in Netscape Navigator

gpeters@ssw.com | Request for Information | Mr. Peters:

¶ Please send information and prices on the security software you recently advertised in *PC Magazine.*

¶ We are interested in implementing a new security program for the personal computers in our main office and would like to study the specifications and features your system provides.

¶ Thank you for your assistance.

C. H. Cox

Correspondence 63-60

Memo With Attachment and Copy Notation

MEMO TO: Edo Dorati Cabaret pops Conductor

FROM: Sam Steele, Executive Director

DATE: March 2, 20--

Subject: Erving Berlin Concert

Our Patron Advisory Program Committtee recommends inits their attached letter that the Erving Berlin concert begin with some pre-World War I hits, followed by music from the '20s and '30s. Favorites from this era are hit songs from Music Box Review, Puttin' on The Ritz, and Follow the the Fleet. After the intermission the committee suggest songs from the '40s and '50s, hits from Annie get Your Gun, Call me Madam, Easter parade. A planning meeting has been scheduled for you, Dolly Carpenter (the Rehearsals Coordinator), and me on Mar. 9 at 10 A.M. at Orchestra Hall. I shall look foreward to seeing you then.

urs

Attachment

c: Dolly Carpenter

Correspondence 63-61

Memo

MEMO TO: Dolly Carpenter, Rehearsals Coordinator
FROM: Sam Steele, Executive Director
DATE: March 3, 20--
SUBJECT: Summer Cabaret Pops Concerts

We are pleased that you will be our rehearsals coordinator for this summer's Cabaret Pops concerts. The five biweekly concerts will run from June 13 through August 8.

As the concert schedule is much lighter during the summer months, I am quite confident that you will be able to use the Orchestra Hall stage for all rehearsals. This is the preference of Edo Dorati, who will be the conductor for this year's Cabaret Pops concerts.

I look forward to seeing you on June 1.

Lesson 64

Skillbuilding and Table Review

GOALS

- Type at least 40wpm/5′/5e
- Format tables

A. Type 2 times.

A. WARMUP

There were two big questions: (1) Would both have to 11
be present to pick up the license? and (2) Is a blood test 23
required? Jeff and Faye were quite dizzy with excitement. 34
| 1 | 2 | 3 | 4 | 5 | 6 | 7 | 8 | 9 | 10 | 11 | 12

SKILLBUILDING

B. PROGRESSIVE PRACTICE: NUMBERS

If you are not using the GDP software, turn to page SB-11 and follow the directions for this activity.

C. Take a 1-minute timing on the first paragraph to establish your base speed. Then take four 1-minute timings on the remaining paragraphs. As soon as you equal or exceed your base speed on one paragraph, advance to the next, more difficult paragraph.

C. SUSTAINED PRACTICE: ALTERNATE-HAND WORDS

The town council decided to shape its destiny when a 11
rich landowner lent a hand by proposing to chair the audit 23
committee. He will be a good chairman, and eight civic 34
club members will work to amend some troublesome policies. 46

One problem relates to the change in profit for many 11
of the firms in the city. As giant property taxes do not 22
relate to income, they wish to make those taxes go down. 33
The result means increases in their sales or income taxes. 45

All eight members of the town council now agree that 11
it is time to join with other cities throughout the state 23
in lobbying with the state legislature to bring about the 35
needed change. The right balance in taxes is the goal. 46

The mayor pointed out that it is not only business 10
property owners who would be affected. Homeowners should 22
see a decrease in property taxes, and renters might see 33
lower rents, as taxes on rental property would be lowered. 45
| 1 | 2 | 3 | 4 | 5 | 6 | 7 | 8 | 9 | 10 | 11 | 12

D. Take two 5-minute timings. Review your speed and errors.

Goal: At least 40wpm/5′/5e

D. 5-MINUTE TIMING

The computer has changed the way you do many things 11
in the office today. Jobs that used to take many hours to 23
complete now can be done in less time. A quick review of 34
ways in which your computer can streamline your work may be 45
in order. 47

Most computer programs include various wizards that 57
will help you through any project. You can use a stored 68
template, or you can create your own style. You do not 79
need to write your thoughts in longhand on paper before 90
you type them. Composing and revising documents as you 101
type them will save you lots of time. 109

Your computer is valuable for more than just writing 120
letters, however. Using various software applications, you 132
can create multimedia presentations that dazzle. You can 143
also build databases for sorting and storing all types of 155
data, format spreadsheets, create personal calendars and 166
colorful charts, and perform calculations. You can even 177
create stationery and publish newsletters. It is exciting 189
to consider all the possibilities for using computers. 200

| 1 | 2 | 3 | 4 | 5 | 6 | 7 | 8 | 9 | 10 | 11 | 12

DOCUMENT PROCESSING

Table 64-23

Three-Column Boxed Table

Go To

Word Processing Manual Review:
L. 36: Table—Create; AutoFit to Contents
L. 37: Table—Merge Cells
L. 38: Center a Table Horizontally and Center Page
L. 39: Table—Align Text in a Column

Reference Manual Review:
R-13A: Boxed Table

$700 COMPOUNDED ANNUALLY FOR 7 YEARS AT 7 PERCENT		
Beginning of Year	**Interest**	**Value**
First	$00.00	$ 700.00
Second	49.00	749.00
Third	52.43	801.43
Fourth	56.10	857.53
Fifth	60.03	917.56
Sixth	64.23	981.79
Seventh	68.72	1,050.51
Eighth	78.68	1,129.19

Table 64-24

Three-Column Open Table

Go To **Word Processing Manual Review:** **L. 37:** Tables—Borders

Reference Manual Review: **R-13B:** Open Table

1. Center the table vertically.
2. Create a table with 3 columns and 9 rows.
3. Center the column headings and type in upper- and lowercase and bold.
4. Automatically adjust the column widths for all columns.
5. Merge the cells in Row 1.
6. Center and type the title in all caps and bold. Press ENTER 1 time.
7. Center and type the subtitle in upper- and lowercase and bold.
8. Press ENTER 1 time after typing the subtitle.
9. Center the table horizontally.

SALES CONFERENCES
All Sessions at Regional Offices

Date	City	Leader
October 7	Boston	D. G. Gorham
October 17	Baltimore	James B. Brunner
October 24	Miami	Becky Taylor
November 3	Dallas	Rodney R. Nordstein
November 10	Minneapolis	Joanne Miles-Tyrell
November 17	Denver	Becky Taylor
November 26	Los Angeles	Rodney R. Nordstein

Table 64-25

Three-Column Ruled Table

Reference Manual Review: **R-13C:** Ruled Table

SECOND HALF-YEAR SALES
Ending December 31, 20--

Month	Sales Quotas ($)	Actual Sales ($)
July	335,400	350,620
August	370,750	296,230
September	374,510	425,110
October	390,270	390,110
November	375,890	368,290
December	360,470	378,690
TOTAL	2,207,290	2,209,050

Lesson 65

Skillbuilding and Employment Document Review

GOALS

- Improve speed and accuracy
- Refine language arts skills in proofreading
- Format employment documents

A. Type 2 times.

A. WARMUP

     Only 6 of the 18 competitors weighed more than 149#. 11
All Big Five matches were scheduled in Gym #3. Amazingly, 23
about 1/3 of the #1 Jaguars were picked to acquire titles. 35
| 1 | 2 | 3 | 4 | 5 | 6 | 7 | 8 | 9 | 10 | 11 | 12

SKILLBUILDING

B. TECHNIQUE PRACTICE: BACKSPACE KEY

Type each word as shown until you reach the backspace sign (←). Then backspace 1 time and replace the previously typed character with the one shown.

First Letter: h←fall s←dash h←lead k←heel p←cage b←rare d←bark l←date t←sold
Middle Letter: has←lf far←te mak←de roo←am do←ive fas←ce war←ve wee←ak yok←lk
Last Letter: sale←t they←m helm←d wall←k pals←e milk←d told←l quip←t main←l

LANGUAGE ARTS

C. Compare this paragraph with the fourth paragraph of Report 61-37 on page 217. Edit the paragraph to correct any errors.

C. PROOFREADING

A successful leader is one who is commited to ideas-ideas for future product and services for improving the firms market position, and for the wellbeing of his or her employes. A leeder possesses a value system that is ethicly and morally sound. leaders who make decisions effecting the firm, employees, and society, have set of beliefs that influence decision-making.

DOCUMENT PROCESSING

Report 65-39

Traditional Resume

Go To

Word Processing Manual Review:
L. 51: Fonts

Reference Manual

Review:
R-12A: Resume

Follow these steps to format this resume correctly:

1. Set alignment at center.
2. Press ENTER 6 times; then center the name in 14-pt. Arial bold.
3. Press ENTER 2 times. Switch to 12-pt. font.
4. Type the street address, followed by a comma.
5. Press the SPACE BAR 1 time; then type the city, state, and ZIP code.
6. Press ENTER 1 time.
7. Type the phone number, followed by a semicolon.
8. Press the SPACE BAR 1 time; then type `email:` and the email address.
9. Press ENTER 2 times.
10. Create an open table with 2 columns and 4 rows. Set alignment to left.
11. Apply a top border to the table, and press ENTER 1 time.
12. Type `OBJECTIVE` in bold in Row 1, Column A.
13. Tab to Column B, press ENTER 1 time, and type your objective.
14. Continue typing the entries in each column as shown. Automatically adjust column widths when finished.

TIMOTHY J. ROBINSON

5816 Foxfire Road, Lawton, OK 73501
Phone: 405-555-3039; email: trobin@lcc.edu

EDUCATION	Lawton Community College, Lawton, Oklahoma Associate in Business degree, Office Systems, June 1998 Specialization in computer application software (Microsoft Word, Excel, Access), business communication, and office systems management. Frederick High School, Frederick, Oklahoma Graduated: May 1996
EXPERIENCE	*Computer Systems Technician*, September 1996-Present Selkirk & Associates, Lawton, Oklahoma Duties include installing and updating computer software programs throughout the firm. *Secretary II*, July 1994-August 1996 (part-time) Kittredge Insurance Agency, Frederick, Oklahoma Duties included typing and word processing while reporting to the administrative assistant to the owner.
ACTIVITIES	College Choir, 1996-1998 Business Students Club, 1996-1998 (Secretary, 1997-1998) Varsity Basketball, 1996-1998 Intramural Soccer, 1996-1998
REFERENCES	References available upon request.

Correspondence 65-62

Application Letter in Block Style With Enclosure Notation

Reference Manual

Review:
R-12B: Application Letter

Current Date | Mrs. Denise F. Klenzman | Director of Human Resources | Cole Enterprises | 3714 Crestmont Avenue | Norman, OK 73069 | Dear Mrs. Klenzman:

¶ Please consider me an applicant for the position of Computer Systems Coordinator with your firm. I became aware of the new position through a friend who is an employee at Cole Enterprises. I have been employed at Selkirk & Associates since graduating from high school in 1996. During this time I have also earned an Assoc. in Business degree at Lawton Community College. The resume enclosed shows that I have had several courses in computer application soft ware and office systems. I am confident that my educational ~~experience~~ background and my computer systems experience make me highly qualified for the position with your firm. You may callme for an interview at 405-555-~~4572~~ 3039.

Sincerely yours, | Timothy J. Robinson | 5816 Foxfire Road | Lawton, OK 73501 | Enclosure

---

Correspondence 65-63

Follow-Up Letter in Block Style

Progress Check
Proofreading Check

Documents designated as Proofreading Checks serve as a check of your proofreading skill. Your goal is to have zero typographical errors when the GDP software first scores the document.

Current Date | Mrs. Denise F. Klenzman | Director of Human Resources | Cole Enterprises | 3714 Crestmont Avenue | Norman, OK 73069

Dear Mrs. Klenzman:

¶ Thank you for the opportunity to meet with you yesterday and to learn of the exciting career opportunities at Cole Enterprises. It was inspiring for me to learn about future plans for your forward-looking company.

¶ I am confident that my education and my experience qualify me in a special way for your position of computer systems coordinator. I am familiar with all of your present equipment and software.

¶ I would very much like to join the professional staff at Cole Enterprises. Please let me know when you have made your decision.

Sincerely yours, | Timothy J. Robinson | 5816 Foxfire Road | Lawton, OK 73501

Unit 14

Reports

LESSON 66
Itineraries

LESSON 67
Agendas and Minutes of Meetings

LESSON 68
Procedures Manual

LESSON 69
Reports Formatted in Columns

LESSON 70
Report Review

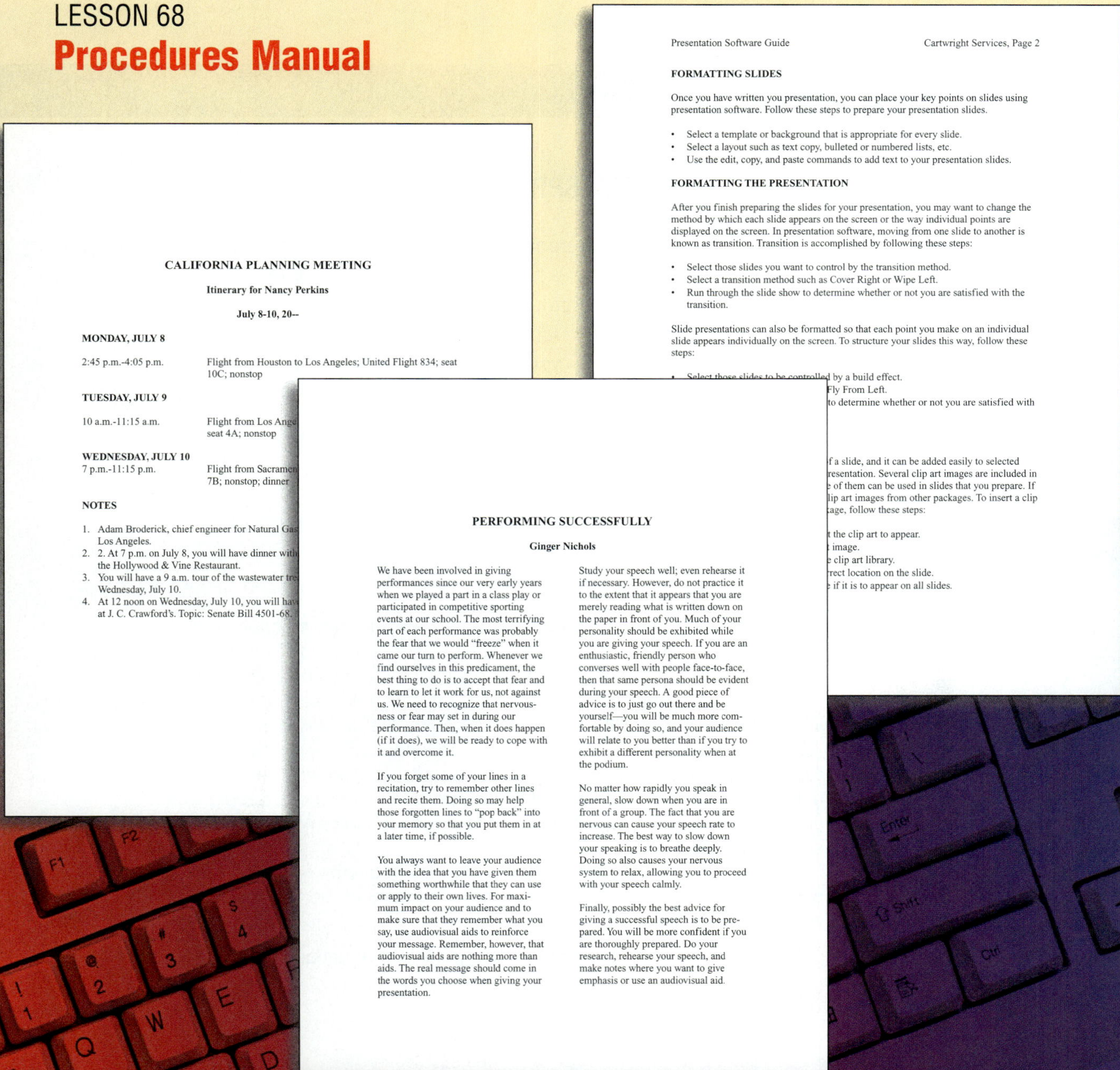

Presentation Software Guide Cartwright Services, Page 2

FORMATTING SLIDES

Once you have written you presentation, you can place your key points on slides using presentation software. Follow these steps to prepare your presentation slides.

- Select a template or background that is appropriate for every slide.
- Select a layout such as text copy, bulleted or numbered lists, etc.
- Use the edit, copy, and paste commands to add text to your presentation slides.

FORMATTING THE PRESENTATION

After you finish preparing the slides for your presentation, you may want to change the method by which each slide appears on the screen or the way individual points are displayed on the screen. In presentation software, moving from one slide to another is known as transition. Transition is accomplished by following these steps:

- Select those slides you want to control by the transition method.
- Select a transition method such as Cover Right or Wipe Left.
- Run through the slide show to determine whether or not you are satisfied with the transition.

Slide presentations can also be formatted so that each point you make on an individual slide appears individually on the screen. To structure your slides this way, follow these steps:

- Select those slides to be controlled by a build effect.
- … Fly From Left.
- … to determine whether or not you are satisfied with

… f a slide, and it can be added easily to selected … resentation. Several clip art images are included in … of them can be used in slides that you prepare. If … lip art images from other packages. To insert a clip … age, follow these steps:

… the clip art to appear.
… image.
… clip art library.
… rect location on the slide.
… if it is to appear on all slides.

CALIFORNIA PLANNING MEETING

Itinerary for Nancy Perkins

July 8-10, 20--

MONDAY, JULY 8

2:45 p.m.-4:05 p.m. Flight from Houston to Los Angeles; United Flight 834; seat 10C; nonstop

TUESDAY, JULY 9

10 a.m.-11:15 a.m. Flight from Los Ange… seat 4A; nonstop

WEDNESDAY, JULY 10

7 p.m.-11:15 p.m. Flight from Sacramen… 7B; nonstop; dinner

NOTES

1. Adam Broderick, chief engineer for Natural Ga… Los Angeles.
2. 2. At 7 p.m. on July 8, you will have dinner with… the Hollywood & Vine Restaurant.
3. You will have a 9 a.m. tour of the wastewater tre… Wednesday, July 10.
4. At 12 noon on Wednesday, July 10, you will hav… at J. C. Crawford's. Topic: Senate Bill 4501-68.

PERFORMING SUCCESSFULLY

Ginger Nichols

We have been involved in giving performances since our very early years when we played a part in a class play or participated in competitive sporting events at our school. The most terrifying part of each performance was probably the fear that we would "freeze" when it came our turn to perform. Whenever we find ourselves in this predicament, the best thing to do is to accept that fear and to learn to let it work for us, not against us. We need to recognize that nervousness or fear may set in during our performance. Then, when it does happen (if it does), we will be ready to cope with it and overcome it.

If you forget some of your lines in a recitation, try to remember other lines and recite them. Doing so may help those forgotten lines to "pop back" into your memory so that you put them in at a later time, if possible.

You always want to leave your audience with the idea that you have given them something worthwhile that they can use or apply to their own lives. For maximum impact on your audience and to make sure that they remember what you say, use audiovisual aids to reinforce your message. Remember, however, that audiovisual aids are nothing more than aids. The real message should come in the words you choose when giving your presentation.

Study your speech well; even rehearse it if necessary. However, do not practice it to the extent that it appears that you are merely reading what is written down on the paper in front of you. Much of your personality should be exhibited while you are giving your speech. If you are an enthusiastic, friendly person who converses well with people face-to-face, then that same persona should be evident during your speech. A good piece of advice is to just go out there and be yourself—you will be much more comfortable by doing so, and your audience will relate to you better than if you try to exhibit a different personality when at the podium.

No matter how rapidly you speak in general, slow down when you are in front of a group. The fact that you are nervous can cause your speech rate to increase. The best way to slow down your speaking is to breathe deeply. Doing so also causes your nervous system to relax, allowing you to proceed with your speech calmly.

Finally, possibly the best advice for giving a successful speech is to be prepared. You will be more confident if you are thoroughly prepared. Do your research, rehearse your speech, and make notes where you want to give emphasis or use an audiovisual aid.

Lesson 66

Itineraries

GOALS

- Type at least 41wpm/5′/5e
- Format itineraries

A. Type 2 times.

A. WARMUP

Had Phil been given a quiz on a subject that had been 11
reviewed by Max and Kay? Frank scored 89 on that quiz; Sue 23
scored 93 (*math only). Both tests were taken on 10/25/01. 35

| 1 | 2 | 3 | 4 | 5 | 6 | 7 | 8 | 9 | 10 | 11 | 12

SKILLBUILDING

B. Take three 12-second timings on each line. The scale below the last line shows your wpm speed for a 12-second timing.

B. 12-SECOND SPEED SPRINTS

This is not the person who is my first choice for this job.
The day was bright as the sun shone on the clear blue lake.
All of you should take a long walk when the sun sets today.
This line has many easy words in it to type your very best.

5 10 15 20 25 30 35 40 45 50 55 60

Keyboarding CONNECTION

Observing Netiquette

Netiquette is proper conduct for email users. It shows courtesy and professionalism and conveys a good impression of you and your company. Since email is nearest to speech, it is the most informal of business documents.

Check your email daily. Try to answer it the same day it arrives. Don't let it accumulate in your mailbox; you risk offending the sender. Use regular capitalization. All caps indicate SHOUTING; all lowercase letters convey immaturity. Most readers tolerate an infrequent typo, but if your message is filled with errors, you appear unprofessional. Use your spell checker, and don't overwhelm people with unnecessary emails. Use discretion. Make sure the information is relevant to each email recipient.

Be considerate. Be professional. Anything you write can wind up in your personnel file. Email that critiques another person can be forwarded to him or her without your knowledge.

YOUR TURN Review your next email message for use of netiquette.

C. Take two 5-minute timings. Review your speed and errors.

Goal: At least 41wpm/5'/5e

C. 5-MINUTE TIMING

Making a successful presentation to an audience is a 11
skill that is absolutely essential in your career. The 22
art of speaking before a group requires planning and very 34
hard work. Although each speaker makes preparation in a 45
different manner, a speaker should follow certain rules. 56
As the speaker, you are quite visible to people in 66
the audience. Therefore, you must make an effort to make 77
a good first impression. Walking to the podium to speak, 88
you give your audience an opportunity to notice your neat 100
appearance, good posture, and confident manner. You will 111
improve the quality of your voice by standing up straight 123
and holding your shoulders back and stomach in. 133
As you talk, use your eyes, face, and hands to help 144
you connect with your listeners. Maintain eye contact by 155
just moving your eyes over the group without focusing on 166
any one person. Use hand movements and facial expressions 178
to convey meanings to your audience. By utilizing these 189
techniques you will improve your speaking skills and your 201
efforts will be noted. 205

| 1 | 2 | 3 | 4 | 5 | 6 | 7 | 8 | 9 | 10 | 11 | 12

FORMATTING

D. ITINERARIES

An itinerary is a proposed outline of a trip that provides a traveler with information such as flight times and numbers, meeting times, travel dates, and room reservations. An itinerary may also include notes of special interest to the traveler.

DOCUMENT PROCESSING

Report 66-40

Itinerary

Reference Manual

Review:
R-11C: Itinerary

Follow these steps to format Report 66-40.

1. Press ENTER 6 times to leave an approximate two-inch top margin.
2. Insert a 2-column, 10-row open table.
3. Merge Row 1 for the main heading and subheading. Remember to insert a hard return between each of the headings and after the date information.
4. Move to Row 2, Column A and type the date; then press Enter 1 time.
5. Move to Row 3 and type the time in Column A. Then type the corresponding information for this time in Column B. Remember to insert a hard return after the final line in Column B.
6. Move to Row 4 and repeat steps 4 and 5 until all dates, times, and entries have been completed. (Do not insert a hard return at the end of the final itinerary entry.)

↓6X

14 pt **PORTLAND SALES MEETING** ↓2X

12 pt↓ **Itinerary for Arlene Gilsdorf** ↓2X

March 12-18, 20-- ↓2X

THURSDAY, MARCH 12 ↓2X

5:10 p.m.-5:55 p.m.	Flight from Detroit to Minneapolis; Northwest 83 (Phone: 800-555-1222); e-ticket; Seat 8D; nonstop ↓2X
6:30 p.m.-8:06 p.m.	Flight from Minneapolis to Portland; Northwest 2363; e-ticket; Seat 15C; nonstop; dinner ↓2X

SUNDAY, MARCH 15

10:35 a.m.-12:22 p.m.	Flight from Portland to Los Angeles; United Airlines 360; e-ticket; Seat 15F; nonstop; breakfast

TUESDAY, MARCH 17

8 a.m.-9:22 a.m.	Flight from San Francisco to Los Angeles; United Airlines 748; e-ticket; Seat 10D; nonstop; snack

WEDNESDAY, MARCH 18

3:40 p.m.-5:50 p.m.	Flight from Los Angeles to Detroit; Southwest 327; e-ticket; Seat 17D; nonstop; snack

Report 66-41

Itinerary

INTERCO SEMINAR

Itinerary for Mrs. Helen Kyslowsky

September 25-29, 20--

WEDNESDAY, SEPTEMBER 25

6:50 p.m.-9:10 p.m. *Flight from Columbus to Boston; America West 2053; Seat 13F; nonstop*

FRIDAY, SEPTEMBER 27

9 a.m.-10:17 a.m. *Flight from Boston to New York City; US Airways 454; Seat 10D; nonstop*

SUNDAY, SEPTEMBER 29

2:07 p.m.-4:18 p.m. *Flight from New York City to Columbus; US Airways 324; Seat 9A; nonstop*

Report 66-42

Itinerary

CALIFORNIA PLANNING MEETING | **Itinerary for Nancy Perkins** | **July 8-10, 20--** | **MONDAY, JULY 8** | Leave at 2:45 p.m. and arrive at 4:05 p.m. Houston to Los Angeles; United Flight 834; Seat 10C; nonstop; | Marriott (310-555-1014) King-sized bed; nonsmoking room; late arrival guaranteed (Reservation No. 45STX78) | **TUESDAY, JULY 9** | Leave at 10 a.m. and arrive at 11:15 a.m. Los Angeles to Sacramento; American Flight 206; Seat 4A; nonstop | **WEDNESDAY, JULY 10** | Leave at 7 p.m. and arrive at 11:15 p.m. Sacramento to Houston; United Flight 307; Seat 7B; nonstop; dinner

Lesson 67

Agendas and Minutes of Meetings

GOALS

- Improve speed and accuracy
- Refine language arts skills in the use of hyphens, abbreviations, and agreement
- Format agendas and minutes of meetings

A. Type 2 times.

A. WARMUP

```
     Rex Yantz was calm before quitting his job at the zoo    11
on 7/10/00. On 8/23/00 he applied for a job at Vance &        22
Walton, "specialists" in corporate law and bankruptcies.      33
| 1 | 2 | 3 | 4 | 5 | 6 | 7 | 8 | 9 | 10 | 11 | 12
```

SKILLBUILDING

B. DIAGNOSTIC PRACTICE: ALPHABET

If you are not using the GDP software, turn to page SB-2 and follow the directions for this activity.

C. DIAGNOSTIC PRACTICE: NUMBERS

If you are not using the GDP software, turn to page SB-5 and follow the directions for this activity.

LANGUAGE ARTS

D. Study the rules at the right.

D. HYPHENS

RULE -compound adjective

Hyphenate compound adjectives that come before a noun (unless the first word is an adverb ending in *-ly*).

We reviewed an up-to-date report on Wednesday.

But: The report was up to date.

But: We reviewed the highly rated report.

Note: A compound adjective is two or more words that function as a unit to describe a noun.

E. AGREEMENT

RULE agreement singular agreement plural

Use singular verbs and pronouns with singular subjects; use plural verbs and pronouns with plural subjects.

I was happy with my performance.

Janet and Phoenix were happy with their performance.

Among the items discussed were our raises and benefits.

F. ABBREVIATIONS

RULE ▶ abbreviate none

In general business writing, do not abbreviate common words (such as *dept.* or *pkg.*), compass points, units of measure, or the names of months, days of the week, cities, or states (except in addresses).

Almost one-half of the audience indicated they were at least 5 feet_8 inches tall.

Note: Do not insert a comma between the parts of a single measurement.

Edit the sentences to correct any errors in grammar.

4 The Queens visited Hickory to look at four bedroom homes.
5 Cindy Wallace has a part time job after school.
6 The accountants was extremely busy from March through April.
7 Lydia and Margaret were invited to present their report.
8 The portfolio include several technology stocks.
9 The planning committee will meet on Tue., Sept. 26.
10 Please credit the acct. for the amt. of $55.48.
11 The mgr. said the org. will move its headquarters to NC.

FORMATTING

G. AGENDAS

An agenda is a list of topics to be discussed at a meeting. It may also include a formal program of a meeting consisting of times, rooms, speakers, and other related information. Follow these steps to format an agenda:

1. Press ENTER 6 times to leave an approximate 2-inch top margin.
2. Center and type the name of the company or committee in all caps, bold, and 14 points.
3. Press ENTER 2 times, and center and type `Meeting Agenda` in upper-and lowercase, bold, and 12 points.
4. Press ENTER 2 times, and center and type the date in upper- and lowercase, bold, and 12 points.
5. Press ENTER 2 times, and change the line spacing to double.
6. Type the first item in the agenda. Number each item using the numbering command.

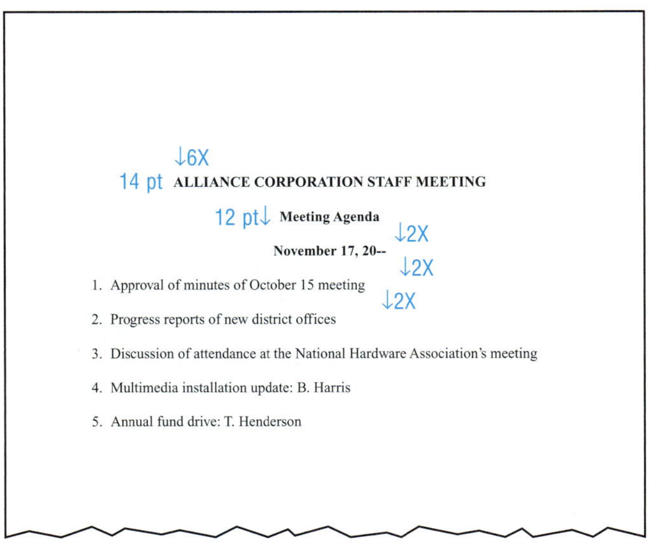

Remember to position the numbers at the left margin.

H. MINUTES OF MEETINGS

Minutes of a meeting are a record of items discussed during a meeting. To format meeting minutes, follow these steps:

1. Press ENTER 6 times to leave an approximate two-inch top margin.
2. Create an open, two-column table that has enough rows to accommodate all of the given information.
3. Merge Row 1 for the main heading, subheading, and date. Format the main heading and subheadings appropriately. (Remember to insert a blank line between each of the headings and after the date information.)
4. Type side headings in all caps and bold.
5. Type all corresponding information in Column B. Remember to insert a hard return after the final line in all Column B entries.
6. Continue typing the minutes as shown in the illustration. Manually adjust column width as needed. Do not insert a hard return at the end of the final minutes entry.

PLANNING COMMITTEE

Minutes of the Meeting

February 10, 20--

ATTENDANCE	The Planning Committee meeting was called to order at 1 p.m. on February 10, 20--, by Michelle North, chairperson. Members present were Cal Anderson, L. T. Braddock, Lisa Samson, Sharon Owens, and J. R. Sterns.
OLD BUSINESS	The committee reviewed bids for the purchase of a new computer for the Cheyenne office. We will accept the lower of two bids that have been submitted.
NEW BUSINESS	The committee reviewed a proposal for a new complex in Helena. After much discussion, the committee agreed to contact the Helena county clerk's office to get information on zoning ordinances.
ADJOURNMENT	The meeting was adjourned at 2:45 p.m. The next meeting is scheduled for March 22 in Room 16.

Respectfully submitted,

L. T. Braddock

L. T. Braddock, Secretary

Go To
Word Processing Manual

I. WORD PROCESSING: HYPHENATION

Study Lesson 67 in your word processing manual. Complete all of the shaded steps while at your computer. Then format the jobs that follow.

Report 67-43

Agenda

Go To
Word Processing Manual Review:
L. 28: Bullets and Numbering

Reference Manual
Review:
R-11A: Meeting Agenda

↓6X
14 pt **ALLIANCE CORPORATION STAFF MEETING** ↓2X

12 pt↓ **Meeting Agenda** ↓2X

November 17, 20-- ↓2X

1. Approval of minutes of October 15 meeting ↓2X
2. Progress reports of new district offices
3. Discussion of attendance at the National Hardware Association's annual meeting
4. Multimedia installation update: B. Harris
5. Annual fund drive: T. Henderson

Report 67-44

Agenda

APEX MULTIMEDIA CORPORATION
Meeting Agenda
October 13, 20--

1. Call to order
2. Approval of minutes of September 10 meeting
3. Progress reports on Sherman contract (Julia Adams)
4. Upgrading of 8.0 presentation media
5. CD-ROM development program (Ray Sanchez)
6. Internet configuration (JoAnn Hubbard)
7. Adjournment

Report 67-45

Minutes of a Meeting

Turn on hyphenation, if needed.

↓6X

14 pt **PLANNING COMMITTEE** ↓2X

12 pt↓ **Minutes of the Meeting** ↓2X

February 10, 20-- ↓2X

ATTENDANCE The Planning Committee meeting was called to order at 1 p.m. on February 10, 20--, by Michelle North, chairperson. Members present were Cal Anderson, L. T. Braddock, Lisa Samson, Sharon Owens, and J. R. Sterns. ↓2X

OLD BUSINESS The committee reviewed bids for the purchase of a new computer for the Cheyenne office. We will accept the lower of two bids that have been submitted.

NEW BUSINESS The committee reviewed a proposal for a new complex in Helena. After much discussion, the committee agreed to contact the Helena county clerk's office to get information on zoning ordinances.

ADJOURNMENT The meeting was adjourned at 2:45 p.m. The next meeting is scheduled for March 22 in Room 16. ↓2X

Respectfully submitted, ↓4X

L. T. Braddock, Secretary

Report 67-46

Minutes of a Meeting

Turn on hyphenation, if needed.

PERSONEL COMMITTEE [N inserted]

Minutes of the Meeting

May 14, 20--

ATTENDENCE [A replaces E] A [special] meeting of the Personnel Committee was held [on May 14, 20--,] in the office of Mr. Cameron. [All] Members present were

(Continued on next page)

except Richard Dixon, who was repre sented by Monica Zick man. The meeting was called to order at 2 p. m.

Old Business A copy of the survey is attached. Eighty-eight employees participated in a survey that had been completed by Andrea Fields. The minutes of the last monthly meeting were read.

NEW BUSINESS Ms. Samuels discussed the need for planning a campaign for job applicants about vacancies occur within the company. Frank Lundquist will draft a flier to be sent to the Park view sentinel. Programs for the N P A convention to be held in Des Moines were distributed to all members. Each committee member were asked to distribute copies to employees in his or her department.

ADJOURN The meeting was adjourned at 3:25 a.m. The next meeting has been scheduled for July 10 in the conference center.

Respectfully submitted,

Brandon Stinson, Secretary

Lesson 68

Procedures Manual

GOALS

- Type at least 41wpm/5′/5e
- Format a procedures manual

A. Type 2 times.

A. WARMUP

```
     Zach sharpened the ax for Quinn just to help him win    10
the $100 tree-cutting event to be held in Kildeer on May 8   23
(if it doesn't rain). The prize will be $250--fantastic!     34
| 1 | 2 | 3 | 4 | 5 | 6 | 7 | 8 | 9 | 10 | 11 | 12
```

SKILLBUILDING

B. MAP

Follow the GDP software directions for this exercise in improving keystroking accuracy.

C. Take two 5-minute timings. Review your speed and errors.

Goal: At least 41wpm/5′/5e

C. 5-MINUTE TIMING

```
     Ergonomics is the science of adapting today's office     11
environment to the human body so that the productivity,       22
health, and safety of employees is at the optimal level.      33
Physical issues, such as proper body posture and support,     45
adjustable office furniture, and adequate lighting are        55
studied to make recommendations for office environments.      67
     Office equipment should be adjusted to ensure safety     78
and health of the workers. Place the monitor at a distance    90
that will allow the eyes to relax. Adjust the lighting and    102
the monitor position to reduce the glare. Lower or raise      113
the keyboard so that the wrists are straight. Place the       124
mouse at the same level next to the keyboard.                 133
     Chair height should allow the feet to rest on the        143
floor and allow the legs to move freely. The height of        154
the chair can be adjusted if the height of the keyboard is    166
not flexible. Remember to walk around the office plaza at     178
regular intervals to provide relief for the body.             188
     When office personnel are comfortable and healthy,       198
they will improve their productivity.                         205
| 1 | 2 | 3 | 4 | 5 | 6 | 7 | 8 | 9 | 10 | 11 | 12
```

FORMATTING

D. PROCEDURES MANUAL

Organizations often prepare procedures manuals to assist employees in identifying the steps or methods they must follow to accomplish particular tasks. To format a procedures manual:

1. Type the manual as a single-spaced report.
2. Place a header on every page except the first page. The header may include such items as the title of the manual (at the left margin) and the company name and page number (at the right margin).
3. Place a footer on every page including the first page. The footer may include the same information as the header or it may identify the content of that page (for example, "Training Program").

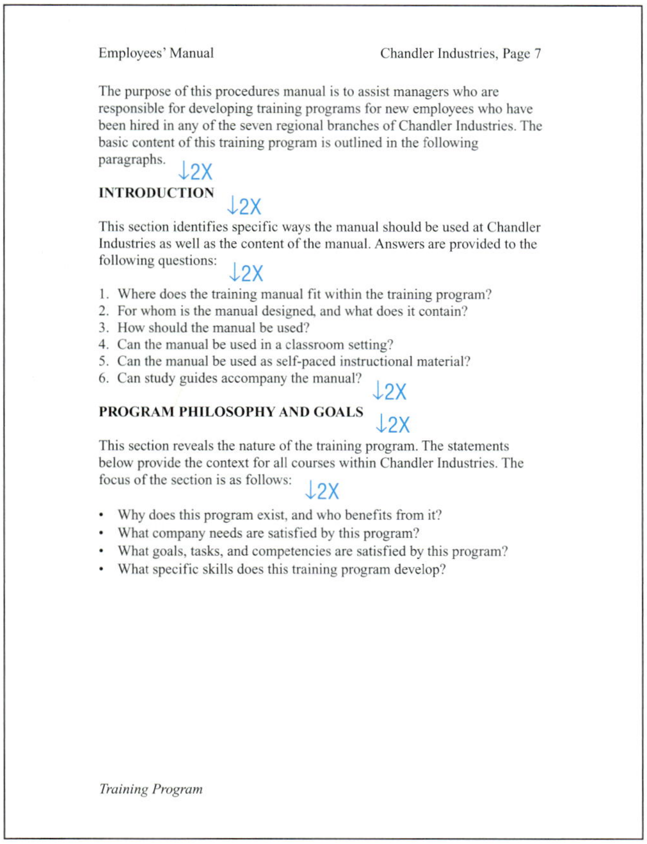

Employees' Manual Chandler Industries, Page 7

The purpose of this procedures manual is to assist managers who are responsible for developing training programs for new employees who have been hired in any of the seven regional branches of Chandler Industries. The basic content of this training program is outlined in the following paragraphs. ↓2X

INTRODUCTION ↓2X

This section identifies specific ways the manual should be used at Chandler Industries as well as the content of the manual. Answers are provided to the following questions: ↓2X

1. Where does the training manual fit within the training program?
2. For whom is the manual designed, and what does it contain?
3. How should the manual be used?
4. Can the manual be used in a classroom setting?
5. Can the manual be used as self-paced instructional material?
6. Can study guides accompany the manual? ↓2X

PROGRAM PHILOSOPHY AND GOALS ↓2X

This section reveals the nature of the training program. The statements below provide the context for all courses within Chandler Industries. The focus of the section is as follows: ↓2X

- Why does this program exist, and who benefits from it?
- What company needs are satisfied by this program?
- What goals, tasks, and competencies are satisfied by this program?
- What specific skills does this training program develop?

Training Program

DOCUMENT PROCESSING

Report 68-47

Procedures Manual

1. Turn on hyphenation.
2. In page numbering, change the page number to start at page 7, then create a header as follows: Type `Employees' Manual` at the left margin. Type `Chandler Industries, Page 7` aligned at the right margin.
3. Create a footer by typing `Training Program` in italic and aligned at the left margin.
4. Type the following portion of a procedures manual.

Go To Word Processing Manual Review:
L. 27: Page Numbering
L. 42: Headers and Footers

Employees' Manual Chandler Industries, Page 7

¶ The purpose of this procedures manual is to assist managers who are responsible for developing training programs for new employees who have been hired in any of the seven regional branches of Chandler Industries. The basic content of this training program is outlined in the following paragraphs.

(Continued on next page)

Remember to single-space the entire list if all items in the list are one line long.

INTRODUCTION

¶ This section identifies specific ways the manual should be used at Chandler Industries as well as the content of the manual. Answers are provided to the following questions:

1. Where does the training manual fit within the training program?
2. For whom is the manual designed, and what does it contain?
3. How should the manual be used?
4. Can the manual be used in a classroom setting?
5. Can the manual be used as self-paced instructional material?
6. Can study guides accompany the manual?

PROGRAM PHILOSOPHY AND GOALS

¶ This section reveals the nature of the training program. The statements below provide the context for all courses within Chandler Industries. The focus of the section is as follows:

- Why does this program exist, and who benefits from it?
- What company needs are satisfied by this program?
- What goals, tasks, and competencies are satisfied by this program?
- What specific skills does this training program develop?

Training Program

Report 68-48

Procedures Manual

1. In page numbering, change the page number to start at page 2.
2. Create a header as follows: Type `Presentation Software Guide` at the left margin. Type `Cartwright Services, Page 2` aligned at the right margin.
3. Type `FORMATTING` as a footer at the left margin.

Presentation Software Guide   Cartwright Services, Page 2

FORMATTING SLIDES

¶ Once you have written your presentation, you can place your key points on slides using presentation software. Follow these steps to prepare your presentation slides.

Remember to insert a blank line between items in a multiline list in a single-spaced document.

- Select a template or background that is appropriate for every slide.
- Select a layout such as text copy, bulleted or numbered lists, etc.
- Use the edit, copy, and paste commands to add text to your presentation slides.

FORMATTING THE PRESENTATION

¶ After you finish preparing the slides for your presentation, you may want to change the method by which each slide appears on the screen or the way individual points are displayed on the screen. In presentation software, moving from one slide to another is known as transition. Transition is accomplished by following these steps:

- Select those slides you want to control by the transition method.
- Select a transition method such as Cover Right or Wipe Left.
- Run through the slide show to determine whether or not you are satisfied with the transition.

(Continued on next page)

¶ Slide presentations can also be formatted so that each point you make on an individual slide appears individually on the screen. To structure your slides this way, follow these steps:

- Select those slides to be controlled by a build effect.
- Select a build effect style such as Fly From Left.
- Run through the slide show again to determine whether or not you are satisfied with the build effect.

Report 68-49

Procedures Manual

1. Open the file for Report 68-48.
2. Remove the third bulleted item under the FORMATING SLIDES heading.
3. Add the following sections to the end of the report.

ADDING CLIP ART

¶ Clipart enhances the appearance of a slide, and it can be easily added to selected slides or to every other slide in your presentation. Several clip art images are included in this presentation package, and any one of them can be used in slides that you prepare. If you choose, however, you can insert clip art images from other packages. To insert a clip art from your presentation package, follow these steps:

- Select the slide on which you want the clip art to appear.
- Click the icon for adding a clip art image. This icon is found on the menu bar.
- Select the image from the software clip art library. The slide can come from the presentation package or you can retrieve it from another clip art package.
- Size and move the image to its correct location on the presentation slide.
- Copy the image to the master slide if it is to appear on all slides.

¶ You can also change the appearance of the clip art image by (1) changing the colors used in the image; (2) flipping the image so that its horizontal or vertical position is reversed (mirror image); (3) changing the contrast or brightness of the image; and (4) cropping the image so that unwanted sections are eliminated from view.

Lesson 69

Reports Formatted in Columns

GOALS
- Improve speed and accuracy
- Refine language arts skills in spelling
- Format magazine articles

A. Type 2 times.

A. WARMUP

```
1      On 12/30/00 Jim gave Alex and Pam a quiz--it was quite   11
2  difficult! Neither scored higher than 82%; their average     22
3  was 79. They should retake the quiz by the 4th or 5th.       32
   | 1 | 2 | 3 | 4 | 5 | 6 | 7 | 8 | 9 | 10 | 11 | 12
```

SKILLBUILDING

B. PACED PRACTICE

If you are not using the GDP software, turn to page SB-14 and follow the directions for this activity.

PPP

PRETEST → PRACTICE → POSTTEST

PRETEST
Take a 1-minute timing. Review your speed and errors.

C. PRETEST: Horizontal Reaches

```
4      Four famous adults gazed at a wren on our farm gate.      11
5  A group of gawking writers wrote facts about an additional   23
6  upward gain in wildlife numbers on their supply of pads.     34
   | 1 | 2 | 3 | 4 | 5 | 6 | 7 | 8 | 9 | 10 | 11 | 12
```

PRACTICE
Speed Emphasis:
If you made no more than 1 error on the Pretest, type each *individual* line 2 times.
Accuracy Emphasis:
If you made 2 or more errors, type each *group* of lines (as though it were a paragraph) 2 times.

D. PRACTICE: In Reaches

```
7  wr wrap wren wreak wrist wrote writer unwrap writhe wreaths
8  ou pout ours ounce cough fouls output detour ousted coupons
9  ad adds dead adult ready blade advice fading admits adheres
```

E. PRACTICE: Out Reaches

```
10 fa fact farm faith sofas fakes faulty unfair famous defames
11 up upon soup upset group upper upturn supply uplift upsurge
12 ga gate gave cigar gains legal gazing legacy gawked garbage
```

POSTTEST
Repeat the Pretest timing and compare performance.

F. POSTTEST: Horizontal Reaches

LANGUAGE ARTS

G. Type this list of frequently misspelled words, paying special attention to any spelling problems in each word.

G. SPELLING

13 personnel information its procedures their committee system
14 receive employees which education services opportunity area
15 financial appropriate interest received production contract
16 important through necessary customer employee further there
17 property account approximately general control division our

Edit the sentences to correct any misspellings.

18 The revised systom was adopted by the finantial division.
19 Four employes want to serve on the new property commitee.
20 Approximatly ten proceedures were included in the contract.
21 Further informasion will be recieved from the customers.
22 Their was much interest shown by the production personal.
23 The services in that aria are necesary for needed control.

FORMATTING

H. MAGAZINE ARTICLES

Magazine articles can be formatted as two-column reports. Follow these steps:

1. Press ENTER 6 times to leave an approximate 2-inch top margin on page 1.
2. Use single spacing and justified alignment; then turn on hyphenation.
3. Create a header to print on all pages except page 1 to identify the author's name and the page number at the top right of every page. Use only the author's last name and the page number in the header (for example, Mysweski 2).
4. Center and type the article title in all caps, bold, and 14 points.
5. Press ENTER 2 times; then center and type the byline in upper- and lowercase, bold, and 12 points.
6. Press ENTER 2 times and change to left-alignment. Then type the article single-spaced in a two-column format.
7. Insert 1 blank line before and after all headings.

↓6X

14 pt **MEMBER BUYING SERVICES** ↓2X

12 pt **Brenda T. Mysweski** ↓2X

Policyholders of AICA (and their dependents) are eligible for a wide range of discount services. These services provide you with a variety of items you can purchase, from automobiles to computers to jewelry. Here are some examples of the merchandise and services that are available to all AICA members. ↓2X

AUTO PRICING ↓2X

You can order the most sophisticated auto information guide on the market. The guide will give you information on retail prices, vehicle specifications, safety equipment, and factory-option packages. ↓2X

When you are ready to place your order for an automobile, a team of company experts will work with you and with the prospective dealer to ensure that you are getting the best possible price through a network of nationwide dealers. You are guaranteed to get the best price for the automobile you have chosen.

Once you have purchased your automobile, AICA will provide your insurance needs. Discounts on policy rates are provided for completion of a driver-training program, for installed antitheft devices, and for installed passive restraint systems such as air bags.

Finally, we can make your purchase decision an easy one by always providing a low-rate finance plan for you. You can be certain that you are getting the most competitive interest rate for the purchase of your automobile when you finance with AICA.

CAR RENTAL DISCOUNTS

When you need to rent an automobile while traveling, special rates and discounts are available to you from five of the largest car rental agencies, and you'll never find better prices!

Mysweski 2

MERCHANDISE BUYING

Each quarter a buying services catalog will be sent to you. This catalog includes a variety of items that can be purchased through AICA. Through the catalog you can purchase jewelry, furniture, sports equipment, electronics, appliances, and computers. To place an order, all you have to do is call AICA toll-free at 1-800-555-3838. Your order will arrive within 10 to 15 days.

Go To Word Processing Manual

I. WORD PROCESSING: COLUMNS

Study Lesson 69 in your word processing manual. Complete all of the shaded steps while at your computer. Then format the jobs that follow.

DOCUMENT PROCESSING

Report 69-50

Magazine Article in Two Columns

MEMBER BUYING SERVICES | Brenda T. Mysweski

¶ Policyholders of AICA (and their dependents) are eligible for a wide range of discount services. These services provide you with a variety of items you can purchase, from automobiles to computers to jewelry. Here are some examples of the merchandise and services that are available to all AICA members.

AUTO PRICING

¶ You can order the most sophisticated auto information guide on the market. The guide will give you information on retail prices, vehicle specifications, safety equipment, and factory-option packages.

¶ When you are ready to place your order for an automobile, a team of company experts will work with you and with the prospective dealer to ensure that you are getting the best possible price through a network of nationwide dealers. You are guaranteed to get the best price for the automobile you have chosen.

(Continued on next page)

¶ Once you have purchased your automobile, AICA will provide all your insurance needs. Discounts on policy rates are provided for completion of a driver-training program, for installed antitheft devices, and for installed passive restraint systems such as air bags.

¶ Finally, we can make your purchase decision an easy one by always providing a low-rate finance plan for you. You can be certain that you are getting the most competitive interest rate for the purchase of your automobile when you finance with AICA.

CAR RENTAL DISCOUNTS

¶ When you need to rent an automobile while traveling, special rates are available to you from five of the largest car rental agencies.

ROAD AND TRAVEL SERVICES

¶ You can enjoy the security of emergency road service through the AICA Road and Travel Plan. This plan also includes discounts on hotels and motels.

¶ As an AICA traveler, you can take advantage of our exclusive discounts and bonuses on cruises and tours. Our travel plan provides daily and weekend trips to over 100 destinations. Take advantage of this wonderful opportunity to let AICA serve all your travel needs.

MERCHANDISE BUYING

¶ Each quarter a buying services catalog will be sent to you. This catalog includes a variety of items that can be purchased through AICA—and you'll never find better prices! Through the catalog you can purchase jewelry, furniture, sports equipment, electronics, appliances, and computers. To place an order, all you have to do is call AICA toll-free at 1-800-555-3838. Your order will arrive within 10 to 15 days.

Report 69-51

Magazine Article in Two Columns

INTERVIEW TECHNIQUES | By Paul Sanford

The interview process allows a company to gather information about you that has not been provided on your resume or application form. This information includes such items as you career goals, appearance, personality, poise, attitudes, and ability to express yourself verbally.

APPEARANCE

There are several things you should keep in mind when going for an interview. You should plan your wardrobe well because first impressions are lasting ones when you walk into the interviewer's office. If you are not quite certain as to what you should wear, dress conservatively. Whatever you select, be sure that your clothing is clean, neat, and comfortable. You should

(Continued on next page)

also pay attention to details such as clean hair, shined shoes, well-groomed nails, and appropriate jewelry and other accessories.

MEETING THE INTERVIEWER

Be sure to arrive at the interview site a few minutes early. Stand when you meet the interviewer for the first time. If a handshake is offered, shake hands in a confident, firm manner. It is also a good idea not to smoke or chew gum during the interview.

THE INTERVIEW PROCESS

Maintain good eye contact with the interviewer when you respond to his or her questions. Listen intently to everything that is said. Be aware of the movements you make with your eyes, your hands, and other parts of your body during the interview. Too much movement may be a signal to the interviewer that you are nervous, that you lack confidence, or that you are not certain of your answers.

During the interview process, the interviewer will judge not only what you say but also how you say it. As you speak, you will be judged on grammar, articulation, vocabulary, and tone of voice. The nonverbal skills that may be judged are your attitude, enthusiasm, listening abilities, and promptness in responding to questions.

ENDING THE INTERVIEW

Let the interviewer determine when it is time to close the interview. When this time arrives, ask the interviewer when he or she expects to make a decision on hiring for this position and when you can expect to hear about the job. Thank the interviewer for taking the time to meet with you, and express a positive desire to work for the company.

After the interview, send a follow-up letter to remind the interviewer of your name and your continued interest in the company. Let that person know how to contact you by providing a telephone number where you can be reached, either at home or at your current work location.

Report 69-52

Magazine Article in Two Columns

Go To
Word Processing Manual Review:
L. 30: Cut/Copy/Paste

Open the file for Report 69-50 and make the following changes:

1. Make yourself the author of the article.
2. Make the MERCHANDISE BUYING section the second paragraph in the article.
3. Add the following section to the end of the article:

```
MISCELLANEOUS SERVICES | In
addition to the above serv-
ices, AICA provides perma-
nent life insurance, pen-
sion plan funding, cash
management, and credit card
programs. At your request,
detailed catalogs will be
sent to you that explain
each of these services.
```

Careers in the publishing field require excellent keyboarding skills.

Lesson 70

Report Review

GOALS
- Type at least 41wpm/5′/5e
- Improve speed and accuracy
- Review report formats

A. Type 2 times.

A. WARMUP

```
     Felix Quayle sat in Seat #14 when he won the jackpot;    11
Van Gill sat in Seat #23 but did not win a prize. Do you      22
think Row 19 (Seats #1560 and #1782) will be lucky for me?    34
| 1 | 2 | 3 | 4 | 5 | 6 | 7 | 8 | 9 | 10 | 11 | 12
```

SKILLBUILDING

B. PROGRESSIVE PRACTICE: ALPHABET

If you are not using the GDP software, turn to page SB-7 and follow the directions for this activity.

C. Take a 1-minute timing on the first paragraph to establish your base speed. Then take four 1-minute timings on the remaining paragraphs. As soon as you equal or exceed your base speed on one paragraph, advance to the next, more difficult paragraph.

C. SUSTAINED PRACTICE: ROUGH DRAFT

```
     The possibility of aging and not being able to live as   11
independently as we want to is a prospect that no one wants   23
to recognize. One resource designed to counter some of the    35
negative realities of aging is called the Handyman Project.   47

     This type of project helps support elders and disabled   12
residents in their efforts to maintain the homes. As the      24
name implies, "handy" volunters per for minor home repairs    36
such as tightning leaky faucets and fixing broken windows.    48

Other type of work include: painting, plumbing, yard          11
work, and carpentery. The volunteers are all as diversfied    23
as the word itself. You may find a retire working next too    35
an executive or a student helping a lisensed electrician.     47
```

(Continued on next page)

Their back ~~grunds~~ grounds may vary, but ~~that~~ what they share is the 11
~~hope~~ desire to put their ~~capabilities~~ abilities to good use. Volunters ~~take~~ find 23
a high level of ~~personnal~~ personal satisfaction after ~~doing~~ finishing a job 35
~~but~~ and spending time with an elder who really needs the help. 47

| 1 | 2 | 3 | 4 | 5 | 6 | 7 | 8 | 9 | 10 | 11 | 12

D. TECHNIQUE PRACTICE: SHIFT/CAPS LOCK

RHONDA KORDICH was promoted on APRIL 1 to SENIOR SECRETARY. The SOLD sign replaced the FOR SALE sign at 1904 ELM DRIVE. The trip to DULUTH was on INTERSTATE 35.

E. Take two 5-minute timings. Review your speed and errors.

Goal: 41wpm/5′/5e

E. 5-MINUTE TIMING

In most offices, many products that are used daily 10
are made of materials that can be recycled. Amazingly, 21
items made of glass, steel, aluminum, plastics, and paper 33
can be recycled to make many products that we need. Also, 45
the recycling process can help save our environment. 56
Some unique examples of the process of recycling the 67
items we throw away regularly are listed here. Used coffee 79
filters can be recycled to make soles for new shoes. Many 91
pieces of paper that are thrown away every day can be used 103
to make tissue paper and paper towels. Most plastics that 115
are used in soda bottles can be recycled for car interiors 127
and insulation for jackets. Used light bulbs and similar 138
glass products can be used to resurface streets. 148
Look around the room in which you are working. If you 159
are not already participating in a recycling program, you 171
may want to recycle some items that you no longer need. 182
Items such as paper, aluminum cans, and file folders can 193
be collected quickly. What additional items can you add? 205

| 1 | 2 | 3 | 4 | 5 | 6 | 7 | 8 | 9 | 10 | 11 | 12

Report 70-53

Agenda

Crandall First National Bank | Meeting Agenda | May 15, 20--

1. Call to Order
2. Approval of minutes of April 17 meeting
3. Mortgage loans (J. William Hokes)
4. Installment loans (Lorraine Hagen)
5. Series EE bonds (Joni Ellickson)
6. Club memberships
7. Certificates of deposit (Louise Abbey)
8. Closing remarks
9. Adjournment

Report 70-54

Minutes of a Meeting

LITTLETON WATERCOLOUR SOCIETY

Minutes of Meeting

October 23, 20--

CALL TO ORDER The meeting was called by Sandra Garvy at 8 in the Littleton library confrence room.

OLD BUSINESS susan Firtz furnished each member with a list of artists and the name of the wtercolor paintings each artist is entering in the Fall Arts Fair.

NEW BUSINESS John Cahmpion informed members a new supply of canvas and oil paint arrived. Members can check out items they need to begin winter projects. Winter Fair will be held December 14.

ADJOURMENT The meeting adjourned at 9:45. The next meeting is November 12.

Respecfully,

Catherine Argetes

Report 70-55

Magazine Article in Two Columns

Type the article in two columns and balance the columns.

Progress Check Proofreading Check

Documents designated as Proofreading Checks serve as a check of your proofreading skill. Your goal is to have zero typographical errors when the GDP software first scores the document.

PERFORMING SUCCESSFULLY

Ginger Nichols

¶ We have been involved in giving performances since our very early years when we played a part in a class play or participated in competitive sporting events at our school. The most terrifying part of each performance was probably the fear that we would "freeze" when it came our turn to perform. Whenever we find ourselves in this predicament, the best thing to do is to accept that fear and to learn to let it work for us, not against us. We need to recognize that nervousness or fear may set in during our performance. Then, when it does happen (if it does), we will be ready to cope with it and overcome it.

¶ If you forget some of your lines in a recitation, try to remember other lines and recite them. Doing so may help those forgotten lines to "pop back" into your memory so that you put them in at a later time, if possible.

¶ You always want to leave your audience with the idea that you have given them something worthwhile that they can use or apply to their own lives. For maximum impact on your audience and to make sure that they remember what you say, use audiovisual aids to reinforce your message. Remember, however, that audiovisual aids are nothing more than aids. The real message should come in the words you choose when giving your presentation.

¶ Study your speech well; even rehearse it if necessary. However, do not practice it to the extent that it appears that you are merely reading what is written down on the paper in front of you. Much of your personality should be exhibited while you are giving your speech. If you are an enthusiastic, friendly person who converses well with people face-to-face, then that same persona should be evident during your speech. A good piece of advice is to just go out there and be yourself—you will be much more comfortable by doing so, and your audience will relate to you better than if you try to exhibit a different personality when at the podium.

¶ No matter how rapidly you speak in general, slow down when you are in front of a group. The fact that you are nervous can cause your speech rate to increase. The best way to slow down your speaking is to breathe deeply. Doing so also causes your nervous system to relax, allowing you to proceed with your speech calmly.

¶ Finally, possibly the best advice for giving a successful speech is to be prepared. You will be more confident if you are thoroughly prepared. Do your research, rehearse your speech, and make notes where you want to give emphasis or use an audiovisual aid.

Unit 15

Correspondence

LESSON 71
Multipage Letters

LESSON 72
Special Letter Features

LESSON 73
More Special Letter Features

LESSON 74
Multipage Memos With Tables

LESSON 75
Memo Reports

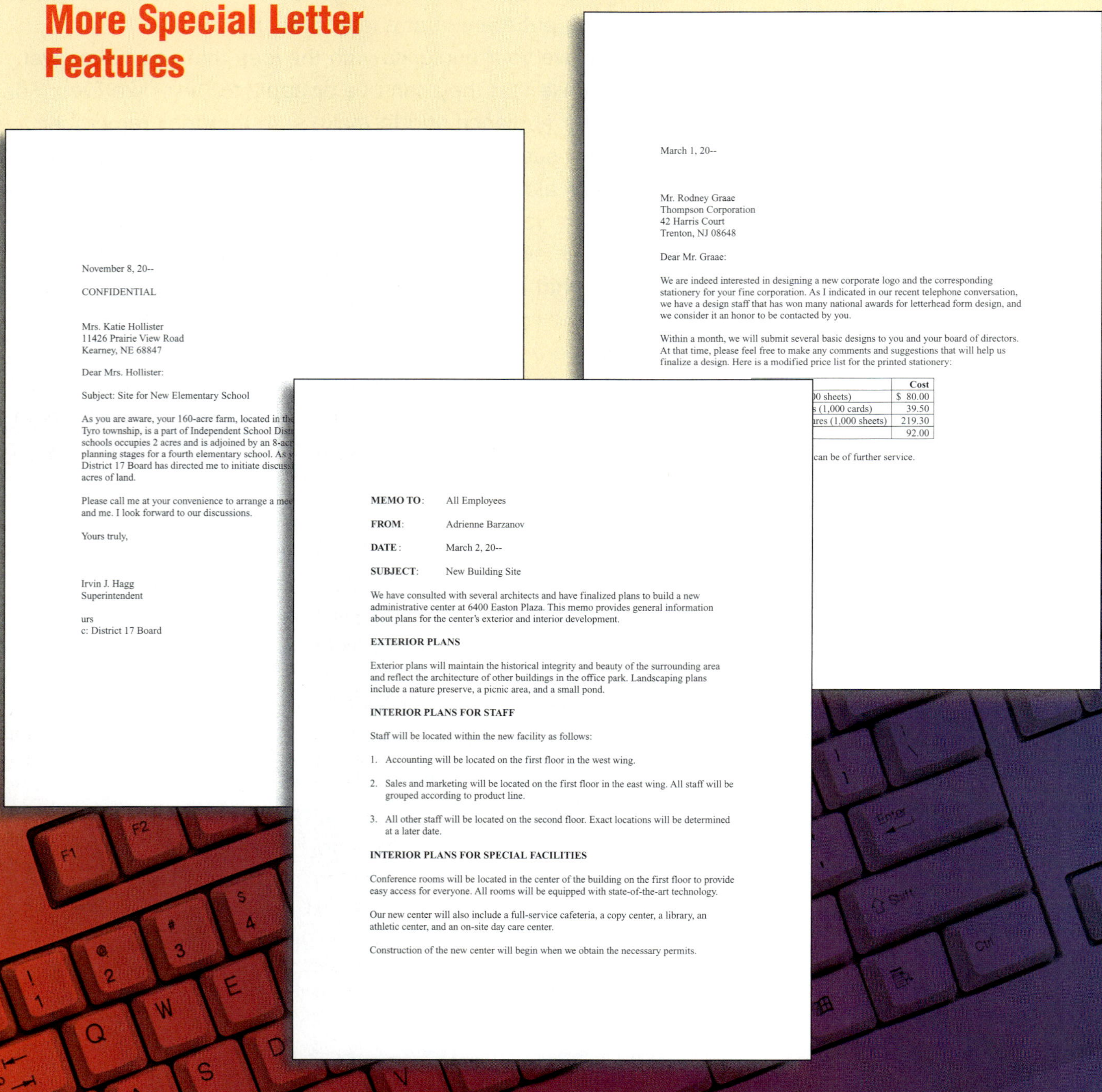

November 8, 20--

CONFIDENTIAL

Mrs. Katie Hollister
11426 Prairie View Road
Kearney, NE 68847

Dear Mrs. Hollister:

Subject: Site for New Elementary School

As you are aware, your 160-acre farm, located in th
Tyro township, is a part of Independent School Distr
schools occupies 2 acres and is adjoined by an 8-acr
planning stages for a fourth elementary school. As y
District 17 Board has directed me to initiate discuss
acres of land.

Please call me at your convenience to arrange a mee
and me. I look forward to our discussions.

Yours truly,

Irvin J. Hagg
Superintendent

urs
c: District 17 Board

March 1, 20--

Mr. Rodney Graae
Thompson Corporation
42 Harris Court
Trenton, NJ 08648

Dear Mr. Graae:

We are indeed interested in designing a new corporate logo and the corresponding stationery for your fine corporation. As I indicated in our recent telephone conversation, we have a design staff that has won many national awards for letterhead form design, and we consider it an honor to be contacted by you.

Within a month, we will submit several basic designs to you and your board of directors. At that time, please feel free to make any comments and suggestions that will help us finalize a design. Here is a modified price list for the printed stationery:

	Cost
)0 sheets)	$ 80.00
s (1,000 cards)	39.50
ires (1,000 sheets)	219.30
	92.00

can be of further service.

MEMO TO: All Employees

FROM: Adrienne Barzanov

DATE: March 2, 20--

SUBJECT: New Building Site

We have consulted with several architects and have finalized plans to build a new administrative center at 6400 Easton Plaza. This memo provides general information about plans for the center's exterior and interior development.

EXTERIOR PLANS

Exterior plans will maintain the historical integrity and beauty of the surrounding area and reflect the architecture of other buildings in the office park. Landscaping plans include a nature preserve, a picnic area, and a small pond.

INTERIOR PLANS FOR STAFF

Staff will be located within the new facility as follows:

1. Accounting will be located on the first floor in the west wing.
2. Sales and marketing will be located on the first floor in the east wing. All staff will be grouped according to product line.
3. All other staff will be located on the second floor. Exact locations will be determined at a later date.

INTERIOR PLANS FOR SPECIAL FACILITIES

Conference rooms will be located in the center of the building on the first floor to provide easy access for everyone. All rooms will be equipped with state-of-the-art technology.

Our new center will also include a full-service cafeteria, a copy center, a library, an athletic center, and an on-site day care center.

Construction of the new center will begin when we obtain the necessary permits.

Multipage Letters

GOALS
- Improve speed and accuracy
- Refine language arts skills in the use of commas
- Format multipage letters

A. Type 2 times.

A. WARMUP

```
1      We were quite dazzled when the plumber drove up in a    11
2  C-150 pickup truck! She was joined by 26 young people (all  23
3  students) who gazed intently as she welded six of the rods. 35
   | 1 | 2 | 3 | 4 | 5 | 6 | 7 | 8 | 9 | 10 | 11 | 12
```

SKILLBUILDING

B. Take three 12-second timings on each line. The scale below the last line shows your wpm speed for a 12-second timing.

B. 12-SECOND SPEED SPRINTS

```
4  Pam knew that five girls in the other car were on the team.
5  The women drove eight blue autos when they made some trips.
6  All the girls in four other autos may go on the same trips.
7  Spring is the time of the year when they have a lot of pep.
   | | | | 5 | | | | 10 | | | | 15 | | | | 20 | | | | 25 | | | | 30 | | | | 35 | | | | 40 | | | | 45 | | | | 50 | | | | 55 | | | | 60
```

LANGUAGE ARTS

C. Study the rules at the right.

C. COMMAS

RULE ▶ ,nonessential expression

Use a comma before and after a nonessential expression.

Andre, who was there, can verify the statement.
But: Anyone who was there can verify the statement.
Van's first book, *Crisis of Management*, was not discussed.
Van's book *Crisis of Management* was not discussed.

Note: A nonessential expression is a group of words that may be omitted without changing the basic meaning of the sentence. Always examine the noun or pronoun that comes before the expression to determine whether the noun needs the expression to complete its meaning. If it does, the expression is *essential* and does *not* take a comma.

RULE ▶ ,adjacent adjective

Use a comma between two adjacent adjectives that modify the same noun.

We need an intelligent, enthusiastic individual for this job.
But: Please order a new bulletin board for our main conference room.

Note: Do not use a comma after the second adjective. Also, do not use a comma if the first adjective modifies the combined idea of the second adjective and the noun (for example, *bulletin board* and *conference room* in the second example).

Edit the sentences by inserting any needed punctuation.

8 The school president Mr. Roberts will address the students.
9 The fall planning meeting which is held in Charlotte has been canceled.
10 Students planning to take the certification test must register for the orientation class.
11 The sleek luxury car is scheduled for delivery next week.
12 Margaret brought her reliable trustworthy laptop to the meeting.
13 A stamped addressed envelope should be included with the survey.

FORMATTING

D. MULTIPAGE LETTERS

To format a multipage letter:

1. Type the first page on letterhead stationery and continuing pages on plain paper that matches the letterhead.
2. Insert a page number at the top right of the second and succeeding pages.

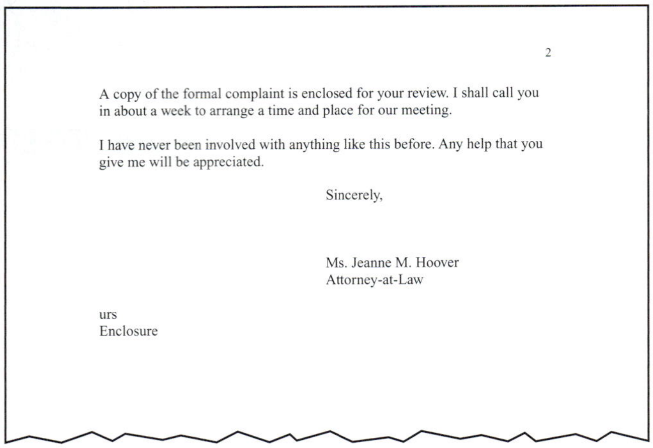
2

A copy of the formal complaint is enclosed for your review. I shall call you in about a week to arrange a time and place for our meeting.

I have never been involved with anything like this before. Any help that you give me will be appreciated.

Sincerely,

Ms. Jeanne M. Hoover
Attorney-at-Law

urs
Enclosure

DOCUMENT PROCESSING

Correspondence 71-64

Multipage Business Letter in Modified-Block Style With Enclosure Notation

Reference Manual

Review:
R-5A and R-5B: Multipage Business Letter

October 16, 20-- | Miss Florence B. Glashan | Attorney-at-Law | 2406 Shadows Glade | Dayton, OH 45426-0348 | Dear Miss Glashan: |

¶ It was good to meet you at the convention for trial attorneys in Detroit last week. In addition to the interesting program highlights of the regular sessions, I find that the informal discussions with people like you are an added plus at these meetings. Your contribution to the program was very beneficial to me.

¶ You may recall that I told you I had just been appointed by the court to defend a woman here in Dayton who has been charged with embezzling large sums of money from her previous employer. The defendant had been employed at a large department store for more than 25 years. Because of her valuable years of experience in accounting with the store, she was in charge of accounts receivable at the store. Her previous employer, the plaintiff in the case, claims that she embezzled $18,634 in 1997; $39,072 in 1998; and $27,045 in 1999.

(Continued on next page)

¶ I feel that it is my responsibility to represent my client and to provide the best defense possible. I recall that you mentioned that you had represented defendants in similar cases in previous years. As I prepare for this defense, perhaps you might help me in the following ways:

1. Please send me the appropriate citations for all similar trials in which you participated.
2. Also, please provide me with any other case citations that you think might be helpful to me in this case.
3. Arrange to meet with me soon so that I can benefit from your experience as I prepare for the trial.

¶ A copy of the formal complaint is enclosed for your review. I shall call you in about a week to arrange a time and place for our meeting. Please let me know if there is additional information that would be helpful in preparing for this case.

¶ I have never been involved with anything like this before. Any help that you give me will be appreciated. I shall look forward to working with you.

Sincerely, | Ms. Jeanne M. Hoover | Attorney-at-Law | urs | Enclosure

! Use the numbering command for the numbered list.

Remember to insert a blank line before and after the list and between each item in a multiline list.

Correspondence 71-65

Multipage Business Letter in Block Style With Copy Notation

April 3, 20-- | Mr. Michael Mc Ginty | District Manager | Sta & Morgan Company | One DuPont cicle | Washington, DC 2006-2133 |

Dear Mike:

¶ It was good to see you at our sales conference last week. Your winning our "golden apple" award for the most sales for the month was well deserved. When you first became part of our sales team, you showed great enthusiasm for you job immediately. There is no doubt that Starr & Morgan is very well represented in the metro Washington area. We particularly want to comment you for otaining the Westminster Account. Acquiting this account has been a major objective for a numbe of years. None of our company's sales represenives have been able to do this feat. Just the idear of a new account of over 500,000 is quite mind-boggling. How did you do it? Did you:

1. sped considerable time with the President Mr. Arch Davis or the Directo of Purchasing, Ms. Betsy Matin?
2. Conduct a series of hands-on workshops for the employees and managers?
3. Develope a special marekting campaign for Westminster it self or use a regular campaign model?
4. Combine various strategies in your efforts to obtain this important account?

(Continued on next page)

¶ Can you let me know what approaches were used to make this sale? Successes of this nature do not happen without a lot of hard work. You are to be commended for putting forth your best efforts to sign the account.

¶ If it can be arranged, a presentation by you at our next sales conference would seem very appropriate. The other sales representatives would benefit much from your success story. Our next meeting will be in late September in Richmond, Virginia. Again, congratulations on your receipt of this award. All of us here in the home office are pleased greatly with the performance of our entire sales team. Indications are that this will be a year when records are broken and we will be in the media spotlight.

Sincerely yours, | Robert D.Miley | Pres. | urs | c: R. Olson, Director of Sales

Correspondence 71-66

Multipage Business Letter in Modified-Block Style With Enclosure Notation

Open the file for Correspondence 71-64 and make the following changes:

1. Change the addressee to `Ms. Cynthia Barnes, Attorney-at-Law.`
2. Change the office address to:
   `4066 Quarry Estates`
   `Dayton, OH 45429-1362`
3. Change the salutation and header as needed.
4. Add this sentence at the end of the second paragraph:
   `The defendant is also being accused of embezzling $35,680 in 2000.`

Lesson 72

Special Letter Features

GOALS

- Type at least 42wpm/5′/5e
- Format special letter features

A. Type 2 times.

A. WARMUP

Six citizens from 14th Avenue East joined 83 other 10
residents to discuss the #794 proposal* for a new swimming 23
pool. Barry Kelm quoted numbers about current pool usage. 34

| 1 | 2 | 3 | 4 | 5 | 6 | 7 | 8 | 9 | 10 | 11 | 12

SKILLBUILDING

B. DIAGNOSTIC PRACTICE: ALPHABET

If you are not using the GDP software, turn to page SB-2 and follow the directions for this activity.

C. MAP

Follow the GDP software directions for this exercise in improving keystroking accuracy.

STRATEGIES FOR *Career Success*

Audience Analysis

Knowing your audience is fundamental to the success of any message. Ask the following questions to help identify your audience.

What is your relationship to your audience? Are they familiar—people with whom you work or people unknown? The latter will prompt you to conduct some research to better communicate your purpose. What is the attitude of your audience? Are they hostile or receptive to your message? How will your message benefit them? What is your anticipated response? Asking these questions first can help prevent message mishap later.

When writing to a diverse audience, direct your message to the primary audience. These key decision makers will make a decision or act on the basis of your message. Determine the level of detail, organization, formality, and use of technical terms and theory.

YOUR TURN Compose a thank you email to a friend. How would it differ from an interview thank you letter?

D. Take two 5-minute timings. Review your speed and errors.

Goal: At least 42wpm/5′/5e

D. 5-MINUTE TIMING

    Imagine that you have just finished college, and you 11
are starting a job in the field of human resources. What 22
are the major qualities you will need to perfect to become 34
successful in your position? While human resource experts 46
display a variety of skills, workers in this field must be 58
competent in their abilities to connect with clients and 69
have the knowledge to counsel them through crises. 79
    Connecting is the process of building good relations 90
with people in an organization. When connecting with an 101
employee, several things are important. The main goal is 112
to determine the needs of the employee and to work toward 124
meeting those needs. The end result should be acceptable 135
to both the company and the employee. 143
    Another goal is to establish open communication with 154
employees. To communicate freely, they must feel they can 166
trust other people. They must be allowed to express their 178
opinions without fear of being criticized. People who help 190
to resolve issues that affect their coworkers contribute 201
significantly to creating a good environment. 210

| 1 | 2 | 3 | 4 | 5 | 6 | 7 | 8 | 9 | 10 | 11 | 12

A career in the design engineering field requires creativity and keyboarding skill.

E. MULTIPLE ADDRESSES

Often a letter may be sent to two or more people at the same address or to different addresses:

1. If a letter is addressed to two people at the same address, type each name on a separate line above the same inside address.
2. If a letter is addressed to two people at different addresses, type each name and address, one under the other. Press ENTER 2 times between the addresses.
3. If a letter is addressed to three or more people, type the names and addresses side by side, with one at the left margin and another beginning at the centerpoint. Insert 1 blank line before typing the third name and address.

November 19, 20-- ↓4X

Dr. Albert Russell, Professor
Department of English
Appalachian State University
Boone, NC 28608 ↓2X

Dr. Kay Smith, Professor
Director of Business
Grove City College
Grove City, PA 16127 ↓2X

Dear Dr. Russell and Dr. Smith:

F. ON-ARRIVAL NOTATIONS

On-arrival notations (such as *Confidential*) should be typed on the second line below the date, at the left margin. Type the notation in all caps. Press ENTER 2 times to begin the inside address.

November 19, 20-- ↓2X

CONFIDENTIAL ↓2X

Mr. and Mrs. Earl Walters
3408 Washington Boulevard
New Tripoli, PA 18066 ↓2X

Dear Mr. and Mrs. Walters:

G. SUBJECT LINES

A *subject* line indicates what a letter is about. Type the subject line below the salutation at the left margin, preceded and followed by 1 blank line. (The term *Re* or *In re* may be used in place of *Subject*.)

November 19, 20-- ↓4X

Mr. and Mrs. Earl Walters
3408 Washington Boulevard
New Tripoli, PA 18066 ↓2X

Dear Mr. and Mrs. Walters: ↓2X

Subject: Insurance Enrollment ↓2X

We are pleased to be able to offer you enrollment in our insurance program.

Go To **Word Processing Manual**

H. WORD PROCESSING: SORT

Study Lesson 72 in your word processing manual. Complete all of the shaded steps while at your computer. Then format the jobs that follow.

DOCUMENT PROCESSING

Correspondence 72-67

Business Letter in Block Style With Subject Line and Copy Notation

November 8, 20--

CONFIDENTIAL

Mrs. Katie Hollister
11426 Prairie View Rd.
Kearney, NE 68847

Dear Mrs. Holister:

Subject: Site For New Elementary School

¶ As you are aware, your 160 acre farm, located in the quarter northeast of Section 25 in Tyro township, is a part of independent School District 17. Each of our elementary schools occupies two acres and is adjoined by an 8-acre park. We are now in the early palnning stages for a third elementary school. As you large farm is centrally located, the District 17 Board has directed me to initiate discussions with you for the purchase of 8 acres of land.

(Continued on next page)

¶ I look forward to our discussions. Please call me at your convenience to arrange a meeting with you and/or your attorney and me.

Yours truly,

Irvin J. Hagg

Superintendent

urs

c: District 17 Board

Correspondence 72-68

Multipage Business Letter in Block Style With Multiple Addresses

Sort each bulleted list in the letter in ascending order.

October 4, 20-- | Ms. Deborah Campbell Wallace | 7835 Virginia Avenue Northwest | Washington, DC 20037 | Mr. Thomas E. Campbell | 3725 Stevens Road Southeast | Washington, DC 20020 | Dear Ms. Wallace and Mr. Campbell:

¶ We received your letter requesting instructions for transferring stock. The most common stock transfer situations are provided below. Determine which type of transfer you require and select the instructions that apply to your stock transfer.

- Name change
- Transferring shares to another individual(s)
- Transfers involving a deceased shareholder (individual ownership)
- Transfers involving a deceased shareholder (multiple owners)
- Transfers involving a minor
- Transfers involving a trust
- Transfers involving a power of attorney

¶ Every transfer requires a letter of instruction specifying how you want your shares transferred. The following items are required for all types of transfers:

- Name and address of new owner(s)
- Social security number or tax payer identification number
- Preferred form of ownership (i.e., joint tenants, tenants in common, etc.)
- Indicate total shares that are being transferred
- Sign and date the form

¶ Please be sure to submit all required documentation and note that all documents submitted become part of the permanent record of transfer and will not be returned.

(Continued on next page)

¶ All transfers must have your signature(s) guaranteed by a financial institution participating in the Medallion Signature Guarantee Program.

¶ If you need additional information, you may visit our Web site for step-by-step instructions or you may call one of our customer service representatives at our toll-free number.

Sincerely, | William J. Shawley | Shareholder Services | urs

Correspondence 72-69

Personal-Business Letter in Block Style With Subject Line

! Format book titles in italic instead of underlining.

November 17, 20--

Dr. Arif Gureshi
8726 East Ridge Drive
Morehead, KY 40351-7268
Dear Dr. Gureshi:
Subject: The Middle East in the Year 2005 Book Discussion
¶ Your new book, The Middle East in the Year 2005, has gotten excellent reviews. The citizens of Morehead are pleased that a respected member of one of our local colleges is receiving national attention.
¶ Our book discussion group in Morehead, composed of members of the AAUW (American Association of University Women), has selected your book for discussion at our May meeting. We would very much like you to be a participant; your attendance at the meeting would be a real highlight.
¶ I shall call you next week. Our members are hoping that you will be able to attend and that an acceptable date can be arranged.
Sincerely,

Theresa A. Gorski
2901 Garfield Court
Morehead, KY 40351-2687

Lesson 73

More Special Letter Features

GOALS

- Improve speed and accuracy
- Refine language arts skills in composing paragraphs
- Format letters with special features

A. Type 2 times.

A. WARMUP

```
1      The 83 Lions Club members raised $6,690 (95% of the     11
2  requested sum) to resurface the tennis courts. Gayle was    22
3  amazed when sixteen jolly members picked up over 10% more.  34
   | 1 | 2 | 3 | 4 | 5 | 6 | 7 | 8 | 9 | 10 | 11 | 12
```

SKILLBUILDING

B. PACED PRACTICE

If you are not using the GDP software, turn to page SB-14 and follow the directions for this activity.

PPP

PRETEST → PRACTICE → POSTTEST

C. PRETEST: Vertical Reaches

PRETEST
Take a 1-minute timing. Review your speed and errors.

```
4      The scents in the trunk scared the rest of the drama    11
5  class. One judge drank juice and ate pecans as the cranky   23
6  coach scolded the best junior and bought the pink dresses.  35
   | 1 | 2 | 3 | 4 | 5 | 6 | 7 | 8 | 9 | 10 | 11 | 12
```

D. PRACTICE: Up Reaches

PRACTICE
Speed Emphasis:
If you made no more than 1 error on the Pretest, type each *individual* line 2 times.
Accuracy Emphasis:
If you made 2 or more errors, type each *group* of lines (as though it were a paragraph) 2 times.

```
7  dr draft drank dryer drain drama dread dream drag drew drug
8  ju judge juice jumpy junks juror julep jumbo judo jump just
9  es essay nests tests less dress acres makes uses best rest
```

E. PRACTICE: Down Reaches

```
10 ca cable caddy cargo scare decay yucca pecan cage calm case
11 nk ankle blank crank blink think trunk brink bank junk sink
12 sc scale scalp scene scent scold scoop scope scan scar disc
```

F. POSTTEST: Vertical Reaches

POSTTEST
Repeat the Pretest timing and compare performance.

LANGUAGE ARTS

G. COMPOSING: PARAGRAPH

Compose a paragraph expressing your opinion on whether or not it is safe to make purchases online. Include precautions and potential dangers.

FORMATTING

H. TABLES WITHIN DOCUMENTS

To format a table that is part of a letter, memo, or report:

1. In a single-spaced document, press ENTER 2 times before and 1 time after the table. Be sure you are outside the table structure before pressing ENTER 1 time.
2. In a double-spaced document, press ENTER 1 time before and after the table.
3. Single-space the body of the table.
4. Adjust the column widths, and center the table within the margins of the document.
5. Never split a table between two pages. If a table will not fit at the bottom of the page on which it is first mentioned, place it at the top of the next page.

MEMO TO: Leo Guthrie

FROM: Paul Forester

DATE: January 10, 20--

SUBJECT: Sales Comparison

Listed below are the sales totals for the last two quarters. Please review the information before our staff meeting on Friday. ↓2X

SALES SUMMARY December 31, 20-- ↓1X		
↓1X **Region**	**Third Quarter**	**Fourth Quarter**
Northeast	456,321	512,980
Southeast	335,765	375,112
Northwest	425,666	457,034
Southwest	388,546	410,478

↓1X

Come to the meeting prepared to discuss plans for the upcoming sales promotions that will take place in our district.

I. COMPANY NAME IN CLOSING LINES

Some business firms show the company name in the closing lines of a letter. The company name is typed in all caps on the second line below the complimentary closing, followed by 3 blank lines before the writer's name.

Thank you for inviting me to participate in the discussion concerning this issue. ↓2X

Sincerely yours, ↓2X

HENDERSON AND SONS, INC. ↓4X

Mark Henderson, President ↓2X

urs

J. BLIND COPY NOTATION

A blind copy (bc:) notation is used when the addressee is not intended to know that one or more other persons are being sent a copy of the letter. Type the bc notation on the file copy at the left margin on the second line after the last item in the letter.

When preparing a letter with a blind copy, print one copy of the letter; then add the blind copy notation and print another.

Thank you for inviting me to participate in the discussion concerning this issue.

Sincerely yours, ↓4X

Mark Henderson
President ↓2X

urs ↓2X

bc: Mary Stevenson

K. DELIVERY NOTATION

Type a delivery notation on the line below the enclosure notation (if used) or on the line below the reference initials. A delivery notation comes before a copy notation.

Sincerely yours, ↓4X

Mark Henderson
President ↓2X

urs
Enclosure
By fax
c: Mary Stevenson

L. POSTSCRIPT

If a postscript is added to a letter, it is typed as the last item in the letter, preceded by 1 blank line. If a blind copy notation and postscript are used, the bc: notation follows the postscript.

urs
Enclosure ↓2X

PS: You will be reimbursed for all expenses. Complete an expense report and submit it to your supervisor. ↓2X

bc: Mary Stevenson

Go To
Word Processing Manual

M. WORD PROCESSING: SHADING

Study Lesson 73 in your word processing manual. Complete all of the shaded steps while at your computer. Then format the jobs that follow.

DOCUMENT PROCESSING

Correspondence 73-70

Business Letter in Block Style With Open Table and Delivery and Blind Copy Notations

March 1, 20-- | Ms. Maureen Testa | Austin Communications | 37 Pittsburgh Road | Franklin, PA 16323 | Dear Ms. Testa:

¶ We are indeed interested in designing a new corporate logo and the corresponding stationery for your fine company. As I indicated in our recent telephone conversation, we have a design staff that has won many national awards for letterhead form design, and we consider it an honor to be contacted by you.

¶ Within a couple of weeks, we will submit to you and your committee several basic designs. Based on your evaluation and suggestions, we can go from there. Here is a modified price list for the printed stationery:

Automatically adjust the column widths and center the table horizontally.

Stationery	**Cost**
Letterhead (500 sheets)	$ 80.00
Business cards (1,000 cards)	39.50
Coated brochures (1,000 sheets)	219.30
Envelopes	92.00

¶ In the meantime, please call me if we can be of further service.

Sincerely yours, | Samantha A. Steele | General Manager | urs | By fax | bc: Design Department

---

Correspondence 73-71

Business Letter in Block Style with Boxed Table and Delivery and Blind Copy Notations

Apply 15% shading to the first row of the table.

Open the file for Correspondence 73-70 from Ms. Steele and make the following changes:

1. Send the letter to `Mr. Rodney Graae | Thompson Corporation | 42 Harris Court | Trenton, NJ 08648`
2. Change the word "company" in the first paragraph to `corporation.`
3. Revise the first two sentences of the second paragraph to say: `Within a month, we will submit several basic designs to you and your board of directors. At that time, please feel free to make any comments and suggestions that will help us finalize a design.`
4. Change the table to a boxed table.

Correspondence 73-72

Multipage Business Letter in Modified-Block Style With Enclosure, Delivery, and Postscript Notations

Current Date | Master Gyms, Inc. | 4201 Castine Court | Raleigh, NC 27613-5981 | Ladies and Gentlemen:

¶ We have 494 apartments at Fountain Ridge. As the recreation coordinator, I have concerns not only about the leisure-time activities of our residents but also about the health and physical fitness of the more than 1,100 people who call Fountain Ridge home.

(Continued on next page)

¶ Our recreation facilities are excellent. In addition to our two outdoor tennis courts and swimming pool, we also have the following indoor facilities: two racquetball courts, swimming pool, whirlpool bath, sauna, steam room, and two billiard tables. However, we have no workout equipment.
¶ During the next few months we will be equipping a new gymnasium. The dimensions of the gym are shown on the enclosed sketch. There will be exercise bicycles, treadmills, and rowing machines. In addition, we would like to install a muscle-toning machine that includes features such as the following: leg press, chest press, shoulder press, arm pull, leg pull, arm lift, leg lift, and sit-up board.
¶ The needs and interests of our residents are varied. Some residents will take full advantage of the equipment we have suggested for the gymnasium. However, many of our residents have expressed interests in an indoor track for walking; others would like to add a track for running. We hope to accommodate as many of the suggestions as we feel are feasible.
¶ The population of the residents in the Fountain Ridge complex consists of a mixture of young and middle-age adult couples as well as single residents. Some of the couples have children who would be old enough to enjoy the facilities. Therefore, safety and durability of the equipment are very important considerations. In addition, we would like to continue to develop our complex in a way that would invite family participation in our recreational activities.
¶ Do you have a sales representative serving this area who could meet with me within a week or ten days? As an alternative, perhaps you have some brochures, including prices, that could be sent to me.
Sincerely yours, | FOUNTAIN RIDGE | Rosa Bailey-Judd | Recreation Coordinator | urs | Enclosure | By fax | PS: Please send a current catalog and price list immediately so that we can prepare for our meeting with the sales representative.

Opportunities in television production studios require keyboarding skill.

Multipage Memos With Tables

GOALS

- Type at least 42wpm/5'/5e
- Format multipage memos with tables

A. Type 2 times.

A. WARMUP

```
     Over 270 cars were backed up near the Baxter & Meintz    11
building after an 18-wheeler jackknifed at an icy junction.  23
About 1/3 to 1/2 of the cars were required to use a detour.  35
| 1 | 2 | 3 | 4 | 5 | 6 | 7 | 8 | 9 | 10 | 11 | 12
```

SKILLBUILDING

B. PROGRESSIVE PRACTICE: ALPHABET

If you are not using the GDP software, turn to page SB-7 and follow the directions for this activity.

C. PROGRESSIVE PRACTICE: NUMBERS

If you are not using the GDP software, turn to page SB-11 and follow the directions for this activity.

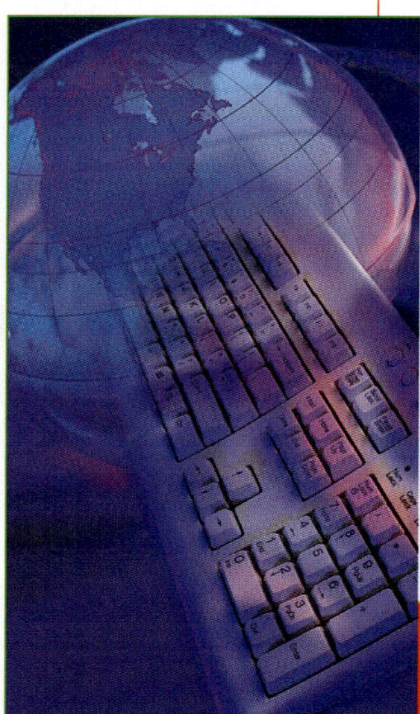

Keyboarding CONNECTION

Virus and Spam Prevention

Use caution when opening email attachments or downloading files from the Internet. Only download files from reliable Web sites. Do not open files attached to an email from an unknown source. Also question files attached to a known source. Some viruses replicate themselves and are sent through email without users' knowledge.

Delete any email with an odd subject, a chain email, or electronic junk mail, commonly known as spam. If you're given the opportunity to unsubscribe from a spammer's list, think twice. Your reply will stop the messages on a reputable mailing list but may incite disreputable list marketers.

To protect against lost data, back up your files on a regular basis. Then you will be prepared if a virus infects your computer. New viruses are discovered daily so update your anti-virus software regularly.

YOUR TURN How do you handle junk mail via post? Do you notice similarities when dealing with spam?

D. Take two 5-minute timings. Review your speed and errors.

Goal: At least 42wpm/5'/5e

D. 5-MINUTE TIMING

Biometric security is used by government agencies 10
and businesses to identify users who access the computer 21
systems. Using a technique of biometric technology, the 32
identity of the user is established. When a user attempts 44
to access the system, the technology is used to search the 56
database for a match. Authentication requires the user to 68
provide a name or personal identification number. 78

Four basic steps are used in biometric technology. 88
First, the images are captured. Then, the features are 99
extracted and converted to a template. Finally, data is 110
matched for authentication. 116

In biometric scanning, images of the fingers, hand, 127
face, or the eye are captured. The unique patterns that 138
exclusively identify the person in an image are extracted, 150
converted to a template, and stored as data. Scans of the 162
retina and iris recognition are most accurate and reliable 174
methods of biometric technology. The blood vessels in the 186
back zone of the eye show unique patterns, and the iris of 198
the eye provides accurate details that identify the person. 210

| 1 | 2 | 3 | 4 | 5 | 6 | 7 | 8 | 9 | 10 | 11 | 12

FORMATTING

Go To **Word Processing Manual**

E. WORD PROCESSING: FIND AND REPLACE

Study Lesson 74 in your word processing manual. Complete all of the shaded steps while at your computer. Then format the jobs that follow.

DOCUMENT PROCESSING

Correspondence 74-73

Multipage Memo With Open Table and Postscript Notation

MEMO TO: L. B. Chinn, Station Manager | **FROM**: Mitzi Grenell, News Director | **DATE**: May 5, 20-- | **SUBJECT**: FCC European Trip

¶ As you requested, this memo is being sent to you as one in a series to keep you informed about my upcoming trip to Europe. I have been invited by the Federal Communications Commission to participate in a study of television news in European countries. The invitation came from Jill Andrews, FCC vice-chair; and I am, of course, delighted to take part in this challenging project.

(Continued on next page)

¶ One function of this study will be to compare the news in countries that have a long history of free-access broadcasting with the programming in newly democratic countries. I have been assigned to lead a study group to six European countries to gather firsthand information on this topic. We will be visiting England, France, Germany, Poland, Romania, and Latvia from August 24 through September 3. In addition to me, our group will consist of the following members:

Arkady Gromov	News Director National Public Radio	Washington, DC
Manuel Cruz	Executive Editor *Miami Herald*	Miami, FL
Katherine Grant	Station Manager WPQR-TV	Boston, MA
Richard Logan	Operations Manager Cable News System	New York, NY

¶ Our initial plans are to spend at least one full day in each of the countries, meeting with the news staff of one or two of the major networks, touring their facilities, viewing recent broadcasts, and becoming familiar with their general operations.

¶ If you need to contact me during my absence, Barbara Brooks, our liaison at the Federal Communications Commission (1919 M Street, NW, Washington, DC 20554; phone: 202-555-3894), will be able to provide a location and phone number.

¶ Arrangements will be made with several different staff members in the News Department to handle my responsibilities here at Channel 5 while I am gone. Dave Gislason will be the contact person for the department. As you can imagine, this is an exciting time for me. Thank you for supporting the project.

| urs | PS: Thanks also for suggesting that this trip be combined with a vacation. My husband and I have discussed the possibility of his joining me for a two-week tour of the Scandinavian countries after the FCC trip has been completed. I shall let you know what our plans are by the end of May.

Correspondence 74-74

Multipage Memo With Open Table and Postscript Notation

Open the file for Correspondence 74-73 and make the following changes:

1. `Jill Andrews` has just been promoted to FCC chair.
2. `Finland` has been added as a seventh country.
3. The trip has been extended through `September 5.`
4. Each occurrence of news (lowercase) has to be changed to `news programming`. (Do not replace News.)
5. `Reggie Jordan, Staff Assistant, FCC, Washington, DC,` will replace Manuel Cruz on the trip.
6. `Gil Friesen` will replace Dave Gislason as contact person.

Correspondence 74-75

Memo With Boxed Table

MEMO TO: Terri Hackworth, Manager

FROM: Rosa Bailey Judd, Recreation Coordinator

DATE: April 14, 20--

SUBJECT: Fitness room

The new Fitness Room will be ready for use in about 1 month. Your leadership in bringing thsi about is sincerely appreciated. After much investigation (much reading and several interviews), I likely will be requesting approval soon to purchase the equipment:

No.	Type
4	exercise bicycles
1	treadmill
1	muscle-toner machine

Three other types of equipment wer considered seriously, but those listed above enable users to reach objectives with out excessive cost. I am not quite ready to recommend the specific brands or the suppliers for these machines. As we expect that there will be very heavy usage, we are concerned with durbility, warranties, and the available of dependable service personnel. Thanks again for your full support and cooperation with this project.

urs

STRATEGIES FOR *Career Success*

Developing Confidence as a Presenter

Public speaking anxiety is quite common. As many as 77 percent of experienced speakers admit to having some anxiety on each speaking occasion. Normally, stage fright decreases with experience.

Even if there are no physical expressions of anxiety, speakers often assume others can see through their smiles to their fears. However, listeners are actually poor judges of the amount of anxiety that speakers experience.

A little anxiety can actually stimulate a better presentation. The best way to control your anxiety is to be well prepared for the presentation. Carefully analyze your audience, research your topic, organize the speech, practice its delivery, and believe in its ideas. Being well prepared puts you in an excellent position to control your anxiety.

YOUR TURN "I'm glad I'm here. I'm glad you're here. I know that I know." What are the benefits of repeating this to yourself before each presentation?

Lesson 75

Memo Reports

GOALS

- Improve speed and accuracy
- Format memo reports

A. Type 2 times.

A. WARMUP

```
     The sizable judge asked three questions: "What's the    11
best time of the day for you to be in court? Can you leave   23
your job at exactly 4 p.m.? If not, 5 p.m. or 7 p.m.?"       34
| 1 | 2 | 3 | 4 | 5 | 6 | 7 | 8 | 9 | 10 | 11 | 12
```

SKILLBUILDING

B. Take a 1-minute timing on the first paragraph to establish your base speed. Then take four 1-minute timings on the remaining paragraphs. As soon as you equal or exceed your base speed on one paragraph, advance to the next, more difficult paragraph.

B. SUSTAINED PRACTICE: SYLLABIC INTENSITY

```
     Each of us has several bills to be paid on a monthly    11
basis. For most of us, a checkbook is the tool that we use   23
to take care of this chore. However, in this electronic      34
age, other ways of doing this have received rave reviews.    45

     You will likely be surprised to learn that the most     11
basic way and the cheapest way to pay bills electronically   23
involves the use of a Touch-Tone phone. The time required    35
is approximately a third of that used when writing checks.   47

     Several banking institutions offer or plan to offer     11
screen phones as a method for paying bills. It is possible   22
to buy securities, make transfers, and determine account     34
balances. You will save time by using a Touch-Tone phone.    45

     A third type of electronic bill processing involves     10
using a microcomputer and a modem. Software programs have    21
on-screen checkbooks linked to bill-paying applications.     34
Other microcomputers use online services through a modem.    46
| 1 | 2 | 3 | 4 | 5 | 6 | 7 | 8 | 9 | 10 | 11 | 12
```

C. TECHNIQUE PRACTICE: SPACE BAR

```
     We will all go to the race if I win my event today.
Do you think that I will be able to finish the race at the
front of the pack, or do you think there are lots of very
fast runners out there who surely can finish ahead of me?
```

LANGUAGE ARTS

D. Edit this paragraph to correct any typing or formatting errors.

D. PROOFREADING: EDITING

```
     Many home computer user like the challenge of haveing the latest in both hardware and software technology. Their are those however, who's needs likely can be satisfied at a very low costs. A used 486-chip personnel computer with color monitor and keyboard might be your's for under $ 300. Check out th Yellow Page, or visit a used-computer store.
```

FORMATTING

E. REPORT HEADINGS IN MEMOS

There are times when a memo report is used rather than preparing a cover memo to accompany a report. The documents are combined into one, and headings are formatted as they are in a report.

DOCUMENT PROCESSING

Report 75-56

Memo Report

Reference Manual

Review:
R-9C: Memo Report

MEMO TO: All Employees | **FROM:** Franklin Coates, Director | **DATE:** February 24, 20-- | **SUBJECT:** Security System

¶ Beginning March 1, we will install a new security access system. Complete installation should occur by the end of March. The system will include new magnetic card readers at all entrances. It will also provide a more secure working environment, especially in the evenings and on weekends. Entrances will lock and unlock automatically each day during working hours. Please carefully read and follow the detailed instructions for using the new system.

RECEIVING A NEW ACCESS CARD

¶ Once the new system is installed, you will need a new access identification card to enter the building during nonworking hours. Human Resources will begin taking pictures for new cards during the week of March 20. When you are called, report immediately. The cards will be issued as soon as they are ready. To receive your new card, you must turn in your old one.

(Continued on next page)

ENTERING THE BUILDING

¶ Entrances will automatically unlock each working day at 8 a.m and lock at 5 p.m. To enter the building during nonworking hours, slide your access identification card (with the magnetic strip facing left) through the card reader at the right of the entrance door. When the green light comes on, open the door. Do not hold the door open longer than 30 seconds.

¶ Once you enter the building during nonworking hours, please proceed immediately to the front desk and sign in. Record in the log book your name, department, extension number, and arrival time.

LEAVING THE BUILDING

¶ Before leaving the building, you must sign out. Please record your departure time beside your name. Do not use the special latch handle to open the door, or the alarm will sound. Instead, use the push bar. Once you have opened the door, do not let it remain open longer than 30 seconds, or the alarm will sound. If you accidentally set off the alarm, return to the front desk and call the security company (the telephone number is at the top of the log book). Be prepared to provide them with your name, extension number, and access card number.

¶ At times you may need to have the door held open for extended periods of time during nonbusiness hours. In these situations, please make arrangements with Building Maintenance by calling extension 4444.

¶ If you have questions about our new security access system and procedures, please contact me.

Report 75-57

Memo Report

Mr. Coates has asked you to revise Report 75-56 as follows:

1. Use February 25 as the date.
2. Change "nonworking" to `nonbusiness` throughout the report.
3. Add the following sentence at the end of the second paragraph:

   `New employees will be asked for a special form, to be provided by their supervisors.`
4. Change "Building Maintenance" to `Building Security.`

Report 75-58

Memo Report

Progress Check
Proofreading Check

Documents designated as Proofreading Checks serve as a check of your proofreading skill. Your goal is to have zero typographical errors when the GDP software first scores the document.

MEMO TO: *All Employees*
FROM: *Adrienne Barzanov*
DATE: *March 2, 20--*
SUBJECT: *New Building Site*

¶ *We have consulted with several architects and have finalized plans to build a new administrative center at 6400 Easton Plaza. This memo provides general information about plans for the center's exterior and interior development.*

EXTERIOR PLANS

¶ *Exterior plans will maintain the historical integrity and beauty of the surrounding area and reflect the architecture of other buildings in the office park. Landscaping plans include a nature preserve, a picnic area, and a small pond.*

INTERIOR PLANS FOR STAFF

¶ *Staff will be located within the new facility as follows:*

1. *Accounting will be located on the first floor in the west wing.*
2. *Sales and marketing will be located on the first floor in the east wing. All staff will be grouped according to product line.*
3. *All other staff will be located on the second floor. Exact locations will be determined at a later date.*

INTERIOR PLANS FOR SPECIAL FACILITIES

¶ *Conference rooms will be located in the center of the building on the first floor to provide easy access for everyone. All rooms will be equipped with state-of-the-art technology.*

¶ *Our new center will also include a full-service cafeteria, a copy center, a library, an athletic center, and an on-site day care center.*

¶ *Construction of the new center will begin when we obtain the necessary permits.*

Unit 16

Tables

LESSON 76
Tables With Footnotes or Source Notes

LESSON 77
Tables With Braced Column Headings

LESSON 78
Tables Formatted Sideways

LESSON 79
Multipage Tables

LESSON 80
Using Predesigned Table Formats

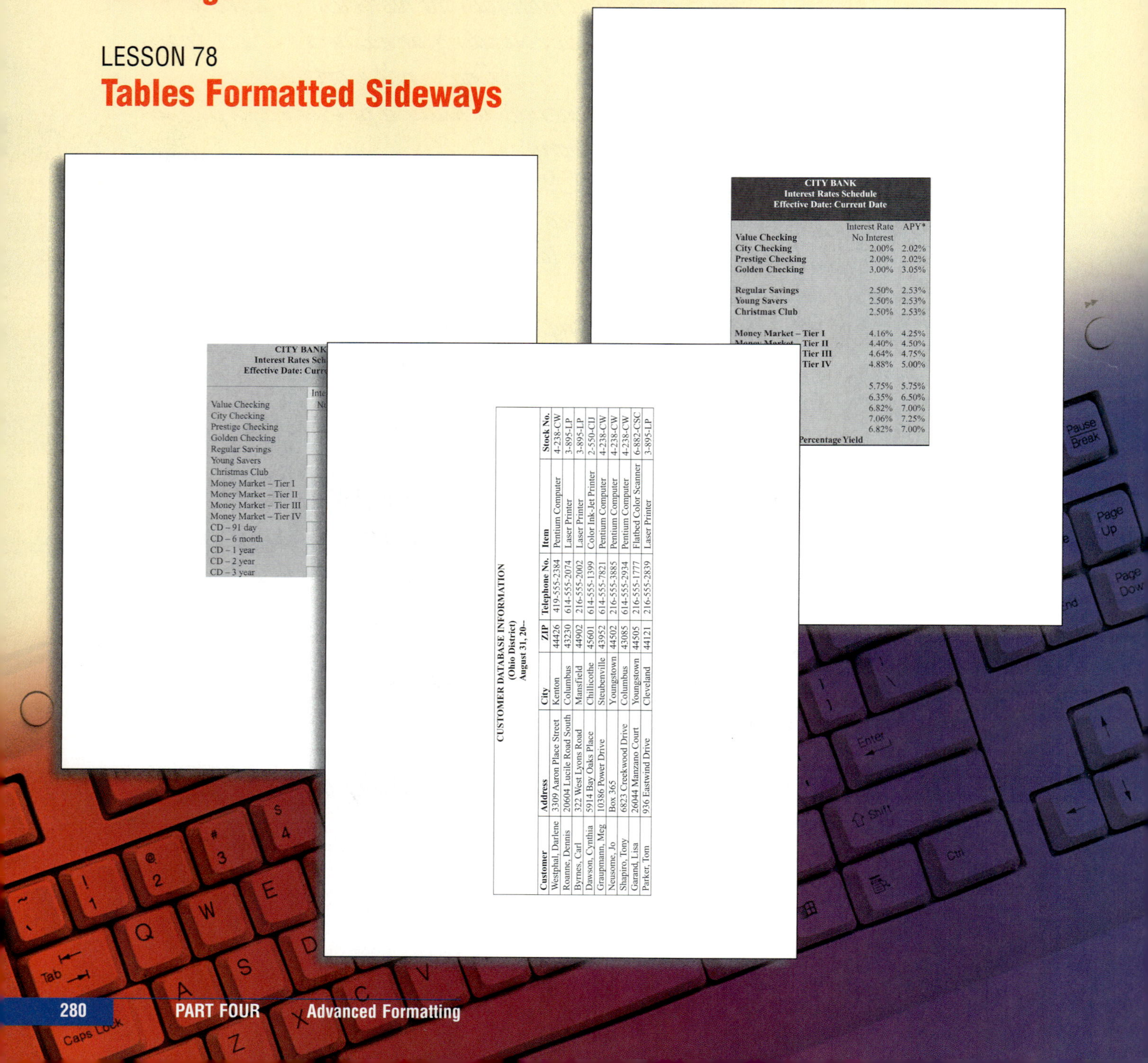

Lesson 76

Tables With Footnotes or Source Notes

GOALS
- Type at least 43wpm/5′/5e
- Change text direction
- Insert or delete rows or columns

A. Type 2 times.

A. WARMUP

```
1       Order #Z391 must be processed "quickly" and exactly     11
2  as specified! In January several orders were sent out by     22
3  mistake; regrettably, one order worth $5,680 was canceled.   34
   | 1 | 2 | 3 | 4 | 5 | 6 | 7 | 8 | 9 | 10 | 11 | 12
```

SKILLBUILDING

B. Take three 12-second timings on each line. The scale below the last line shows your wpm speed for a 12-second timing.

B. 12-SECOND SPEED SPRINTS

```
4  You paid for the ruby that she owned when he was just five.
5  Toby wishes to thank all eight of the girls for their time.
6  Yale is a very fine place to learn about the world of work.
7  She has a theory that the icy roads will cause a bad wreck.
   5 10 15 20 25 30 35 40 45 50 55 60
```

C. DIAGNOSTIC PRACTICE: ALPHABET

If you are not using the GDP software, turn to page SB-2 and follow the directions for this activity.

STRATEGIES FOR *Career Success*

Cellular Phone Manners Matter

Mind your cell phone manners! While the cellular phone allows you to keep in touch with your boss, coworkers, and clients, it also requires you to consider your communication etiquette. One of the worst violations of etiquette and safety is driving and talking at the same time. It is much safer to pull off the road to make a call.

Consider others when you use the cellular phone in a public place (e.g., a restaurant). If you use the phone in public, talk quietly and watch what you say. Cellular phones in meetings can distract others; some companies prohibit them in business meetings.

Since cellular phone use is costlier than a traditional phone, when you call a cell phone user, keep your message brief.

YOUR TURN Observe cellular phone users in a public place. Are they mindful of others when they use their phones?

D. Take two 5-minute timings. Review your speed and errors.

Goal: At least 43wpm/5'/5e

D. 5-MINUTE TIMING

```
     Several years ago many corporations in the business          11
world adopted a policy called casual Friday. This trend           22
enabled employees to dress down each Friday. Employers            33
distributed guidelines for appropriate casual clothing.           44
Advocates for casual Friday justified the change by citing        56
increased productivity and better employee morale.                66
     A controversy regarding the casual Friday policy is          78
being addressed currently. Many businesses are questioning        90
the effect of casual dress on productivity. Studies are          101
being analyzed to determine if casual dress has an adverse       113
effect on the attitudes of employees toward attendance,          124
tardiness, and professional image.                               131
     Apparently, some managers believe that workers are          141
not following the guidelines. The managers want to adopt         152
stricter standards for an acceptable dress code that would       164
prohibit employees from appearing too relaxed when they          175
report for work. Some employees with concerns about the          186
casual dress code are suggesting that Friday should be a         197
day to dress up for the office. They intend to foster a          208
more productive office environment.                              215
| 1 | 2 | 3 | 4 | 5 | 6 | 7 | 8 | 9 | 10 | 11 | 12
```

FORMATTING

Reference Manual

Refer to pages R-8A and R-13A of the Reference Manual.

E. TABLES WITH FOOTNOTES OR SOURCE NOTES

To format tables with footnotes:

1. Include a separator row for the footnote reference at the bottom when you are creating the table structure.
2. Select the cells in the bottom row and merge the cells.
3. Type an asterisk (or another symbol) at the appropriate point within the table to indicate that there is a footnote.
4. Type the footnote.

Go To Word Processing Manual

F. WORD PROCESSING: TABLE—TEXT DIRECTION, AND TABLE—INSERT OR DELETE ROWS OR COLUMNS

Study Lesson 76 in your word processing manual. Complete all of the shaded steps while at your computer. Then format the jobs that follow.

DOCUMENT PROCESSING

Table 76-26

Seven-Column Boxed Table With Table Note

Your completed table will look different from the one shown.

1. Center the table vertically.
2. Create a boxed table with 7 columns and 6 rows, and type the table.
3. Merge cells in Row 6 for the table note.
4. Right-align the text in the number columns.
   Note: Do not change the left alignment of the column headings.

(Continued on next page)

Your completed table will look different from the one shown.

5. Bold Row 1 and Column A, excluding the table note.
6. Select Row 1 and change the text direction to display vertically top-to-bottom.
7. Drag down on the bottom border of Row 1 until the column headings display in one continuous line without wrapping.
8. Automatically adjust the column widths for all columns.
9. Center the table horizontally.

Account Number	Blue Sierra Letterhead	Italian Renaissance Letterhead	Sonoma Desert Letterhead	Watercolor Wash Letterhead	Sandstone Marble Letterhead	Greek Acropolis Letterhead
GV-11	3,500	500	750	1,000	250	1,250
GV-29	2,500	250	250	500	500	250
GV-37	750	1,000	500	2,500	250	2,500
GV-10	250	500	1,000	250	1,500	250
Note: This information is subject to change.						

Table 76-27

Seven-Column Boxed Table

Open the file for Table 76-26 and make the following changes:

1. Delete the table note row.
2. Delete Column G.
3. Insert a column to the left of Column B.
4. Insert a row above Row 3. Type: GV-72 | 1,250 | 500 | 1,000 | 250 | 750 | 2,000
5. Type: French Patina Letterhead | 750 | 1,250 | 250 | 1,000 | 500
6. Right-align the text in the numbers columns as needed.
7. Apply 10% shading to Row 1.

Table 76-28

Six-Column Boxed Table With Source Note

Your completed table will look different from the one shown.

1. Center the table vertically.
2. Create a boxed table with 5 columns and 6 rows, and type the table.
3. Merge cells in Row 6 for the source note.
4. Right-align the text in the number columns.
   Note: Do not change the left alignment of the column headings
5. Select Row 1 and change the text direction to display vertically top-to-bottom.
6. Drag down on the bottom border of Row 1 until the column headings display in one continuous line without wrapping.
7. Automatically adjust the column widths for all columns.
8. Center the table horizontally.

Office Supply Account	LED Laser Printer	Internal Fax Modem	Cash Management System	Plain-paper Laser Fax
OE-9	$405	$181	$199	$249
DD-7	395	150	205	234
US-2	410	125	183	252
OB-1	420	167	179	245
Source: March invoices				

Lesson 77

Tables With Braced Column Headings

GOALS

- Improve speed and accuracy
- Refine language arts skills in capitalization
- Format braced headings in tables

A. Type 2 times.

A. WARMUP

```
1      Six citizens from 14th Avenue East joined 83 other       10
2  residents to discuss the #794 proposal* for a new swimming   22
3  pool. Barry Kelm quoted numbers about current pool usage.    33
   | 1 | 2 | 3 | 4 | 5 | 6 | 7 | 8 | 9 | 10 | 11 | 12
```

SKILLBUILDING

B. DIAGNOSTIC PRACTICE: NUMBERS

If you are not using the GDP software, turn to page SB-5 and follow the directions for this activity.

C. MAP

Follow the GDP software directions for this exercise in improving keystroking accuracy.

LANGUAGE ARTS

D. Study the rules at the right.

D. CAPITALIZATION

RULE ≡ noun #

Capitalize nouns followed by a number or letter (except for the nouns *line, note, page, paragraph,* and *size*).

Please read Chapter 5, which begins on page 94.

RULE ≡ compass point

Capitalize compass points (such as *north, south,* or *northeast*) only when they designate definite regions.

From Montana we drove south to reach the Southwest.

Edit the sentences to correct any errors in capitalization.

```
4  The marketing manager had a reservation on flight 505 to Atlanta.
5  Please order two model 6M printers.
6  The desktop publishing seminar will be held in Room 101.
7  Study pages 120-230 for the unit test.
8  Please contact all representatives in the northern states.
9  Have you visited the city of Pittsburgh?
10 The population of the south continues to increase.
```

FORMATTING

E. BRACED COLUMN HEADINGS

A braced column heading is a heading that applies to more than one column (for example, *Retirement Account* in the table shown below):

1. To create a braced column heading, position the insertion point where you want the braced heading to appear.
2. Merge the cells to create space for the braced heading.
3. Center the braced column headings over the columns.

DOCUMENT PROCESSING

Table 77-29

Six-Column Boxed Table With Braced Column Headings

1. Center the table vertically.
2. Create a boxed table with 6 columns and 6 rows.
3. Center and type the braced and regular column headings in upper- and lowercase and bold.
4. Block column headings and right-align the text in columns containing numbers.
5. Follow the standard table format.
6. Merge cells and columns as necessary.

INSURED ACCOUNT DEPOSITS **For Melanie and Frank Bush**					
First World Savings		**Individual Account**		**Retirement Account**	
Month	**Branch**	**M. Bush**	**F. Bush**	**M. Bush**	**F. Bush**
January	Reseda	$5,500	$2,350	$2,000	$10,000
February	Valencia	7,950	5,700	5,500	4,300
March	Van Nuys	2,400	7,300	9,300	2,550

Table 77-30

Four-Column Boxed Table With Braced Column Headings

1. Center the table vertically.
2. Create a boxed table with 4 columns and 6 rows.
3. Center and type the braced and regular column headings in upper- and lowercase and bold; right-align the number columns.
4. Follow the standard table format.
5. Merge cells as necessary.

CINEPLEX VIDEOS **Sales Trends**			
Western Region		**Total Sales**	
State	**Manager**	**Last Year**	**This Year**
California	George Lucas	$1,956,250	$2,135,433
Nevada	Marjorie Matheson	859,435	1,231,332
Washington	Valerie Harper	737,498	831,352

Table 77-31

Four-Column Boxed Table With Braced Column Headings

Open the file for Table 77-30 and make the following changes.

1. Change the column heading "Western Region" to Eastern Region.
2. Change the state names to New York | New Jersey | Delaware.
3. Change the manager's names to Robert DeLuca | Doris Lynch | Megan Bennett.
4. Change last year's amounts to $2,052,659 | 534,958 | 894,211.
5. Change this year's amounts to $3,345,312 | 2,311,478 | 925,138.

Excellent keyboarding skills are among the many qualifications required for an exciting career in television news reporting.

Lesson 78

Tables Formatted Sideways

GOALS

- Type at least 43wpm/5'/5e
- Format tables in landscape orientation

A. Type 2 times.

A. WARMUP

```
     This week order a monitor with a resolution of 1280 x   11
1024 that supports an optimal refresh rate from V & Q Inc.   23
It will cost $573* (*a 9% savings) if ordered before July!   35
| 1 | 2 | 3 | 4 | 5 | 6 | 7 | 8 | 9 | 10 | 11 | 12
```

SKILLBUILDING

B. PACED PRACTICE

If you are not using the GDP software, turn to page SB-14 and follow the directions for this activity.

Keyboarding **CONNECTION**

Finding People on the Internet

Remember that long-lost friend from high school? Well, he or she may not be lost for long if you use the Internet's assistance. It is easy to search for a person on the Net by following a few simple steps.

Access a search engine. Click hyperlinks pertaining to finding people such as People Finder or People Search. Enter the information requested about the person, and press the Search button.

Conduct a search for Web sites where you can also find email addresses. Enter the information about the person you are seeking. Click the Search button. Your search should list any names and email addresses that match the name you entered.

YOUR TURN Access a search engine and try to locate the address of a high school friend.

C. Take two 5-minute timings. Review your speed and errors.

Goal: At least 43wpm/5'/5e

C. 5-MINUTE TIMING

```
     Virtual office workers conduct their work in settings      11
having different requirements from the ordinary workplace.      23
They may rely extensively on telecommuting to transmit and      35
access data to and from corporate offices. They often use       47
a company Web site, which is protected by a password, for       58
electronic communication. By connecting to the site, they       70
can use services such as office support and Web research.       82
     Access to the Internet, telephones, and fax lines          92
are among the basic tools required for the virtual office.     104
To succeed in the virtual office environment, workers must     116
be competent and very organized, work well without being       127
supervised, and be skilled in effective time management.       138
     Coping skills for virtual office workers may include      149
maintaining a good balance between work and personal life,     161
preserving contact with office coworkers and customers,        172
solving hardware and software problems, and scheduling         183
vacations. Home office workers may also have to deal with      195
feelings of being isolated and distracted. Many workers,       206
however, enjoy the nontraditional job setting.                 215
| 1 | 2 | 3 | 4 | 5 | 6 | 7 | 8 | 9 | 10 | 11 | 12
```

FORMATTING

Go To **Word Processing Manual**

D. WORD PROCESSING: PAGE ORIENTATION

Study Lesson 78 in your word processing manual. Complete all of the shaded steps while at your computer. Then format the jobs that follow.

DOCUMENT PROCESSING

Table 78-32

Seven-Column Boxed Table in Landscape

1. Format the table in landscape orientation.
2. Set 0.5-inch side margins for the page.
3. Create a boxed table with 7 columns and 11 rows.
4. Type the following column headings in bold:

   Customer | Address | City | ZIP | Telephone No. | Item | Stock No.
5. In Column A, type the customer's last name followed by a comma; then type the first name.

(Continued on next page)

CUSTOMER DATABASE INFORMATION

(Ohio District)

August 31, 20---

Maria Westphal | 3309 aaron Place Avenue | Kenton | 44426 | 419-555-2384 | Pentium computer | 4-238-cw

Dennis Roanne | 20604 Lucile Rd. South | Columbus | 43230 | 614-555-2074 | laser printer | 3-895-LP

Carl Byrnes | 322 W. Lyons Road | Mansfield | 44902 | 216-555-2002 | Color Laser Printer | 3-895-LP

Cynthia Dawson | 5914 Bay Oaks Place | Chilicothe | 45610 | 614-555-1399 | Color Ink-Jet Printer | 2-550-cij

Meg Graupmann | 10386 power Dr. | Steubenville | 43952 | 614-555-7821 | Pentium Computer | 4-238-CW

Jo Neusome | Box 365 | Youngtown | 44502 | 216-555-3885 | Pentium computer | 4-238-CW

Tony Shapiro | 6823 Creekwood Lane | Columbus | 43085 | 614-555-2934 | Pentium Computer | 5-987-PC

Lisa Garand | 26044 Manzano Court | Youngstown | 44505 | 216-555-1777 | FlatBed Color Scanner | 6-8820-CSC

Tom Parker | 936 East wind Drive | Cleveland | 44121 | 216-555-2839 | Lasser Printer | 3-895-LP

Table 78-33

Seven-Column Boxed Table in Landscape

Open the file for Table 78-32, and make the following changes:

1. Change the date to `August 19, 20--`.
2. Sort the table alphabetically by the customers' last names.
3. Change the font for the column headings to Arial Narrow, and shade the headings with a 10% fill.

Table 78-34

Seven-Column Boxed Table in Landscape

1. Create a boxed table using landscape orientation.
2. Use 1-inch margins for top, bottom, left, and right margins.
3. Center the table vertically and horizontally.
4. Center-align headings, and apply standard table format.
5. Insert a row above Row 1.
6. Type `REGIONAL SALES OFFICES` in bold and uppercase. Center the heading.
7. Type `General Information` as a subtitle for the table.

REGIONAL SALES OFFICES
General Information

Region	**Street Address**	**City**	**State**	**ZIP**	**Telephone**	**Fax**
East	8787 Orion Place	Columbus	OH	43240-4027	614-555-4951	614-555-4999
Mid-Continent	1415 Elbridge Payne Road	Chesterfield	MO	63017-8522	636-555-9940	636-555-9034
Southeast	3100 Breckinridge Boulevard	Duluth	GA	30096	770-555-7007	770-555-7422
West	21600 Oxnard Street	Woodland Hills	CA	91367	818-555-2675	818-555-2697

Multipage Tables

GOALS

- Improve speed and accuracy
- Refine language arts skills in spelling
- Format multipage tables

A. Type 2 times.

A. WARMUP

```
     Please request this key item by June: an XYZ 2000        10
motherboard with 512-MB RAM. I don't expect delivery until    22
7/5; I realize this is a "great" investment for the money!    34
| 1 | 2 | 3 | 4 | 5 | 6 | 7 | 8 | 9 | 10 | 11 | 12
```

SKILLBUILDING

PPP

PRETEST → PRACTICE → POSTTEST

B. PRETEST: Alternate- and One-Hand Words

PRETEST
Take a 1-minute timing. Review your speed and errors.

```
     They both blame the fight on the visitor. The girl       10
had no right to imply that the proxy was brave enough to      21
draw you into the unholy case. The union will reward you.     32
| 1 | 2 | 3 | 4 | 5 | 6 | 7 | 8 | 9 | 10 | 11 | 12
```

C. PRACTICE: Alternate-Hand Words

PRACTICE
Speed Emphasis:
If you made no more than 1 error on the Pretest, type each *individual* line 2 times.
Accuracy Emphasis:
If you made 2 or more errors, type each *group* of lines (as though it were a paragraph) 2 times.

```
also angle field bushel ancient emblem panel sight fish big
both blame fight formal element handle proxy signs girl and
city chair giant island visitor profit right their laid cut
```

D. PRACTICE: One-Hand Words

```
acts hilly award uphill average poplin refer jolly adds him
area jumpy based homily baggage you'll serve union beat ink
case brave extra limply greater unholy wages imply draw you
```

E. POSTTEST: Alternate- and One-Hand Words

POSTTEST
Repeat the Pretest timing and compare performance.

F. PROGRESSIVE PRACTICE: ALPHABET

If you are not using the GDP software, turn to page SB-7 and follow the directions for this activity.

LANGUAGE ARTS

G. Type this list of frequently misspelled words, paying special attention to any spelling problems in each word.

G. SPELLING

13 assistance compliance initial limited corporation technical
14 operating sufficient operation incorporated writing current
15 advice together prepared recommend appreciated cannot based
16 benefit completing analysis probably projects before annual
17 issue attention location association participation proposed

Edit the sentences to correct any misspellings.

18 The complience by the corporation was sufficient to pass.
19 I cannot reccomend the project based on the expert advise.
20 The location of the proposed annual meeting was an issue.
21 Your assistance in completeing the project is appreciated.
22 Together we prepared an analysis of their current operation.
23 The writing was incorporated in the initial asociation bid.

FORMATTING

H. MULTIPAGE TABLES

Tables should generally be formatted to fit on one page. However, if a table extends to another page, follow these formatting rules:

1. Repeat the column headings at the top of each new page.
2. Number all pages in the upper right-hand corner.

1

75 TALLEST MOUNTAINS OF NORTH AMERICA
(Ranked by Height in Feet)

Name	Place	Rank	Height
McKinley	Alaska	1	20,320
Logan	Yukon	2	19,850
Pico de Orizaba	Mexico	3	18,555
St. Elias	Alaska/Yukon	4	18,008
Popocatepetl	Mexico	5	17,930
Foraker	Alaska	6	17,400
Iztaccihuatl	Mexico	7	17,343
Lucania	Yukon	8	17,147
King	Yukon	9	16,971
Steele	Yukon	10	16,644
Bona	Alaska	11	16,550
Blackburn	Alaska	12	16,390
Kennedy	Alaska	13	16,286
Sanford	Alaska	14	16,237
Vancouver	Alaska/Yukon	15	15,979
South Buttress	Alaska	16	15,885
Wood	Yukon	16	15,885
Churchill	Alaska	18	15,638
Fairweather	Alaska/British Columbia	19	15,300
Zinantecatl (Toluca)	Mexico	20	15,016
Hubbard	Alaska/Yukon	21	15,015
Bear	Alaska	22	14,831
Walsh	Yukon	23	14,780
East Buttress	Alaska	24	14,730
Matlalcueyetl	Mexico	25	14,636
Hunter	Alaska	26	14,573
Alverstone	Alaska/Yukon	27	14,565
Browne Tower	Alaska	28	14,530
Whitney	California	29	14,494
Elbert	Colorado	30	14,433
Massive	Colorado	31	14,421
Harvard	Colorado	32	14,420
Rainier	Washington	33	14,410
University Peak	Alaska	33	14,410
Williamson	California	35	14,375
La Plata Peak	Colorado	36	14,361
Blanca Peak	Colorado	37	14,345
Uncompahgre Peak	Colorado	38	14,309
Crestone Peak	Colorado	39	14,294

2

75 TALLEST MOUNTAINS OF NORTH AMERICA
(Ranked by Height in Feet)

Name	Place	Rank	Height
Lincoln	Colorado	40	14,286
Grays Peak	Colorado	41	14,270
Antero	Colorado	42	14,269
Torreys Peak	Colorado	43	14,267
Castle Peak	Colorado	44	14,265
Quandary Peak	Colorado	44	14,265
Evans	Colorado	46	14,264
Longs Peak	Colorado	47	14,255
McArthur	Yukon	48	14,253
Wilson	Colorado	49	14,246
White Mt. Peak	California	49	14,246
North Palisade	California	51	14,242
Cameron	Colorado	52	14,238
Shavano	Colorado	53	14,229
Belford	Colorado	54	14,197
Princeton	Colorado	54	14,197
Crestone Needle	Colorado	54	14,197
Yale	Colorado	57	14,196
Bross	Colorado	58	14,172
Kit Carson	Colorado	59	14,165
Wrangell	Alaska	60	14,163
Shasta	California	61	14,162
El Diente Peak	Colorado	62	14,159
Point Success	Washington	63	14,158
Maroon Peak	Colorado	64	14,156
Tabegauche	Colorado	65	14,155
Oxford	Colorado	66	14,153
Sill	California	66	14,153
Sneffels	Colorado	68	14,150
Democrat	Colorado	69	14,148
Capitol Peak	Colorado	70	14,130
Liberty Cap	Washington	71	14,112
Pikes Peak	Colorado	72	14,110
Snowmass	Colorado	73	14,092
Russell	California	74	14,088
Eolus	Colorado	75	14,083

Go To Word Processing Manual

I. WORD PROCESSING: REPEATING TABLE HEADING ROWS

Study Lesson 79 in your word processing manual. Complete all of the shaded steps while at your computer. Then format the jobs that follow.

DOCUMENT PROCESSING

Table 79-35

Multipage Four-Column Boxed Table

Follow these steps to create a multipage table:

1. Create a boxed table with 4 columns and 77 rows.
2. Type the table as shown.
3. Include column headings on all pages.
4. Apply 10% shading to the column headings row.
5. Number the pages in upper right-hand corner.

1

75 TALLEST MOUNTAINS OF NORTH AMERICA
(Ranked by Height in Feet)

Name	Place	Rank	Height
McKinley	Alaska	1	20,320
Logan	Yukon	2	19,850
Pico de Orizaba	Mexico	3	18,555
St. Elias	Alaska/Yukon	4	18,008
Popocatepetl	Mexico	5	17,930
Foraker	Alaska	6	17,400
Iztaccihuatl	Mexico	7	17,343
Lucania	Yukon	8	17,147
King	Yukon	9	16,971
Steele	Yukon	10	16,644
Bona	Alaska	11	16,550
Blackburn	Alaska	12	16,390
Kennedy	Alaska	13	16,286
Sanford	Alaska	14	16,237
Vancouver	Alaska/Yukon	15	15,979
South Buttress	Alaska	16	15,885
Wood	Yukon	16	15,885
Churchill	Alaska	18	15,638
Fairweather	Alaska/British Columbia	19	15,300
Zinantecatl (Toluca)	Mexico	20	15,016
Hubbard	Alaska/Yukon	21	15,015
Bear	Alaska	22	14,831
Walsh	Yukon	23	14,780
East Buttress	Alaska	24	14,730
Matlalcueyetl	Mexico	25	14,636
Hunter	Alaska	26	14,573
Alverstone	Alaska/Yukon	27	14,565
Browne Tower	Alaska	28	14,530
Whitney	California	29	14,494
Elbert	Colorado	30	14,433
Massive	Colorado	31	14,421
Harvard	Colorado	32	14,420
Rainier	Washington	33	14,410
University Peak	Alaska	33	14,410
Williamson	California	35	14,375
La Plata Peak	Colorado	36	14,361
Blanca Peak	Colorado	37	14,345
Uncompahgre Peak	Colorado	38	14,309
Crestone Peak	Colorado	39	14,294

2

75 TALLEST MOUNTAINS OF NORTH AMERICA
(Ranked by Height in Feet)

Name	Place	Rank	Height
Lincoln	Colorado	40	14,286
Grays Peak	Colorado	41	14,270
Antero	Colorado	42	14,269
Torreys Peak	Colorado	43	14,267
Castle Peak	Colorado	44	14,265
Quandary Peak	Colorado	44	14,265
Evans	Colorado	46	14,264
Longs Peak	Colorado	47	14,255
McArthur	Yukon	48	14,253
Wilson	Colorado	49	14,246
White Mt. Peak	California	49	14,246
North Palisade	California	51	14,242
Cameron	Colorado	52	14,238
Shavano	Colorado	53	14,229
Belford	Colorado	54	14,197
Princeton	Colorado	54	14,197
Crestone Needle	Colorado	54	14,197
Yale	Colorado	57	14,196
Bross	Colorado	58	14,172
Kit Carson	Colorado	59	14,165
Wrangell	Alaska	60	14,163
Shasta	California	61	14,162
El Diente Peak	Colorado	62	14,159
Point Success	Washington	63	14,158
Maroon Peak	Colorado	64	14,156
Tabegauche	Colorado	65	14,155
Oxford	Colorado	66	14,153
Sill	California	66	14,153
Sneffels	Colorado	68	14,150
Democrat	Colorado	69	14,148
Capitol Peak	Colorado	70	14,130
Liberty Cap	Washington	71	14,112
Pikes Peak	Colorado	72	14,110
Snowmass	Colorado	73	14,092
Russell	California	74	14,088
Eolus	Colorado	75	14,083

Table 79-36

Multipage Four-Column Boxed Table

Open the file for Table 79-35, and make the following changes:

1. Sort the table alphabetically by state in ascending order.
2. Delete the subtitle (Ranked by Height in Feet).

Table 79-37

Five-Column Boxed Table in Landscape

Follow these steps to create a boxed table:

1. Use landscape orientation.
2. Create a boxed table with 5 columns and 7 rows.
3. Type the table as shown.
4. Apply 10% shading to the heading row.
5. Apply 100% shading (black) to the title row.

INVESTMENT SUMMARY				
Limited Partnership	**Date of Issue**	**Initial Cost**	**Annual Dividend***	**Owner**
HS Properties	January 2001	$50,000	$6,066	Alpha Association
Northern Lumber	May 2001	50,000	8,750	CXT Corporation
ST1	February 2001	50,000	7,500	Smith & Sons, Incorporated
ST2	December 2001	100,000	12,250	Q and S Company
*Annual dividends based on current market analysis.				

Lesson 80

Using Predesigned Table Formats

GOALS

- Type at least 43wpm/5′/5e
- Format tables using TableAutoFormat

A. Type 2 times.

A. WARMUP

```
     "Just when can we expect to realize a profit of 5% or   11
more?" This kind of question will be important to 2/3 of    22
the shareholders; they own over 89% of the prime holdings.   34
| 1 | 2 | 3 | 4 | 5 | 6 | 7 | 8 | 9 | 10 | 11 | 12
```

SKILLBUILDING

B. Take a 1-minute timing on the first paragraph to establish your base speed. Then take four 1-minute timings on the remaining paragraphs. As soon as you equal or exceed your base speed on one paragraph, advance to the next, more difficult paragraph.

B. SUSTAINED PRACTICE: NUMBERS AND SYMBOLS

```
     There is a need at this time to communicate our new      11
pricing guidelines to our franchise outlets. In addition,    23
they must be made aware of inventory implications. They      34
will then be in a position to have a successful operation.   46

     Franchise operators could be requested to use either     11
a 20% or a 30% markup. A $50 item would be marked to sell    23
for either $60 or $65. Depending on future prospects for     34
sales, half of the articles would be priced at each level.   46

     Ms. Aagard's suggestion is to assign items in Groups     11
#1470, #2830, and #4560 to the 20% category. The Series 77   23
items* would be in the 30% markup category except for the    35
items with a base rate under $100. What is your reaction?    46

     Mr. Chavez's recommendation is to assign a 30% markup    11
to Groups #3890, #5290, #6480, and #7180. About 1/4 of the   22
remainder (except for soft goods) would also be in the 30%   34
category. Groups #8340 and #9560 would have a 20% markup.    46
| 1 | 2 | 3 | 4 | 5 | 6 | 7 | 8 | 9 | 10 | 11 | 12
```

C. Type each sentence on a separate line by pressing ENTER after each sentence.

C. TECHNIQUE PRACTICE: ENTER KEY

```
     Start a business. See the banker. Rent a building.
Check state codes. Check city codes. Get needed licenses.
Contact suppliers. Call utility companies. Buy furniture.
Hire the employees. Open the doors. Hope for customers.
```

D. Take two 5-minute timings. Review your speed and errors.

Goal: At least 43wpm/5'/5e

D. 5-MINUTE TIMING

Finding a job may be more difficult today with the 10
rapid changes in technology. Students just entering the 21
workforce must complete specialized classes to compete for 33
the new technology jobs. However, completing a course of 44
study does not guarantee employment. 51

A candidate who is ready for employment must build 61
a resume and prepare for the interview process. A resume 72
is a written statement of you and your qualifications. When 84
you have completed your resume, you are ready to market 95
yourself to prospective employers. 102

After you have scheduled an interview appointment 112
with a potential employer, take time to become familiar 123
with the job and the company. Research the products or 134
services the company provides. Make a list of questions 145
to ask during the interview. Plan to wear clothing that is 157
appropriate for the company you are visiting. 166

During the interview, be prepared to answer questions 177
that relate to travel, relocation, your goals, strengths 188
and weaknesses, and why you should be hired. After the 199
interview, express your interest in the job and thanks for 211
the time to interview. 215

1 2 3 4 5 6 7 8 9 10 11 12

FORMATTING

Go To Word Processing Manual

E. WORD PROCESSING: TABLE—AUTOFORMAT

Study Lesson 80 in your word processing manual. Complete all the shaded steps while at your computer. Then format the jobs that follow.

DOCUMENT PROCESSING

Table 80-38

Three-Column Table

1. Change the orientation to landscape and, create a table with 3 columns and 18 rows.
2. Apply the 3D effects 3 Table AutoFormat—or one of your choice.
3. Remove bold formatting from the last line, if necessary.

CITY BANK Interest Rates Schedule Effective Date: [Current Date]		
	Interest Rate	APY
Value Checking	0.00%	0.00%
City Checking	2.00%	2.02%
Prestige Checking	2.00%	2.02%
Golden Checking	3.00%	3.05%
Regular Savings	2.50%	2.53%
Young Savers	2.50%	2.53%
Christmas Club	2.50%	2.53%
Money Market—Tier I	4.16%	4.25%
Money Market—Tier II	4.40%	4.50%
Money Market—Tier III	4.64%	4.75%
Money Market—Tier IV	4.88%	5.00%
CD—91 day	5.75%	5.75%
CD—6 month	6.35%	6.50%
CD—1 year	6.82%	7.00%
CD—2 year	7.06%	7.25%
CD—3 year	7.15%	7.50%

Table 80-39

Three-Column Table With Table Note

Open the file for Table 80-38 and make the following changes:

1. Change the orientation to portrait.
2. Add 1 blank row between Golden Checking and Regular Savings.
3. Add 1 blank row between Christmas Club and Money Market—Tier I.
4. Add 1 blank row between Money Market—Tier IV and CD—91 day.
5. Merge the cells in the inserted rows.
6. Apply a Table AutoFormat of your choice.
7. Type an * after APY.
8. Insert 1 blank row at the bottom of the table and type `*APY=Annual Percentage Yield`.

Table 80-40

Four-Column Table

Follow these steps to create a table using Table AutoFormat.

1. Create the following table in default format.
2. Apply the Contemporary Table AutoFormat option—or one of your choice.

BUILDING DIRECTORY Paulding Meeting Facility			
No.	Room Name	Seating	Square Feet
102	Alabama	35	400
104	Colorado	150	1,600
106	Delaware	25	350
108	Georgia	50	600
202	Montana	35	400
204	Nevada	50	600
206	New Jersey	300	3,200
208	Pennsylvania	350	3,600

Progress Check
Proofreading Check

Documents designated as Proofreading Checks serve as a check of your proofreading skill. Your goal is to have zero typographical errors when the GDP software first scores the document.

Architectural designers use their keyboarding skills continually.

Test 4

Skills Assessment on Part 4

5-Minute Timing

Many business firms and agencies are publishing their 11
own publications by using various software packages that 22
are available today. These packages have been created to 33
enable persons with limited knowledge to design pages very 45
easily. The big challenge, however, is for the person to 56
design the pages effectively so that the reader will read 68
the pages. After all, the main reason for investing time 79
and money in the publication is to read the articles. 90
Designing pages that are easy to read is not as easy 101
as it seems. For example, a reader may be confused if a 112
page has too many headlines and stories. However, a reader 124
may prefer to read fewer headlines with longer articles 135
that are printed in larger type. 142
Desktop publishers need a few good tools to interest 153
readers. A good plan to capture attention is to place the 165
most important articles at the top of the first page and 176
the less important stories on the inside pages. Listings 187
and subheadings are excellent tools to guide the reader 198
through the pages. Also, pictures and graphics are good 209
tools for capturing attention. 215

| 1 | 2 | 3 | 4 | 5 | 6 | 7 | 8 | 9 | 10 | 11 | 12

Correspondence Test 4-76

Memo Report With Four-Column Boxed Table

MEMO

TO: All employees

FROM: Paula Sullivan

Date: January 15, 20--

SUBJECT: Capital Communication Co.

Capital Communication Co. (CCC) operates the fourth largest network in the U.S. In addition CCC owns 8 television stations, 3 radio stations, and 4 newspapers.

HISTORY

CCC was started in 1962 by a subsidiary of Heartland Publications as a public service network. It began with three radio stations and added both radio and television stations until it went public in 1956. In 1987 it merged with Pacific

(Continued on next page)

Media Company and added 4 newspapers. CCCs largest paper, *The San Antonio Times*, won a pulitzer Prize for writing last year.

EARNINGS With sales of $4.9 billion dollars for the most recent 12-month period and income of $486 million, it continues to lead the "buy" list of most stock brokers. The table shows a break down of its earnings.

CAPITAL COMMUNICATION COMPANY			
Company	Last Year	This Year	Next Year*
Radio	#1.3	$1.4	$1.4
Television	$1.8	$2.1	$2.2
Newspapers	$1.4	$1.5	$2.0
*Projected			

Correspondence Test 4-77

Business Letter in Block Style With Blind Copy and Postscript Notations

Current Date | Mr. Owen F. Austin | 1734 Perry Street | Flint, MI 48504 | Dear Mr. Austin:

¶ I am sorry that time constraints shortened our telephone conversation yesterday. Given the circumstances as you presented them, you would be wise to consider drafting a General Durable Power of Attorney as described in Section 495 of the new act.

¶ A Power of Attorney, under the old law, is effective only up to the time that a person is disabled or incompetent. Now the General Durable Power of Attorney, under the new statute, will remain in effect until a person either revokes it or passes away.

¶ The new law will be very helpful to many elderly and infirm people. Sincerely yours, | C. F. Storden | Attorney-at-Law | urs | PS: You may want to discuss this matter with your children before calling my office for an appointment. | bc: Peggy Austin, Walter Austin

Table Test 4-41

Four-Column Boxed Table

Add 20% shading to the title row and 10% shading to column headings and total rows.

AMERICAN TRADE (As a Percentage of Total)			
Exports		**Imports**	
Canada	22	Japan	20
Japan	12	Canada	19
Mexico	7	Mexico	6
United Kingdom	6	Germany	5
Germany	5	Taiwan	5
South Korea	4	South Korea	4
Other Countries	44	Other Countries	41
TOTAL	100	TOTAL	100

PART 5

Specialized Applications

OBJECTIVES

KEYBOARDING

- Type at least 47 words per minute on a 5-minute timing with no more than 5 errors.

LANGUAGE ARTS

- Refine proofreading skills and correctly use proofreaders' marks.
- Use abbreviations, capitals, and punctuation correctly.
- Improve composing and spelling skills.
- Recognize subject/verb agreement.

WORD PROCESSING

- Use the word processing commands necessary to complete the document processing activities.

DOCUMENT PROCESSING

- Format formal report projects, international business documents, medical office documents, and legal office documents.

TECHNICAL

- Answer at least 90 percent of the questions correctly on an objective test.

KEYBOARDING IN PUBLIC ADMINISTRATION/ GOVERNMENT SERVICES

Career Opportunities

Occupations in this cluster involve supplying services to the public. Jobs center around such areas as city and town services, protective services, the armed services, postal services, public utilities, education, and social services. Schoolteachers, members of the armed services, firefighters, police officers, school counselors, and social workers are all examples of public service positions.

City and town administrators must be well-organized and work well with people. Protective service employees need to be physically fit, must have a sense of fairness and honesty, and are obligated to use good judgment. Educational professionals must be compelled to motivate people, be able to establish and maintain good relationships, and think creatively. Social workers should demonstrate a basic concern for others, employ a sense of objectivity, and work well with people. The keyboard is undoubtedly a useful tool for anyone working in public services—an arena abound with employment opportunities.

Unit 17

Formal Report Project

LESSON 81
Formal Report Project

LESSON 82
Formal Report Project

LESSON 83
Formal Report Project

LESSON 84
Formal Report Project

LESSON 85
Formal Report Project

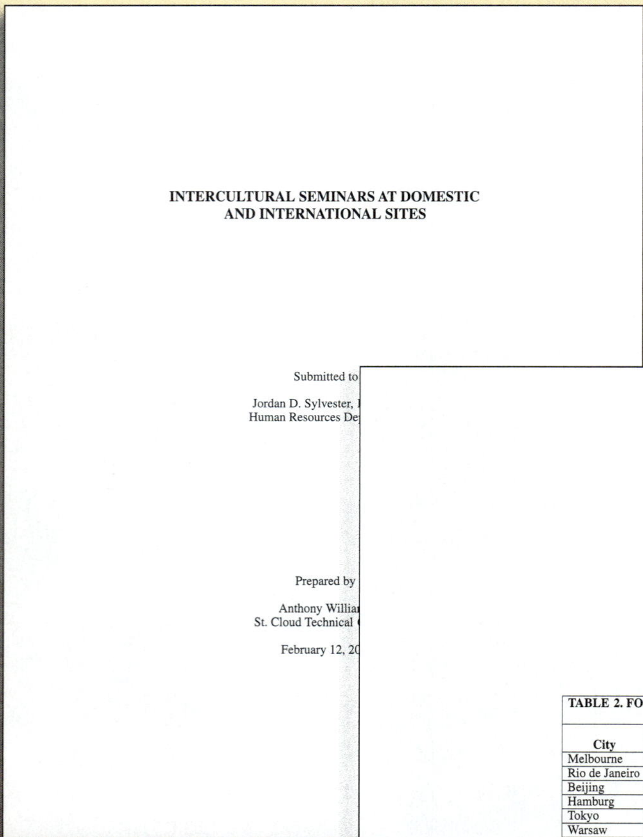

INTERCULTURAL SEMINARS AT DOMESTIC
AND INTERNATIONAL SITES

Submitted to

Jordan D. Sylvester,
Human Resources De

Prepared by

Anthony Willia
St. Cloud Technical

February 12, 2

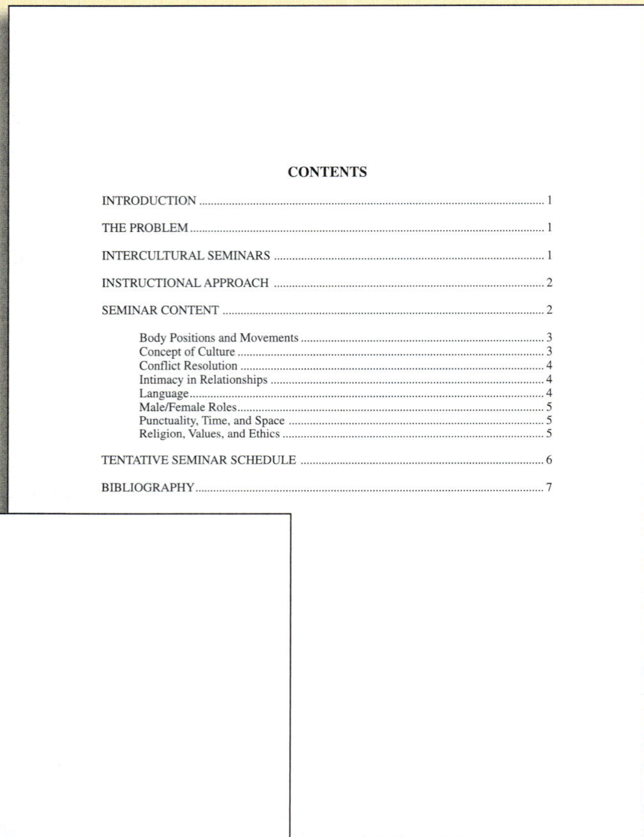

CONTENTS

INTRODUCTION 1
THE PROBLEM 1
INTERCULTURAL SEMINARS 1
INSTRUCTIONAL APPROACH 2
SEMINAR CONTENT 2
Body Positions and Movements 3
Concept of Culture 3
Conflict Resolution 4
Intimacy in Relationships 4
Language 4
Male/Female Roles 5
Punctuality, Time, and Space 5
Religion, Values, and Ethics 5
TENTATIVE SEMINAR SCHEDULE 6
BIBLIOGRAPHY 7

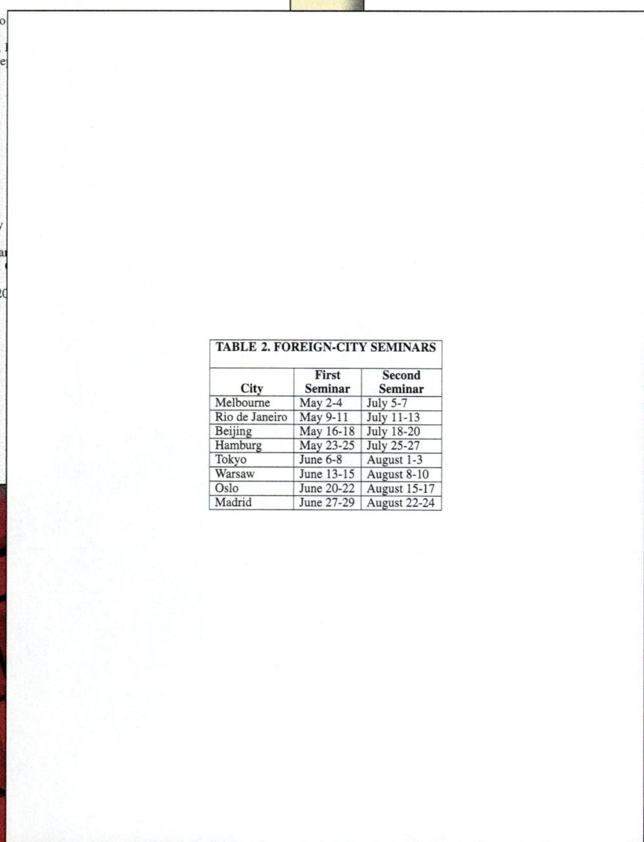

TABLE 2. FOREIGN-CITY SEMINARS

City	First Seminar	Second Seminar
Melbourne	May 2-4	July 5-7
Rio de Janeiro	May 9-11	July 11-13
Beijing	May 16-18	July 18-20
Hamburg	May 23-25	July 25-27
Tokyo	June 6-8	August 1-3
Warsaw	June 13-15	August 8-10
Oslo	June 20-22	August 15-17
Madrid	June 27-29	August 22-24

Lesson 81

Formal Report Project

GOALS

- Improve speed and accuracy
- Refine language arts skills in grammar
- Format a formal report

A. Type 2 times.

A. WARMUP

```
     The jalopy quivered as it crossed over the 1/5-mile      11
long bridge on Route 267 about 14 miles south @ Granite       22
Falls. The axle on Richard's truck broke as he whizzed by.    34
| 1 | 2 | 3 | 4 | 5 | 6 | 7 | 8 | 9 | 10 | 11 | 12
```

SKILLBUILDING

B. MAP

Follow the GDP software directions for this exercise in improving keystroking accuracy.

C. Take a 1-minute timing on the first paragraph to establish your base speed. Then take four 1-minute timings on the remaining paragraphs. As soon as you equal or exceed your base speed on one paragraph, advance to the next, more difficult paragraph.

C. SUSTAINED PRACTICE: CAPITALIZATION

```
     A visit to Europe is a vacation that many people dream     11
of doing. There are many countries to visit and hundreds of     23
sites to see if you can spend at least four weeks on the        34
continent. A trip to Europe is one you will never forget.       45

     If you decide to visit Europe, the months of June and      11
July would probably be the prettiest, but they would also       23
be the busiest. England, France, and Germany are popular        34
countries to visit; Spain is popular for Americans as well.     46

     In England you will want to visit St. Paul's Cathedral     11
and Big Ben. And, of course, when you are in England, you       23
do not want to pass up the opportunity to see Buckingham        34
Palace. Plan on staying a few days to see all the sites.        45

     France certainly is a highlight of any European visit.     11
Paris offers many sites such as the Arc de Triomphe, the        22
Louvre, the Eiffel Tower, and the Gothic Cathedral of Notre     34
Dame. Other cities to visit are Nice, Lyon, and Versailles.     46
| 1 | 2 | 3 | 4 | 5 | 6 | 7 | 8 | 9 | 10 | 11 | 12
```

LANGUAGE ARTS

D. Study the rules at the right.

D. AGREEMENT

RULE ▶ agreement pronouns

Some pronouns (*anybody, each, either, everybody, everyone, much, neither, no one, nobody,* and *one*) are always singular and take a singular verb. Other pronouns (*all, any, more, most, none,* and *some*) may be singular or plural, depending on the noun to which they refer.

Each of the employees has finished his or her task.
Much remains to be done.
Most of the pie was eaten, but most of the cookies were left.

RULE ▶ agreement intervening words

Disregard any intervening words that come between the subject and verb when establishing agreement.

The box containing the books and pencils has not been found.
Alex, accompanied by Tricia, is attending the conference and taking his computer.

Edit the sentences to correct any errors in grammar.

```
20 Everybody who signed up for the trip are to be at Building 16.
21 All the tourists are sending cards to us from their hotels.
22 Everyone on the trip, including spouses, have been having fun.
23 Some of the postcards from their vacations are not arriving.
24 Two of the sales reps from Region 4 were given cash bonuses.
25 The fastest runner from all five teams are receiving a trophy.
```

FORMATTING

Go To Word Processing Manual

E. WORD PROCESSING: STYLES

Study Lesson 81 in your word processing manual. Complete all of the shaded steps while at your computer. Then format the job that follows.

DOCUMENT PROCESSING

Report 81-59 ▶

Multipage Business Report

Reference Manual

Refer to Reference Manual pages R-8A and R-8B to review the correct format for business reports.

The business report that starts in this lesson is continued through Lesson 85. Use the following guidelines to format the report:

1. Create a style named `Report Title` for the title of the report. The title is to be formatted in all caps, bold, and 14 points.
2. Create a style named `Subtitle` for the subtitle, byline, and date at the beginning of the report. This information is to be formatted in upper- and lowercase, bold, and 12 points.
3. Create a style named `Side` for the side headings. Side headings are to be formatted in all caps, bold, and 12 points.
4. Create a style named `Paragraph` for the paragraph headings. Paragraph headings are to be formatted in upper- and lowercase, bold, and 12 points.
5. Create a header for all pages except the first page. Use 10-point Arial italic font. Type `Human Resources Department` at the left margin. At the right margin, type `Page` followed by 1 space, and insert automatic page numbering. Add a bottom border/line.

Note: The same instructions for adding a border to a table apply to adding a border to a header. Click Format, Borders and Shading, and then click Horizontal Line. Refer to Lesson 37 in the Word Manual for additional instruction.

Apply the *Title* style.

INTERCULTURAL SEMINARS AT DOMESTIC AND INTERNATIONAL SITES

Apply the *Subtitle* style.

Jordan D. Sylvester, Director

Human Resources Department

February 12, 20--

Apply the *Side* style.

INTRODUCTION

agreement intervening words

¶ The marketing department has been doing surveys of our world wide offices, foriegn customers, and prospective foriegn customers over the last several months. Information received through the use of questionnaires has made us aware of an urgent need to improve our communication skills as we conduct our operations at the international level.

Apply the *Side* style.

THE PROBLEM

agreement pronouns

¶ Some incidents have been reported to us in which we have failed to negotiate contract with foreign customers and prospective foreign customers because of serious break downs in comunication. Very few of these setbacks have been the result of conscious negative acts on the part of our employees. The main culprit seems to be lack of awareness of cultural differences and a lack of appreciation for the nuances that reflect these cultural differences. Indeed there almost are unlimited possibilities for misunderstandings, insults, miscues, and avenues for people of good intent to miscommunicate.

Apply the *Side* style.

INTERCULTURAL SEMINARS

agreement intervening words

¶ Three day seminars designed to improve intercultural communication skills will be held at regional sites in the U. S. and in foreign cities where we have offices:

- Beijing
- Hamburg
- Madrid
- Melbourne

(Continued on next page)

- Oslo
- Rio de Janeiro
- Tokyo
- Warsaw

agreement intervening words

¶ It will be our intend [t] that all employees who have direct contact with people from other countries will participate in these seminars over a four-month period.

¶ It would be unreasonable to assume that a small team of people from our company would have the breadth [of knowledge] needed to conduct these seminars in (8) foreign countries. However, Christin Zapoola, Terrence Mazlowski, and Nadene Andropolis have agreed to work together as the coordinating team for this effort. Each of these individuals has worked over the past (2) months with the managers of our international offices as well as natives in specific countries to formulate a preliminary plan for these in-service programs. ~~There~~ [Their] plan will utilize the expertise of our employees who have had negotiating experience in each country and who have knowledge of [local] customs as demonstrated by natives. We are confident that through this team approach [,] everyone will gain an understanding of problems only not from the position of our company but also from the perspective of those with whom they conduct business.

agreement pronouns

agreement pronouns

Save this unfinished report. You will resume work on it in Lesson 82.

Formal Report Project

GOALS

- Type at least 44wpm/5′/5e
- Format a formal report

A. Type 2 times.

A. WARMUP

1 The path will be covered by approximately 30 pieces 11
2 of slate from Quarry #19. Schreiner & Zimmer (the general 23
3 contractor) took the joint bid of $638, including delivery. 35

| 1 | 2 | 3 | 4 | 5 | 6 | 7 | 8 | 9 | 10 | 11 | 12

SKILLBUILDING

B. Take three 12-second timings on each line. The scale below the last line shows your wpm speed for a 12-second timing.

B. 12-SECOND SPEED SPRINTS

4 There are many things to think about if you buy a used car.
5 Two of the main things are its age and the number of miles.
6 Take the car for a test drive in town and on the open road.
7 Pay a fee to an auto expert who will check it over for you.

5 10 15 20 25 30 35 40 45 50 55 60

C. PROGRESSIVE PRACTICE: ALPHABET

If you are not using the GDP software, turn to page SB-7 and follow the directions for this activity.

STRATEGIES FOR *Career Success*

Letter of Complaint

Is poor product or bad service getting you down? By writing a concise, rational letter of complaint, you have the possibility of the reader honoring your request.

In the first paragraph, give a precise description of the product or service (e.g., model, serial #). Include a general statement of the problem (e.g., "It is not working properly."). In the middle section, provide the details of what went wrong (e.g., when it happened, what failed). Refer to copies of invoices, checks, etc. Describe how you were inconvenienced, with details about time and money lost. State what you want (e.g., refund, repair, replace). In the closing paragraph, ask for a timely response to the complaint (e.g., "Please resolve this problem within the next two weeks.").

YOUR TURN Think about the last time that you experienced poor product or service. Did you write a letter of complaint?

D. Take two 5-minute timings. Review your speed and errors.

Goal: At least 44wpm/5′/5e

D. 5-MINUTE TIMING

Critical thinking is a skill that can be learned and 11
applied to many life situations. Many definitions are used 23
to describe critical thinking skill. The common theme that 35
is expressed in these definitions is associated with using 47
cognitive skill. With this skill, the person thinks with a 59
purpose in mind and usually directs his or her thoughts 70
toward goals. The person looks at a situation and decides 82
rationally what to believe or not believe. In critical 93
thinking, the goal is to achieve understanding, evaluate 104
viewpoints, and solve problems. After evaluating all the 115
elements of the problem, a decision is made based on the 126
evidence and concrete findings. Emotions, prejudices, and 138
biases should not sway the final outcome. 146

Critical thinking is useful in reading, speaking, 156
writing, and listening. A critical thinker asks pertinent 168
questions and looks for new solutions. He or she listens 179
carefully to others and gives feedback. A critical thinker 191
zealously searches out the truth and willingly accepts 202
change when new facts are presented. Critical thinking is 213
very important for solving problems. 220

| 1 | 2 | 3 | 4 | 5 | 6 | 7 | 8 | 9 | 10 | 11 | 12

DOCUMENT PROCESSING

Report 81-59

(Continued)

Continue working on Multipage Business Report 81-59.

INSTRUCTIONAL APPROACH

¶ Connors and Saggett suggest a framework of instruction with the following: three components

1. The cognitive component includes information about communicating with people. of other cultures
2. The effective component is the area in which attention is given to attitudes, emotions, and resulting behaviors as they are effected by human interaction in a multi-cultural environment.

(Continued on next page)

3. The experiential component is the "hands-on" element which suggests different possibilities. Others have found that the use of simulations is a natural for this type of experience. The writing of letters, memos, and reports to persons in other cultures also provides beneficial learning experiences. In addition, the use of tutors can be very helpful to workers unfamiliar with a particular culture.[1]

SEMINAR CONTENT

¶ The cognitive, affective, and experiential frames would be applied as appropriate for each of the topics included. The coordinating team members have utilized the resources available to them at our 3 local universities. Most colleges and universities now provide instruction in international communication. While the content at times is integrated into several business administration courses, there has been a trend in recent years to provide a course or courses specifically designed for business interaction in an intercultural setting. The very nature of this type of study makes it very difficult to segment the broad topical areas as all elements are so closely intertwined. However, the tentative seminar plan is to cover the content as described below.

¶ The seminars must reflect the broad involvement of our international operations. There is a need for many workers in our domestic offices to develop an appreciation of the intercultural chalenge. This is true not only for those in the marketing and sales areas. Those in our Finance Department and our Legal Department are involved not only with foreign companies but also with huge multinational corporations that at times are as large as or larger than the biggest companies in the entire United States.

¶ Zapoola, Mazlowski, and Andropolis suggest the following as tentative instructional topics:[2]

[1]James C. Connors and Paul T. Saggett, "Communicating With World Cultures," *World of Business*, April 2000, pp. 25-28.

[2]Christin Zapoola, Terrence Mazlowski, and Nadene Andropolis, *Conducting Intercultural Seminars*, Northeast Publishing, Boston, Mass., 2001.

(Continued on next page)

Reference Manual

Review the format for placing a table in a report on page R-8B of the Reference Manual.

TABLE 1. SEMINAR TOPICS	
Instructional Topic	**Time**
Body Movements	2 hours
Concept of Culture	3 hours
Language	2 hours
Conflict Resolution	3 hours
Intimacy in Relationships	3 hours
Male/female Roles	3 hours
Punctuality, Time, and Space	2 hours
Religion, Values, and ethics	4 hours

¶ **Body Positions and Movements.** Body language that is, facial expressions, gestures, and body movements conveys messages about attitude and may be interpreted differently by people in cultures. For example, firm handshakes are the norm in the U.S.; loose handshakes are the custom in some other countries. The way we stand, sit, and hold our arms may convey different messages in different cultural settings.

¶ **Concept of culture.** This session will be an over view of the various cultures in which we conduct our business affairs. Perreault identifies the need for varied marketing strategies within the different economic, political, and cultural environments:

> International marketing is complicated because these environments—in particular, the cultural environment—often consist of elements familiar to american marketing executives. A further complication is the tendency for people to use their own cultural values as a frame of reference when in a foreign environment.[3]

Case studies will be reviewed that are considered classics in the field of international communication. Summaries of some of our own successes and failures will be reported.

Save this unfinished report. You will resume work on it in Lesson 83.

[3]William D. Perreault, "The World Is Our Market," *E-Market USA Home Page*, January 2001, http://www.emarket.com/newstoday.htm (March 18, 20--).

Formal Report Project

GOALS
- Improve speed and accuracy
- Refine language arts skills in composing
- Format a formal report

A. Type 2 times.

A. WARMUP

```
1      The 16 young farmers (only 50% over 30 years of age)     11
2  gathered in Room 209 to begin discussing the earthquake      22
3  threat; an extra door prize was given as a "joke present."   34
   | 1 | 2 | 3 | 4 | 5 | 6 | 7 | 8 | 9 | 10 | 11 | 12
```

SKILLBUILDING

PPP

PRETEST → PRACTICE → POSTTEST

PRETEST
Take a 1-minute timing. Review your speed and errors.

B. PRETEST: Common Letter Combinations

```
4      The insurance agent read the report before giving it     11
5  to your deputy director. This weekly action showed that      22
6  the agent really knew the actual input on a daily basis.     33
   | 1 | 2 | 3 | 4 | 5 | 6 | 7 | 8 | 9 | 10 | 11 | 12
```

PRACTICE
Speed Emphasis:
If you made no more than 1 error on the Pretest, type each *individual* line 2 times.
Accuracy Emphasis:
If you made 2 or more errors, type each *group* of lines (as though it were a paragraph) 2 times.

C. PRACTICE: Word Beginnings

```
7  re- repel renew remit relax refer ready react really reveal
8  in- inept inert inset input infer index incur inches insert
9  be- bears beams beach below being began befit beauty beside
```

D. PRACTICE: Word Endings

```
10 -ly truly madly lowly early daily apply hilly simply weekly
11 -ed sized hired dated cited based acted added opened showed
12 -nt plant meant giant front event count agent amount fluent
```

POSTTEST
Repeat the Pretest timing and compare performance.

E. POSTTEST: Common Letter Combinations

F. PROGRESSIVE PRACTICE: NUMBERS

If you are not using the GDP software, turn to page SB-11 and follow the directions for this activity.

LANGUAGE ARTS

G. COMPOSING A DOCUMENT

Compose a one-page document in which you describe how you can use the Styles command in a resume you are preparing for a job search. You might include features such as fonts, font sizes, indentations, spacing, etc., to control the appearance of your resume. Use default margins, double spacing, and two paragraphs in your document. Provide a title, and type your name at the top of the document.

In paragraph 1, you could include information on using styles for those items you want to highlight in your resume such as (1) your name and address at the top of the resume, (2) the section headings that often run down the left side of the resume, and (3) any bullets you want to include for items that contain multiple entries.

In paragraph 2, you could include a brief discussion on (1) the margins to use for your resume, (2) line spacing to use for individual entries, and (3) line spacing to use between entries.

A brief summary statement should be included to emphasize the importance of proofreading your document and the need for accuracy in a resume.

FORMATTING

Go To **Word Processing Manual**

H. WORD PROCESSING: INSERT CLIP ART AND FILES

Study Lesson 83 in your word processing manual. Complete all of the shaded steps while at your computer. Then format the job that follows.

DOCUMENT PROCESSING

Report 81-59

(Continued)

Continue working on Report 81-59.

Insert "conversation.wmf" from the People category in the Microsoft Clip Art Gallery (or insert a similar piece of clip art).

Set the clip art at a size of 1-inch square, and place it at the right margin at the beginning of the **Language** paragraph.

¶ **Conflict Resolution.** Whether in negotiating a contract, working together to remedy product quality issues, or resolving contract interpretations, the need for tact and skill is particularly important in the foreign setting. Many of the seminar topics discussed above have implications in the area of conflict resolution. While every effort should be made to prevent conflict, there is a need for guidance in resolving disagreements in foreign cultures.

¶ **Intimacy in Relationships.** The degree of physical contact that is acceptable varies considerably. Hugs and kisses are the standard, even in the business office, in some countries. By contrast, the act of touching a person is considered an extreme invasion of privacy in other places. The use of first names may or may not be acceptable. To ask a personal question is extremely offensive in some cultures. While socializing with business clients is to be expected in some countries, that would be highly inappropriate in others. These are only a few of the relationship concerns that will be explored.

¶ **Language.** It is obvious that language differences play a major part in business miscommunication. Whenever there is an interpreter or a written translation involved, the chances for error are increased. There are over 3,000 languages used on the earth. Just as with English, there are not only

(Continued on next page)

grammar rules but also varied meanings as words are both spoken and written. Even with the English language, there are differences in usage between the English used in the United States and that used in England. Although English is the language usually used in international communication, the topics identified in Table 1 above illustrate the complexity of communicating accurately; and the problem continues to grow. For example, literal translations of American advertising and labeling have sometimes resulted in negative feelings toward products. As world trade increases, so does the need for American businesses to understand the complexities of cultural differences. Ober offers this excellent example:

> Businesspeople in both Asian and Latin American countries tend to favor long negotiations and slow deliberations. They exchange pleasantries at some length before getting down to business. Likewise, many non-Western cultures use the silent intervals for contemplation, whereas businesspeople from North America tend to have little tolerance for silence in business negotiations. As a result, North Americans may rush in and offer compromises and counterproposals that would have been unnecessary if they had shown more patience.[4]

¶ A good sense of humor is an asset not only in our personal lives but also in the business environment. However, it probably should be avoided in multicultural settings because the possibilities for misinterpretation are compounded. Do not use humor that makes fun of a particular individual, group, or culture. Remember that what may appear to be humorous to you may have a negative connotation in another culture.

¶ **Male/Female Roles.** There are major contrasts in the ways male and female roles are perceived in different cultures. The right to vote is still withheld from women in countries all over the world. Opportunities for female employment in the business environment vary considerably. Pay differentials for men and women continue to exist even when they are performing the same tasks. Opportunities for advancement for men and women often are not the same.

Insert "alarmclock. gif" from the Web Bullets and Buttons category in the Microsoft Clip Art Gallery (or insert a similar piece of clip art).

Set the clip art at a size of 1-inch square, and place it at the right margin at the beginning of the **Punctuality, Time, and Space** paragraph.

¶ **Punctuality, Time, and Space.** A meeting that is scheduled for 9 a.m. likely will start on time in the United States, but in some other cultures the meeting may not start until 9:30 or even 10 o'clock. Punctuality and time concepts vary with the customs and practices of each country. Patience really can be a virtue.

¶ There is also the element of space—the distance one stands from someone when engaged in conversation. If a person stands farther away than usual, this may signal a feeling of indifference or even a negative feeling. Standing too close is a sign of inappropriate familiarity. However, it should be recognized that different cultures require a variety of space for business exchanges to take place. In the United States, that space is typically from three to five feet, but in the Middle East and in Latin American countries, this distance is considered too far.

Save this unfinished report. You will resume work on it in Lesson 84.

---

[4]Scot Ober, *Contemporary Business Communication*, 3rd ed., Houghton-Mifflin Company, Boston, 1998, p. 49.

Lesson 84

Formal Report Project

GOALS

- Type at least 44wpm/5′/5e
- Format a formal report

A. Type 2 times.

A. WARMUP

```
     The new schedule* has the Lynx at their home park on    11
July 27 with the zany Waverley Blackhawks. The Lynx scored   23
five fourth-quarter goals in their last game to win 8 to 4!  35
| 1 | 2 | 3 | 4 | 5 | 6 | 7 | 8 | 9 | 10 | 11 | 12
```

SKILLBUILDING

B. DIAGNOSTIC PRACTICE: ALPHABET

If you are not using the GDP software, turn to page SB-2 and follow the directions for this activity.

Careers in the public administration/government services career cluster offer many opportunities to use keyboarding skills, at times in unconventional locations.

C. Take two 5-minute timings. Review your speed and errors.

Goal: At least 44wpm/5′/5e

C. 5-MINUTE TIMING

Proofreading skill is developed with practice. You 10
may want to master several techniques that will help you 21
develop and improve your proofreading skills. 30
In order to be a successful proofreader, you will 40
want to schedule time to read through the completed job 51
several times. At the first reading, check your work to 62
see if the margins are correct and the page numbers are in 74
the right places. Determine if the spacing and font styles 86
are correct. With each reading, zone in on a specific type 98
of error. If possible, read your work out loud and only 109
read one word at a time. You may find that placing a ruler 121
under each line as you read it will give your eyes a more 133
manageable amount of text to read. 140
At the next reading, ascertain that the content of 150
the document follows a logical order. If cited works are 161
included, be sure the citations are in the proper format 172
with complete and accurate data. Check to be sure that all 184
the basic rules of grammar, spelling, and punctuation have 196
been followed. Proofread your document when you are fresh 208
and alert. Remember, proofreading takes time and patience. 220

| 1 | 2 | 3 | 4 | 5 | 6 | 7 | 8 | 9 | 10 | 11 | 12

Keyboarding CONNECTION

Sending Email Attachments

Your email program will tell you if an attachment has been sent, but the attachment may arrive in unusable or partially usable form. Often the sender and recipient need to use the same or compatible software to open and use each other's documents, especially if the files contain visuals, records, or spreadsheets.

Send a test email by attaching a test document and ask your receiver to send you one in return. If the test fails with a word processing document, open your word processor, and save the document again as a text file. You may lose some formatting (indents, bold, bullets), but any email program, as well as any word processor, can usually read the file.

YOUR TURN Open a word processing file. Save it as a text file. Open the text file in your word processor. What formatting has changed? Send both files to yourself as email attachments. Open them and note any changes.

Table 84-42

Three-Column Boxed Table

TABLE 2. FOREIGN-CITY SEMINARS		
City	**First Seminar**	**Second Seminar**
Melbourne	May 2-4	July 5-7
Rio de Janeiro	May 9-11	July 11-13
Beijing	May 16-18	July 18-20
Hamburg	May 23-25	July 25-27
Tokyo	June 6-8	August 1-3
Warsaw	June 13-15	August 8-10
Oslo	June 20-22	August 15-17
Madrid	June 27-29	August 22-24

Report 81-59

(Continued)

Continue working on Report 81-59.

¶ **Religion, Values, and Ethics.** While we can recognize the difficult challenge presented by language differences, this category (religion, values, and ethics) is in some ways the area that can bring about the most serious breakdowns in relations with those from other cultures.

- The very nature of religious beliefs suggests that this is a delicate area for those involved in business transactions in foreign countries. Also, religious beliefs affect the consumption of certain products throughout the world. Examples are tobacco, liquor, pork, and coffee.
- Values are a reflection of religious beliefs for most people. We often hear references to right and wrong as applied to the ideals and customs of a society. Values relate to a range of topics, and they may pertain to areas such as cleanliness, education, health care, and criminal justice.
- Ethics can be considered as standards of conduct that reflect moral beliefs as applied to both one's personal life and one's business life. Camp and Satterwhite suggest a definition for ethical behavior and the use of a code of ethics within the business environment:

> Being ethical means being honest, fair, and objective in all forms of communication. The true test of being ethical is to work toward the good of all rather than towards the good of a specialized group at the expense of some other group. Some organizations and companies develop a written code of ethics so employees and customers or clients have a written record of the philosophy of the group. A code of ethics states the goals of the group in terms of how the business operates and how it treats customers and competitors.[5]

[5]Sue C. Camp and Marilyn L. Satterwhite, *College English & Communication,* Glencoe/McGraw-Hill Book Company, New York, 1998, p. 53.

Insert "world.wmf" from the Maps category in the Microsoft Clip Art Gallery (or insert a similar piece of clip art).

Set the clip art at a size of 1-inch square, and place it at the right margin at the beginning of the first paragraph.

Save this unfinished report. You will resume work on it in Lesson 85.

TENTATIVE SEMINAR SCHEDULE

¶ As indicated earlier, it is our intent that all employees who have direct contact with people in other cultures will participate in these seminars. For that reason there will be two identical three-day seminars scheduled at each foreign site. Only selected employees in our regional sites in the United States will participate. These people have been tentatively identified on the basis of the extent of their involvement with persons from other countries.

¶ As all employees in our foreign offices will participate, a decision has been made to schedule these seminars through the summer. A tentative schedule for these seminars is shown in Table 2.

(Insert Table 84-42 here)

The Marketing Department is to be commended for calling our attention to the seriousness of our international communication problem. Christin Zapoola, Terrence Mazlowski, and Nadene Andropolis also deserve our sincere thanks for their planning efforts for our intercultural communication seminars. As can be seen, special attention is being given to the seminar topics for these in-service programs. Efforts are also being made to identify instructors and resource persons who will develop instructional strategies that will be effective, interesting, and well received by the participants. These seminars will help significantly in increasing our market share in the international market.

Lesson 85

Formal Report Project

GOALS
- Improve speed and accuracy
- Refine language arts skills in proofreading
- Format a formal report

A. Type 2 times.

A. WARMUP

Bev ordered the following: 24 #794 napkin boxes, 48 11
#265B quarts of ketchup, and 72 reams of 20-lb white print 23
paper. Did you receive the prize jalapeno peppers we sent? 35
| 1 | 2 | 3 | 4 | 5 | 6 | 7 | 8 | 9 | 10 | 11 | 12

SKILLBUILDING

B. Type the columns 2 times. Press TAB to move from column to column.

B. TECHNIQUE PRACTICE: TAB

M. A. Barnes	Julie Herden	Lynn Masica	Don Trueblood
Nathan Favor	Brett Irvin	Lisa O'Keefe	Matthew Utbert
Lee Chinn	Rick Kenwood	J. E. Perry	Jill Voss-Walin
Xavier Saxon	Lance King	Chad Quinn	Robin Yager

C. PACED PRACTICE

If you are not using the GDP software, turn to page SB-14 and follow the directions for this activity.

LANGUAGE ARTS

D. Compare this paragraph with lines 4-7 on page 305.

D. PROOFREADING

A visitt to Europe is a vacation that many people dreem
of takking. There are many countrys to visit and hundreds
of sights to see if you can spend at least for weeks on the
continnent. A trip too Europe is one you will never forget.

DOCUMENT PROCESSING

Report 85-60

Title Page

Reference Manual

Refer to page R-7B of the Reference Manual to format the title page.

Create a title page for Report 81-59 as a separate document. Use the copy in the illustration.

↓Center page

14 pt **INTERCULTURAL SEMINARS AT DOMESTIC AND INTERNATIONAL SITES** ↓12X

12 pt↓ Submitted to ↓2X

Jordan D. Sylvester, Director
Human Resources Department ↓12X

Prepared by ↓2X

Your Name ↓2X

February 12, 20--

Report 85-61

Table of Contents

Reference Manual

Refer to page R-7D of the Reference Manual to format the Table of Contents.

Create a Table of Contents page for Report 81-59. Use the following guidelines to prepare the Table of Contents page:

1. Type the entries using the side and paragraph headings from the report.
2. Type the side headings in all caps; type the paragraph headings in upper- and lowercase.
3. Paragraph headings are indented 0.5 inch from the left margin.
4. Do not include the header on the Table of Contents page.
5. Use the page numbers from your report to complete each entry in the Table of Contents page.

(Continued on next page)

Use the model for reference to format the Table of Contents. Refer to your report to prepare the Table of Contents.

↓6X

14 pt **CONTENTS** ↓2X

12 pt INTRODUCTION 1

THE PROBLEM 1

INTERCULTURAL SEMINARS 1

INSTRUCTIONAL APPROACH 2

SEMINAR CONTENT . . . . 2 ↓2X

→tab Body Positions and Movements 3
Concept of Culture 3
Conflict Resolution . . . . 4 ↓2X

TENTATIVE SEMINAR SCHEDULE 6

BIBLIOGRAPHY 7

Report 85-62

Bibliography

Reference Manual

Refer to page R-9B of the Reference Manual to format the Bibliography page.

Spell-check your report for errors. Proofread it for omitted or repeated words, errors that form a new word, and formatting errors.

Create a Bibliography for Report 81-59 as a separate document. Study the illustration below. Use the footnote references plus the following entry for the Bibliography page: Locker, Kitty O., *Business and Administrative Communication,* 4th ed., Irwin McGraw-Hill Book Company, New York, 1997. Remember that bibliographic entries are arranged alphabetically by last name of the author.

↓6X

BIBLIOGRAPHY ↓2X

hanging indent

Camp, Sue C., and Satterwhite, Marilyn L., *College English & Communication,* 0.5" Glencoe/McGraw-Hill Book Company, New York, 1998, p. 53 ↓2X

Connors, James C., and Saggett, Paul T., "Communicating With World Cultures," *World of Business,* April 2000, pp. 25-28.

Locker, Kitty O., *Business and Administrative Communication,* 4th ed., Irwin McGraw-Hill Book Company, New York, 1997.

Progress Check Proofreading Check

Documents designated as Proofreading Checks serve as a check of your proofreading skill. Your goal is to have zero typographical errors when the GDP software first scores the document.

Finalize the report project:

- Proofread all the pages for format and typing errors.
- Assemble the pages in this order: title page, table of contents, body, bibliography, and a blank page for a back cover sheet.
- Staple the report at three places along the left edge.

Unit 18

INTERNATIONAL FORMATTING

LESSON 86
International Formatting (Canada)

LESSON 87
International Formatting (Mexico)

LESSON 88
International Formatting (France)

LESSON 89
International Formatting (Germany)

LESSON 90
International Formatting (Japan)

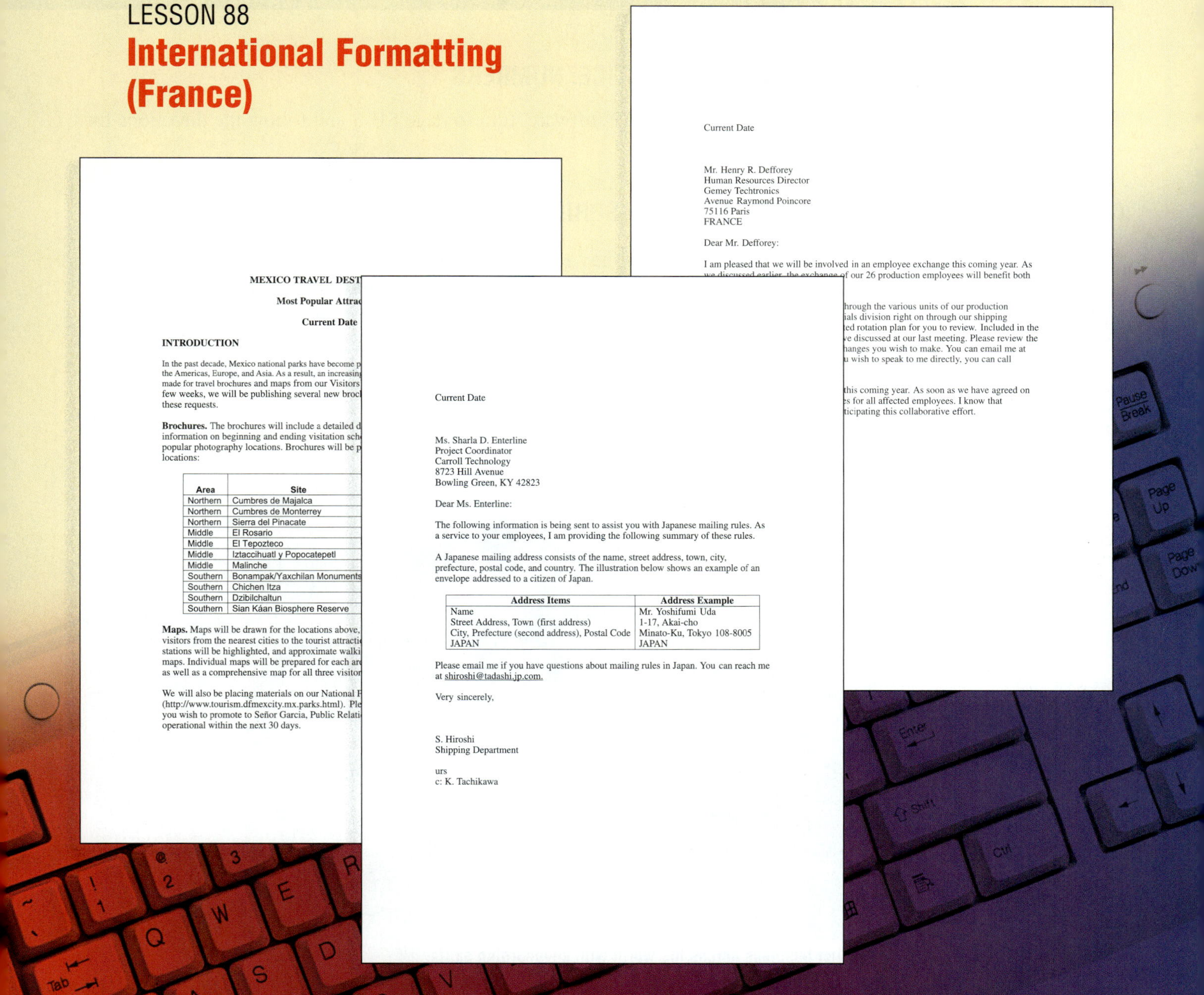

Lesson 86

International Formatting (Canada)

GOALS

- Type at least 45wpm/5′/5e
- Format international documents

A. Type 2 times.

A. WARMUP

```
     The lynx at the zoo fought wildly and had to be moved    11
quickly to a new cage (#248-I or #357-II). These adjoining    23
cages place the lynx (all of them) into individual areas.     34
| 1 | 2 | 3 | 4 | 5 | 6 | 7 | 8 | 9 | 10 | 11 | 12
```

SKILLBUILDING

B. DIAGNOSTIC PRACTICE: NUMBERS

If you are not using the GDP software, turn to page SB-5 and follow the directions for this activity.

C. Take three 12-second timings on each line. The scale below the last line shows your wpm speed for a 12-second timing.

C. 12-SECOND SPEED SPRINTS

```
The auto will now have to turn off on the lane to the lake.
Mark must type these lines fast and press for a high speed.
We had a lunch at the lake and went for a walk in the park.
Take this disk to have it fixed by the end of your workday.
 5  10  15  20  25  30  35  40  45  50  55  60
```

Conduct business across the world with keyboarding skills.

D. Take two 5-minute timings. Review your speed and errors.

Goal: At least 45wpm/5'/5e

D. 5-MINUTE TIMING

During good economic times businesses have trouble 10
finding and retaining skilled workers. As a result, some 21
companies may offer exceptional benefit packages to their 33
employees. Benefit packages can include such items as life 45
insurance, profit sharing, sick leave, paid vacation and 56
holidays, and flextime. 61

The concept of flextime was introduced to the work 71
force many years ago. Companies adopted this policy for a 83
variety of reasons. Among the reasons for flexible work 94
schedules are relieving traffic congestion, attracting 105
women back into the workforce, and helping the employees 116
meet family needs and responsibilities. 124

Organizations can manage flexible scheduling in many 135
ways. Employees may have flexible arrival and departure 146
times. This policy allows people who like to work early in 158
the day to start early and end early in the afternoon, and 170
vice versa. Other companies may allow their employees to 181
work extended hours for four days and then have three days 193
off. This type of benefit has been quite beneficial to 204
workers and companies. Companies have found that workers 215
are usually more productive and have fewer absences. 225

| 1 | 2 | 3 | 4 | 5 | 6 | 7 | 8 | 9 | 10 | 11 | 12

Keyboarding CONNECTION

Effective Teleconferencing for Meetings

Teleconferencing is a useful way to conduct meetings with businesspersons across the globe. To make the best use of teleconference meetings, follow these guidelines.

Since sound quality varies greatly, use the best equipment available. Allow individual participants enough time to use their technology. Participants should select a conference leader and alternate that leadership. Distribute agendas to everyone in advance, possibly via email.

Be sensitive to time zone differences. Since it is possible someone will experience an inconvenient time, consider rotating the times of the meetings. Assign someone to prepare and email to the participants a brief summary covering the main discussion topics and action items of the teleconference.

YOUR TURN List what you think are the advantages and disadvantages of conducting meetings via teleconference.

E. METRIC PAPER SIZE

Paper size for correspondence in the United States is typically 8.5 × 11 inches. However, correspondence in many foreign countries is often formatted on metric-sized paper. The most popular of these is called A4 paper, and it measures 210 × 297 millimeters—approximately 8.25 × 11.75 inches.

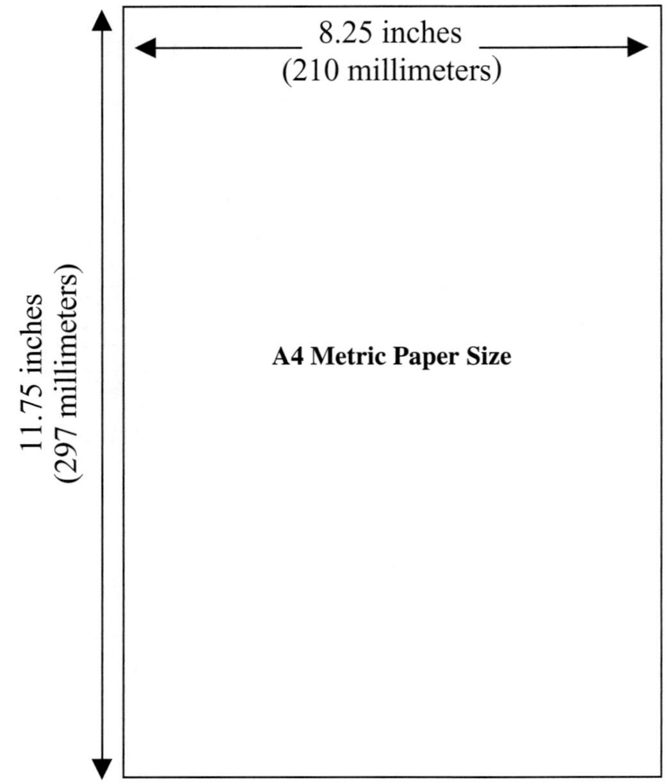

F. METRIC ENVELOPE SIZE

A standard large envelope (No. 10) measures 9.5 × 4.125 inches. A large envelope for metric size paper is called DL, and it measures 110 × 220 millimeters—approximately 4.33 inches by 8.67 inches. The metric envelope is not as deep as a No. 10 envelope, but it is slightly wider.

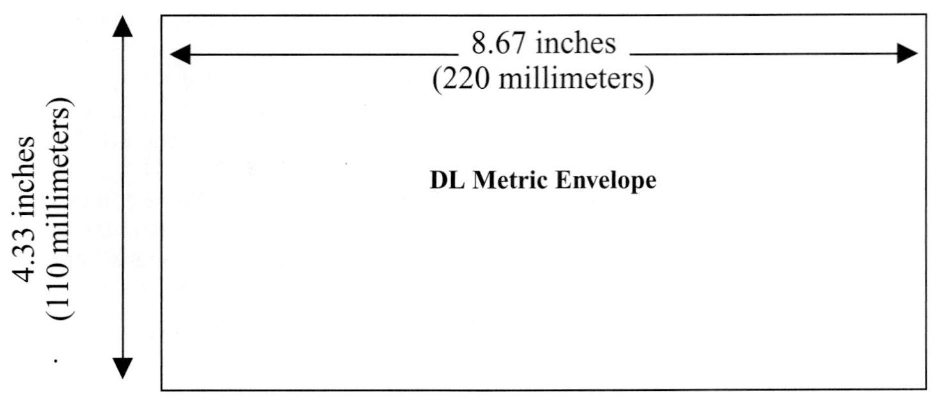

G. INTERNATIONAL ADDRESSES IN LETTERS

International addressing is becoming more common with the advent and popularity of Internet communications. International addresses frequently require slight modifications to the address lines, such as the addition of special codes, abbreviations, and capitalization. Examples of these modifications are illustrated below.

Canada Address Example:

8437 Dixie Road	Street Address [street number followed by street name]
Brampton, ON L6T 5P6	City/Province/Postal Code [1 space between first 3 and last 3 characters]
CANADA	Country Name [typed in all capitals]

Mexico Address Example:

AV. Chapultepec 28	Street Address [street name followed by street number]
06724 MEXICO D.F.	Postal Code/City [postal code and city name; "MEXICO D.F." denotes Mexico City]
MEXICO	Country Name [typed in all capitals]

France Address Example:

14, RUE ROYALE	Street Address [street number followed by a comma, then street name]
75008 PARIS	Postal Code/City [postal code and city name]
FRANCE	Country Name [typed in all capitals]

Germany Address Example:

MANNESMANNUFER 2	Street Address
D-40213 DUESSELDORF	Postal Code/City [Postal code and city name]
GERMANY	Country Name [typed in all capitals]

Japan Address Example:

10-1, TORANOMON 2-CHOME	Division of the City
MINATO-KU TOKYO 105-8436	Additional Division of the City, plus the City Name and Postal Code
JAPAN	Country Name [typed in all capitals]

Go To
Word Processing Manual

H. WORD PROCESSING: PAPER SIZE

Study Lesson 86 in your word processing manual. Complete all of the shaded steps while at your computer. Then format the jobs that follow.

DOCUMENT PROCESSING

Situation: You work for World-Tech Industries, an international computer manufacturer, and are employed in their Vancouver, Canada, office. Your customer base consists primarily of companies located in northwestern states of the United States, but you also maintain several accounts with Canadian firms in Western Canada.

With your Canadian customers, you prepare written communications on A4 metric paper because Canadian corporations use A4 letterhead and DL metric envelopes. You also adhere to Canadian mailing guidelines by using two-letter province codes and postal codes. Prepare the following correspondence, which appears in your in-basket for today.

Correspondence 86-78

Business Letter in Modified-Block With Copy and Postscript Notations

Current Date | Mr. Alec R. Cousins | Manager, Computer Services | Columbia Enterprises, Ltd. | 338 Dunsmuir Street | Vancouver, BC V4B 5R9 | CANADA | Dear Mr. Cousins:

¶ Thank you for your recent computer order. As you requested, we have added the DVD drives to the 50 computers. There will be no extra charge for exchanging the DVD drives for the ZIP drives that come standard with the C-420 model you ordered.

¶ Your order will be shipped 10 business days from the date of your order. Our order processing and shipping departments are online, and you can check the progress of your order by going to www.worldtech.com and clicking on Customer Orders.

¶ We look forward to the opportunity to serve your computer needs for many years to come.

Sincerely, | Sharon T. Yates | Sales Manager | urs | c: T. D. Mourieux, P. M. Phillips | PS: The special software you ordered with your computers will be installed at our factory, ready for your use when your computers arrive.

Table 86-43

Five-Column Boxed Table in Landscape

Prepare Table 86-42 on A4 paper, in landscape orientation. **Note:** Entries are arranged by kilometers from Vancouver, British Columbia.

CUSTOMER SHIPPING ADDRESSES AND DISTANCE
(Distance Appears in Kilometers from Vancouver—"As the Crow Flies")

Name	**Address**	**City/Province**	**Postal Code**	**Kilometers**
Francis Stevens	17820 Attwood Road	Prince George, BC	V2N 653	520
Helene Abrams	269 Acadia Drive, SE	Calgary, AB	T2J 0A6	673
Connie Visocki	39 Blackburn Drive, SW	Edmonton, AB	T6W 1C5	817
Clarence Brewer	157 Caribou Street, E.	Moose Jaw, SK	S6H 0R4	1,266
Christine Osborn	P.O. Box 613	The Pas, MB	R9A 1K7	1,597
Andrew Svenson	14 Island Drive	Flin Flon, MB	R8A 058	1,850
Gary Fitzpatrick	635 Agnes Street	Winnipeg, MB	R3E 1X8	1,869
Lazo Aida	P.O. Box 1016	Churchill, MB	R0B 0E0	2,152

Table 86-44

Five-Column Boxed Table in Landscape

Open the file for Table 86-43 and make the following changes:

1. Rearrange the entries in Column A so that they appear as follows: (last name, comma, first name)
2. Rearrange the entries in the table, placing them in alphabetical order by the last name of the customer.

Keyboarding skills can be a very important part of your job—anywhere and anytime.

Lesson 87

International Formatting (Mexico)

GOALS

- Improve speed and accuracy
- Refine language arts skills in the use of abbreviations
- Format international documents

A. Type 2 times.

A. WARMUP

On 4/25/00 Jamie exercised by "power walking" on the 11
athletic tracks. She also zipped along the city's favorite 23
route (Polk Street & Bell Avenue). It was a quick walk! 34

| 1 | 2 | 3 | 4 | 5 | 6 | 7 | 8 | 9 | 10 | 11 | 12

SKILLBUILDING

B. PROGRESSIVE PRACTICE: ALPHABET

If you are not using the GDP software, turn to page SB-7 and follow the directions for this activity.

C. Type the paragraph 2 times, concentrating on each letter typed.

C. TECHNIQUE PRACTICE: CONCENTRATION

El uso de la bicicleta es muy popular en Barranquilla. Cuando el tiempo es bueno a toda la gente joven le gusta ir a pasear en bicicletas. Me gusta ir a montar en bicicleta, especialmente cuando hace sol y el tiempo es agradable.

LANGUAGE ARTS

D. Study the rules at the right.

D. ABBREVIATIONS

RULE abbreviate measure

In technical writing, on forms, and in tables, abbreviate units of measure when they occur frequently. Do not use periods.

14 oz   5 ft 10 in   50 mph   2 yrs 10 mo

RULE abbreviate lowercase

In most lowercase abbreviations made up of single initials, use a period after each initial but no internal spaces.

a.m.	p.m.	i.e.	e.g.	e.o.m.
Exceptions:	mph	mpg	wpm	

RULE abbreviate =

In most all-capital abbreviations made up of single initials, do not use periods or internal spaces.

OSHA	PBS	NBEA	WWW	VCR	MBA
Exceptions:	U.S.A.	A.A.	B.S.	Ph.D.	P.O.
	B.C.	A.D.			

Edit the sentences to correct any errors in the use of abbreviations.

```
8  A mixture of 25 lb of cement and 100 lb of gravel was used.
9  The desk height must be reduced from 2 ft. 6 in. to 2 ft 4 in.
10 The 11 a. m. meeting was changed to 1 p. m. because of a conflict.
11 The eom statement was published over the Internet on the W.W.W.
12 She enlisted in the U.S.M.C. after she received her MBA degree.
13 His Ph. D. dissertation deals with the early history of NATO.
```

FORMATTING

E. INTERNATIONAL URLs

Uniform Resource Locators (URLs) identify a site on the World Wide Web where specific information can be found. In international URLs, an abbreviation for a country is often included in the URL, as shown below.

Country	Uniform Resource Locator (URL)
Canada	http://www.pearlson.animate.chap2.ca
France	http://www.education.grad.up.fr
Germany	http://www.mercedes.de
Japan	http://www.sushi.co.jp
Mexico	http://www.reloj.baja.mx

F. WORD PROCESSING: INSERT SYMBOL

Special symbols are used frequently in foreign languages to provide readers with a special accent that must be used to pronounce words correctly. Some examples of special accent symbols used in Mexico in the Spanish language are shown below.

Symbol	Spanish Word	English Translation
ñ	Señor, Señorita	Mr., Mrs
í	el río	river
ó	adiós	goodbye

DOCUMENT PROCESSING

Correspondence 87-79

Email Message

Send an email message to Medina Noriega (mnoriega@riobravo.net), with a subject as follows: New Manufacturing Plants. Type an appropriate greeting for Mr. Noriega and a closing and signature line for yourself. Type the body as shown below. Proofread your email message for typing, spelling, and formatting errors.

¶ As you know, sales in our international divisions have been accelerating since the advent of our new Jefe automobile. As a result, several new manufacturing plants will open in the next eight years. The first five of these plants will open in France and Germany.

¶ To market our new manufacturing plants and promote the Jefe, our Marketing Division is planning to open new Web sites on the Jefe home page. The following links will be added to advertise our plant expansion:

Bordeaux, France: http://www.bordeaux.fr.jefe.new.html
Toulouse, France: http://www.toulouse.fr.jefe.new.html
Grenoble, France: http://www.grenoble.fr.jefe.new.html
Hamburg, Germany: http://www.hamburg.de.jefe.new.html
Stuttgart, Germany: http://www.stuttgart.de.jefe.new.html

abbreviate lowercase

¶ You will be notified when the Web sites go online. Until then, plan to work with your Marketing Division personnel to implement the marketing plan we discussed at our meeting last month (i.e., the Henderson Proposal). When the sites go online, we hope to maximize our exposure on the WWW. If they are as successful as we believe they will be, our promotional campaign may also be implemented at our plants in Piedras Negras, Morelia, and Cancun.

abbreviate ≡

Report 87-63

Business Report With Four-Column Boxed Table

Type the report on A4-size paper.

MEXICO TRAVEL DESTINATIONS

Most Popular Attractions

(Current Date)

INTRODUCTION

¶ In the past decade, Mexico national parks have become popular tourist sites for visitors from the Americas, Europe, and Asia. As a result, an increasing number of requests have been made for travel brochures and maps from our Visitors' Bureau. Therefore, in the next few weeks, we will be publishing several new brochures and maps to accommodate these requests.

¶ Brochures. The brochures will include a detailed description of the site, providing information on beginning and ending visitation schedules, highlights of the site, and popular photography locations. Brochures will be prepared on the following sites and locations:

Type the copy at the right in table format, inserting the table into the report.

abbreviate measure

Accent symbol used in Sian Káan

Area	Site	Location	Top 10 Ranking
Northern	Cumbres de Majalca	Chihuahua	2 yrs
Northern	Cumbres de Monterrey	Nuevo Leon	2 yrs
Northern	Sierra del Pinacate	Mexicali	4 yrs
Middle	El Rosario	Mexico City	1 yr
Middle	El Tepozteco	Morelos	10 yrs
Middle	Iztaccihuatl y Popocatepetl	Morelos	10 yrs
Middle	Malinche	Puebla	3 yrs
Southern	Bonampak/Yaxchilan Monuments	Chiapas	7 yrs
Southern	Chichen Itza	Merida	15 yrs
Southern	Dzibilchaltun	Yucatan	5 yrs
Southern	Sian Káan Biosphere Reserve	Quintana Roo	4 yrs

(Continued on next page)

¶ Maps. Maps will be drawn for the locations above, with detailed inserts to guide visitors from the nearest cities to the tourist attractions. Walking trails and resting stations will be highlighted, and approximate walking times will be noted on the maps. Individual maps will be prepared for each area (northern, middle, and southern) as well as a comprehensive map for all three visitor areas.

¶ We will also be placing materials on our National Parks Web site (http://www.tourism.dfmexcity.mx.parks.html). Please send any advertising pieces you wish to promote to Señor Garcia, Public Relations Director. These sites will be operational within the next 30 days.

Accent symbol used in Señor

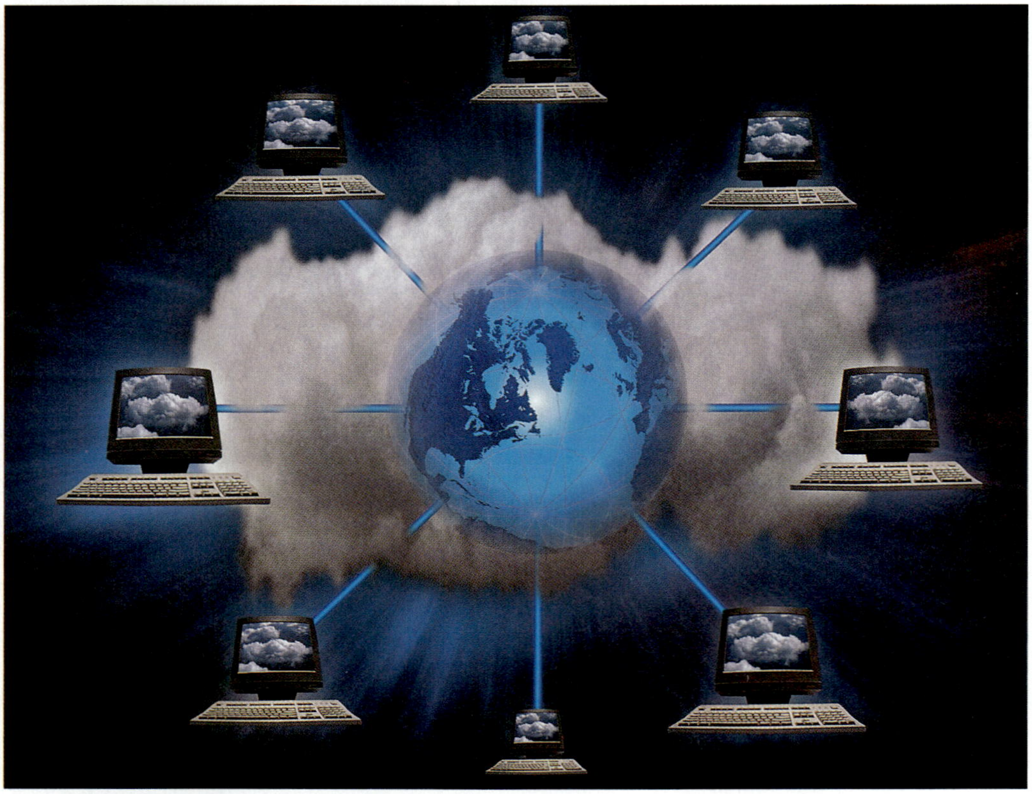

The keyboard connects us to the world.

Lesson 88

International Formatting (France)

GOALS

- Type at least 45wpm/5′/5e
- Format international documents

A. Type 2 times.

A. WARMUP

```
     On May 4, 2000, Kaye gave a dazzling talk on graphics;   11
it was quite fantastic! She is also writing an excellent      22
book about graphics with text. It might sell for $23.85.      33
| 1 | 2 | 3 | 4 | 5 | 6 | 7 | 8 | 9 | 10 | 11 | 12
```

SKILLBUILDING

B. DIAGNOSTIC PRACTICE: ALPHABET

If you are not using the GDP software, turn to page SB-2 and follow the directions for this activity.

C. PACED PRACTICE

If you are not using the GDP software, turn to page SB-14 and follow the directions for this activity.

Keyboarding CONNECTION

Protecting Your Files With Anti-Virus Programs

A virus is a computer program intentionally written to contaminate your computer system. Viruses can enter your system from files downloaded from the Internet or can be acquired from infected files sent to you via email, diskette, or other storage media.

You can protect your computer by purchasing an anti-virus program. These programs periodically scan your computer system for viruses. They also scan files that you bring into the system. Some anti-virus manufacturers allow you to download a trial copy of their software from their Web site. You can try the software for a few days before you decide if you want to buy it.

If you want to visit anti-virus sites to find out what they have to offer, search for ***anti-virus software*** on your search engine.

YOUR TURN From your browser, access *www.thefreesite.com/antivirus.htm* for a listing and overview of some free anti-virus software.

D. Take two 5-minute timings. Review your speed and errors.

Goal: At least 45wm/5′5e

D. 5-MINUTE TIMING

```
     Technology surrounds us. It is everywhere you look.      10
People use their cell phones to have conversations just       21
about anywhere. They carry their pagers so that they can      32
be reached at any time. Everyone, from busy executives to     44
the college students, has become accustomed to always being   56
available, at all hours, day or night.                        64
     In recent years, busy travelers have become used to      74
using their laptops everywhere. They use computer ports       86
in airports, hotel rooms and lobbies, and even taxis. The     98
technology allows the busy traveler to have access to the    110
Internet while on the go. Using the laptop, the user can     121
access the latest weather report, sports scores, and news,   133
almost as soon as they happen.                               139
     Using the latest technology, you can keep up with       149
your work and maintain contact with your office. You can     160
even access your bank accounts and pay bills while waiting   172
in traffic. Also, if you are in an unfamiliar area, you can  184
locate a restaurant or call for directions. The technology   196
options that have become available to almost everyone are    208
quite amazing. We are living in a small world that seems     219
to be getting smaller each day.                              225
| 1 | 2 | 3 | 4 | 5 | 6 | 7 | 8 | 9 | 10 | 11 | 12
```

FORMATTING

E. DAY/MONTH/YEAR FORMAT

Software Note: So that the software scores properly, insert a 0 before the date if it is the 1st through the 9th of the month.

In international correspondence, the date line is often formatted as follows: day, month, year. Thus, the first line of a letter to a foreign recipient may appear as shown in the illustration.

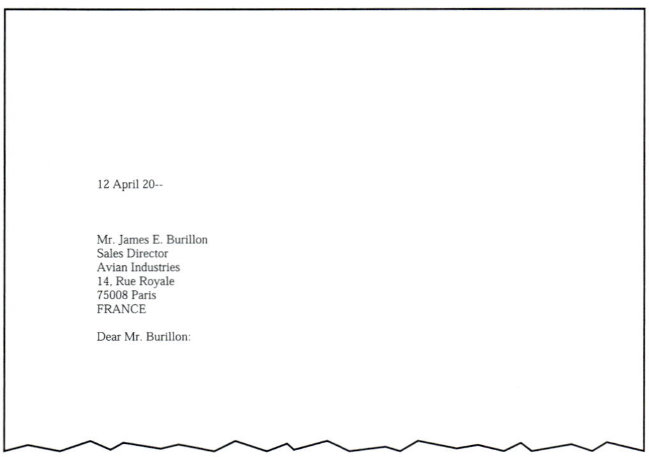
12 April 20--

Mr. James E. Burillon
Sales Director
Avian Industries
14, Rue Royale
75008 Paris
FRANCE

Dear Mr. Burillon:

F. DOT-STYLE TELEPHONE NUMBERS

Telephone numbers in the United States use a format that places hyphens after the area code and after the 3-digit prefix for a 7-digit telephone number. Another format for displaying telephone numbers used in many countries is to replace the hyphens with periods. Examples of this format are as follows: 701.555.4832 or 818.555.3424.

G. INTERNATIONAL TELEPHONE ACCESS CODES

International phone numbers require a series of special access codes. Each country is assigned a unique access code. Some of the more common access codes are displayed in the table below. Note that the United States and Canada share the same access code: 1. (**Note:** An access code of "011" is used for calls made from the United States or Canada to other countries. For calls made from other countries to the United States or Canada, the access code is "1.")

When listing a United States telephone number in a document going to an international address, precede the access code with a plus sign. For example, if a telephone number in Boston was listed in a document being sent to a foreign address, it would appear as follows: "+1.617.555.8923."

Country	Access Code	Country	Access Code
Canada	1	Taiwan	886
Japan	81	Germany	49
Denmark	45	United Kingdom	44
Mexico	52	Italy	39
France	33	United States	1

DOCUMENT PROCESSING

Correspondence 88-80

Business Letter in Block Style With Enclosure and Copy Notations

Type the letter on A4-size paper.

Current Date (use day/month/year format) | Mr. Henry R. Defforey | Human Resources Director | Gemey Techtronics | Avenue Raymond Poincore | 75116 Paris | FRANCE | Dear Mr. Defforey:

¶ I am pleased that we will be involved in an employee exchange this coming year. As we discussed earlier, the exchange of our 26 production employees will benefit both companies.

¶ We plan to rotate all 26 employees through the various units of our production process, starting from the raw materials division right on through our shipping operations. I have enclosed a projected rotation plan for you to review. Included in the plan are all the employee rotations we discussed at our last meeting. Please review the plan and email me if there are any changes you wish to make. You can email me at ssouthern@techgroup.com, or, if you wish to speak to me directly, you can call +1.214.555.9090.

(Continued on next page)

¶ I look forward to working with you this coming year. As soon as we have agreed on the rotation plan, we can make copies for all affected employees. I know that everyone from our end is eagerly anticipating this collaborative effort.

Sincerely, | Sheila T. Southern | Human Resources Manager | urs | Enclosure | c: T. Lambeer, S. Gouet

Table 88-45

Three-Column Boxed Table

Type the table on A4-size paper.

Apply 20% shading to the column headings.

ROTATION PLAN Tech-Group Inc. and Gemey Techtronics		
Department	**Rotation Start Date**	**Rotation End Date**
Raw Materials	3 July 20--	August 11 20--
Board assembly	14 August 20--	22 September 20--
Drive and Assembly	25 Sept. 20--	3 November 20--
Power Unit	6 November 20--	15 December 20--
Testing & Evaluation	18 December 20--	2 Feburary 20--
Shiping	5 Feb. 20--	16 March 20--

Correspondence 88-81

Email Message

Send an email message to Henry R. Defforey (hdefforey@techtron.com) with a subject as follows: Rotation Plan Revision. Type an appropriate greeting for Mr. Defforey and a closing and signature line for yourself. Type the body as shown below. Proofread your email message for typing, spelling, and formatting errors.

¶ I am sending you this email to alert you to a change we must make in the rotation plan I sent you last week. We will have to refit several of our board assembly production unit relay systems during the week of 14 August through 18 August. To avoid significantly altering the remaining rotation plan, I would like to suggest that we use one-half of the drive assembly rotation period to complete the board assembly rotation.

¶ Please respond to my email as soon as possible so that we can make whatever changes are necessary.

Lesson 89

International Formatting (Germany)

GOALS

- Improve speed and accuracy
- Refine language arts skills in spelling
- Format international documents

A. Type 2 times.

A. WARMUP

```
     Did Jacqueline get 62% of the vote in the election on   11
9/04/00? I think Buzz* (*Kelly) voted for her at 7:35 p.m.   23
that evening, and she was really excited when Jackie won.    34
| 1 | 2 | 3 | 4 | 5 | 6 | 7 | 8 | 9 | 10 | 11 | 12
```

SKILLBUILDING

B. MAP

Follow the GDP software directions for this exercise in improving keystroking accuracy.

C. Take a 1-minute timing on the first paragraph to establish your base speed. Then take four 1-minute timings on the remaining paragraphs. As soon as you equal or exceed your base speed on one paragraph, advance to the next, more difficult paragraph.

C. SUSTAINED PRACTICE: PUNCTUATION

```
     One of the strengths you must have if you are going to  11
be a success in business is good writing skills. You must    23
practice your writing skills every day if you want them to   35
improve. Perfection of writing skills takes much practice.   47

     You must always strive to write clearly, concisely,     11
and accurately. Remember always that your writing can be     22
examined by more people than just the one to whom you have   34
written. It's often looked at by other readers as well.      45

     You want to be sure that your letters always convey a   11
positive, helpful attitude. Don't forget, you represent      23
more than yourself when you write--you also represent your   35
company! This is an important, useful rule to remember.      46

     Try to stay away from negative words like "can't" or    11
"won't." Readers also do not like phrases such as "because   23
of company policies" or "due to unforeseen circumstances."   35
Using these words and phrases never helps resolve problems.  47
| 1 | 2 | 3 | 4 | 5 | 6 | 7 | 8 | 9 | 10 | 11 | 12
```

LANGUAGE ARTS

D. Type this list of frequently misspelled words, paying special attention to any spelling problems in each word.

D. SPELLING

means valve entry patient officer similar expenses industry
quality judgment academic provisions previously cooperation
foreign closing indicated secretary especially construction
monitoring assessment continuing registration manufacturing
products policies capacity presently accordance implemented

Edit the sentences to correct any misspellings.

Every company offiser will have simaler expenses next week.
In my judgement, we must insist on co-operation from all.
My secretery said that she traveled to a foriegn country.
We must continue monitering the progress for assesment.
The new policeis must be implimented for all products.

FORMATTING

E. METRIC UNITS OF MEASUREMENT

The metric unit of measurement was devised in 1670. It is based on units of 10 and is used by almost every nation in the world. The five common measurements in the metric system are length, area, volume, weight, and temperature. The table below shows a comparison of the basic units of measure used in the metric and U.S. systems.

Metric Unit	Metric Units of Measure	U.S. Units of Measure
Length	millimeter, centimeter, meter, kilometer	inch, foot, yard, mile
Area	square centimeter, square meter, hectare	square inch, square foot, square yard
Volume	cubic centimeter, cubic decimeter, cubic meter, liter, hectoliter	cubic inch, cubic foot, fluid ounce, pint, gallon
Weight	milligram, gram, kilogram, tonne	ounce, pound, ton
Temperature	Celsius	Fahrenheit

DOCUMENT PROCESSING

Correspondence 89-82

Email Message

Send an email message to Klaus Neubuerger (kneubuerger@deutschecomp.de.com) with a subject as follows: Metric Conversions. Type an appropriate greeting for Mr. Neubuerger and a closing and signature line for yourself. Type the body as shown below. Proofread your email message for typing, spelling, and formatting errors.

¶ The total conversion of our processing plant in Wiesbaden to a metric system is now only six months away. To prepare our employees who will be transferring to the Wiesbaden plant, I would like you to send me the brief summary report we completed for plant supervisors when we were planning for the conversion last year.
¶ The metric system will be quite foreign to many of our younger employees who were not involved in the planning stages of the conversion, and the summary report will give them a head start on metrication before their transfer.
¶ Call me on Thursday morning (+1.702.555.1839) so that we can discuss the Frankfurt plant closing. As you recall, the operations at that plant will be transferred to Wiesbaden in July; we need to monitor that operation closely until the transfer has been completed.

Correspondence 89-83

Business Letter in Block Style

Type the letter on A4-size paper.

Current Date (use day/month/year format) | Ms. Geraldine Sommer | Marketing Department | Deutsch Lebensmittel, Inc. | Mannesmannufer 2 | D-40213 Duesseldorf | GERMANY | Dear Ms. Sommer:
¶ Student's first and last name has asked that I send a copy of the summary report on metrics that we completed last year. As you recall, I sent you that report previously to share with the new employees at our Stuttgart plant.
¶ If you wish, you can email me the disk copy that accompanied the report, and my secretary will run a hard copy from my office.
Sincerely, | Klaus Neubuerger | Human Resources Manager | trl

Report 89-64

Multipage Report In Business Style

Type the report on A4 size paper.

Insert "bd05089. wmf" from the Academic category in the Microsoft Clip Art Gallery or insert a similar piece of clip art. Change the clip art height to 1.16 inches; place it at the left margin at the beginning of the first paragraph.

METRIC SUMMARY REPORT

July 30, 20--

¶ The metric system was devised by Gabriel Mouton, a French man, in 1607. It is a system based on units of 10 and is considered by some many to be more accurate and easier to use than the imperial system of measure used in the United States. When it was first defined, a meter was considered to be 1/10,000,000 of the distance from the Pole to the Equator

¶ The most common metric measurements are for length, area, volume, weight, and temperature. For our wiesbaden plant, the most crucial measurements for new employees from the U.S. will be volume and weight. Comparisons between these two measures appear in Table 1 (comparing volume measures) and Table 2 (comparing weight measures).

Table 1. METRIC/U.S. COMPARISONS FOR VOLUME

Metric Unit	Metric Measure	U.S. Measure
Cubic Centimeter	1 cubic centimeter	0.061 cubic inches
Cubic Decimeter	1,000 cubic centimeters	0.053 cubic ft
Cubic Meter	1,000 cubic decimeters	1.31 cubic yards
Liter	1 cubic decimeter	1.76 pints
Hectoliter	100 Liters	21.99 gal gallons

Table 2. METRIC/U.S. COMPARISONS FOR WEIGHT

Metric Unit	Metric Measure	U.S. Measure
Miligram	1 milligram	0.015 grain
gram	1,000 milligrams	0.035 ounces
Kilogram	1,000 grams	2.205 lbs pounds
Tonne	1,000 kilograms	0.984 tons

(Continued on next page)

¶ Employees will quickly adapt to the metric system when they use it on a daily basis. Although we encourage all employees to make calculations in the metric system, it may be helpful for the first few days if they are aware of the conversion factors involved in comparing the 2 measurement systems. The following conversions may, therefore, be helpful to them:

- Multiply inches by 2.45 to get centimeters
- Multiply feet by 0.305 to get meters
- Multiply miles by 1.6 to get kilometers
- Divide lbs. by 2.2 to get kilograms
- Multiply ounces by 28 to get grams
- Multiply fluid ounces by 30 to get milliliters
- Multiply gallons by 3.8 to get liters

¶ More detailed conversions and metric information can be obtained by visiting the web site for the U.S. metric association at http://lamar.colostate.edu/~hillger/.

The keyboard is an integral component in the growth of our global economy.

Lesson 90

International Formatting (Japan)

GOALS

- Type at least 45wpm/5′/5e
- Format international documents

A. Type 2 times.

A. WARMUP

James used a dozen of Harold's power trucks to quickly 11
move over 17 large boxes on 11/30/00. I think these trucks 23
(just the diesels) may need maintenance work on 3/24/01. 34

| 1 | 2 | 3 | 4 | 5 | 6 | 7 | 8 | 9 | 10 | 11 | 12

SKILLBUILDING

PPP

PRETEST → **PRACTICE** → **POSTTEST**

PRETEST
Take a 1-minute timing. Review your speed and errors.

B. PRETEST: Close Reaches

Uncle Bert chased a fast, weary fox into the weeds of 11
the swamp. He hoped to grab the old gray fox under the 22
bridge with a rope as he darted swiftly from his cold lair. 34

| 1 | 2 | 3 | 4 | 5 | 6 | 7 | 8 | 9 | 10 | 11 | 12

PRACTICE
Speed Emphasis:
If you made no more than 1 error on the Pretest, type each *individual* line 2 times.
Accuracy Emphasis:
If you made 2 or more errors, type each *group* of lines (as though it were a paragraph) 2 times.

C. PRACTICE: Adjacent Keys

as asked asset based basis class least visas ease fast mass
op opera roped topaz adopt scope troop shops open hope drop
we weary wedge weigh towed jewel fewer dwell wear weed week

D. PRACTICE: Consecutive Fingers

sw swamp swift swoop sweet swear swank swirl swap sway swim
un uncle under undue unfit bunch begun funny unit aunt junk
gr grade grace angry agree group gross gripe grow gram grab

POSTTEST
Repeat the Pretest timing and compare performance.

E. POSTTEST: Close Reaches

F. Take two 5-minute timings. Review your speed and errors.

Goal: At least 45wpm/5'/5e

F. 5-MINUTE TIMING

Anyone with a supervisory position will occasionally 11
have to deal with a problem employee. Learning to deal 22
positively with this type of worker can benefit everyone 33
within the organization. As a manager, you should address 45
the problem as soon as you become aware of it. However, if 57
you are extremely upset, it may be best to wait until you 69
calm down and have time to plan what you will say. Avoid 80
using an approach based on reaction, which can often be 91
ineffective and too emotional. Speaking too quickly and 102
without thinking may bring unwanted consequences. 112

When you talk to the employee, be sure you get to 122
the real issue. Present the facts and tell the employee 133
exactly what he or she is doing wrong on the job. Do not 144
express your own personal opinion. You need to present a 155
positive and mutually fair solution to the employee in 166
order to solve the problem. At the end of the meeting, ask 178
the employee to explain the problem to you and the changes 190
that are necessary. By following this procedure, you know 202
that everyone understands what is happening. Set up a time 214
to meet in a few weeks to follow up with the employee. 225

| 1 | 2 | 3 | 4 | 5 | 6 | 7 | 8 | 9 | 10 | 11 | 12

DOCUMENT PROCESSING

Correspondence 90-84

Business Letter in Block Style With Copy Notations

Type the letter on A4-size paper.

Current Date (use day/month/year format) | Mr. Kouji Tachikawa | Chief Technology Officer | Tadashi Corporation | 7-1, Shiba 5-Chome | Minato-Ku, Tokyo 108-8001 | JAPAN | Dear Mr. Tachikawa:

¶ It is a distinct pleasure to learn that we will be working together to develop the training manual to be used in our joint venture. Your company has long been known for its excellence in developing instructional materials, and Carroll Technology is pleased to play a collaborative part with you in this venture.

¶ Our development teams have been working with their counterparts in Tadashi over the past several weeks. Your suggestion that we pool our personnel resources was indeed an excellent one that will give us a head start in the development stage.

(Continued on next page)

¶ If I may make one suggestion, I believe it would be helpful for the personnel in our mailing and shipping department to have a better understanding of the labeling procedures used in Japan for distributing the training manuals. Could you please send me some information that might be helpful in this regard? I will do the same for you by sending you the labeling procedures used at Carroll Technology.
Sincerely | Sharla D. Enterline | Project Coordinator | urs | c: Mr. R. Akiyama, Mr. S. Hiroshi, Mr. C. Brandenburger

---

Correspondence 90-85

Email Message

Send an email message to Sharla Enterline (senterline@carroll.com) with a subject as follows: Labeling Procedures. Type a greeting for Ms. Enterline and a closing and signature line for yourself. Type the following copy as the body.

¶ It is my pleasure to inform you that Mr. S. Hiroshi will be forwarding to your office a summary of the package labeling procedures used at Tadashi Inc. Employees from many different foreign countries have used these procedures to help them understand mailing requirements in Japan.
¶ After receiving the procedures, feel free to email Mr. Hiroshi with any questions you may have. You can reach him at shiroshi@tadashi.jp.com. If you prefer, you can call Mr. Hiroshi at +81.3.34543113.

Correspondence 90-86

Business Letter in Block Style With Illustration and Copy Notation

Type the letter on A4-size paper.

Military dates should have a 0 inserted before the date if it is the 1st through the 9th of the month.

Current Date (use day/month/year format) | Ms. Sharla D. Enterline | Project Coordinator | Carroll Technology | 8723 Hill Avenue | Bowling Green, KY 42823 | Dear Ms. Enterline:

¶ The following information is being sent to asist you with Japanese mailing rules. As a service to your employees, I am providing the following summary of these rules.

¶ A Japanese mailing address consists ~~mainly~~ of the name, street address, town, city, pre fecture, postal, and country. The illustration below shows an example of envelope addressed to a citizen of Japan.

(Continued on next page)

Address Items	Address Example
Name	Mr. Yoshifumi Uda
~~St.~~ Street Address, Town (1st address)	1-17, Akai-cho
City, Prefecture (2d address), Postal Code	Minato-Ku, Tokyo 108-8005
JAPAN	JAPAN

¶ Please Email me if you have questions about mailing rules in japan. You can reach me at shiroshi@tadashi.jp.com.

Very sincerely, | S. Hiroshi | Shipping Dept. | urs | c: K. Tachikawa

---

Table 90-46

Two-Column Boxed Table

JAPANESE POSTAL CODE REGULATIONS
Prepared by Student Name

Postal Code Rule	Example
The first line of a Japanese address can be used for the addressee's name.	Mr. Takashi Imaizumi Mr. Kazuki Terada
The second line may include a street name or building number.	Kifune 3-402 (this represents building 402 on the 3rd street within the Kifune neighborhood)
The third line represents the city and prefecture (an area within the city).	Meito-ku, Nagoya 112-3844 Minato-Ku, Tokyo 105-8436
The fourth line can be used to identify the country to where the document or package is being mailed.	JAPAN

Correspondence 90-87

Business Letter in Block Style With Enclosure Notation

Type the letter on A4-size paper.

Progress Check
Proofreading Check

Documents designated as Proofreading Checks serve as a check of your proofreading skill. Your goal is to have zero typographical errors when the GDP software first scores the document.

Current Date | Mr. Fujio Okuda | Sales Manager | Naruto Publishing Company | 7-35, Kitashinagawa 6-Chome | Shinagawa-Ku, Tokyo 141-0001 | JAPAN | Dear Mr. Okuda:

¶ We are pleased to have this opportunity for two of our computer textbooks to be translated into Japanese and for you to do the same for two of your textbooks in the computer area. As we agreed at our meeting in Takasaki last week, sales for both of our book companies should improve substantially with these translations.

¶ I am enclosing with this letter the first three units of *Computer Essentials* so that your editors can begin the translation process. We will do the same here at Globe Publishing when your first three units from *Global Computers* arrive in Chicago.

¶ Should your editorial staff have any questions during the translation, they can email me at shaddock@globe.com or telephone me at +1.402.555.3848.

Sincerely, | Shannon Haddock | Editorial Director | urs | Enclosure

Unit 19

Medical Office Applications

LESSON 91
Medical Office Applications

LESSON 92
Medical Office Applications

LESSON 93
Medical Office Applications

LESSON 94
Medical Office Applications

LESSON 95
Medical Office Applications

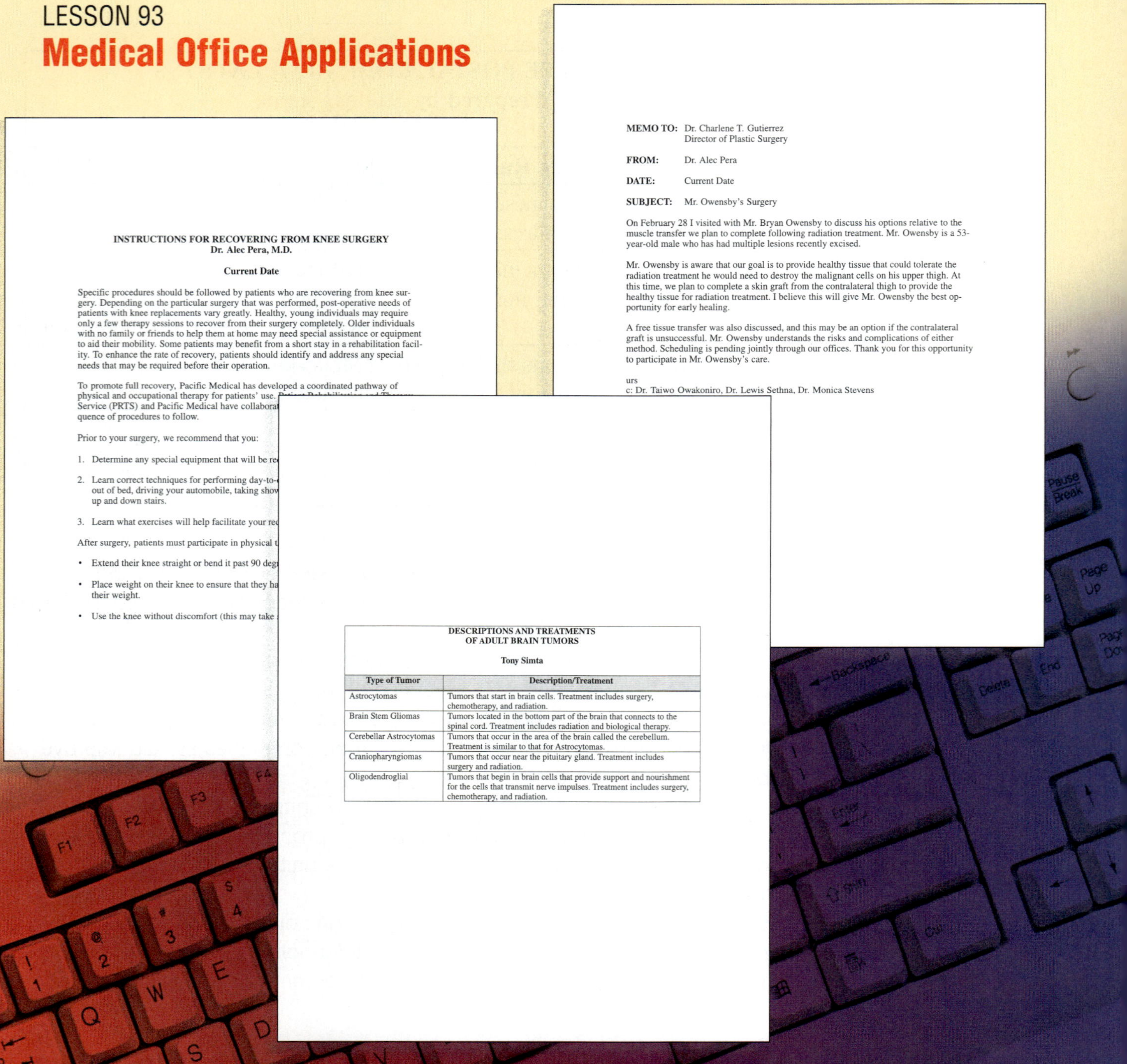

INSTRUCTIONS FOR RECOVERING FROM KNEE SURGERY
Dr. Alec Pera, M.D.

Current Date

Specific procedures should be followed by patients who are recovering from knee surgery. Depending on the particular surgery that was performed, post-operative needs of patients with knee replacements vary greatly. Healthy, young individuals may require only a few therapy sessions to recover from their surgery completely. Older individuals with no family or friends to help them at home may need special assistance or equipment to aid their mobility. Some patients may benefit from a short stay in a rehabilitation facility. To enhance the rate of recovery, patients should identify and address any special needs that may be required before their operation.

To promote full recovery, Pacific Medical has developed a coordinated pathway of physical and occupational therapy for patients' use. Patient Rehabilitation and Therapy Service (PRTS) and Pacific Medical have collaborat... quence of procedures to follow.

Prior to your surgery, we recommend that you:

1. Determine any special equipment that will be re...
2. Learn correct techniques for performing day-to-... out of bed, driving your automobile, taking show... up and down stairs.
3. Learn what exercises will help facilitate your re...

After surgery, patients must participate in physical t...

- Extend their knee straight or bend it past 90 deg...
- Place weight on their knee to ensure that they ha... their weight.
- Use the knee without discomfort (this may take ...

MEMO TO: Dr. Charlene T. Gutierrez
Director of Plastic Surgery

FROM: Dr. Alec Pera

DATE: Current Date

SUBJECT: Mr. Owensby's Surgery

On February 28 I visited with Mr. Bryan Owensby to discuss his options relative to the muscle transfer we plan to complete following radiation treatment. Mr. Owensby is a 53-year-old male who has had multiple lesions recently excised.

Mr. Owensby is aware that our goal is to provide healthy tissue that could tolerate the radiation treatment he would need to destroy the malignant cells on his upper thigh. At this time, we plan to complete a skin graft from the contralateral thigh to provide the healthy tissue for radiation treatment. I believe this will give Mr. Owensby the best opportunity for early healing.

A free tissue transfer was also discussed, and this may be an option if the contralateral graft is unsuccessful. Mr. Owensby understands the risks and complications of either method. Scheduling is pending jointly through our offices. Thank you for this opportunity to participate in Mr. Owensby's care.

urs
c: Dr. Taiwo Owakoniro, Dr. Lewis Sethna, Dr. Monica Stevens

DESCRIPTIONS AND TREATMENTS OF ADULT BRAIN TUMORS

Tony Simta

Type of Tumor	Description/Treatment
Astrocytomas	Tumors that start in brain cells. Treatment includes surgery, chemotherapy, and radiation.
Brain Stem Gliomas	Tumors located in the bottom part of the brain that connects to the spinal cord. Treatment includes radiation and biological therapy.
Cerebellar Astrocytomas	Tumors that occur in the area of the brain called the cerebellum. Treatment is similar to that for Astrocytomas.
Craniopharyngiomas	Tumors that occur near the pituitary gland. Treatment includes surgery and radiation.
Oligodendroglial	Tumors that begin in brain cells that provide support and nourishment for the cells that transmit nerve impulses. Treatment includes surgery, chemotherapy, and radiation.

Lesson 91

Medical Office Applications

GOALS

- Improve speed and accuracy
- Refine language arts skills in punctuation
- Format medical office documents

A. Type 2 times.

A. WARMUP

```
     The taxes* were quickly adjusted upward by 20 percent   11
because of the improvements to her house (built in 1901).   23
A proposed law might not penalize good homeowners like her.   35
| 1 | 2 | 3 | 4 | 5 | 6 | 7 | 8 | 9 | 10 | 11 | 12
```

SKILLBUILDING

B. MAP

Follow the GDP software directions for this exercise in improving keystroking accuracy.

C. Take a 1-minute timing on the first paragraph to establish your base speed. Then take four 1-minute timings on the remaining paragraphs. As soon as you equal or exceed your base speed on one paragraph, advance to the next, more difficult paragraph.

C. SUSTAINED PRACTICE: ALTERNATE-HAND WORDS

```
     A downturn in world fuel prices signals a lower profit   11
for giant oil firms. In fact, most downtown firms might   22
see the usual sign of tight credit and other problems. The   34
city must get down to business and make plans in the fall.   46

     The hungry turkeys ate eight bushels of corn that were   11
given to them by our next door neighbors. They also drank   22
the eight bowls of water that were left in the yard. All in   34
all, the birds caused quite a bit of chaos early that day.   46

     A debate on what to do about that extra acreage in the   11
desert dragged on for four hours. One problem is what the   23
effect may be of moving the ancient ruins to a much safer   35
place. City officials must always protect our environment.   47

     Molly was dressed in a plain pink dress at the annual   11
meeting that was taking place at the hotel in Tempe later   23
that last week in September. The agenda included four very   35
controversial topics that have often generated much debate.   47
| 1 | 2 | 3 | 4 | 5 | 6 | 7 | 8 | 9 | 10 | 11 | 12
```

LANGUAGE ARTS

D. Study the rules at the right.

D. PUNCTUATION

RULE : explanatory material

Use a colon to introduce explanatory material that follows an independent clause.

The computer satisfies three criteria: speed, cost, and power.

But: The computer satisfies the three criteria of speed, cost, and power.

Remember this: only one coupon is allowed per customer.

Note: An independent clause can stand alone as a complete sentence. Do not capitalize the word following the colon.

RULE . polite request

Use a period to end a sentence that is a polite request.

Will you please call me if I can be of further assistance.

Note: Consider a sentence a polite request if you expect the reader to respond by doing as you ask rather than by giving a yes-or-no answer.

Edit the sentences to correct any errors in punctuation.

```
20 We need the following items, pens, pencils, and paper.
21 May I suggest that you send the report by Tuesday?
22 These are some of your colleagues: Bill, Mary, and Ann.
23 Would you please pay my bills when I am on vacation?
24 Our flag is these three colors; red, white, and blue.
25 Would you please start my car to warm it up for me.
```

DOCUMENT PROCESSING

Situation: You work for a temporary agency in Eugene, Oregon. This week you are employed by McKenzie-Willamette Hospital, 1460 G Street, Springfield, OR 97477. For the next five days you will be working in various units within the hospital: Admissions Office, Billing Office, Dermatology, Oncology, and Surgery.

Your administrative assignments require you to format various documents such as letters, memos, medical reports, surgery reports, visitation reports, doctors' reports, etc.

You will spend today in the Admissions Office at McKenzie-Willamette. Complete the jobs that have been assigned to you in the order in which they appear below.

Proofread your work carefully and check for spelling, punctuation, grammar, and formatting errors so that your documents are mailable and free of errors.

Correspondence 91-88

Block Style Letter With Enclosure Notation

Current Date | Ms. Nancy J. Dodson | 3727 Harris Street | Eugene, OR 97405-4246 | Dear Ms. Dodson:

¶ Thank you for contacting us and considering us as your primary care provider. We are confident that you will be pleased with our services and our patient care, and we look forward to many years of serving your health needs.

¶ Now that you have made your final selection, we would like you to complete the enclosed Patient Information Form and send it back to us at your earliest convenience. As you can see, the form asks mostly for personal information so that we can contact you or your employer if necessary. In addition, the form requests the following information: the name, address, and telephone number of your insurance company, and your insurance policy number.

: explanatory material

(Continued on next page)

¶ Again, welcome to McKenzie-Willamette! If there is any additional information we can provide about our services, do not hesitate to call us at 555-2300 or email us at mckenzie@pacific.net.
Sincerely, | Lucille R. Medford | Office Manager | urs | Enclosure

Table 91-47

Three-Column Boxed Table With Shaded Cells

Remember to hold down the CTRL key as you press TAB to position the words (Last), (First), and (Initial) correctly in the table.

Create a patient information form, using the illustration below and these guidelines:

1. Create a table with 3 columns and 13 rows.
2. Merge cells in selected rows to provide room for each individual entry.
3. Insert 1 blank line above and below the centered section headings.
4. Merge three cells into two cells in Rows 2, 5, 8, and 13.
5. Use the ENTER key to increase the depth of each row.
6. Use default Tab settings to type the "Last/First/Initial" entries in Row 1.
7. Use Arial, 12 pt. for the entire table.
8. Use 10% shading for the centered section heading cells.

<table>
<tr><th colspan="3">Patient Information</th></tr>
<tr><td colspan="2">Name: (Last)   (First)   (Initial)</td><td>Birth Date:</td></tr>
<tr><td colspan="3">Address:</td></tr>
<tr><td>City:</td><td>State:</td><td>ZIP:</td></tr>
<tr><td>Phone:</td><td colspan="2">Social Security Number:</td></tr>
<tr><th colspan="3">Employer Information</th></tr>
<tr><td colspan="3">Employer:</td></tr>
<tr><td colspan="2">Address:</td><td>Phone:</td></tr>
<tr><td>City:</td><td>State:</td><td>ZIP:</td></tr>
<tr><th colspan="3">Insurance Information</th></tr>
<tr><td colspan="3">Name of Company:</td></tr>
<tr><td colspan="3">Address:</td></tr>
<tr><td>Phone:</td><td colspan="2">Policy Number:</td></tr>
</table>

Correspondence 91-89

Memo With Copy Notation

MEMO TO: Dr. Abraham Kramer
FROM: Paula Campbell
DATE: Current Date
SUBJECT: Radiology Lab Closing

¶ Next week the Radiology Lab in Building D will be closed for repairs. I realize that this is the week you were going to take a group of interns from McKenzie-Willamette to see our new equipment.

¶ I have arranged to have the Radiology Lab in Building C open for you to use so that you do not have to postpone the meeting with the interns. I am sending over a passkey for the lab with security. The passkey will open three doors: main entry, hall entry, lab door.

¶ Would you please give me a call on Ext. 75 if this lab substitution is not satisfactory with you.

urs

c: Dr. Arnold, Dr. Kazinofski

: explanatory material

. polite request

Laptop computers are becoming more widely used in the office setting because of the flexibility they offer to employees for working at home and traveling on business.

Lesson 92

Medical Office Applications

GOALS

- Type at least 46wpm/5′/5e
- Format medical office documents

A. Type 2 times.

A. WARMUP

```
     Missy examined these items: the #4261 oil painting, a    11
Bowes & Elkjer porcelain vase, and the 86-piece collection    23
of glazed antique pitchers. There were 337 people present.    35
| 1 | 2 | 3 | 4 | 5 | 6 | 7 | 8 | 9 | 10 | 11 | 12
```

SKILLBUILDING

B. Take three 12-second timings on each line. The scale below the last line shows your wpm speed for a 12-second timing.

B. 12-SECOND SPEED SPRINTS

```
Their home is on a lake that is right south of the prairie.
They have a boat and motor and spend a lot of time fishing.
Kay caught so many fish that she gave some to the old lady.
She was so pleased that a young girl would do this for her.
''''5''''10''''15''''20''''25''''30''''35''''40''''45''''50''''55''''60
```

C. PROGRESSIVE PRACTICE: ALPHABET

If you are not using the GDP software, turn to page SB-7 and follow the directions for this activity.

STRATEGIES FOR *Career Success*

Business Communication

There are five components to the communication process, whether written or oral.

The **sender** is the person who initiates the communication process. The **message** is the information that needs to be communicated (e.g., There will be a meeting at...). The **channel** is the method for transmitting the message (e.g., email, letter, memo, orally). The **audience** is the person(s) who receives the message. **Feedback** is the response given to the sender by the audience that enables the sender to determine if the message was received as intended.

The most effective communication within companies must flow, not only downward but also upward.

YOUR TURN Suppose you send a memo to 20 people in your department announcing a meeting to discuss your company's new policy on flex time. Who is the sender? What is the message? What is the channel you use to transmit the message? Who is the audience? What is the ultimate feedback?

D. Take two 5-minute timings. Review your speed and errors.

Goal: At least 46wpm/5'/5e

D. 5-MINUTE TIMING

```
     The first impression you make on a job interview will   11
be a lasting one, and you will want it to be favorable. A    23
safe choice is to dress conservatively. If you have time,    35
find out what people who are currently employed at this      46
company wear to work. You can acquire this information by    58
simply calling the human resources office. Or, you could     69
observe what the current employees are wearing when you      80
pick up a job application from the company.                  89
     As you plan the details of your appearance before       99
your job interview, be cognizant of all the details. You    110
will want to present a neat and clean appearance. Your      121
clothing should be clean and neatly pressed. Your hair and  133
your nails should be neatly groomed, and your shoes should  145
be clean and polished. You should use only a small amount   157
of perfume or cologne and wear only basic jewelry. Plan to  169
arrive for the appointment in time to make a final check    180
of your appearance before your interview.                   188
     Your appearance may not be the sole factor that will   199
secure the job, but it will help you make a positive first  211
impression. Remember to dress for the position you would    222
like rather than the position you have.                     230
| 1 | 2 | 3 | 4 | 5 | 6 | 7 | 8 | 9 | 10 | 11 | 12
```

DOCUMENT PROCESSING

Report 92-65

Multipage Business Report

This is now Day 2 in your temporary work assignment at McKenzie-Willamette Hospital. Today you are assigned to the Billing Office, where you will complete documents related to the activities in that office. Your first assignment is to prepare a report describing the billing process at McKenzie-Willamette.

MCKENZIE-WILLAMETTE BILLING PROCESS

Student's Name

Current Date

Determining Fees

¶ Fees that a physician charges for services should be fair both to the patients that are under his or her care as well as to the medical profesion. A doctors' fees should be based on the following critera:

(Continued on next page)

- the amount of time involved in providing the service.
- the level of skill required in providing the service.
- the degree of expertise required to interpret the results of the service provided.

¶ Fees should be identified in a fee schedule that lists procedures performed and the charges assessed for those procedures. The fee schedule should be made available to patients if it's requested. If patients inquire as to amount of the fee an estimate should be given to the patient. In all instances, this estimate should be made available to the patient before treat ment begins.

RECORDING TRANSACTIONS

¶ A record of all patient visits must be maintained. A chargeslip should be used to record procedures. The charge slip includes information such as a check list of all procedures; a checklist of all diagnosis; space for additional information; and an area for all previous charges, payments, As the doctor performs procedures, anotations and changes are made to the charge slip so that it is always kept current. The charge slip should be attached to the patients' chart. When all procedures have been completed, a copy of the charge slip is sent to the patient to indicate the charges incurred during the patient's visit.

MAKING PAYMENT ARRANGEMENTS

¶ A patient's bill can be paid by one of the following methods:

- A patient can pay the bill by cash or check at the conclusion of the visit.
- A patient can pay fixed amounts of the bill at any designated times, weekly or monthly.
- A bill can be sent to the patient at the conclusion of the visit.
- A bill can be sent to the Health Insurance Carrier.

COLLECTING OVERDUE ACCOUNTS

¶ There are a number of reasons why a patient might pay a bill. What ever the reason, however, steps must be taken to collect delinquent accounts. Depending on the number of days the acount has been over due, here are some suggestions for steps that can be taken to collect payment:

(Continued on next page)

1. Attach a reminder when the bill is sent if payment is over ~~thirty~~ 30 days overdue (this is the usual grace period given to accounts).
2. If payment is not received after the reminder is sent, it may be necessary to call the patient to request payment.
3. The next step would be to attach a personal note to a statement that is over due, possibly as long as 60 days.
4. Make one further attempt to telephone the patient for payment.
5. Send a collection letter for payment. The letter should be friendly, but firm. Remind the patient that the account is overdue. Offer to assist the patient in making payments on a fixed schedule by establishing a payment plan. Leave your telephone number so the patient can call you if there are any questions that need to be answered regarding the bill.
6. The final alternative in collecting an unpaid bill is to turn over the account to a collection agency or go to court for legal action. This is a costly step for both caregivers and patients and it should be used only as a last resort.

Table 92-48

Five-Column Boxed Table

Press the SPACE BAR 10 times between the phone number and the email address.

STATEMENT

WENDY NEWMAN, M.D.
McKenzie-Willamette Hospital
1460 G Street
Springfield, OR 97477
Phone: 541-555-2300 Email: mckenzie@pacific.net

Patient:	Marion W. Fleming			
Address:	852 East 26th Avenue			
City/State/ZIP:	Eugene, OR 97405-4104			
Date	**Description**	**Charge**	**Payment**	**Balance**
3/18/01	EKG	185.00	50.00	135.00
3/18/01	Laboratory Work	125.00	25.00	100.00
3/19/01	X-Ray	85.00	0.00	85.00
3/21/01	Cholesterol Check	75.00	25.00	50.00
3/21/01	Laboratory Work	80.00	25.00	55.00
Total Due				**425.00**

Lesson 93

Medical Office Applications

GOALS
- Improve speed and accuracy
- Refine language arts skills in composing
- Format medical office documents

A. Type 2 times.

A. WARMUP

```
1      Did you hear the excellent quartet of junior cadets?   11
2  Everybody in that crowd (estimated at over 500) applauded  23
3  "with gusto." The sizable crowd filled the 3/4-acre park.  34
   | 1 | 2 | 3 | 4 | 5 | 6 | 7 | 8 | 9 | 10 | 11 | 12
```

SKILLBUILDING

PPP

PRETEST → PRACTICE → POSTTEST

B. PRETEST: Discrimination Practice

PRETEST
Take a 1-minute timing. Review your speed and errors.

```
4      Did the new clerk join the golf team? James indicated  11
5  to me that Patricia invited her prior to last Wednesday. He 23
6  believes she must give you a verbal commitment at once.    34
   | 1 | 2 | 3 | 4 | 5 | 6 | 7 | 8 | 9 | 10 | 11 | 12
```

C. PRACTICE: Left Hand

PRACTICE
Speed Emphasis:
If you made no more than 1 error on the Pretest, type each *individual* line 2 times.
Accuracy Emphasis:
If you made 2 or more errors, type each *group* of lines (as though it were a paragraph) 2 times.

```
7  vbv bevy verb bevel vibes breve viable braves verbal beaver
8  wew went week weans weigh weave wedges thawed weaker beware
9  ded dent need deals moved ceded heeded debate edging define
```

D. PRACTICE: Right Hand

```
10 klk kale look kilts lakes knoll likely kettle kernel lacked
11 uyu buys your gummy dusty young unduly tryout uneasy jaunty
12 oio oils roil toils onion point oriole soiled ration joined
```

E. POSTTEST: Discrimination Practice

POSTTEST
Repeat the Pretest timing and compare performance.

F. PROGRESSIVE PRACTICE: NUMBERS

If you are not using the GDP software, turn to page SB-11 and follow the directions for this activity.

LANGUAGE ARTS

G. COMPOSING AN EMAIL MESSAGE

Compose an email message to your employer (Dr. Natalie Benson—nbenson@docmed.com), informing Dr. Benson of the appointments you have scheduled for Tuesday, April 17, 20--. The first appointment is with James Mitchell, who is coming for his annual physical—make this appointment at 9 a.m. The second appointment is with Karen McDaniels, who is going to have her blood pressure and cholesterol checked. She will see Dr. Benson at 10 a.m. The final appointment is with Mary Ann Bradley, who will see the doctor about flu symptoms. Be sure you use an appropriate signature line in your closing. Print but do not save or send this email message.

DOCUMENT PROCESSING

Correspondence 93-90

Business Letter in Modified-Block Style With Enclosure and Postscript Notations

This is the third day of your temporary assignment, and it is the first experience you will gain working in a specialty area—the Dermatology Unit. Dermatology is a branch of science dealing with the skin and its structure, functions, and diseases.

Current Date | Dr. Stanley G. Streisand | Professor of Medical Science | Hillside Medical College | 110 Sunset Drive | Eugene, OR 97403-2120 | Dear Dr. Streisand:

¶ Thank you for the invitation to address the students in your medical science class on the topic of dermatology. As you know, this is my specialty; I am especially interested in the topic of skin rashes and their causes and treatments.

¶ I recognize that your students are beginning medical school students, so my presentation will focus on a very general talk about dermatology. I am enclosing a copy of a paper I presented at the AMA meeting in San Francisco last week that I think would be appropriate for your students. The audience at my AMA presentation was primarily first-year nursing students who were interested in a general background of the more common types of skin rashes.

¶ Please send me a copy of your program with directions on how to reach your classroom on the day of my presentation. I look forward to meeting with your students.

Sincerely yours, | Angela Miller, M.D. | urs | Enclosure | PS: Please let me know how many students you have in your class so I can prepare an adequate number of handouts for them.

Report 93-66

Multipage Business Report With Side and Paragraph Headings

COMMON SKIN RASHES
(Their Causes and Cures)
Dr. Stanley G. Streisand

¶ Skin rashes are caused by many different things. They are often recognized by symptoms of reddening, itching, blistering, dryness, or scabbing of the skin. Some of the more common ailments that fall into the category of skin rashes are dermatitis, eczema, and psoriasis. This paper will discuss these three common types of skin rashes.

DERMATITIS

¶ Dermatitis is often referred to as contact dermatitis. Some of the more common substances that cause dermatitis are soaps, rubber, jewelry, plants, household and industrial chemicals, cosmetics, and perfumes. Contact dermatitis is further classified as either allergic contact dermatitis or irritant contact dermatitis.

Instead of underlining a word, use italic.

¶ Allergic Contact Dermatitis. This skin rash occurs after contact is made with certain substances, called allergens. The rash occurs as a reaction of the body's immune system to expel the allergen from your skin. Some common allergens are metals in jewelry, cosmetics, and rubber boots.

¶ Irritant Contact Dermatitis. This skin rash does not require exposure to an allergen but can develop when you come in contact with certain substances—skin cleansers, detergents, solvents, and oils.

(Continued on next page)

ECZEMA

¶ Eczema, also known as atopic dermatitis, causes the skin to appear red and blotchy all over. The disease occurs at any age but mainly from infancy to childhood. It affects about 3 percent of the United States population. There are two types of eczema–atopic eczema and hand eczema.

¶ Atopic Eczema. This form of eczema is caused by the house dust mite, by heat, by contact with woolen clothing, by detergents, and by stress.

¶ Hand Eczema. Hand eczema is caused by sensitive skin, too much exposure to wet work, detergents, oils, and greases.

PSORIASIS

¶ Psoriasis is a chronic skin disease characterized by inflammation and skin scaling. This disease affects about 5.5 million people in the United States. It occurs in all age groups and affects both men and women. When psoriasis develops, patches of skin redden and become covered with scales. The skin then cracks and may cause severe irritation in places like the elbows, knees, face, scalp, and lower back.

¶ It is believed that psoriasis is a disorder of the immune system in which there are not enough white blood cells to help protect the body against infection and diseases of this type.

Lesson 94

Medical Office Applications

GOALS

- Type at least 46wpm/5′/5e
- Format a formal report

A. Type 2 times.

A. WARMUP

```
     Mr. Baxter will move to 1749 Larkin Street; his old     11
home is in Gray's Woods, just east of the corner of Parson   23
and 167th Avenue. The house sizes are quite different!       34
| 1 | 2 | 3 | 4 | 5 | 6 | 7 | 8 | 9 | 10 | 11 | 12
```

SKILLBUILDING

B. DIAGNOSTIC PRACTICE: ALPHABET

If you are not using the GDP software, turn to page SB-2 and follow the directions for this activity.

A career in pharmacy requires fast and accurate keyboarding skills.

C. Take two 5-minute timings. Review your speed and errors.

Goal: At least 46wpm/5'/5e

C. 5-MINUTE TIMING

Innovative technology may bring new problems for our 10
homes and businesses. The use and overuse of cell phones 21
is causing many people to look at the etiquette of cell 32
phone usage. Are there times and places where a cell phone 44
should not be used? 48
People want to be able to stay in touch, no matter 58
where they are or what they are doing. However, in some 69
places cell phone usage is inappropriate or simply not 80
allowed. For example, you would not want a ringing cell 91
phone to disrupt the entire production if you are enjoying 103
a concert or play. As a consideration to everyone in the 114
audience, the management may make an announcement asking 125
audience members to turn off their cell phones or pagers 136
before the production begins. Making this request gives 147
everyone the opportunity to enjoy the show. 156
Often you see someone driving a car while talking on 167
a cell phone. Talking on the phone while you are driving 178
is not a good idea. When you are talking on the phone and 190
not concentrating on driving, you may cause an accident. 201
Driving a vehicle in traffic deserves your full attention. 213
Be cognizant of this fact, and do not use your cell phone 225
when driving your vehicle. 230

| 1 | 2 | 3 | 4 | 5 | 6 | 7 | 8 | 9 | 10 | 11 | 12

DOCUMENT PROCESSING

Table 94-49

Two-Column Open Table

This is the Day 4 of your temporary assignment. Today you are working in the Oncology Unit. Oncology is a branch of science dealing with the study of tumors.

DESCRIPTIONS AND TREATMENTS OF ADULT BRAIN TUMORS

Type of Tumor	**Description/Treatment**
Astrocytomas	Tumors that start in brain cells. Treatment includes surgery, chemotherapy, and radiation.

(Continued on next page)

Brain Stem Gliomas	Tumors located in the bottom part of the brain that connects to the spinal cord. Treatment includes radiation and biological therapy.
Cerebellar Astrocytomas	Tumors that occur in the area of the brain called the cerebellum. Treatment is similar to that for Astrocytomas.
Craniopharyngiomas	Tumors that occur near the pituitary gland. Treatment includes surgery and radiation.
Oligodendroglial	Tumors that begin in brain cells that provide support and nourishment for the cells that transmit nerve impulses. Treatment includes surgery, chemotherapy, and radiation.

Correspondence 94-91

Business Letter in Block Style With Subject Line

Current Date | Dr. Samuel Abbott | Sacred Heart Medical Center | 267 Ferry Street | Eugene, OR 97401-2409 | Dear Sam: | Subject: Paul R. Williams

¶ On March 3 I examined Mr. Williams and discovered a Stage 1A, Cleaved B cell follicular lymphoma in the left inguinal region. I conducted a surgical excision and recommended radiation therapy. Mr. Williams completed his radiation therapy four weeks ago and feels well at this time. He has no complaints, his appetite and energy are normal, and he looks good. His weight is down five pounds upon my recommendation four weeks ago that he lose some excess weight.

¶ There are no abdominal or inguinal lymph nodes to his scrotal sac exam. There are, however, three to four millimeter nodes in the right inguinal region that appear totally unchanged from his original exam on March 3. His lungs are clear, his heartbeat is regular, the liver and spleen are not enlarged, and there are no palpable masses.

¶ It appears to me that Mr. Williams has recovered satisfactorily from his radiation therapy. He has requested a second opinion, and I am therefore recommending that he make an appointment with you at his earliest convenience. We will prepare a referral for Mr. Williams and forward it to your office in a day or two.

Sincerely, | Donna Stensland, M.D. | urs

Table 94-50

Two-Column Boxed Table

Open the file for Table 94-49 and make the following changes:

1. Change the format to a boxed table.
2. Shade the cells in Row 2 at 10 percent.
3. Remove the extra hard return at the bottom of each cell.
4. Change the bottom border style in Row 2 to a double line.
5. After the title, press the ENTER key 2 times; then type your name.

Lesson 95

Medical Office Applications

GOALS
- Improve speed and accuracy
- Refine language arts skills in proofreading
- Format medical office documents

A. Type 2 times.

A. WARMUP

1 The extra black vacuum cleaners with the large-sized 11
2 grips were just lowered to $160 from $240 (a 33 1/3% mark- 23
3 down). Jay's #57 quilts were marked down to $98 from $108. 35

| 1 | 2 | 3 | 4 | 5 | 6 | 7 | 8 | 9 | 10 | 11 | 12

SKILLBUILDING

B. Type each word as shown until you reach the backspace sign (←). Then backspace 1 time and replace the previously typed character with the character shown. For example, if you see "hi←at," type "hi," backspace 1 time, and then type "at," resulting in the word "hat." *Technique Tip:* Press the BACKSPACE key with the sem finger, without looking at your keyboard.

B. TECHNIQUE PRACTICE: BACKSPACE KEY

4 p←cat c←tab b←peg p←but p←tie m←say t←car s←tea s←mad f←car
5 di←ye be←ag ge←um ri←ob mu←ad pa←it ca←rt fa←it fa←in pa←od
6 ham←d any←t new←t was←r sea←t mad←t gag←p tab←r tax←p ant←d
7 cheat←p scalp←e charm←t peace←h chart←m trace←k hub←t bib←t

C. PACED PRACTICE

If you are not using the GDP software, turn to page SB-14 and follow the directions for this activity.

LANGUAGE ARTS

D. Edit this paragraph to correct any keyboarding or formatting errors.

D. PROOFREADING

8 Suprising as it may seem, their has been a good deal
9 of interest in comunicating with a computer thruogh the
10 human voice for about fourty years. Researchers haev spent
11 millions ofdollars in hteir efforts to improve voice input
12 tecknology. It is likly that in the next decade we will
13 see many use ful applications in busness and in education.

DOCUMENT PROCESSING

Table 95-51

Two-Column Boxed Table

This is the final day of your five-day temporary assignment, and today you are working in the Surgery Unit. The specialty within this unit is knee surgery. Your first assignment is to create a table displaying various medical terms and their definitions.

MEDICAL TERMS AND THEIR DEFINITION s

Student's Name

Current Date

Adenopathy	Swelling or morbid enlargement of the lymph nodes
Ausultation (c)	Listening to sounds made by (the various) body structures as a diagnostic method
Cholecystectomy	Surgical removal of the gall bladder
Enterostomies	Incisions into the intestines that produce a small hole in the abdomen which through the intestines are emptied
Femur	The long bone of the thigh
Fibroperitonal (e)	Related to the tissue that lines the abdominal cavity (which) ~~and~~ covers most of the viscera
Laparoscopic	A minimally invasive surgical technique using a fiber optic instrument
Hemostasis	The arrest of bleeding
Laprаotomy	incision into the loin
Trocars	Instruments for withdrawing fluid from a cavity

Report 95-67

Business Report With Numbered and Bulleted Lists

INSTRUCTIONS FOR RECOVERING FROM KNEE SURGERY

Dr. Alec Pera, M.D.

Current Date

¶ Specific procedures should be followed by patients who are recovering from knee surgery. Depending on the particular surgery that was performed, post-operative needs of patients with knee replacements vary greatly. Healthy, young individuals may require only a few therapy sessions to recover from their surgery completely. Older individuals with no family or friends to help them at home may need special assistance or equipment to aid their mobility. Some patients may benefit from a short stay in a rehabilitation facility. To enhance the rate of recovery, patients should identify and address any special needs that may be required before their operation.

¶ To promote full recovery, Pacific Medical has developed a coordinated pathway of physical and occupational therapy for patients' use. Patient Rehabilitation and Therapy Service (PRTS) and Pacific Medical have collaborated on recommending a specific sequence of procedures to follow.

¶ Prior to your surgery, we recommend that you:

1. Determine any special equipment that will be required to promote your recovery.
2. Learn correct techniques for performing day-to-day activities such as getting in and out of bed, driving your automobile, taking showers, getting up from a seat, and going up and down stairs.
3. Learn what exercises will help facilitate your recovery.

¶ After surgery, patients must participate in physical therapy to ensure that they can:

- Extend their knee straight or bend it past 90 degrees.
- Place weight on their knee to ensure that they have the strength and stability to hold their weight.
- Use the knee without discomfort (this may take several months).

Correspondence 95-92

Email message

Send an email message to Dr. Sandra Lockhart (slockhart@sacredheart.com), with a subject as follows: Patient File for P. R. Walden. Type an appropriate greeting for Dr. Lockhart and a closing and signature line for yourself. Type the body as shown below. Proofread your email message for typing, spelling, and formatting errors.

Mr. Walden came in today with a crusted lesion in his back. Lesion was removed using 1% Xylocaine with Epinephrine loc. Wound was closed with 4.0 nylon sutures. Stitches should be removed in approximately 10 days. Sutures should be kept dry for 3 days. Mr. Walden is to call if he has questions or if problems arise.

Correspondence 95-93

Memo With Copy Notations

Progress Check
Proofreading Check

Documents designated as Proofreading Checks serve as a check of your proofreading skill. Your goal is to have zero typographical errors when the GDP software first scores the document.

Dr. Charlene T. Gutierrez, Director of Plastic Surgery, was asked to assist Dr. Alec Pera with surgery on Bryan Owensby. After an office visit with Mr. Owensby, Dr. Gutierrez dictated the following memo to Dr. Pera. Use the current date and a subject of *Mr. Owensby's Surgery*.

On Friday I visited with Mr. Bryan Owensby to discuss his options relative to the muscle transfer we plan to complete following radiation treatment. Mr. Owensby is a 53-year-old male who has had multiple lesions recently excised.

¶ Mr. Owensby is aware that our goal is to provide healthy tissue that could tolerate the radiation treatment he would need to destroy the malignant cells on his upper thigh. At this time, we plan to complete a skin graft from the contralateral thigh to provide the healthy tissue for radiation treatment. I believe this will give Mr. Owensby the best opportunity for early healing.

¶ A free tissue transfer was also discussed, and this may be an option if the contralateral graft is unsuccessful. Mr. Owensby understands the risks and complications of either method. Scheduling is pending jointly through our offices. Thank you for this opportunity to participate in Mr. Owensby's care.

urs | c: Dr. Taiwo Owakoniro, Dr. Lewis Sethna, Dr. Monica Stevens

Unit 20

Legal Office Applications

LESSON 96
Legal Office Applications

LESSON 97
Legal Office Applications

LESSON 98
Legal Office Applications

LESSON 99
Legal Office Applications

LESSON 100
Legal Office Applications

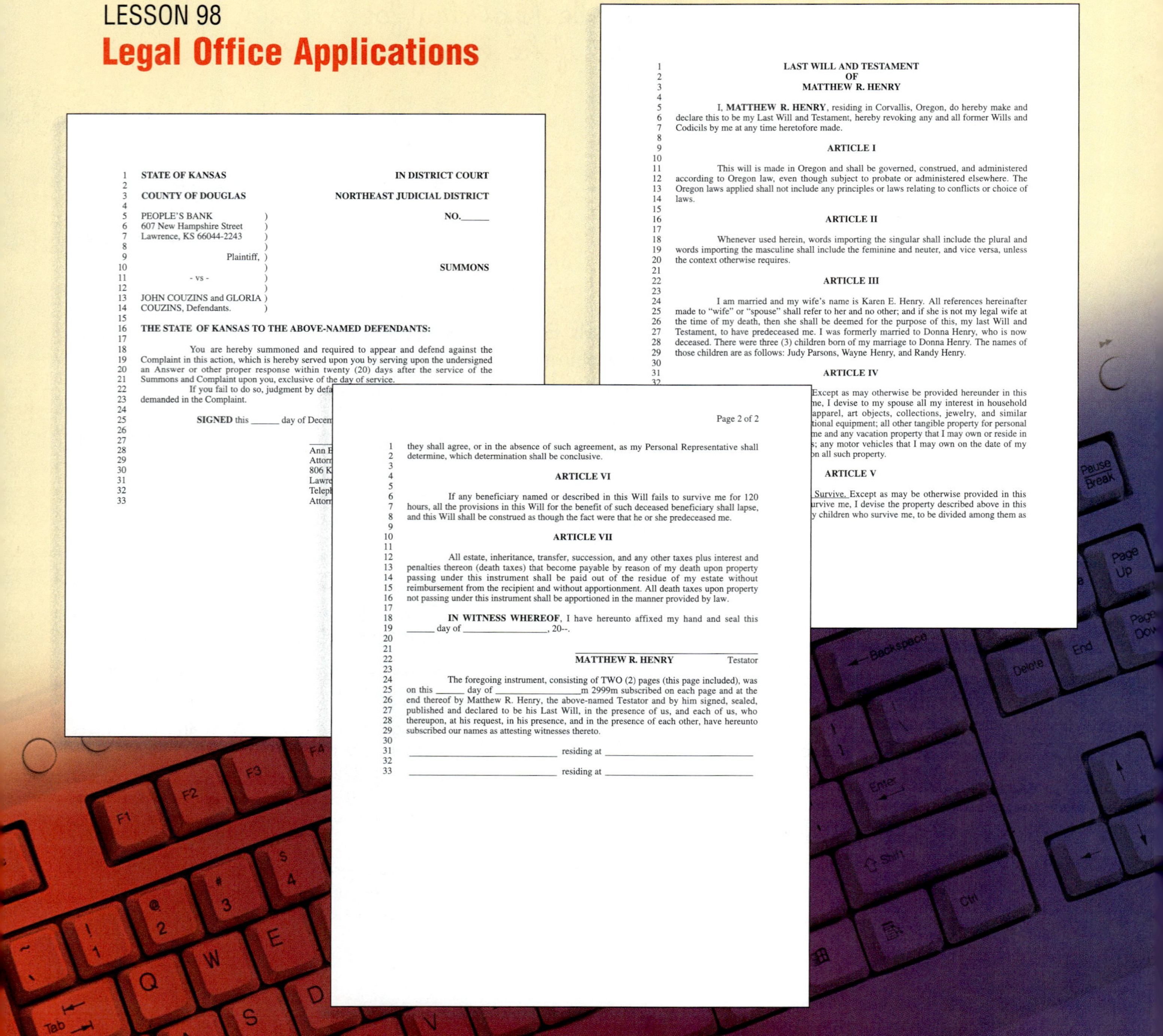

LAST WILL AND TESTAMENT
OF
MATTHEW R. HENRY

I, **MATTHEW R. HENRY**, residing in Corvallis, Oregon, do hereby make and declare this to be my Last Will and Testament, hereby revoking any and all former Wills and Codicils by me at any time heretofore made.

ARTICLE I

This will is made in Oregon and shall be governed, construed, and administered according to Oregon law, even though subject to probate or administered elsewhere. The Oregon laws applied shall not include any principles or laws relating to conflicts or choice of laws.

ARTICLE II

Whenever used herein, words importing the singular shall include the plural and words importing the masculine shall include the feminine and neuter, and vice versa, unless the context otherwise requires.

ARTICLE III

I am married and my wife's name is Karen E. Henry. All references hereinafter made to "wife" or "spouse" shall refer to her and no other; and if she is not my legal wife at the time of my death, then she shall be deemed for the purpose of this, my last Will and Testament, to have predeceased me. I was formerly married to Donna Henry, who is now deceased. There were three (3) children born of my marriage to Donna Henry. The names of those children are as follows: Judy Parsons, Wayne Henry, and Randy Henry.

ARTICLE IV

...Except as may otherwise be provided hereunder in this ...me, I devise to my spouse all my interest in household ...apparel, art objects, collections, jewelry, and similar ...tional equipment; all other tangible property for personal ...me and any vacation property that I may own or reside in ...s; any motor vehicles that I may own on the date of my ...n all such property.

ARTICLE V

...Survive. Except as may be otherwise provided in this ...rvive me, I devise the property described above in this ...y children who survive me, to be divided among them as

---

STATE OF KANSAS	**IN DISTRICT COURT**
COUNTY OF DOUGLAS	**NORTHEAST JUDICIAL DISTRICT**

PEOPLE'S BANK)
607 New Hampshire Street)
Lawrence, KS 66044-2243)
Plaintiff,) **NO.______**
\- vs -) **SUMMONS**
JOHN COUZINS and GLORIA)
COUZINS, Defendants.)

THE STATE OF KANSAS TO THE ABOVE-NAMED DEFENDANTS:

You are hereby summoned and required to appear and defend against the Complaint in this action, which is hereby served upon you by serving upon the undersigned an Answer or other proper response within twenty (20) days after the service of the Summons and Complaint upon you, exclusive of the day of service.

If you fail to do so, judgment by defa... demanded in the Complaint.

SIGNED this ______ day of Decem...

Ann ...
Attorn...
806 K...
Lawre...
Teleph...
Attorn...

Page 2 of 2

they shall agree, or in the absence of such agreement, as my Personal Representative shall determine, which determination shall be conclusive.

ARTICLE VI

If any beneficiary named or described in this Will fails to survive me for 120 hours, all the provisions in this Will for the benefit of such deceased beneficiary shall lapse, and this Will shall be construed as though the fact were that he or she predeceased me.

ARTICLE VII

All estate, inheritance, transfer, succession, and any other taxes plus interest and penalties thereon (death taxes) that become payable by reason of my death upon property passing under this instrument shall be paid out of the residue of my estate without reimbursement from the recipient and without apportionment. All death taxes upon property not passing under this instrument shall be apportioned in the manner provided by law.

IN WITNESS WHEREOF, I have hereunto affixed my hand and seal this ______ day of _________________, 20--.

____
MATTHEW R. HENRY Testator

The foregoing instrument, consisting of TWO (2) pages (this page included), was on this ______ day of _________________m 2999m subscribed on each page and at the end thereof by Matthew R. Henry, the above-named Testator and by him signed, sealed, published and declared to be his Last Will, in the presence of us, and each of us, who thereupon, at his request, in his presence, and in the presence of each other, have hereunto subscribed our names as attesting witnesses thereto.

__________________________ residing at __________________________

__________________________ residing at __________________________

Lesson 96

Legal Office Applications

GOALS

- Type at least 47wpm/5′/5e
- Format legal office applications

A. Type 2 times.

A. WARMUP

1 Marshal bought five chances for the contest. He won 11
2 six prizes and was given a check for $2,350--these prizes 23
3 are equal to 1/4th of Jill's winnings for all of last year. 35
| 1 | 2 | 3 | 4 | 5 | 6 | 7 | 8 | 9 | 10 | 11 | 12

SKILLBUILDING

B. DIAGNOSTIC PRACTICE: NUMBERS

If you are not using the GDP software, turn to page SB-5 and follow the directions for this activity.

C. Take three 12-second timings on each line. The scale below the last line shows your wpm speed for a 12-second timing.

C. 12-SECOND SPEED SPRINTS

4 They saw the sun shine through after days and days of rain.
5 She hopes to get a much higher math score on the next test.
6 Jo did not study for the math exam she took late last week.
7 This time he spent at least ten days studying for the test.
5 | 10 | 15 | 20 | 25 | 30 | 35 | 40 | 45 | 50 | 55 | 60

Keyboarding CONNECTION

Capturing an Image From the Internet

Would you like to copy an image or graphic from the Internet? It's easy!

Point to the image or graphic and press the right mouse button. When the shortcut menu appears, choose Save Picture As (or Save Image As). The Save Picture dialog displays. Select the appropriate drive and name the file if necessary. Click Save. The image is usually saved with a .gif, .jpg, or .bmp file extension. To insert the image into a Word document, choose Picture from the Insert menu, and select From File. Locate the file, and click Insert.

YOUR TURN Conduct a Web search and locate an image or graphic to save. Right-click the image, and choose Save Picture As; name the file; and save the image. Insert the image into a word processing document.

D. Take two 5-minute timings. Review your speed and errors.

Goal: At least 47wpm/5′/5e

D. 5-MINUTE TIMING

Many businesses across the country are adopting a 10
new trend called business casual. Depending on the type of 22
organization for which you work, business casual can have 34
various interpretations. Most corporations allow their 45
employees to dress down a notch from what was expected 56
previously. If people wore suits and ties previously, then 68
the business casual code would allow them to eliminate 79
wearing ties and suit jackets. It is quite necessary for 90
businesses to formulate dress code guidelines for their 101
employees to follow when business casual is introduced. 112
Surveys of various companies show mixed results when 123
employees are given the option of dressing more casually. 135
Some companies feel business casual is a perk that works 146
for employees. However, other companies report that job 157
productivity rates decrease when workers are allowed to 168
dress down. 170
When you feel good about the way you look, you will 181
show this attitude in your performance. If your company 192
has adopted a business casual dress code, you must keep in 204
mind that business casual does not mean that you can dress 216
in a sloppy manner. A neat appearance and good grooming 227
always enhance a business casual look. 235

| 1 | 2 | 3 | 4 | 5 | 6 | 7 | 8 | 9 | 10 | 11 | 12

FORMATTING

E. LEGAL DOCUMENTS

Legal documents are typed on either 8½-inch by 14-inch legal paper or 8½-inch by 11-inch standard paper. Many firms today use standard paper for their legal documents.

Legal cap, vertical rules running from top to bottom on a page, have been used for years to identify the left and right margins of legal documents. Whether or not legal cap is used, the left margin is typically set at 1.25 inches and the right margin maintains a default 1.0 inch. The top and bottom margins in a legal document are usually set at 1 inch but may vary from firm to firm.

It is also common practice to number the lines in a legal document to enable an attorney to make reference to particular lines or sections in the document.

(Continued on next page)

Pages in a legal document are often numbered as "*Page 1 of 7*" to indicate the total number of pages in the document. Paragraphs are usually indented from 0.5 inch to 1.0 inch. Full justification is frequently used.

Legal documents come in numerous formats such as affidavits, wills, deeds, summons, indictments, etc. The illustration below shows a sample of an affidavit. An affidavit is a written statement made under oath.

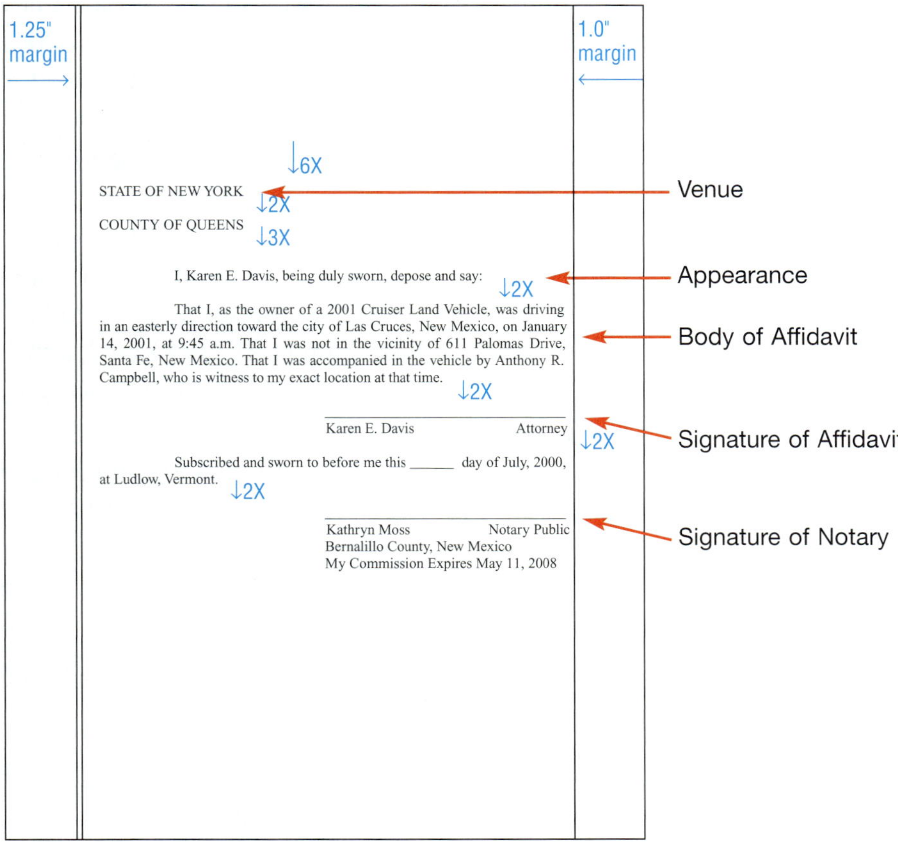

STATE OF NEW YORK

COUNTY OF QUEENS

I, Karen E. Davis, being duly sworn, depose and say:

That I, as the owner of a 2001 Cruiser Land Vehicle, was driving in an easterly direction toward the city of Las Cruces, New Mexico, on January 14, 2001, at 9:45 a.m. That I was not in the vicinity of 611 Palomas Drive, Santa Fe, New Mexico. That I was accompanied in the vehicle by Anthony R. Campbell, who is witness to my exact location at that time.

Karen E. Davis Attorney

Subscribed and sworn to before me this ______ day of July, 2000, at Ludlow, Vermont.

Kathryn Moss Notary Public
Bernalillo County, New Mexico
My Commission Expires May 11, 2008

Go To
Word Processing Manual

F. WORD PROCESSING: LINE NUMBERING

Study Lesson 96 in your word processing manual. Complete all of the shaded steps while at your computer. Then format the jobs that follow.

DOCUMENT PROCESSING

Report 96-68

Affidavit of Possession

Insert line numbering for all lines.

Double-space between all paragraphs.

Indent paragraphs 1 inch.

AFFIDAVIT OF POSSESSION ↓1DS

STATE OF VERMONT ↓1DS

COUNTY OF WINDSOR ↓1DS

¶ (1") Eric Wesley, being first duly sworn, deposes and says:

¶ (1") That he is an adult person and is a resident of Windsor County, Vermont, and that his mailing address is P.O. Box 801, Ludlow, VT 05149.

(Continued on next page)

That he knows and is well acquainted with the history, ownership and occupancy of the following-described property situated in Windsor County, Vermont, to-wit:

All that part of the Southeast Quarter of the Northeast Quarter of Section Nine (9), Township Seventy-two (72), further described as follows: Beginning at the Northeast corner of said Southeast Quarter of the Northeast Quarter; thence South along the East line of said quarter 1000.00 feet; thence west 575.00 feet; thence North 200.00 feet; thence West 204.00 feet; thence North 800.00 feet; thence East 979.00 feet.

That the record title holder in fee simple of the above property is Eric Wesley, a single person; that he is presently in possession of the above-described premises;

That ownership of the aforesaid property is based upon an unbroken chain of title through immediate and remote grantors by deed of conveyance which has been recorded for a period of more than twenty-one (21) years, to-wit: Since August 21, 1943, at 2 a.m.;

That the owner(s) and his predecessors in title to the aforementioned property have had open, actual, adverse, notorious and continuous possession against all persons and have paid taxes in open and adverse possession for more than twenty-one (21) years; and

That the purpose of this Affidavit of Possession is to show proof of ownership by providing and recording evidence of possession for marketable title as required by the Marketable Record Title Act of the State of Vermont.

Underscore is 6 characters wide.

DATED this ______ day of August, 20--, at Ludlow, Vermont.

↓1DS

Underscore starts at a left tab of 3.0 inches and ends at the right margin.

3" Tab

____

Blake Crawford Attorney-at-Law

Subscribed and sworn to before me this ______ day of August, 20--. ↓1DS

Underscore starts at a left tab of 3.0 inches and ends at the right margin.

3" Tab

____

Shirley Blakely Notary Public
Windsor County, Vermont
My Commission Expires July 17, 2008

Correspondence 96-94

Business Letter in Block Style With Enclosure and Copy Notations

Current Date | Mr. Eric Wesley | P.O. Box 801 | Ludlow, VT 05149 | Dear Mr. Wesley:

¶ Enclosed is your copy of the Affidavit of Possession that was filed on your behalf with the Windsor County Courthouse.

¶ As you can see, only the Southeast Quarter of your property was included in the affidavit. We will have to file an additional affidavit if you want to add the Northwest Quarter as well as your Franklin County properties. All affidavits must be completed prior to your property being advertised in the *Windsor News.*

¶ I will be out of the office all of next week. If you have questions, please call my associate, Emily Waters.

Sincerely, | Blake Crawford | urs | Enclosure | c: Marvin Steele, Beverley Perez

Lesson 97

Legal Office Applications

GOALS
- Improve speed and accuracy
- Refine language arts skills in the use of punctuation
- Format legal office applications

A. Type 2 times.

A. WARMUP

```
     Jacqueline kept prize #2490 instead of #3761 because   11
it was worth 58.5% more value. That was a great prize! Last 23
year the law firm of Adams & Day donated all grand prizes.  34
| 1 | 2 | 3 | 4 | 5 | 6 | 7 | 8 | 9 | 10 | 11 | 12
```

SKILLBUILDING

B. PROGRESSIVE PRACTICE: ALPHABET

If you are not using the GDP software, turn to page SB-7 and follow the directions for this activity.

C. PACED PRACTICE

If you are not using the GDP software, turn to page SB-14 and follow the directions for this activity.

LANGUAGE ARTS

D. Study the rules at the right.

D. SEMICOLONS

RULE ▶ ; no conjunction

Use a semicolon to separate two closely related independent clauses that are not connected by a conjunction (such as *and, but,* or *nor*).

Management favored the vote; stockholders did not.

But: Management favored the vote, but stockholders did not.

RULE ▶ ; series

Use a semicolon to separate three or more items in a series if any of the items already contain commas.

Staff meetings were held on Thursday, May 7; Monday, June 7; and Friday, June 12.

Note: Be sure to insert the semicolon between (not within) the items in a series.

Edit the sentences to correct any errors in the use of semicolons.

```
Paul will travel to Madrid, Spain; Lisbon, Portugal, and
Nice, France.
Mary's gift arrived yesterday, Margie's did not.
Bring your textbook to class; I'll return it tomorrow.
The best days for the visit are Monday, May 10, Tuesday,
May 18, and Wednesday, May 26.
Jan is the president; Peter is the vice president.
```

DOCUMENT PROCESSING

Report 97-69

Warranty Deed

A warranty deed is one in which a seller warrants (or guarantees) that he or she has full ownership of the property with the right to sell it. The seller also guarantees all rights of the property to the buyer.

Insert line numbers for all lines.

Underscore is 6 characters wide.

WARRANTY DEED ↓1DS

1" tab → **THIS INDENTURE,** Made this ______ day of October, 20--, between **Thomas J. Wallace**, **Grantor,** whether one or more, and **Barbara Denman, Grantee,** whether one or more, whose post office address is 315 Clark Avenue, Ames IA 50010-3314. ↓2X

WITNESSETH, for and in consideration of the sum of **SEVENTY-FIVE THOUSAND and 00/100 DOLLARS ($75,000),** Grantor does hereby **GRANT** to Grantee, all of the following real property lying and being in the County of Story, State of Iowa, and described as follows, to-wit:

Lots Seventeen (17) and Eighteen (18), Block Seventy-three (73), Original Townsite of Ames, Iowa, **SUBJECT TO** easements, special or improvement taxes and assessments, mineral conveyances, rights-of-way and reservations of record.

(THIS DEED IS IN FULFILLMENT OF THAT CERTAIN CONTRACT FOR DEED ENTERED INTO BY AND BETWEEN THE SAME PARTIES ON THE DATE HEREOF.)

And the said Grantor for himself, his heirs, executors and administrators, does covenant with the Grantee that he is well seized in fee of the land and premises aforesaid and has good right to sell and convey the same in manner and form aforesaid: that the same are free from all encumbrances, except installments of special assessments or assessments for special improvements which have not been certified to the County Treasurer for collection, and the above granted lands and premises in the possession of said Grantee, against all persons lawfully claiming or to claim the whole or any part thereof, the said Grantor will warrant and defend.

WITNESS, the hand of the Grantor.

3" tab → ______________________________

Thomas J. Wallace ↓2X

(Continued on next page)

STATE OF IOWA ↓2X

County of Story ↓2X

On this ______ day of October, 20--, before me, a notary public within and for said County and State, personally appeared Thomas J. Wallace, to me known to be the person described in and who executed the within and foregoing instrument and acknowledged to me that he executed the same as his free act and deed. ↓2X

3-inch tab →

____
Boyd H. Fraser Notary Public
Story County, Iowa
My Commission Expires June 15, 2008

Table 97-52

Two-Column Boxed Table

WARRANTY DEED TERMINOLOGY State of Iowa	
Term	Definition
Appurtenance	Something attached to the land
Consideration	The value of the property
Escrow	A system of document transfer in which the document is given to a third party to hold until the conditions of the agreement have been met
Grantee	The person who is buying the property
Grantor	The person who owns the property
Mortgage	The pledging of property as security for a loan
Tenement	Something that can be possessed, such as land or a building
Warranty Deed	A deed in which the seller forever guarantees clear title to the land

Correspondence 97-95

Email Message

Send an email message to David Barinowski, (dbarinowski@legal.com) with a subject as follows: Foreclosure Property. Type a closing and signature line for yourself. Type the body as shown below. Proofread your email message for typing, spelling, and formatting errors. Print but do not save or send this email message.

¶ David, you might recall last week that I indicated there might be some fore closure property available and that it would be auctioned at the Story County Courthouse. On September 9 3 properties in southern Story county will be auctioned as foreclosures. These properties are located adjacent to the lots you purchased last year I know that you would be interested in expanding your lot size with this purchase. Specifically, they are located in Spring Township, Lot 23; Aiken Township, Lot 17; and Andrews Township, Lot 9.

; no conjunction

; series

; no conjunction

¶ I expect these properties will sell for around $36,000 each; their excellent location may force the bidding into the $40,000 or $50,000 range. If you cannot be present for the auction but would like to place a bid on the properties, please let me know so that I can act on your behalf as your agent. If you ~~want~~ elect to do this, send me the bidding range you wish to present for each of the Properties or for all 3 as one combined property. I need confirmation from you no later than September 7 so that I can register as your agent to present your bid.

Keyboarding skills are essential for any career in the legal field.

Lesson 98

Legal Office Applications

GOALS
- Type at least 47wpm/5′/5e
- Format legal office applications

A. Type 2 times.

A. WARMUP

```
     Janet bought dozens of disks (5 or 6) to store her        10
article, "The Internet Sanctions." She quickly sent it to      23
her editor, Max Pavlow, on the 18th or 19th of September.      34
| 1 | 2 | 3 | 4 | 5 | 6 | 7 | 8 | 9 | 10 | 11 | 12
```

SKILLBUILDING

B. DIAGNOSTIC PRACTICE: ALPHABET

If you are not using the GDP software, turn to page SB-2 and follow the directions for this activity.

C. Type the paragraph 2 times, concentrating on each letter typed.

C. TECHNIQUE PRACTICE: SHIFT/CAPS LOCK

```
     Raymond and Karen must travel through TENNESSEE and
KENTUCKY on TUESDAY and WEDNESDAY. Raymond will speak in
NASHVILLE on the topic of COMPUTER AWARENESS; Karen will
speak in LOUISVILLE, and her talk is on INTERNET ACCESS.
```

STRATEGIES FOR *Career Success*

Enhance Your Presentation With Visual Aids

Visual aids capture people's attention while increasing their retention. Use visual aids to present an outline of your presentation, explain detailed technical or numeric information, and summarize your key points.

Be selective. Don't bombard your audience with visuals. Your visual aids should support and clarify your verbal presentation. Consider the size of your audience and the size of the room before selecting your visuals. Audiences have little patience for visuals that are too small to read. Types of visual aids are overhead transparencies, slides, photographs, flip charts, maps, flowcharts, posters, handouts, and computer graphics including tables, graphs, and charts.

Limit the amount of information on a visual. Use simple graphics. Continue displaying the current visual until you are ready to discuss the next one. Always keep the projector or overhead on.

YOUR TURN In what ways would your visual aids differ if your audience had 10 people or 110?

D. Take two 5-minute timings. Review your speed and errors.

Goal: At least 47wpm/5′/5e

D. 5-MINUTE TIMING

From the time you start attending school, you begin 10
to develop the skills in making friends and getting along 23
with people. These skills are used throughout your life 34
journey. If you want to be successful in any business or 45
career, you can't be a loner. You must learn skills for 56
working successfully with people from all cultures. 66
In a corporation, people use their unique skills 76
to work as a team in order to accomplish their goals. Like 88
a finely tuned orchestra or a football team, all members 99
must work together to achieve the desired objective. If a 111
person does not work efficiently within the group, then 122
other team members may have to work harder to compensate 133
so that the effort of the team will not fall short. 143
Working with others allows you the opportunity to 153
learn from other people. You may also learn some things 164
about yourself. To get along with your coworkers, you may 176
have to overlook the personal faults of others. Everyone 187
has faults, and your faults may be just as disconcerting 198
to other people as their faults are to you. Your ability 209
to work with people will enhance your quest for career 220
advancement. You can expect amazing results when you work 232
with your team. 235

| 1 | 2 | 3 | 4 | 5 | 6 | 7 | 8 | 9 | 10 | 11 | 12

Lawyers, as well as other professionals, find a laptop computer a valuable resource while traveling on business.

DOCUMENT PROCESSING

Report 98-70

Summons

A summons is a document that notifies a defendant that a lawsuit has been filed and an appearance must be made before the court, at a specified time, to answer the charges.

Insert line numbers for all lines.

Underscore is 6 characters wide.

Use a right tab setting of 2.25" for the closing parentheses of the venue information.

STATE OF KANSAS ↓2X **IN DISTRICT COURT**

COUNTY OF DOUGLAS ↓2X **NORTHEAST JUDICIAL DISTRICT**

PEOPLE'S BANK) **NO.______**
607 New Hampshire Street)
Lawrence, KS 66044-2243) ↓2X
)
Plaintiff,) ↓2X **SUMMONS**
)
- vs -)
) ↓2X
JOHN COUZINS and GLORIA)
COUZINS, Defendants.) ↓2X

THE STATE OF KANSAS TO THE ABOVE-NAMED DEFENDANTS: ↓2X

Tab at 1" → You are hereby summoned and required to appear and defend against the Complaint in this action, which is hereby served upon you by serving upon the undersigned an Answer or other proper response within twenty (20) days after the service of the Summons and Complaint upon you, exclusive of the day of service.

If you fail to do so, judgment by default will be taken against you for the relief demanded in the Complaint. ↓2X

SIGNED this ______ day of December, 20--. ↓2X

Tab at 3" → ______________________________
Ann Barfield
Attorney at Law
806 Kentucky St.
Lawrence KS 66044-2648
Telephone: (785) 555-8226
Attorney for Plaintiff

Correspondence 98-96

Memo With Enclosure and Copy Notations

MEMO TO: Raymond Ruzi

FROM: Charlotte Libretto

DATE: Current Date

SUBJECT: Client listing

¶ As you requested, I am now enclosing an up-to-date new client list for our Atlanta area clients. This list is curent as of last week, and it includes clients in the counties of Carroll, Cobb, Douglas, Fulton, and paulding. Please note that the billing hours are shown in this list.

¶ Douglas and Cobb counties represent the greatest number of clients over all, although this list doesn't reveal the total number of clients per county. Just in the past quarter, these two counties represented nearly eighty % of our client base. Cobb County clients do not represent a sizable percentage of our client base, but the opening of three new law offices in that county will most certainly generate considerable business in the coming months.

¶ We will send you an updated list bi-weekly. The next list will most certainly show substantial gains in Cobb County, and we expect business in Douglas and Fulton counties to continue growing because of the growth in the area West of Atlanta. If you have any questions about any of our new clients please call our main office at 770-555-1843.

urs | Enclosure | c: Blair Kiplan

Much of the work done in a legal office is transcribed by administrative support staff.

Table 98-53

Four-Column Boxed Table

CLIENT LIST Current Date			
Name	**Address**	**County**	**Billing Hours**
Gary Baxter	128 Holly St.	Douglas	25
Carroll Bryan	323 Newnan St.	Carroll	28
Margie Coulon	301 Bradley St.	Paulding	15
Thomas Henry	2900 Shady Grove	Cobb	22
Debra Johnson	215 Griffin Dr.	Cobb	34
Sean Lowe	156 Cypress Circle	Fulton	10
Luther Nicholson	6703 Burns Rd.	Paulding	12
Pearl Nix	106 Alice Lane	Douglas	18
James Presley	622 North Ave.	Carroll	23
Janie Ramey	1202 Park St.	Fulton	32
Heather Sanders	248 Lakeshore Dr.	Cobb	12
Thomas Tarpley	2950 Chapel Hill Rd.	Douglas	29
Vickie Thomas	4821 Hope Rd.	Carroll	9
Jack West	111 Pierce St.	Fulton	18
Ray Young	108 Waverly Way	Douglas	30
Tong Zhen	286 Laurel Terrace	Paulding	35

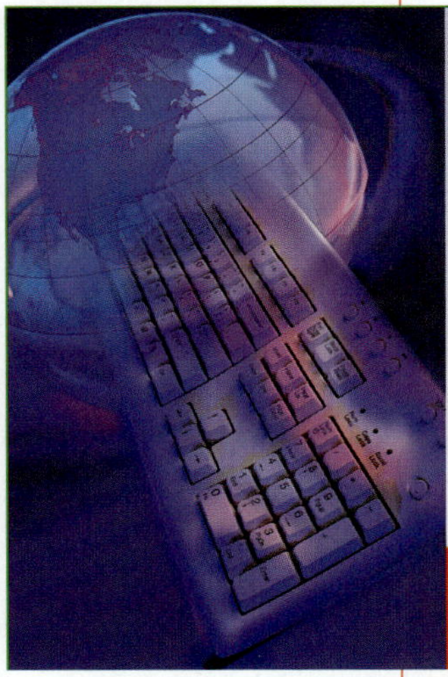

Keyboarding CONNECTION

Coping With Spam

Have you received heaps of unsolicited email, commonly known as spam? Everyone wants to get rid of those irritating online sales pitches. Contrary to popular advice, however, there is not much you can do about them. You can make use of various filters, but they aren't foolproof.

If you end up on a spammer's list and receive a courteous email asking you to reply if you wish to be removed from the list, DO NOT REPLY. The spammer may take your reply as someone who's reading the mail, and you may be put on the hot list. The best action is to try to avoid divulging your email address to spam. Most importantly, use an alternate account if posting to any kind of online forum.

YOUR TURN How do you deal with postal "junk mail" that you receive? Are there similarities in dealing with spam?

Lesson 99

Legal Office Applications

GOALS

- Improve speed and accuracy
- Refine language arts skills in spelling
- Format legal office applications

A. Type 2 times.

A. WARMUP

Zeke sharpened his ax so that he could quite easily 11
saw through 15 very large pine trees. Each load will sell 23
for $175 (to Blake & James Inc.) at next Friday's auction. 35

| 1 | 2 | 3 | 4 | 5 | 6 | 7 | 8 | 9 | 10 | 11 | 12 |

SKILLBUILDING

B. MAP

Follow the GDP software directions for this exercise in improving keystroking accuracy.

C. Take a 1-minute timing on the first paragraph to establish your base speed. Then take four 1-minute timings on the remaining paragraphs. As soon as you equal or exceed your base speed on one paragraph, advance to the next, more difficult paragraph.

C. SUSTAINED PRACTICE: ROUGH DRAFT

The pattern of employment in our country is undergoing 11
some major changes. Companies are slowly decreasing their 23
permanent staff to just a core group of managers and other 35
high-powered people and are using temporaries for the rest. 47

This trend is creating an ac[c]ordion aftermath in many 11
firms: the ability to expand and contract as the time ~~or~~ [and] 23
the balance sheets dictate. ~~Have~~ [Having] this range of flexibility 35
~~would~~ [will] be a key ingredient in the compet~~a~~[i]tive fight to come. 47

All of these changes ~~would~~ [will] make it tough for ~~all~~ [the] unions 11
to stay a float. They do not have a satisfact~~e~~[o]ry method of 23
organizing such employe[e]s. Unions ~~can~~ [could] try to change in to 35
social agenc(ei)s, providing aid to members outside of work. 47

Such services as elder or child care, counseling, debt 11
manag[e]ment, and even health care may[ ]be of great as[s]istance 23
as employers find it more and more dif[f]icult to offer these 35
ben[e]fits. [Unions may find their niche by filling this gap.] 47

| 1 | 2 | 3 | 4 | 5 | 6 | 7 | 8 | 9 | 10 | 11 | 12 |

LANGUAGE ARTS

D. Type this list of frequently misspelled words, paying special attention to any spelling problems in each word.

D. SPELLING

20 distribution executive extension requested specific carried
21 recommended alternative programs access budget issued seize
22 objectives indicated calendar family could these until your
23 administrative accommodate possibility students fiscal past
24 transportation employee's categories summary offered estate

Edit the sentences to correct any misspellings.

25 The execitive requested an extention on spicific programs.
26 I have recomended alternitive programs for early next week.
27 These objectives were indacated for the new calender year.
28 These passed administrative goals will accomodate the team.
29 These catagories could be included in the employee summery.

DOCUMENT PROCESSING

Report 99-71

Last Will and Testament

Add line numbers to entire document; restart line numbering on the second page.

Add page number for page 2 in this format: Page 2 of 2.

Use a 1-inch tab for new paragraphs.

Press ENTER 2 times before and after the Articles.

A last will and testament is a legal document stating how a person wants his or her property distributed after death.

LAST WILL AND TESTAMENT
OF
MATTHEW R. HENRY

I, **MATTHEW R. HENRY**, residing in Corvallis, Oregon, do hereby make and declare this to be my Last Will and Testament, hereby revoking any and all former Wills and Codicils by me at any time heretofore made.

ARTICLE I

This will is made in Oregon and shall be governed, construed, and administered according to Oregon law, even though subject to probate or administered elsewhere. The Oregon laws applied shall not include any principles or laws relating to conflicts or choice of laws.

ARTICLE II

Whenever used herein, words importing the singular shall include the plural and words importing the masculine shall include the feminine and neuter, and vice versa, unless the context otherwise requires.

(Continued on next page)

ARTICLE III

I am married and my wife's name is Karen E. Henry. All references hereinafter made to "wife" or "spouse" shall refer to her and no other; and if she is not my legal wife at the time of my death, then she shall be deemed for the purpose of this, my last Will and Testament, to have predeceased me. I was formerly married to Donna Henry, who is now deceased. There were three (3) children born of my marriage to Donna Henry. The names of those children are as follows: Judy Parsons, Wayne Henry, and Randy Henry.

ARTICLE IV

If My Spouse Survives. Except as may otherwise be provided hereunder in this Article IV, if my spouse survives me, I devise to my spouse all my interest in household furniture and furnishings, books, apparel, art objects, collections, jewelry, and similar personal effects; sporting and recreational equipment; all other tangible property for personal use; all other like contents of my home and any vacation property that I may own or reside in on the date of my death; all animals; any motor vehicles that I may own on the date of my death; and any unexpired insurance on all such property.

ARTICLE V

If My Spouse Does Not Survive. Except as may be otherwise provided in this Article IV, if my spouse does not survive me, I devise the property described above in this Article (except motor vehicles) to my children who survive me, to be divided among them as they shall agree, or in the absence of such agreement, as my Personal Representative shall determine, which determination shall be conclusive.

ARTICLE VI

If any beneficiary named or described in this Will fails to survive me for 120 hours, all the provisions in this Will for the benefit of such deceased beneficiary shall lapse, and this Will shall be construed as though the fact were that he or she predeceased me.

ARTICLE VII

All estate, inheritance, transfer, succession, and any other taxes plus interest and penalties thereon (death taxes) that become payable by reason of my death upon property passing under this instrument shall be paid out of the residue of my estate without reimbursement from the recipient and without apportionment. All death taxes upon property not passing under this instrument shall be apportioned in the manner provided by law.

(Continued on next page)

The first underscore is 6 characters wide; the second underscore is 20 characters wide.

IN WITNESS WHEREOF, I have hereunto affixed my hand and seal this ______ day of ____________________, 20--.

Set left tab at 3.0 inches for signature line; set right tab for "Testator."

____

MATTHEW R. HENRY Testator

The foregoing instrument, consisting of TWO (2) pages (this page included), was on this ______ day of ____________________, 20--, subscribed on each page and at the end thereof by Matthew R. Henry, the above-named Testator and by him signed, sealed, published and declared to be his Last Will, in the presence of us, and each of us, who thereupon, at his request, in his presence, and in the presence of each other, have hereunto subscribed our names as attesting witnesses thereto.

Each underscore is 25 characters wide.

_________________________ residing at _________________________

_________________________ residing at _________________________

Correspondence 99-97

Business Letter in Block Style with Subject Line, Bulleted List, Enclosure, and Copy Notations

Current Date | Mr. Matthew R. Henry | 768 Southwest Adams Avenue | Corvallis, OR 97333-4523 | Dear Mr. Henry: | Subject: Will Provisions
¶ Your last will and testament has been drafted and is enclosed for your review. Please review it carefully for any specific omissions or deletions.
¶ Although your will has been drafted as you indicated, there are still a couple of alternative inclusions that I would recommend.

- Do you wish to include a fiduciary powers summary in the will?
- What division of estate do you wish to include for your family?

¶ These inclusions could be rather comprehensive. Therefore, could we schedule a meeting for next Tuesday to accommodate these changes? Please call my administrative assistant so she can put you on my calendar. Sincerely, | Andrea L. Grainger | Attorney-at-Law | urs | Enclosure | c: T. Carter, S. Rohrer, A. Winchester

Lesson 100

Legal Office Applications

GOALS
- Type at least 47wpm/5′/5e
- Format legal office applications

A. Type 2 times.

A. WARMUP

```
     Val Lopez and Jack Drew quickly bought six tickets for  11
Sam's $24,600 collector's auto (a 1957 Chevrolet). Over the  23
past month, its value increased by 1.5%. That is fantastic!  35
| 1 | 2 | 3 | 4 | 5 | 6 | 7 | 8 | 9 | 10 | 11 | 12
```

SKILLBUILDING

PPP

PRETEST → PRACTICE → POSTTEST

PRETEST
Take a 1-minute timing. Review your speed and errors.

B. PRETEST: Horizontal Reaches

```
     Bart enjoyed his royal blue race car. He bragged about  11
how he learned to push for those speed spurts that helped    23
him win those races. The car had a lot of get-up-and-go.     34
| 1 | 2 | 3 | 4 | 5 | 6 | 7 | 8 | 9 | 10 | 11 | 12
```

PRACTICE
Speed Emphasis:
If you made no more than 1 error on the Pretest, type each *individual* line 2 times.
Accuracy Emphasis:
If you made 2 or more errors, type each *group* of lines (as though it were a paragraph) 2 times.

C. PRACTICE: In Reaches

```
oy toy ahoy ploy loyal coyly royal enjoy decoy annoy deploy
ar fare arch mart march farms scars spear barns learn radar
pu pull push puts pulse spurt purge spuds pushy spurs pupil
```

D. PRACTICE: Out Reaches

```
ge gear gets ages getup raged geese lunge pages cagey forge
da dare date data dance adage dazed sedan daubs cedar daily
hi high hick hill hinge chief hires ethic hiked chili hitch
```

POSTTEST
Repeat the Pretest timing and compare performance.

E. POSTTEST: Horizontal Reaches

F. Take two 5-minute timings. Review your speed and errors.

Goal: At least 47wpm/5'/5e

F. 5-MINUTE TIMING

Company loyalty may be a thing of the past. A worker 11
who stayed and worked for one corporation for thirty or 22
more years is a rarity these days. People are moving to 33
different jobs at a faster pace than in the past. Changing 45
jobs many times over a career no longer carries the stigma 57
of the past. People are looking for new challenges. 67

Workers who change jobs are able to market their 77
skills and get significant salary increases. Hopping from 89
job to job can pay amazing dividends for some careers. 100
Corporations are quite willing to offer higher salaries 111
and more perks to attract the most talented people. People 123
who are changing jobs frequently have the experience and 134
knowledge that other companies are willing to employ. 145

The opportunity to change jobs is available not only 156
to younger workers but also to the older workers who are 167
well into their careers. For example, computer technology 179
is currently experiencing a boom. The Internet industry 190
has placed a high demand for computer programmers. People 202
with experience in this area can request higher salaries. 214
A company may even offer additional benefits in order to 225
attract experienced workers with great credentials. 235

| 1 | 2 | 3 | 4 | 5 | 6 | 7 | 8 | 9 | 10 | 11 | 12

STRATEGIES FOR *Career Success*

Letter of Resignation

When you plan to leave a job, you should write a resignation letter, memo, or email to your supervisor and send a copy to Human Resources. Follow these guidelines to write an effective resignation.

Start a resignation letter positively, regardless of why you are leaving. Include how you benefited from working for the company, or compliment your coworkers.

In the middle section, state why you are leaving. Provide an objective, factual explanation and avoid accusations. Your resignation becomes part of your permanent company record. If it is hostile, it could backfire on you when you need references. Stipulate the date your resignation becomes effective (provide at least a two-week notice).

End the letter of resignation with a closing of goodwill (e.g., "I wish all of you the best in the future.").

YOUR TURN List the benefits of NOT "burning your bridges" (showing anger or bitterness) in your letter of resignation.

Report 100-72

Complaint

A complaint is the initial document filed with a court by a plaintiff to begin an adversarial or action at law proceeding. A judgment is the decision of the court.

Review the format of a summons in Lesson 98 before typing the introductory lines in the complaint.

COMPLAINT is aligned at the right on the same line as – *vs*-.

Use a right tab setting of 2.31" for the closing parentheses of the venue information.

Press ENTER 2 times before each Roman numeral.

All Roman numerals are centered between the margins.

STATE OF NORTH DAKOTA — **IN DISTRICT COURT**

COUNTY OF WALSH — **NORTHEAST JUDICIAL DISTRICT**

WALSH COUNTY BANK)
170 Main Street)
Adams, ND 58210)
)
Plaintiff,)
)
- vs -) **COMPLAINT**
)
KENNEDY FARMERS, INC.)
JAMES D. KENNEDY and)
CAROL KENNEDY, Defendants)

NO. ______

PLAINTIFF FOR ITS CAUSE OF ACTION AND COMPLAINT AGAINST THE DEFENDANTS, COMPLAINS, ALLEGES AND SHOWS TO THE COURT:

I.

That defendants owe plaintiff $5,685.00, plus interest and charges, under the terms of a promissory note executed April 10, 20--, a copy of which is attached hereto and incorporated by reference as “Exhibit A.”

II.

That defendants have not, upon due demand, satisfied their obligation under the terms of the promissory note.

III.

That Kennedy Farmers, Inc., is a North Dakota for-profit corporation duly organized under the corporate laws of the State of North Dakota.

IV.

That the registered agent of Kennedy Farmers, Inc., is James D. Kennedy.

V.

That James D. Kennedy executed a Commercial Guaranty for the note dated April 10, 20--, a copy of which is attached hereto and incorporated herein by reference as “Exhibit B.”

(Continued on next page)

VI.

That the indebtedness was the renewal of a prior promissory note executed by Kennedy Farmers, Inc., to Walsh County Bank on June 17, 20--, which was in the original principal amount of $6,685.00, a copy of which is attached hereto and incorporated by reference as "Exhibit C."

VII.

That Carol Kennedy executed a Commercial Guaranty on the prior promissory note No. 7249, and the Commercial Guaranty provides that the guaranty extends to " . . . all renewals of, extensions of, modifications of, refinancings of, consolidations of, and substitutions for the promissory note or agreement." A copy of that Commercial Guaranty is attached hereto and incorporated hereby by reference as "Exhibit D."

VIII.

That James D. Kennedy and Carol Kennedy are personally liable for the amount of the debt, as is the corporation, Kennedy Farmers, Inc.

Be sure to use bold type in selected words and phrases of the complaint.

WHEREFORE, PLAINTIFF DEMANDS JUDGMENT AGAINST THE DEFENDANTS, AND EACH OF THEM, AS FOLLOWS:

Numbered items are indented to the same point as the paragraphs.

1. For the amount of $3,585.00, plus interest on that amount from and after April 10, 20--, at the rate of 10.75% per annum; and for its costs, late charges, and disbursements in this action;
2. For such other and further relief as the Court may deem appropriate.

SIGNED this ______ day of December, 20--.

Set a left tab at 3.0 inches for the signature lines and attorney description.

____

Harold E. Jensen
Attorney at Law
405 1st Street
Adams, ND 58210
Telephone: (701) 555-4832
Attorney for Plaintiff

Report 100-73

Judgment

A Judgment uses the same format as a Complaint, shown in Report 100-72 on pages 388–389.

Be sure to use bold type in selected words of the judgment.

Use a right tab setting of 2.88" for the closing parentheses of the venue information.

Format all-caps text in bold.

STATE OF ARIZONA — **IN DISTRICT COURT**

COUNTY OF MARICOPA — **CENTRAL JUDICIAL DISTRICT**

Timothy Barnes d/b/a Barnes Computers)
1651 West Baseline Road)
Tempe, AZ 85283)
)
Plaintiff,)
)
- vs -)
)
Maricopa Hospital Association)
d/b/a Maricopa Nursing Care)
Defendant)

CIVIL NO. 43-89-D-00145

JUDGMENT

¶ The defendant, Maricopa Hospital Association, d/b/a Maricopa Nursing Care, having been regularly served with process, and having failed to appear and answer the plaintiff's Complaint filed herein, and the default of said defendant having been duly entered, and it appearing that said defendant is not an infant nor an incompetent person, and an affidavit of nonmilitary service having been filed herein, and it appearing by the affidavits of plaintiff that plaintiff is entitled to judgment herein,

¶ IT IS THEREFORE ORDERED AND ADJUDGED, that the plaintiff have and recover from the defendant, Maricopa Hospital Association d/b/a Maricopa Nursing Care, the sum of $8,000.00 plus interest thereon from and after August 10, 20--, until paid, together with costs in the sum of $252.75.

¶ SIGNED this _____ day of __________, 20___.

____
Clerk of the District Court

Report 100-74

Affidavit

Progress Check
Proofreading Check

Documents designated as Proofreading Checks serve as a check of your proofreading skill. Your goal is to have zero typographical errors when the GDP software first scores the document.

AFFIDAVIT OF POSSESSION

STATE OF OREGON

COUNTY OF LINN

¶ I, MARILYN T. HUGGINS, being first duly sworn, depose and say:

¶ That I am the petitioner in the above-entitled suit.

¶ That the respondent, RICHARD M. HUGGINS, and I are the parents of BENJAMIN T. HUGGINS. That BENJAMIN T. HUGGINS is currently residing exclusively with me. Respondent is currently residing away from the home at 1529 South Oak Street, Albany, Oregon. That I am a fit and proper person to have immediate and temporary custody of BENJAMIN T. HUGGINS.

¶ I believe that these pending dissolution proceedings will aggravate this situation; therefore, I believe that it is necessary and appropriate for the Court to issue an Order restraining and enjoining respondent from physically or verbally abusing or harassing me or our child in any way.

The first underscore is 6 characters wide; the second underscore is 20 characters wide.

¶ Subscribed and sworn to before me this ______ day of ____________________, 20--.

____

Notary Public for Oregon
My commmission expires: 1/7/20--

Legal teams frequently work together on documentation review, using the keyboard to track revisions.

Test 5

Skills Assessment on Part 5

5-Minute Timing

When you submit your resume to apply for a job, you 10
want your resume to be noticed. Here are some things you 22
can do to make certain your resume receives the attention 34
it deserves. 36

First, be neat. Review the resume to make sure there 47
are no spelling or typographical errors. Check your resume 59
for correct grammar. Remember, this document will make the 71
first impression with a potential employer; you want the 82
document to represent you in the best way. Use white paper 94
of good quality to print your resume. 102

Second, try to be creative. Make your resume unique. 113
A potential employer may be looking for specific criteria 125
when he or she scans the elements of your resume. Be sure 137
to provide information that explains exactly what skills 148
you have acquired in positions you have held in the past. 160
Avoid using the buzzwords that everyone else uses. 170

Finally, state a career objective on your resume. 180
Some experts suggest that by stating a career objective, 191
you are showing a career path. Others think that stating 202
a career objective may limit many job possibilities. If 213
you state a career objective, make sure the objective is 224
in line with the specific job for which you are applying. 235

| 1 | 2 | 3 | 4 | 5 | 6 | 7 | 8 | 9 | 10 | 11 | 12

Correspondence Test 5-98

Business Letter in Block Style With Copy Notations

Current Date (use day/month/year format) | Mr. Antoine Lauvergeon | Marketing Director | Alatel Inc. | 54 Rue la Boetie | 75382 Paris cedex 08 | France | Dear Mr. Lauvergeon:

¶ As we predicted, our jefe effort marketing was a tremendous success in the 5 new plants opened last Spring in France and Germany. In fact, sales at those two plants have surpassed our Switzerland and Italy sales over the same period. Much of this sucess is due to your timely marketing campaign that was conducted during the first quarter. Congratulations to you and your staff on this fine effort.

Because of this positive experience, we have decided to expand our promotional campaign at our plants in Negras Piedras, Morelia, and Cancun. Would you please put together a proposal for these plants and send it to me by the end of next week. We are excited about this oportunity and look forward to recieving your proposal.

¶ Again, nice work on the France and Germany effort.

Sincerely, | Harold Deforey | V.P., Marketing | c: Mari Lynn Somnolet, James Lafforgue

Table Test 5-54

Two-Column Open Table

HEMATOLOGY REPORT

Name ______________________ **Doctor** ______________________

Test Results ____

____ WBC	____ Glucose
____ Hemoglobin	____ Cholesterol
____ PMN	____ BUN
____ Bands	____ Calcium
____ Lymphs	____ Phosphorous
____ Mono	____ Bilirubin
____ Eos	____ Uric acid
____ Baso	____ Alkaline phosphatase
____ Platelets	____ Albumin
____ Thyroid	____ Protein, total

Productivity for the voluminous research involved in the legal profession is enhanced by the use of a keyboard.

Report Test 5-75

Summons

Use a right tab setting of 2.18" for the closing parentheses of the venue information.

STATE OF NEBRASKA	**IN DISTRICT COURT**
COUNTY OF WAYNE	**NORTHEAST JUDICIAL DISTRICT**

PAUL C. CREWS)
610 Thorman St)
Wayne, NE 68787)
)
Plaintiff,)
)
- vs -)
)
ANGELINA WASHINGTON)
Defendant.)

NO.______

SUMMONS

THE STATE OF NEBRASKA TO THE ABOVE-NAMED DEFENDANT:

You are hereby required to appear and defend the complaint filed against you in the above-entitled action within thirty (30) days from the date of service of this summons upon you, and in case of your failure to do so, for want thereof, plaintiff(s) will apply to the court for the relief demanded in the complaint.

SIGNED this ______ day of May, 20--

____

Jeremy Richfield
Attorney at Law
Box 148
Wayne, NE 68787
Telephone: (402) 555-3832
Attorney for Plaintiff

PART 6

Using and Designing Business Documents

OBJECTIVES

KEYBOARDING

- Type at least 50 words per minute on a 5-minute timing with no more than 5 errors.

LANGUAGE ARTS

- Refine proofreading skills and correctly use proofreaders' marks.
- Use capitals, punctuation, and grammar correctly.
- Improve composing and spelling skills.
- Recognize subject/verb agreement.

WORD PROCESSING

- Use the word processing commands necessary to complete the document processing activities.

DOCUMENT PROCESSING

- Design office forms, office publications, and Web pages.

TECHNICAL

- Answer at least 90 percent of the questions correctly on an objective test.

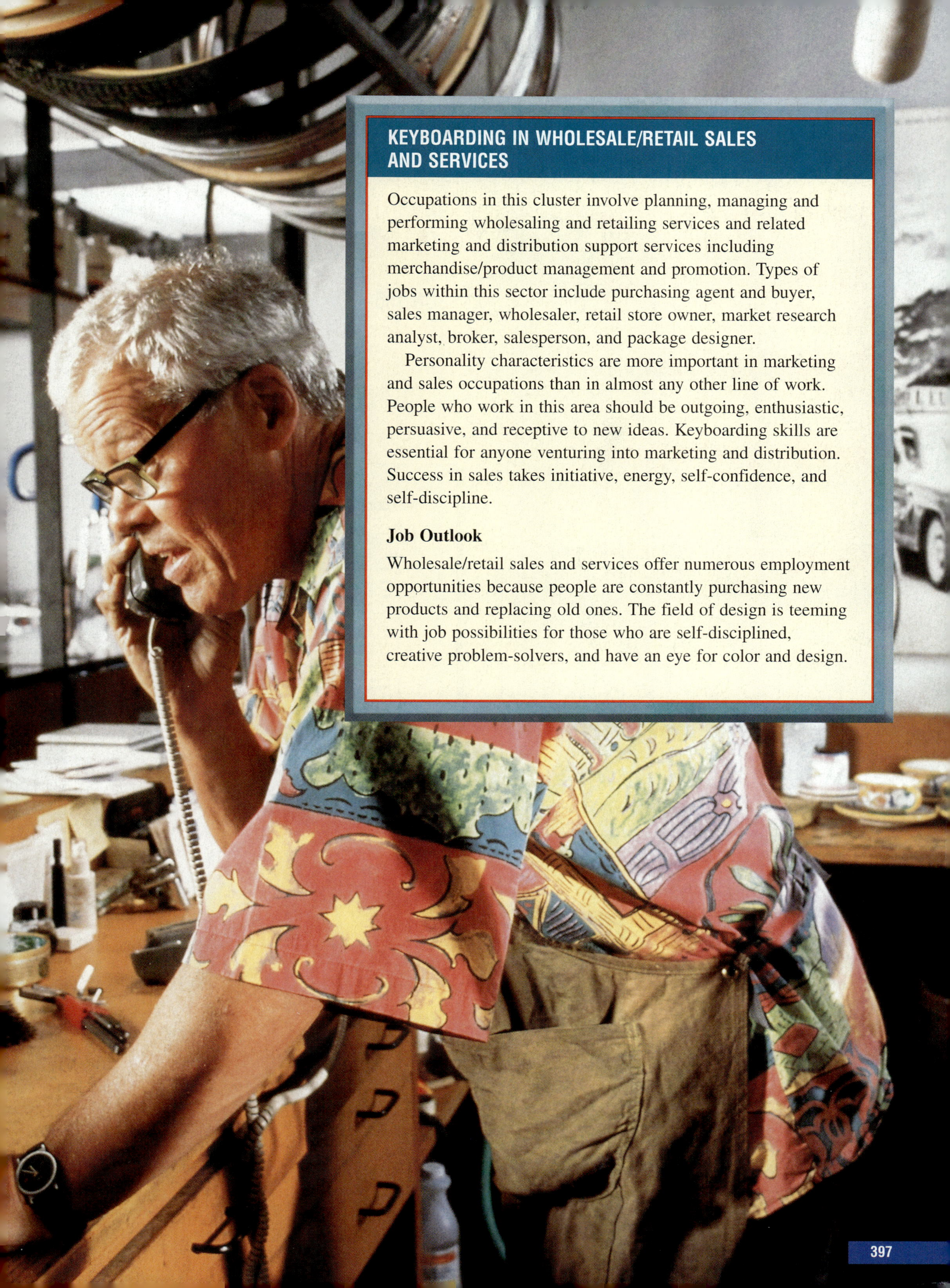

KEYBOARDING IN WHOLESALE/RETAIL SALES AND SERVICES

Occupations in this cluster involve planning, managing and performing wholesaling and retailing services and related marketing and distribution support services including merchandise/product management and promotion. Types of jobs within this sector include purchasing agent and buyer, sales manager, wholesaler, retail store owner, market research analyst, broker, salesperson, and package designer.

Personality characteristics are more important in marketing and sales occupations than in almost any other line of work. People who work in this area should be outgoing, enthusiastic, persuasive, and receptive to new ideas. Keyboarding skills are essential for anyone venturing into marketing and distribution. Success in sales takes initiative, energy, self-confidence, and self-discipline.

Job Outlook

Wholesale/retail sales and services offer numerous employment opportunities because people are constantly purchasing new products and replacing old ones. The field of design is teeming with job possibilities for those who are self-disciplined, creative problem-solvers, and have an eye for color and design.

Unit 21

Using and Designing Office Forms

LESSON 101
Using Correspondence Templates

LESSON 102
Using Report Templates

LESSON 103
Designing Letterheads

LESSON 104
Designing Notepads

LESSON 105
Designing Miscellaneous Office Forms

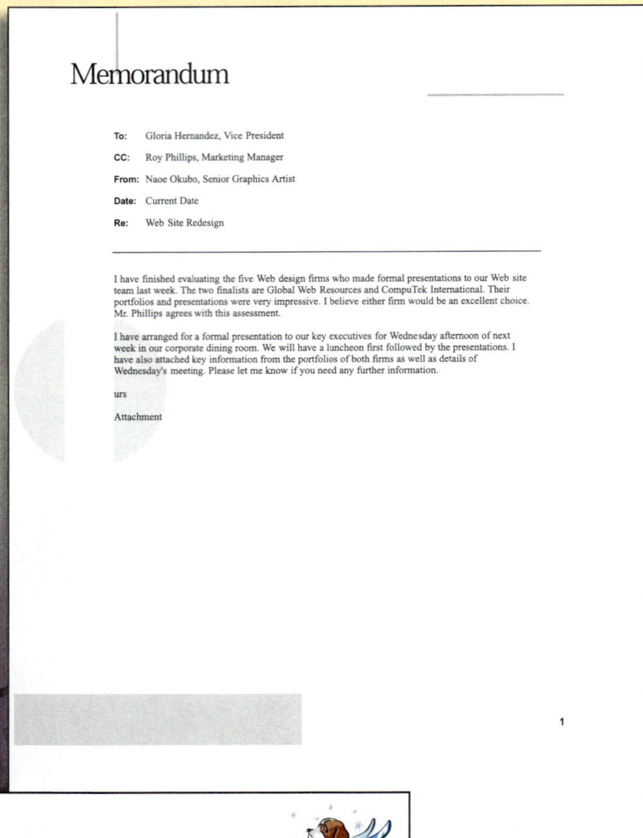

Memorandum

To: Gloria Hernandez, Vice President

CC: Roy Phillips, Marketing Manager

From: Naoe Okubo, Senior Graphics Artist

Date: Current Date

Re: Web Site Redesign

I have finished evaluating the five Web design firms who made formal presentations to our Web site team last week. The two finalists are Global Web Resources and CompuTek International. Their portfolios and presentations were very impressive. I believe either firm would be an excellent choice. Mr. Phillips agrees with this assessment.

I have arranged for a formal presentation to our key executives for Wednesday afternoon of next week in our corporate dining room. We will have a luncheon first followed by the presentations. I have also attached key information from the portfolios of both firms as well as details of Wednesday's meeting. Please let me know if you need any further information.

urs

Attachment

1

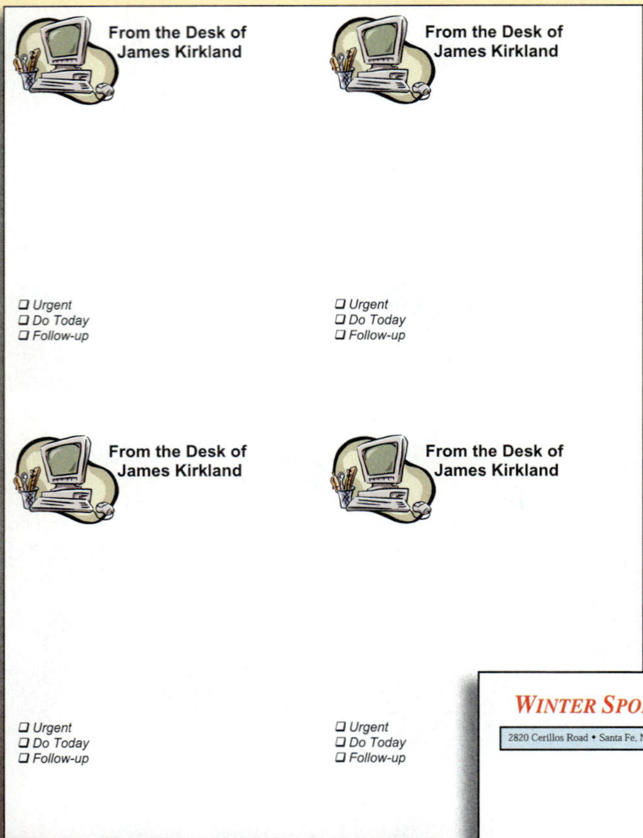

From the Desk of James Kirkland

❑ Urgent
❑ Do Today
❑ Follow-up

From the Desk of James Kirkland

❑ Urgent
❑ Do Today
❑ Follow-up

From the Desk of James Kirkland

❑ Urgent
❑ Do Today
❑ Follow-up

From the Desk of James Kirkland

❑ Urgent
❑ Do Today
❑ Follow-up

WINTER SPORTS

2820 Cerillos Road • Santa Fe, NM 87505 • 505-555-3496 • www.wintersports.com

Lesson 101

Using Correspondence Templates

GOALS

- Improve speed and accuracy
- Refine language arts skills in grammar
- Format correspondence using a template

A. Type 2 times.

A. WARMUP

```
     The secretary made a reservation on Flight #847; it        11
departs at exactly 3:05 on July 6. A sizable number of          22
key executives (about 1/2) requested seats in Rows G to M.      34
| 1 | 2 | 3 | 4 | 5 | 6 | 7 | 8 | 9 | 10 | 11 | 12
```

SKILLBUILDING

B. Take three 12-second timings on each line. The scale below the last line shows your wpm speed for a 12-second timing.

B. 12-SECOND SPEED SPRINTS

```
Bob will lend all the keys to you if you will fix the leak.
Ruth wanted to thank you for all of the work you did today.
Both of the books will have to be sent to her by next week.
Dick paid her half of the money when she signed the papers.
| | | | 5 | | | | 10 | | | | 15 | | | | 20 | | | | 25 | | | | 30 | | | | 35 | | | | 40 | | | | 45 | | | | 50 | | | | 55 | | | | 60
```

C. PROGRESSIVE PRACTICE: ALPHABET

If you are not using the GDP software, turn to page SB-7 and follow the directions for this activity.

D. PROGRESSIVE PRACTICE: NUMBERS

If you are not using the GDP software, turn to page SB-11 and follow the directions for this activity.

LANGUAGE ARTS

E. Study the rules at the right.

E. ADJECTIVES AND ADVERBS AND AGREEMENT

RULE ▶ , adjective/adverb

Use comparative adjectives and adverbs (*-er, more,* and *less*) when referring to two nouns or pronouns; use superlative adjectives and adverbs (*-est, most,* and *least*) when referring to more than two.

The shorter of the two training sessions is the more helpful one.

The longest of the three training sessions is the least helpful one.

RULE , agreement nearer noun

If two subjects are joined by *or, either/or, neither/nor,* or *not only/but also,* make the verb agree with the subject nearer to the verb.

Neither the coach nor the players are at home.
Not only the coach but also the referee is at home.
But: Both the coach and the referee are at home.

Edit the sentences to correct any errors in grammar.

8 Of the three printers, the faster one was the most expensive.
9 Of the two phones purchased, the first one is the better model.
10 The quietest of the five printers is also the less expensive.
11 Not only the manager but also the employees wants to attend.
12 Neither the printer nor the monitors is in working order.
13 Either Mr. Cortez or his assistants have to sign the order.
14 Coffee or soft drinks is available for the afternoon session.
15 Not only the manual but also the software were mailed.

FORMATTING

F. FILLING IN FORMS

Many business forms can be created by using templates that are provided within word processing software. When a template is opened, a generic form is displayed on the screen. Specific information that is appropriate for that form may then be added.

Template forms contain data fields that correspond to blank sections on printed forms. For example, a memo template may include the guide words *To:*, *CC:*, *From:*, *Date:*, and *Re*: for the subject. Templates are usually designed so that you can replace data in fields easily by clicking in the field and typing or by selecting the information you want to replace and typing. Built-in styles are also readily available.

You can customize a generic template by filling in repetitive information (such as the company name and telephone number) and save it as a new template. Then each time you open that newly created template, the customized information appears automatically.

Go To Word Processing Manual

G. WORD PROCESSING: CORRESPONDENCE TEMPLATES

Study Lesson 101 in your word processing manual. Complete all of the shaded steps while at your computer. Then format the jobs that follow.

DOCUMENT PROCESSING

Form 101-1
Memo Template

Note: You may want to read and print the information in the template before deleting it.

1. Select the first memo template listed in your word processing software.
2. Follow the directions on the template to type the information for this memo using the built-in styles as needed.
3. Use the default style for the current date.
4. Type the rest of the information in the copy shown on the next page.

(Continued on next page)

To: Naoe Okubo Senior Graphic Artist

CC: Mr. Roy Phillips, Marketing Manager

From: Gloria Hernandez, Vice President

Date: Current Date

Re: Website Redesign

¶ Our web site needs a complete redesign and reorganization. I know this assignment is a major challenge, and I have full confidence in your skill and ability. Within the next week, you should contact 5 web design firms and make arrangements for a formal presentation to you and your staff. Please invite Roy Phillips and his staff in Marketing as well. When you have chosen the two best candidates, submit your findings to key executives in a presentation. The better of the two will then be chosen.

adjective/adverb

adjective/adverb

¶ Because our web site is crucial to our sales and marketing efforts you must make this assignment a top priority. If you need temporary help to support you in your efforts, let me know. Thank you for your continued good work, Naoe. I look forward to your presentation and your recomendations.

urs

Form 101-2

Letter Template With Enclosure Notation

1. Select the first letter template listed in your word processing software.
2. Follow the template directions to type the information for this letter using the built-in styles as needed.
   Note: There is no company slogan.
3. The company name is `Global Web Resources`.
4. Type each line of the return address on a separate line similar to the inside address on the letter.

   The return address is as follows:
   `575 Eighth Avenue, Suite 1104`
   `New York, NY 10018`
   `212-555-3495`
   `www.globalwebresources.com`
5. Use the default spacing provided by the template between the date and the inside address.
6. Type the rest of the information into the template as indicated in the copy below using standard business letter format for a block-style letter.

Current Date | Naoe Okubo | Contempo Fashions | 22802 Soledad Canyon | Santa Clarita, CA 91355 | Dear Ms Okubo:

¶ Thank you for your request for more information on Web page design, layout, and graphics. I have enclosed some brochures that address some of your questions.

¶ Ms. Ina Phillips is our senior account manager in your area. Either her staff members or Ms. Phillips is going to schedule an appointment with you and your staff for a formal presentation of our design portfolios this week. The best way to answer your questions and to help you reach a decision is to

agreement nearer noun

(Continued on next page)

have you see examples of some of the Web sites we have developed for other clients in the fashion industry. I know you will be impressed by the creativity and innovative concepts that Global Web Resources is known for in this business.

¶ If you would like a preview now, please go to www.globalwebresources.com and click the link entitled Professional Images to see some of our best designs. Again, thank you for your interest in our services.

adjective/adverb

Sincerely, | Linda Vigil | Vice President | urs | Enclosures

Form 101-3

Memo Template With Attachment Notation

To: Roy Phillips, Marketing Manager | **CC:** Gloria Hernandez, Vice President | **From:** Naoe Okubo, Senior Graphics Artist | **Date:** Current Date | **Re:** Web Site Redesign

¶ I have contacted five Web design firms for formal presentations in our executive boardroom. A schedule of the meeting dates and times is attached. Because Ms. Hernandez has indicated that this assignment is to take top priority, not only current projects but also future work is to be put on hold. If you need any temporary help with any projects in progress, let me know.

agreement nearer noun

¶ The Web design firms that have been scheduled are very innovative and creative. The presentations should be exciting. Ask your staff to prepare for the meeting by visiting the Web sites and doing some research on each company. Please forward this memo to the members of your staff.

urs | Attachment

Select the first memo template listed in your word processing software.

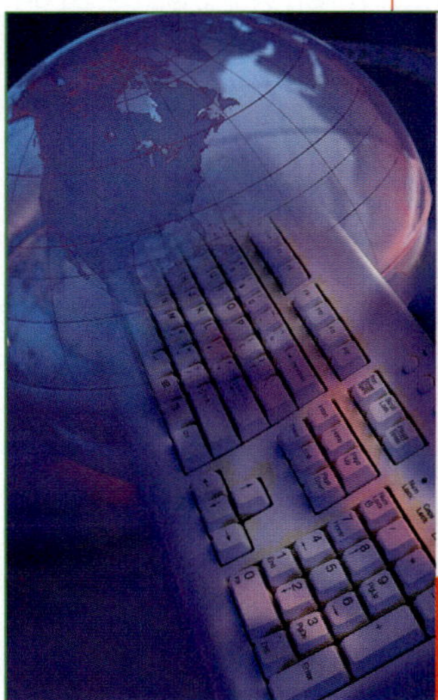

Keyboarding CONNECTION

Transferring Text From a Web Page

Have you ever wished you could copy the text from a Web page? You can!

To select the desired text to copy, click in front of the text and drag to the end of it. (If the text won't highlight, try to click at the end of the desired text and drag backwards.) To copy the Web text, from the Edit menu, select Copy. Open your word processing document. Position the cursor where you want to paste the text. From the Edit menu of the word processor, select Paste. The text appears in the word processing document.

When you copy text information from the Web, you must cite the source in your word processing document by giving the URL (Web page address), Web page name, and author, if given.

YOUR TURN Open a Web page. Copy some text and paste it in a word processing document.

Using Report Templates

GOALS

- Type at least 48wpm/5'/5e
- Format reports using a template

A. Type 2 times.

A. WARMUP

```
     I am glad the office measures just 15 x 23* (*feet)      11
because the carpet is quite expensive! At $64/yard, we        21
can't afford any mistakes; contact v&zcarpets@mail.com.       33
| 1 | 2 | 3 | 4 | 5 | 6 | 7 | 8 | 9 | 10 | 11 | 12
```

SKILLBUILDING

B. PACED PRACTICE

If you are not using the GDP software, turn to page SB-14 and follow the directions for this activity.

Careers in wholesale businesses use keyboard input to get products to customers quickly and efficiently.

C. Take two 5-minute timings. Review your speed and errors.

Goal: At least 48wpm/5′/5e

C. 5-MINUTE TIMING

In their quest to complete school and enter the job 11
market, students will discover quickly that they have more 23
to learn about office politics. At the beginning of their 35
careers, students become acquainted with the importance of 47
power, the office grapevine, and building relationships. 58
Power can be defined as the possession of control or 69
command over others. In any type of business there are two 81
types of power, formal and informal. The people listed in 93
the company directory in positions of authority have the 104
formal power. Support personnel, such as secretaries and 115
office assistants, have informal power. 123
Students understand quickly the importance of the 133
grapevine in office politics. Sometimes the grapevine is 144
portrayed as gossip, and workers need to determine that 155
this type of information could be harmful. However, the 166
grapevine can be a good source for learning procedures for 178
working within the organization; this type of information 190
is vital for career success. 196
Building good relationships with coworkers is also 206
important. Successful workers assist others in becoming a 218
part of the team. They realize that working together will 230
develop a strong team spirit that gets things done. 240

| 1 | 2 | 3 | 4 | 5 | 6 | 7 | 8 | 9 | 10 | 11 | 12

FORMATTING

Go To Word Processing Manual

D. WORD PROCESSING: REPORT TEMPLATES

Study Lesson 102 in your word processing manual. Complete all of the shaded steps while at your computer. Then format the jobs that follow.

DOCUMENT PROCESSING

Form 102-4

Report Template

Note: You may want to read and print the information in the template before deleting it.

1. Select the first report template listed in your word processing software.
2. Type the information for this report using the built-in template styles as needed.
3. On the title page, type the following address:
   `575 Eighth Avenue, Suite 1104`
   `New York, NY 10018`
   `212-555-3495`
   `www.globalwebresources.com.`
4. The company name is `Global Web Resources`.
5. The title is `Web Design Proposal`.
6. The subtitle is `Strategies for the Online Presence of Contempo Fashions`.
7. Use the same title and subtitle on the second page of the report.
8. Type the rest of the information into the template as indicated in the copy below.

Introduction

¶ Two major issues need addressing in terms of the website design for Contempo Fashions. The sites most obvious weakness is a lack of unity. The content seems to be out of sync with the design. The division is definitely noticeable to the casual observe.

¶ Often those in charge of content don't have any background in html or coding of any kind, and fell locked into the current design because they simply don't know what there options are. Those in charge of the design can get caught up in trying to create an attractive page that doesn't really effectively work with the content. Global Web Resources is in it business of providing workable solutions that will address both of these needs.

Content Issues

¶ The content is by far the first and most important element in a web site. If the content is not effective, it doesnt matter how attractive the design is because noone will bother to read beyond the first page or even the first line. Spelling and grammar must be checked with meticuluos care. The credibility of your company is at stake. The readability of the web site can be improved dramatically. Headings, subheadings, bullets and numbers are critical in making your pages readable. Visitors to your site scan for major headings and want to move quickly and efficiently to any items of interest. Visual separation between paragraphs is critical for readability. The use of

(Continued on next page)

whitespace created by inserting blank lines between paragraphs is generally more effective than indenting paragraphs. Short lines and short pages make readers want to look at your site pages rather than avoid them.

Design Issues

¶ The design of the web site is done well overall. Appropriate fonts, colors, and art were used in a manner that complements the image of Contempo Fashions. The site's navigation is intuitive and easy to use. However, the design is dated and needs a new look.

¶ The 2 groups that are now managing the site must be given guidance in working together to produce a unified site that is both attractive and effective. The goals of the design group and those in charge of content must be brought into alignment in order to make the content work within the context of the current design. Global Web Resources has a web design solution that will bring the needs of both these groups into alignment. Your redesigned site will be visually appealing, informative, and intuitive to the visitor. We I look forward to our meeting detailed presentation this week.

Form 102-5

Report Template

Open the file for Form 102-4 and make the following changes:

1. On the title page, change the address as follows:
   8502 N. Ashley Street
   Tampa, FL 33604
   813-555-1205
   www.CTI.com.
2. The company name is CompuTek International.
3. Change the report title both on the title page and on the first page of the report to Web Site Proposal.
4. Change the report subtitle both on the title page and on the first page of the report to Content and Design Recommendations for Contempo Fashions.
5. Delete the second paragraph under the heading "Introduction."
6. Delete the second paragraph under the heading "Content Issues."
7. Delete the last paragraph of the report.
8. Move the insertion point to the end of the first paragraph under the heading "Design Issues," and press ENTER 1 time.
9. Use the Heading 1 style to add the heading Solutions.
10. Move to the end of the report, and add the following paragraphs.
    Paragraph 1:
    Your Web site should always have new and updated content so that your visitors will have good reason to return. If you continue with your current Web site plan, the maintenance of your site will become a major responsibility. Hundreds of files will need to be maintained whenever you want to make a fundamental change to your site.

(Continued on next page)

The best approach is to let your writers post new content themselves without having to worry about design issues. This is accomplished through a database-driven Web site.

Paragraph 2:

Building a database-driven Web site requires a great deal of technical expertise and tools such as scripting languages and relational database software. Your operating system must be compatible with these languages and databases. Server-side programming is also critical here. CompuTek International would build a database-driven site design and host the site to minimize technical troubleshooting issues. We look forward to our meeting this week.

A career in the exciting and ever-changing fashion industry demands an eye for color and design as well as keyboarding skills.

Lesson 103

Designing Letterheads

GOALS

- Improve speed and accuracy
- Refine language arts skills in composing
- Design letterheads

A. Type 2 times.

A. WARMUP

```
     Does Quentin know if 1/2 of the January order will be   11
ready? At 5:30 about 46% of the orders still hadn't been      22
mailed! Mr. Gray expects a very sizable loss this month.      33
| 1 | 2 | 3 | 4 | 5 | 6 | 7 | 8 | 9 | 10 | 11 | 12
```

SKILLBUILDING

B. DIAGNOSTIC PRACTICE: ALPHABET

If you are not using the GDP software, turn to page SB-2 and follow the directions for this activity.

C. These paragraphs are made up of very short words, requiring the frequent use of the SPACE BAR. Do not pause before or after pressing the SPACE BAR. Type the paragraph 2 times.

C. TECHNIQUE PRACTICE: SPACE BAR

```
     He had the car in the shop and knew that the cost for
the work might be high. If the bill for the work was to be
more than he could pay, he knew that he would skip it. It
did not make any sense to put more money into the old car.
     If you are near the old shop, come in to see if you can
pay the bill at that time. If you are not able to pay it at
that time, you can come back to see us when you are able.
```

LANGUAGE ARTS

D. COMPOSING A MEMO

Compose the body of a memo to explain basic design guidelines. Refer to page 409—Section E, Designing a Form—frequently. Use the following suggestions for composing each paragraph:

Paragraph 1. Explain that a simple, balanced design is essential and that typefaces, attributes, and sizes should be limited.

Paragraph 2. Explain that white space should be used to make text easier to read and graphics easier to see.

Paragraph 3. Explain that word processing software is a powerful tool that makes experimenting easy.

FORMATTING

E. DESIGNING A FORM

Use the following guidelines to design an attractive, effective form:

1. Keep all elements of your design simple and balanced.
2. Limit the number of typefaces (fonts), attributes (bold, italics, etc.), and sizes. Using two typefaces is a good rule of thumb.
3. Use white space liberally to separate and open up text and graphics.
4. Use different alignments (left, center, right, and full) to add interest and emphasis.
5. Experiment and change—word processing software makes both easy to do.

Go To Word Processing Manual

F. WORD PROCESSING: SMALL CAPS AND TEXT BOXES

Study Lesson 103 in your word processing manual. Complete all of the shaded steps while at your computer. Then format the jobs that follow.

DOCUMENT PROCESSING

Form 103-6

Letterhead Form

Note: When creating, sizing, or positioning a text box, switch to a whole-page view. When typing text, switch to a page-width view or larger as desired. As you add information to the text box, adjust the size of the text box as needed.

1. Change the left and right margins to 0.25 inch, and press ENTER 2 times.
2. Apply a border to the bottom of the second blank line.
3. Insert a picture of an elementary school or kindergarten.
4. Drag and size the picture so that it looks like the one in the illustration.
5. Create a text box about the size and in the same position as the one in the illustration to hold the business name.
6. Remove the line around the text box, and change the fill to none.
7. Change to Arial 18 point small caps, and center and type `Tutor Time`.
8. Change the font color as desired to coordinate with the picture.
9. Create a text box about the size and in the same position as the one in the illustration to hold the address of the business.
10. Remove the line around the text box, and change the fill to none.
11. Change the font to Arial 10 point, and right-align and type the lines of the address:

```
4219 Richmond Ave., Suite 205
Houston, TX 77027
713-555-7337
www.tutortime.com
```

(Continued on next page)

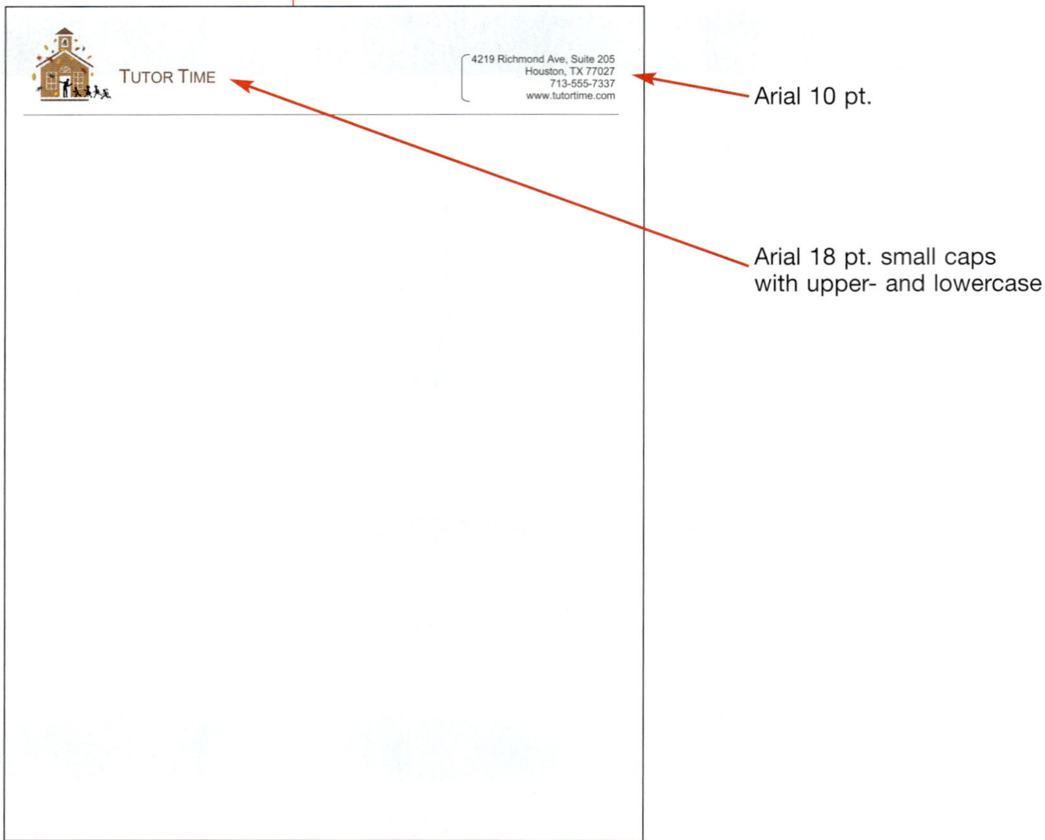
TUTOR TIME

4219 Richmond Ave, Suite 205
Houston, TX 77027
713-555-7337
www.tutortime.com

Form 103-7

Letterhead Form

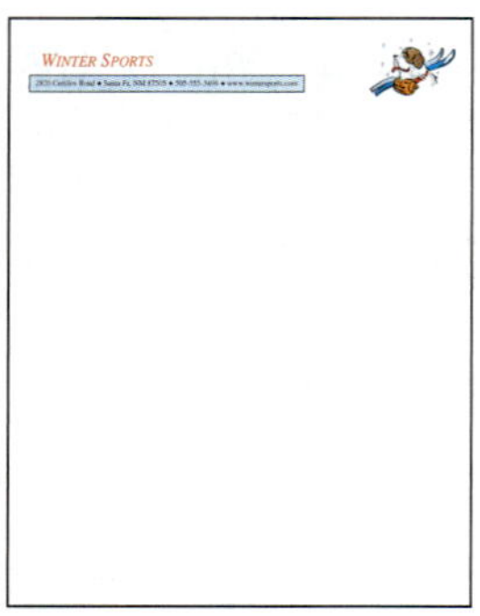

1. Press ENTER 2 times, and insert a picture of your favorite winter sport.
2. Drag and size the picture so that it looks like the one in the illustration.
3. Create a text box about the size and in the same position as the one in the illustration to hold the name of the business.
4. Remove the line around the text box, and change the fill to none.
5. Change to Times New Roman 24 point small caps, and type `Winter Sports` with upper- and lowercase.
6. Change the font color of the business name to coordinate with one of the colors in the picture.
7. Create a text box about the size and in the same position as the one in the illustration to hold the address of the business.
8. Change the font to Times New Roman 10 point and center and type the lines of the address:
   `2820 Cerillos Road`
   `Santa Fe, NM 87505`
   `505-555-3496`
   `www.wintersports.com.`
9. Insert a diamond-shaped symbol between each item in the address block as shown in the illustration. Insert 1 space before and after the symbol.
10. Add a fill to the textbox to coordinate with one of the colors in the picture.

(Continued on next page)

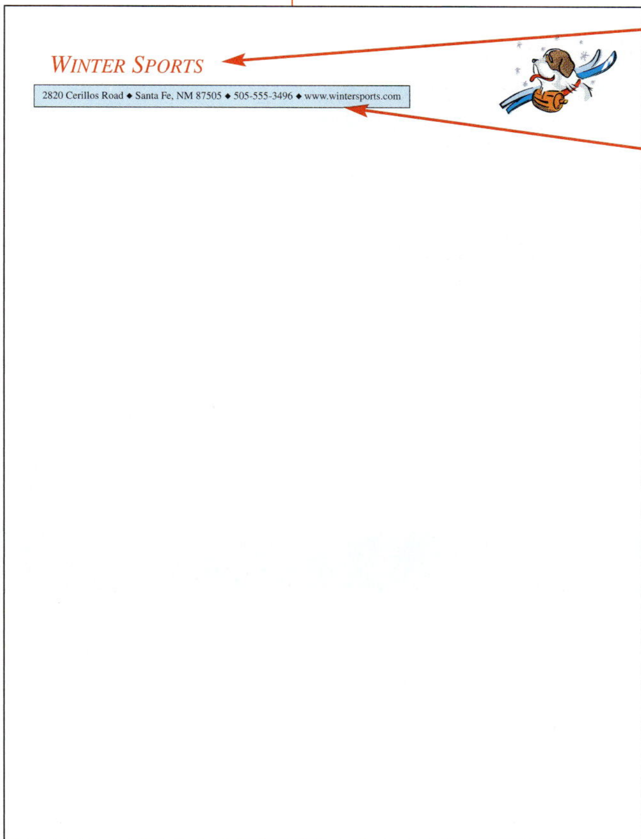

Form 103-8

Letterhead Form

1. Create a letterhead design of your own—for you personally, for your school, or for a business.
2. Insert at least one picture that enhances the theme of the letterhead.
3. Remember to include complete information in the address block.
4. Try using other fonts that you have not yet applied—experiment with point sizes and attributes.

STRATEGIES FOR *Career Success*

Designing the Page for Readability

A well-designed document is appealing to the eye, easy to read, and shows you are professional and competent. Follow these simple guidelines to increase the readability of your documents.

Use white space (e.g., empty space) to make material easier to read by separating it from the other text. Side margins should be equal. Create white space by varying paragraph length. The first and last paragraphs should be short—three to five typed lines.

Use bulleted or numbered lists to emphasize material. Lists are normally indented on the left. Make sure all the items in the list are grammatically parallel in structure. Use headings to introduce new material. Use full caps sparingly. Consider desktop publishing software to visually enhance your document. Remember to balance graphics, lists and text.

YOUR TURN Review a document you have recently written. What page design and format techniques did you use to make the document more readable?

Lesson 104

Designing Notepads

GOALS

- Type at least 48wpm/5'/5e
- Design notepads

A. Type 2 times.

A. WARMUP

```
     This series* (*6 films, 28 minutes) by J Zeller goes     11
beyond the "basics" of computers. Viewers keep requesting     23
an extension on the dates; this includes 3/2, 5/5, and 8/9.   35
| 1 | 2 | 3 | 4 | 5 | 6 | 7 | 8 | 9 | 10 | 11 | 12
```

SKILLBUILDING

B. MAP

Follow the GDP software directions for this exercise in improving keystroking accuracy.

Retail sales management opportunities require excellent keyboarding skills in the day-to-day business operation.

C. Take two 5-minute timings. Review your speed and errors.

Goal: At least 48wpm/5′/5e

C. 5-MINUTE TIMING

Employers are always searching for people who have 10
saleable skills. Having saleable skills makes you unique 21
and desirable as an employee. Developing skills such as 32
tenacity, a good sense of humor, positive attitude, ability 44
to get along with coworkers, a pleasing personality, and 55
the ability to manage your time and prioritize your work 66
could help you find a good job. 72

A tenacious person is persistent and maintains strong 83
work habits. He or she does not give up on any task easily 95
and always expects to complete the assigned tasks. 105

A good sense of humor and a positive attitude are two 116
traits that can help a person advance on the job. Although 128
there are times to be serious at work, sometimes you have 140
to look at things humorously. If you maintain a positive 151
attitude, other workers will like working with you. 162

When you acquire the skills to manage your time and 172
prioritize your work, you will be successful in anything 183
you try to do. When you are given an assignment, ask for 195
guidelines so that you will know what needs to be done and 207
in what order. Then try to complete the assignment in a 218
timely fashion. The skills may be difficult to learn, but 230
you will be glad you can manage your time and work. 240

| 1 | 2 | 3 | 4 | 5 | 6 | 7 | 8 | 9 | 10 | 11 | 12

FORMATTING

Go To Word Processing Manual

D. WORD PROCESSING: PRINT OPTIONS

Study Lesson 104 in your word processing manual. Complete all of the shaded steps while at your computer. Then format the jobs that follow.

DOCUMENT PROCESSING

Form 104-9

Notepad Form

Many ink jet printers do not print beyond the bottom half inch on a sheet of paper. Keep this in mind when positioning objects at the bottom of a page.

1. Press ENTER 2 times, and insert a picture of an office desk or some picture related to an office notepad.
2. Drag and size the picture so that it looks similar to the one in the illustration.
3. Create a text box about the size and in the same position as the one in the illustration to hold the words "From the Desk of Your Name."
4. Remove the line around the text box, and change the fill to none.
5. Change to Arial Bold 36 point, and center and type `From the Desk of Your Name` inside the text box.
6. Create a text box about the size and in the same position as the one in the illustration to hold the checkbox list at the bottom of the notepad.
7. Remove the line around the text box, and change the fill to none.
8. Insert a checkbox symbol using Wingdings Italic 28 point. Space 1 time.
9. Change to Arial Italic 28 point, type `Urgent` inside the text box, and press ENTER 1 time.
10. Repeat Steps 8 and 9 for the remaining lines in the checkbox list, adding the words `Do Today` and `Follow-up`.
11. Change to a whole-page view, and select and copy the entire document.
12. Move to the end of the document and insert 3 hard page breaks to create 3 additional blank pages.
13. Paste the copied document into each of the 3 newly created pages.
14. Use the print option to print 4 pages per sheet on 8.5- by 11-inch paper.

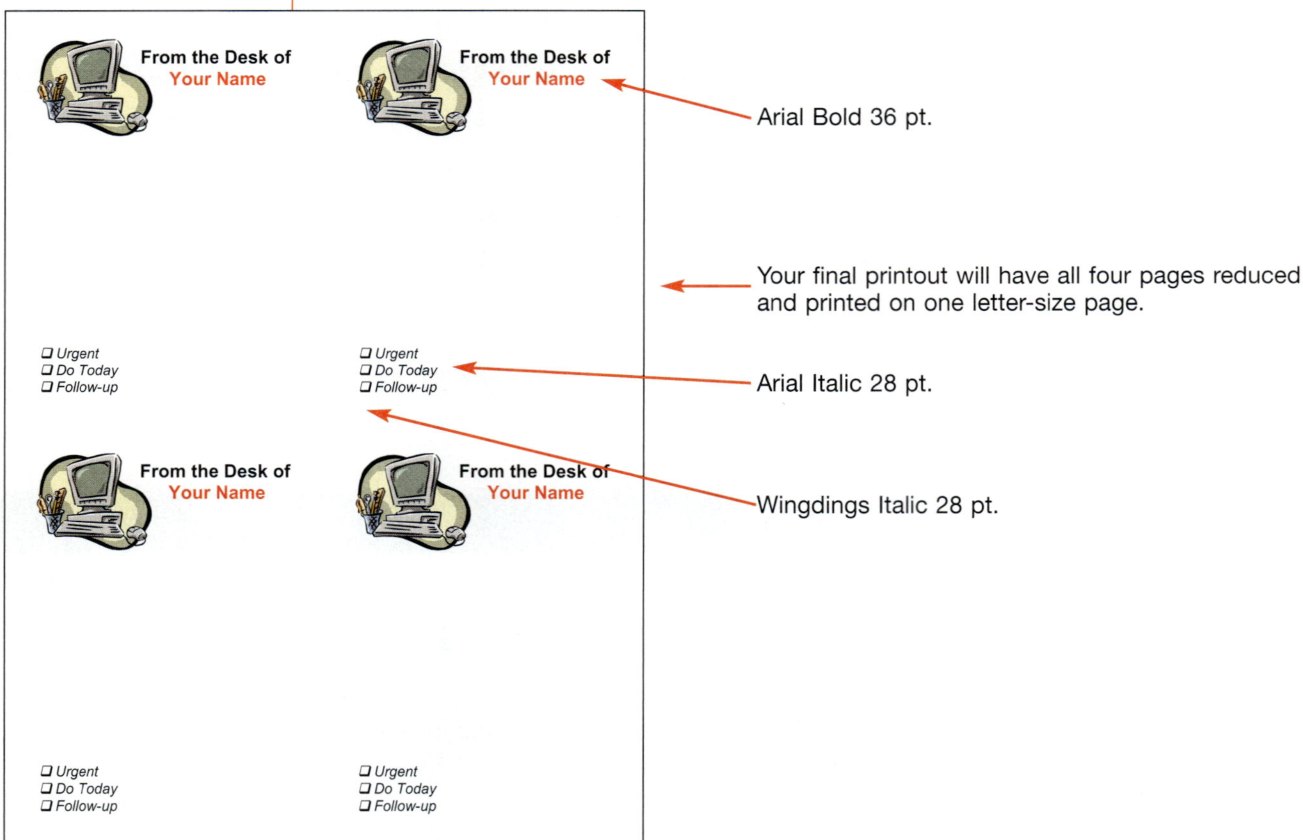

Form 104-10

Notepad Form

1. Press ENTER 2 times, and insert a picture of an office desk or some picture related to a musical note or a personalized office note.
2. Drag and size the picture so that it looks similar to the one in the illustration.
3. Create a text box about the size and in the same position as the one in the illustration to hold the words "Just a Note to Say."
4. Remove the line around the text box, and change the fill to none.
5. Change to a script font of your choice in 48 point bold and italic.
6. Center and type `Just a Note to Say` followed by 1 space and 3 periods with 1 space after each period except the last.
7. Create a text box about the size and in the same position as the one in the illustration to hold the words at the bottom of the notepad.
8. Change to the same script font used in the first text box in 36 point, and center and type `From the Desk of First Name` inside the text box.
9. Change to a whole-page view, and select and copy the entire document.
10. Move to the end of the document, and insert 3 hard page breaks to create 3 additional blank pages.
11. Paste the copied document into each of the 3 newly created pages.
12. Use the print option to print 4 pages per sheet on 8.5- by 11-inch paper.

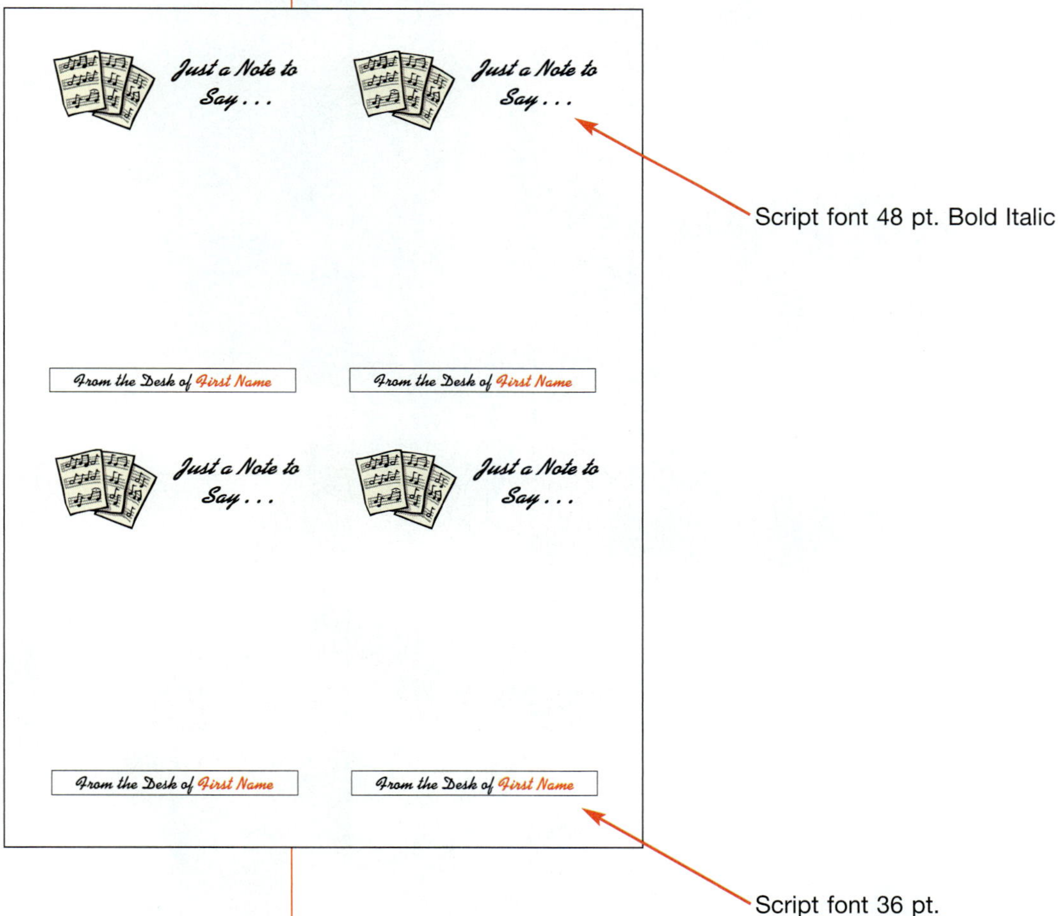

Form 104-11

Notepad Form

1. Create a notepad design of your own—for you personally, for your school, or for a business.
2. Insert at least one picture that enhances the theme of the notepad.
3. Insert at least one text box with a fill.
4. Try using other fonts that you have not yet applied. Experiment with point sizes and attributes.

Careers in retail sales and service may use scanning input for some tasks, but the keyboard is a necessary component to complete business transactions.

Lesson 105

Designing Miscellaneous Office Forms

GOALS

- Improve speed and accuracy
- Refine language arts skills in proofreading
- Design miscellaneous office forms

A. Type 2 times.

A. WARMUP

```
1      Item #876 won't be ordered until 9/10. Did you gather   11
2  all requests and input them exactly as they appeared? Zack  23
3  will never be satisfied until he contacts jack@orders.com.  35
   | 1 | 2 | 3 | 4 | 5 | 6 | 7 | 8 | 9 | 10 | 11 | 12
```

SKILLBUILDING

PPP

PRETEST → PRACTICE → POSTTEST

PRETEST
Take a 1-minute timing. Review your speed and errors.

B. PRETEST: Vertical Reaches

```
4      The man knelt on the lawn and used a knife with skill   11
5  to raise the valve away from the brace. His back ached in   23
6  vain as he crawled over the knoll to fix the flawed valve.  35
   | 1 | 2 | 3 | 4 | 5 | 6 | 7 | 8 | 9 | 10 | 11 | 12
```

PRACTICE
Speed Emphasis:
If you made no more than 1 error on the Pretest, type each *individual* line 2 times.
Accuracy Emphasis:
If you made 2 or more errors, type each *group* of lines (as though it were a paragraph) 2 times.

C. PRACTICE: Up Reaches

```
7  aw away award crawl straw drawn sawed drawl await flaw lawn
8  se self sense raise these prose abuse users serve send seem
9  ki kind kites skill skier skims skips skits kilts king skid
```

D. PRACTICE: Down Reaches

```
10 ac ache track paced brace races facts crack acute back aces
11 kn knob knife kneel knows knack knelt known knoll knot knew
12 va vain vague value valve evade naval rival avail vats vase
```

POSTTEST
Repeat the Pretest timing and compare performance.

E. POSTTEST: Discrimination Practice

F. Take a 1-minute timing on the first paragraph to establish your base speed. Then take four 1-minute timings on the remaining paragraphs. As soon as you equal or exceed your base speed on one paragraph, advance to the next, more difficult paragraph.

F. SUSTAINED PRACTICE: SYLLABIC INTENSITY

```
     People continue to rent autos for personal use or for     11
their work, and the car-rental business continues to grow.     23
When you rent a car, look carefully at the insurance cost.     35
You might also have to pay a mileage charge for the car.       46

     It is likely that a good deal of insurance coverage is    11
part of the standard rental cost. But you might be urged       22
to procure extra medical, property, and collision coverage.    34
If you accept, be ready to see your rental charge increase.    46

     Perhaps this is not necessary, as you may already have    11
the kind of protection you want in a policy that you have      23
at the present time. By reviewing your own auto insurance      35
policy, you may easily save a significant amount of money.     47

     Paying mileage charges could result in a really large     11
bill. This is especially evident when the trips planned        22
involve destinations that are many miles apart. Complete a     34
total review of traveling plans before making a decision.      45
```

LANGUAGE ARTS

G. Compare these lines with lines 25-28 in the Sustained Practice drill above. Edit the lines to correct any errors.

G. PROOFREADING

```
     Paying milage charges could result in a very large
bill. This is especially evident when the trips planned
involve destinations that are manymiles apart. complete a
total review of traveling plans before making a decsion.
```

DOCUMENT PROCESSING

Form 105-12

Directory Form

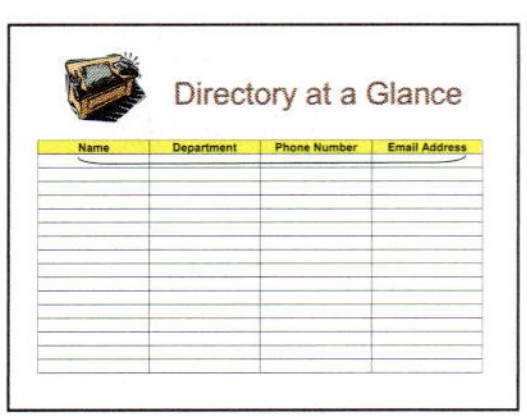

1. Change the page orientation to landscape.
2. Change the top margin to 2.3 inches and the remaining margins to 0.75 inch.
3. Press ENTER 1 time.
4. Create a boxed table with 4 columns and 17 rows.
5. Select the entire table and change the font to Arial Bold 18 point.
6. Type these column headings in Row 1: `Name` | `Department` | `Phone Number` | `Email Address`. Change the alignment in the row to center.
7. Move to the top of the document, and insert a picture associated with a directory in the same position as the one in the illustration.
8. Insert a text box about the size and in the same position as the one in the illustration to hold the heading.
9. Change to Arial 48 point, and center and type `Directory at a Glance` inside the text box.
10. Remove the line around the text box, and change the fill to none.
11. Add shading to the cells in Row 1 of the boxed table, using a color that complements the picture.

(Continued on next page)

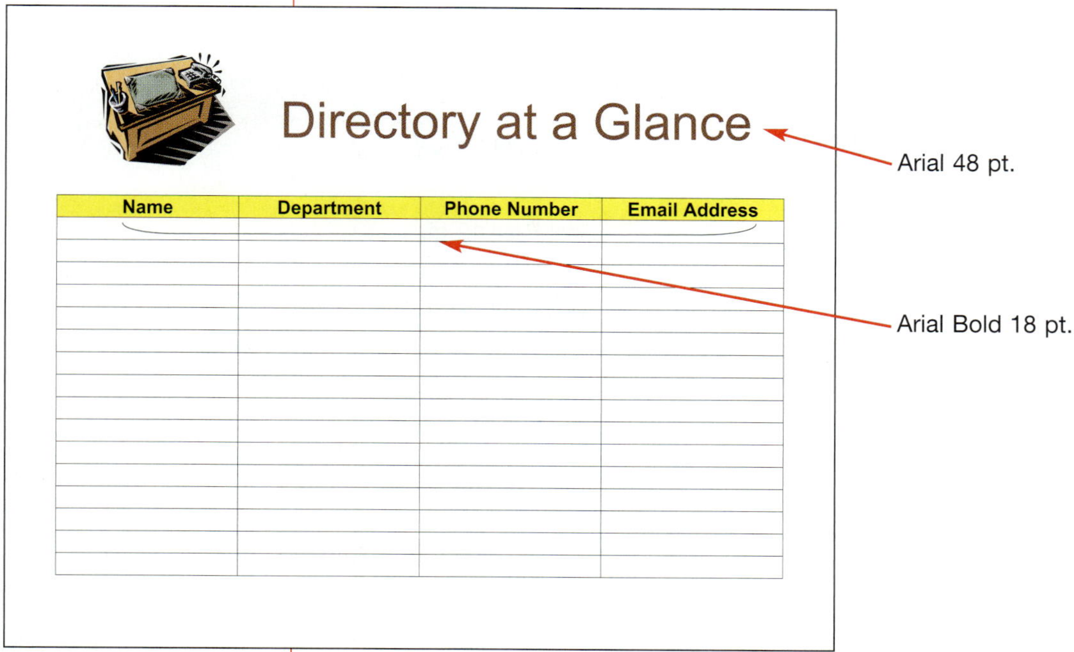

Form 105-13

Sign-In Form

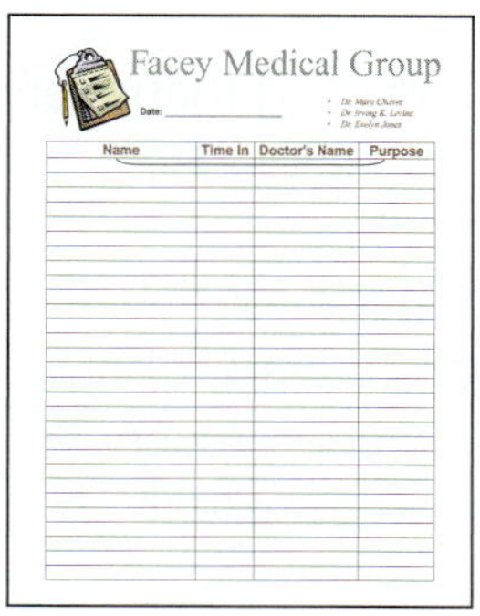

1. Change the top margin to 2 inches and the remaining margins to 0.75 inch.
2. Create a boxed table with 4 columns and 29 rows.
3. Select Row 1 and change the font to Arial Bold 18 point.
4. Type these column headings in Row 1: `Name` | `Time In` | `Doctor's Name` | `Purpose`. Change the alignment in the row to center.
5. Adjust the column widths manually so they appear similar to the illustration.
6. Select Rows 2-29 and change the font to Arial Bold 12 point.
7. Insert a text box about the size and in the same position as the one in the illustration to hold the name of the medical group.
8. Change to Times New Roman 48 point, and center and type `Facey Medical Group`.
9. Remove the line around the text box, and change the fill to none.
10. Insert a picture of an office desk or some clip art related to an office notepad.
11. Create a text box about the size and in the same position as the one in the illustration to hold the date line.
12. Change to Arial Bold 12 point, and type `Date:` followed by a series of underlines to form a signature line similar to the one in the illustration.
13. Remove the fill and the lines around the text box.
14. Create a text box about the size and in the same position as the one in the illustration to hold the names of the doctors.
15. Change to Times New Roman Italic 12 point, and type the following doctors' names in a bulleted list:
    `Dr. Mary Chavez`
    `Dr. Irving K. Levine`
    `Dr. Evelyn Jones`
16. Remove the line around the text box, and change the fill to none.
17. Change the font color of the words on the form as desired to coordinate with the picture.

(Continued on next page)

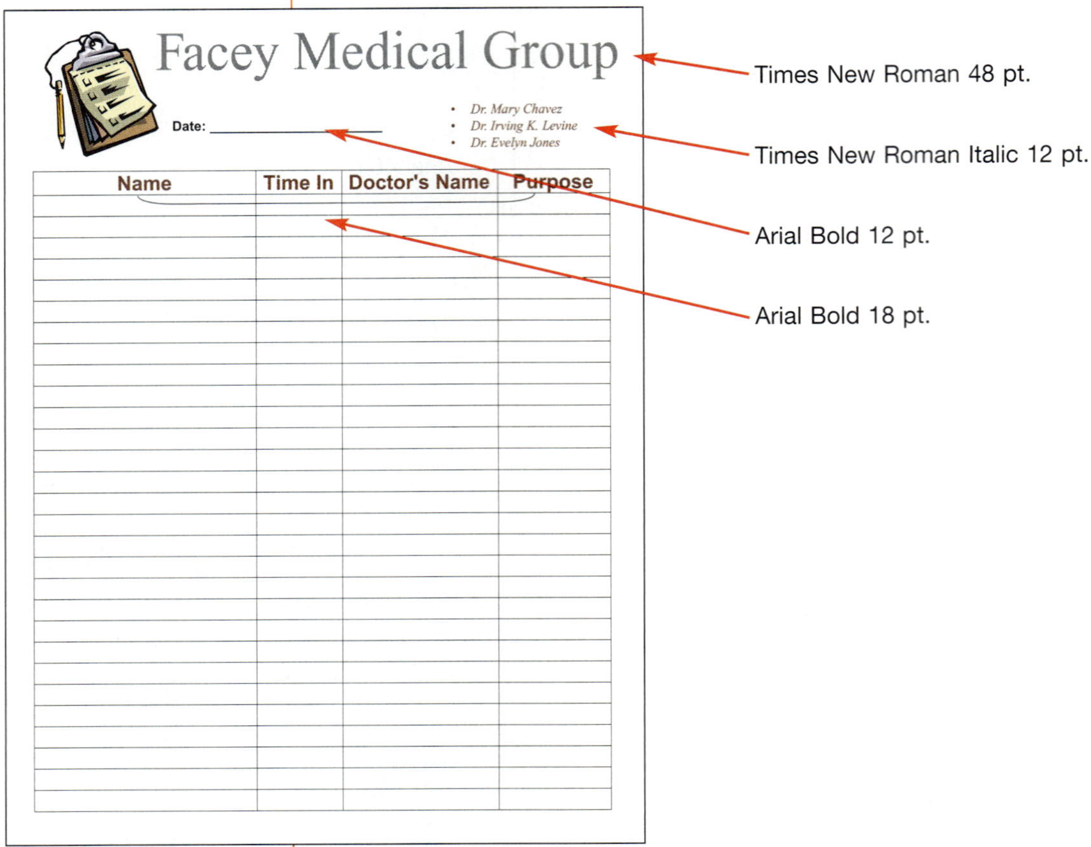

Form 105-14

Memo Template With Attachment Notation

Select the first memo template listed in your word processing software.

Progress Check
Proofreading Check

Documents designated as Proofreading Checks serve as a check of your proofreading skill. Your goal is to have zero typographical errors when the GDP software first scores the document.

To: Gloria Hernandez, Vice President | **CC:** Roy Phillips, Marketing Manager | **From:** Naoe Okubo, Senior Graphics Artist | **Date:** Current Date | **Re:** Web Site Redesign

¶ I have finished evaluating the five Web design firms who made formal presentations to our Web site team last week. The two finalists are Global Web Resources and CompuTek International. Their portfolios and presentations were very impressive. I believe either firm would be an excellent choice. Mr. Phillips agrees with this assessment.

¶ I have arranged for a formal presentation to our key executives for Wednesday afternoon of next week in our corporate dining room. We will have a luncheon first followed by the presentations. I have also attached key information from the portfolios of both firms as well as details of Wednesday's meeting. Please let me know if you need any further information.

urs | Attachment

Unit 22

Designing Office Publications

LESSON 106
Designing Cover Pages

LESSON 107
Designing Announcements and Flyers

LESSON 108
Designing Newsletters: A

LESSON 109
Designing Newsletters: B

LESSON 110
Designing Newsletters: C

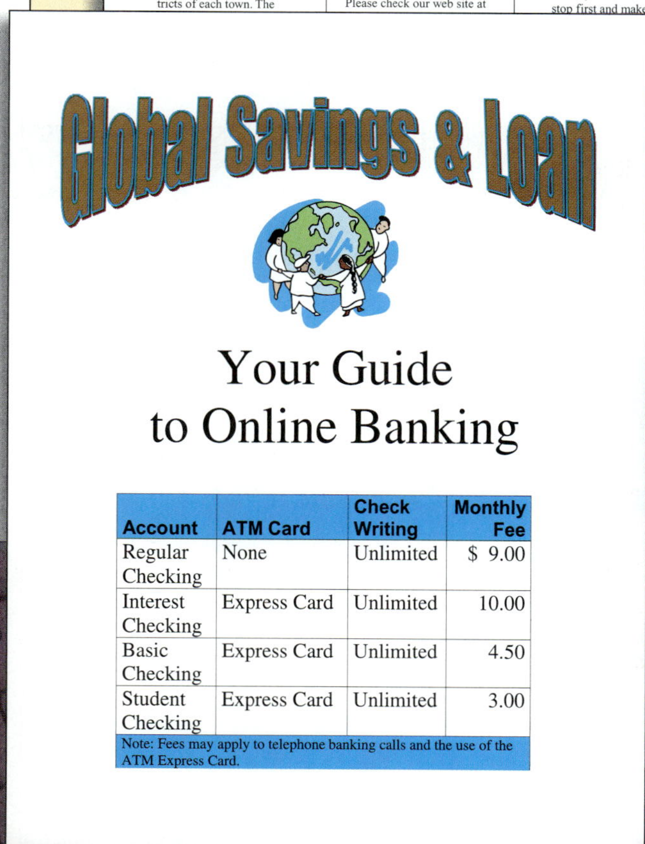

Account	ATM Card	Check Writing	Monthly Fee
Regular Checking	None	Unlimited	$ 9.00
Interest Checking	Express Card	Unlimited	10.00
Basic Checking	Express Card	Unlimited	4.50
Student Checking	Express Card	Unlimited	3.00
Note: Fees may apply to telephone banking calls and the use of the ATM Express Card.			

Lesson 106

Designing Cover Pages

GOALS

- Type at least 49wpm/5′/5e
- Design cover pages

A. Type 2 times.

A. WARMUP

```
     Buzz told us that Flight #7864 got into Phoenix just        11
3 minutes before Vick's! This is quite remarkable when           22
you realize that we never planned for such a "coincidence."      34
| 1 | 2 | 3 | 4 | 5 | 6 | 7 | 8 | 9 | 10 | 11 | 12
```

SKILLBUILDING

B. PROGRESSIVE PRACTICE: ALPHABET

If you are not using the GDP software, turn to page SB-7 and follow the directions for this activity.

Keyboarding CONNECTION

Searching the Yellow Pages

Do you find the Yellow Pages of your phone directory handy? Try the Internet as an alternate source. Many of the Web's search engines have a Yellow Pages feature that is quite useful.

You can use the Yellow Pages feature to search for mailing addresses and phone numbers of businesses and organizations. The Yellow Pages link appears in most leading Internet search engines. These search engines may also provide a map of the location of the business or organization.

The Yellow Pages feature of a search engine is like having all the phone directories in the United States at your fingertips.

YOUR TURN Click the Yellow Pages feature on one of your favorite search engines. Search for a business in your city by name and then by category. Did you retrieve the address and phone number of the business using both search methods?

C. Take two 5-minute timings. Review your speed and errors.

Goal: At least 49wpm/5′/5e

C. 5-MINUTE TIMING

```
     Are women better at some jobs than men? In one recent   11
study, researchers found that women might be better sales    23
managers. Women are better suited for organizations that     34
have a collaborative style of management. The study found    46
other interesting tendencies among women managers.           56
     Females were able to build sales teams that had more    67
commitment to company goals. They could motivate, direct,    79
evaluate, and reward their sales force better than their     90
male counterparts. The study found that the managers were   102
able to reduce stress levels by working closely with their  114
teams, and workers were more satisfied with their jobs and  126
happier with their pay. Staff turnover was also reduced.    137
The team building and nurturing skills of female sales      148
managers may be what some companies need to be successful.  160
     This study also compared sales in companies using      170
controls based on behavior with sales in companies using    181
controls based on outcome. Companies with sales based on    192
behavior want to make sales, but they also want to acquire  204
closer relationships with their customers. However, in      215
companies using controls based on outcomes, sales reps are  227
not given exact directions by their managers, and they are  239
usually paid only commissions.                              245
| 1 | 2 | 3 | 4 | 5 | 6 | 7 | 8 | 9 | 10 | 11 | 12
```

FORMATTING

Go To **Word Processing Manual**

D. WORD PROCESSING: WORD ART

Study Lesson 106 in your word processing manual. Complete all of the shaded steps while at your computer. Then format the jobs that follow.

DOCUMENT PROCESSING

Report 106-76

Cover Page

! To ensure that your document is scored properly, you will insert 2 spaces at the beginning of the document.

1. Press the SPACE BAR 2 times, and insert a picture related to vision or reading.
2. Drag and size the picture so that it looks similar to the one in the illustration.
3. Insert word art about the size and in the same position as the one at the top of the illustration with the words `Preferred Optical Vision Plan` in 2 lines as shown. Use the default font.

(Continued on next page)

Many ink jet printers do not print beyond the bottom half inch on a sheet of paper. Keep this in mind when positioning objects at the bottom of a page.

4. Choose a style and color to coordinate with the picture.
5. Create a text box about the size and in the same position as the one at the bottom of the illustration to hold the directory information.
6. Remove the line around the text box, and change the fill to none.
7. Change to Arial Bold 20 point, center and type `Directory of Participating Vision Care Specialists` in 2 lines as shown in the illustration, and press ENTER 2 times.
8. Change to Arial 16 point, center, and type `for all salaried employees of the San Francisco Community College District` in 2 lines as shown in the illustration, and press ENTER 2 times.
9. Change to Arial 18 point, center, and type `September 20--`.
10. Change any of the font colors to coordinate with the picture as desired.

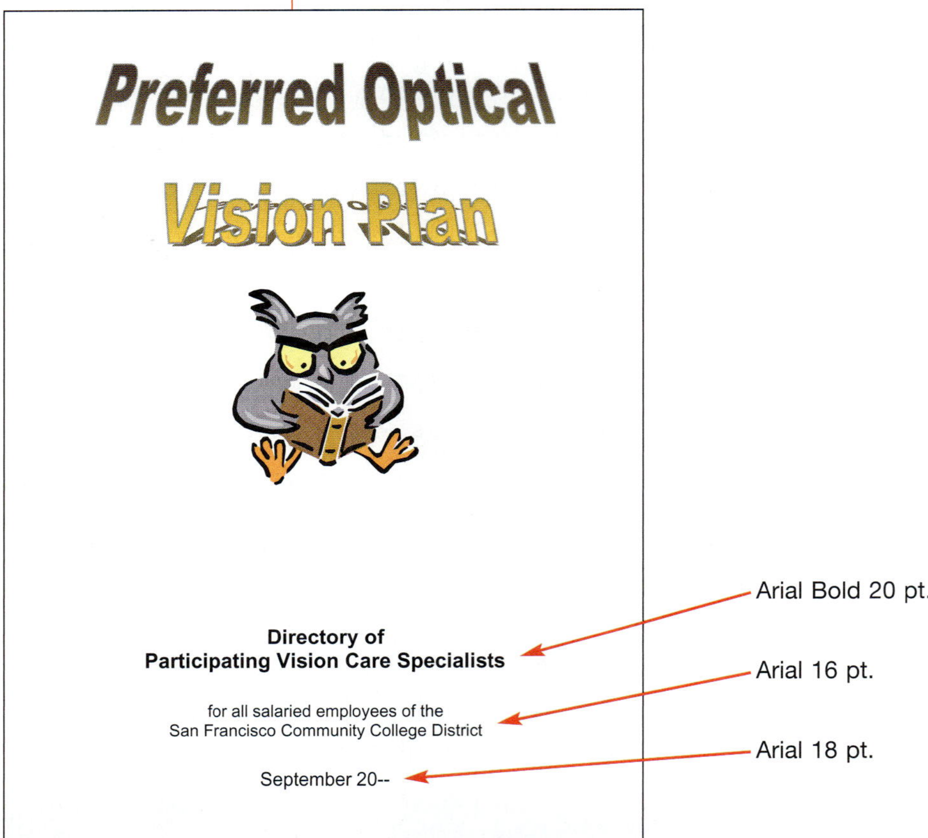

Report 106-77

Cover Page

1. Press the SPACE BAR 2 times, and insert a picture related to dining.
2. Drag and size the picture so that it looks similar to the one in the illustration on page 425.
3. Insert word art about the size and in the same position as the one at the top of the illustration with the words `Sonoma County's Dining Guide` in 2 lines as shown.
4. Choose a style and color for the word art to coordinate with the picture, and use the default font.
5. Create a text box about the size and in the same position as the one at the bottom of the illustration to hold the bulleted list.
6. Remove the line around the text box, and change the fill to none.
7. Change to Arial Bold 24 point, and type the following list unformatted (without bullets):

```
Fine Dining
Midrange
Bargain
```

8. Apply bullets to the list.

(Continued on next page)

9. Create a text box about the size and in the same position as the one at the bottom of the illustration to hold the date.
10. Add a line around the text box, and change the fill to a color that coordinates with the picture.
11. Change to Arial Bold Italic 26 point, and type `Summer 20--`.
12. Change any of the font colors to coordinate with the picture as desired.

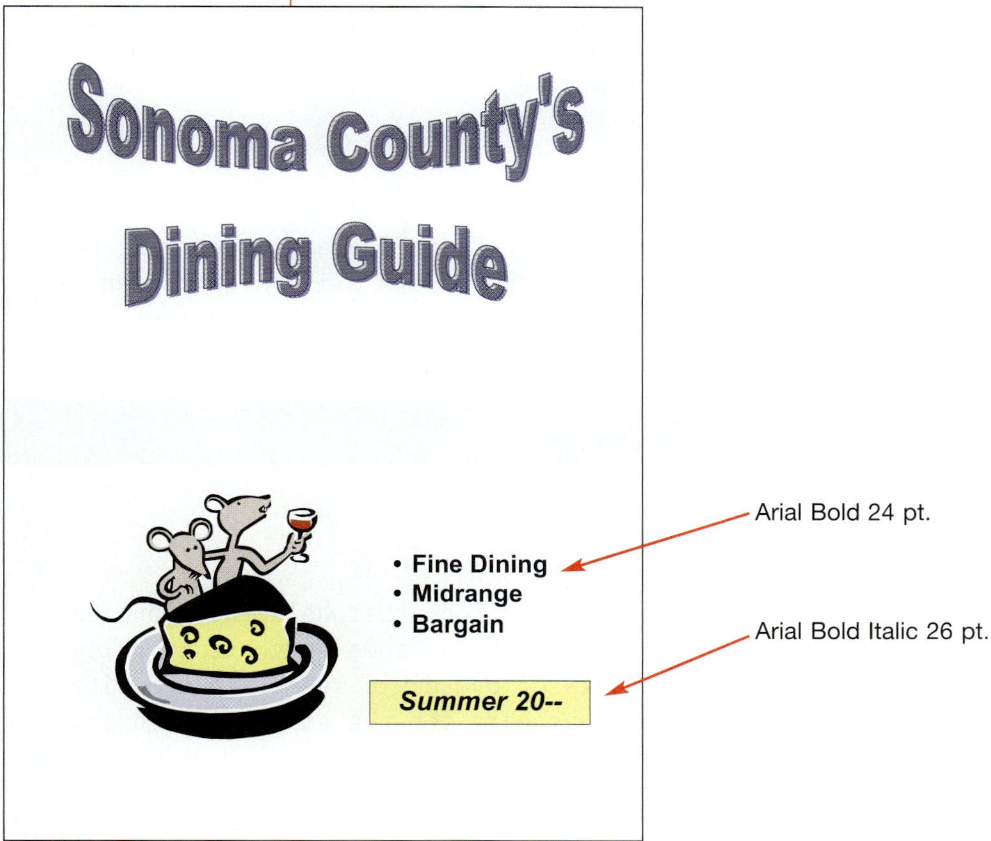

Report 106-78

Cover Page

1. Create a cover page design of your own to be used as the insert for a view binder that holds information for one of your courses.
2. Insert at least one picture related to the subject of the course.
3. Insert at least one text box with a fill.
4. Insert some word art.
5. Change any of the font colors to coordinate with the picture or word art as desired.

Lesson 107

Designing Announcements and Flyers

GOALS

- Improve speed and accuracy
- Refine language arts skills in grammar
- Design announcements and flyers

A. Type 2 times.

A. WARMUP

```
     Does Quentin know if 1/2 of the January order will be   11
ready? At 5:30 about 46% of the orders still hadn't been     22
mailed! Mr. Gray expects a very sizable loss this month.     33
| 1 | 2 | 3 | 4 | 5 | 6 | 7 | 8 | 9 | 10 | 11 | 12
```

SKILLBUILDING

B. Take three 12-second timings on each line. The scale below the last line shows your wpm speed for a 12-second timing.

B. 12-SECOND SPEED SPRINTS

```
Rico will rush to tidy the big room that held the supplies.
Yale is a very fine school that has some very strict rules.
Helen will audit the books of one civic leader in the city.
The man had a name that was hard for the small girl to say.
| | | | 5 | | | | 10 | | | | 15 | | | | 20 | | | | 25 | | | | 30 | | | | 35 | | | | 40 | | | | 45 | | | | 50 | | | | 55 | | | | 60
```

C. Type each sentence on a separate line by pressing ENTER after each sentence. Type 2 times.

C. TECHNIQUE PRACTICE: ENTER

```
Decorate the room. Attend the seminar. Go to the theater.
Watch the inauguration. Go to the rally. See the recital.
Run in the marathon. Bake the bread. Vacuum the bedrooms.
Visit the nursing home. Sell the ticket. Drive the truck.
```

D. DIAGNOSTIC PRACTICE: ALPHABET

If you are not using the GDP software, turn to page SB-2 and follow the directions for this activity.

LANGUAGE ARTS

E. Study the rules at the right.

E. PRONOUNS

RULE ▶ nominative pronoun

Use nominative pronouns (such as *I, he, she, we, they,* and *who*) as subjects of a sentence or clause.

The programmer and <u>he</u> are reviewing the code.

Barb is a person <u>who</u> can do the job.

(Continued on next page)

RULE ▶
objective pronoun

Use objective pronouns (such as *me, him, her, us, them,* and *whom*) as objects of a sentence, clause, or phrase.

The code was reviewed by the programmer and <u>him</u>.
Barb is the type of person <u>whom</u> we can trust.

Edit the sentences to correct any errors in the use of pronouns.

12 We hope they will take all of them to the concert tomorrow.
13 John gave the gift to she on Monday; her was very pleased.
14 If them do not hurry, Mary will not finish her work on time.
15 The book was proofread by her; the changes were made by he.
16 It is up to them to give us all the pages they read today.
17 Me cannot assure they that it will not rain for the picnic.

FORMATTING

Go To
Word Processing Manual

F. WORD PROCESSING: TABLE—MOVE

Study Lesson 107 in your word processing manual. Complete all of the shaded steps while at your computer. Then format the jobs that follow.

DOCUMENT PROCESSING

Report 107-79 ▶
Announcement

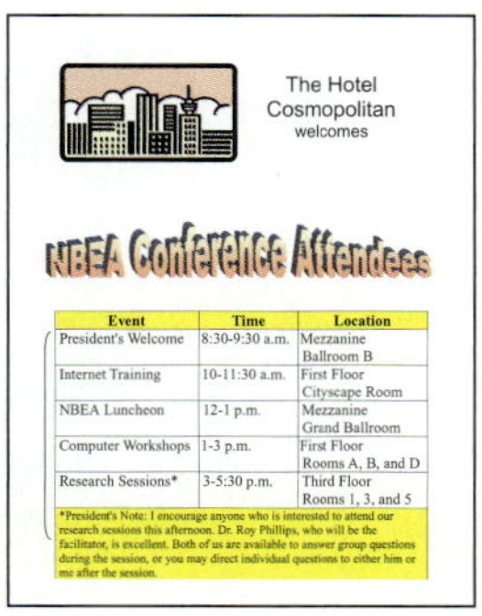

The Hotel
Cosmopolitan
welcomes

NBEA Conference Attendees

Event	Time	Location
President's Welcome	8:30-9:30 a.m.	Mezzanine Ballroom B
Internet Training	10-11:30 a.m.	First Floor Cityscape Room
NBEA Luncheon	12-1 p.m.	Mezzanine Grand Ballroom
Computer Workshops	1-3 p.m.	First Floor Rooms A, B, and D
Research Sessions*	3-5:30 p.m.	Third Floor Rooms 1, 3, and 5
*President's Note: I encourage anyone who is interested to attend our research sessions this afternoon. Dr. Roy Phillips, who will be the facilitator, is excellent. Both of us are available to answer group questions during the session, or you may direct individual questions to either him or me after the session.		

1. Change the left and right margins to 0.5 inch.
2. Press the SPACE BAR 2 times, and insert a picture associated with a large city.
3. Drag and size the picture so that it looks similar to the one in the illustration.
4. Create a text box about the size and in the same position as the one at the top of the illustration to hold the welcoming message.
5. Remove the line around the text box, and change the fill to none.
6. Change to Arial 28 point, center, and type `The Hotel Cosmopolitan` in 2 lines as shown in the illustration, and press ENTER 1 time.
7. Change to Arial 22 point, and center and type `welcomes`.
8. Insert word art about the size and in the same position as the one at the top of the illustration with the words `NBEA Conference Attendees`.
9. Drag and size the word art so that it looks similar to the word art shown in the illustration.
10. Change the word art font for readability if desired.
11. Choose a style and color for the word art to coordinate with the picture.
12. Insert a boxed table with 3 columns and 7 rows, and drag it into position as shown in the illustration.
13. Change to Times New Roman Bold 20 point, and type the centered column headings.
14. Change to Times New Roman 20 point, and type the left-aligned column entries.
15. Type the information in Column C in 2 lines as shown.
16. Merge the cells in Row 7, change to Times New Roman 16 point, and type the information as shown.
17. Automatically adjust the column width for all entries, and drag the table into position again.
18. Add a shading color to the first and last row to coordinate with the word art and picture.

(Continued on next page)

Event	Time	Location
President's Welcome	8:30-9:30 a.m.	Mezzanine Ballroom B
Internet Training	10-11:30 a.m.	First Floor Cityscape Room
NBEA Luncheon	12-1 p.m.	Mezzanine Grand Ballroom
Computer Workshops	1-3 p.m.	First Floor Rooms A, B, and D
Research Sessions*	3-5:30 p.m.	Third Floor Rooms 1, 3, and 5

nominative pronoun
nominative pronoun
objective pronoun
nominative and objective pronouns

*President's Note: I encourage anyone who is interested to attend our research sessions this afternoon. Dr. Roy Phillips, who will be the facilitator, is excellent. Both of us are available to answer group questions during the session, or you may direct individual questions to either him or me after the session.

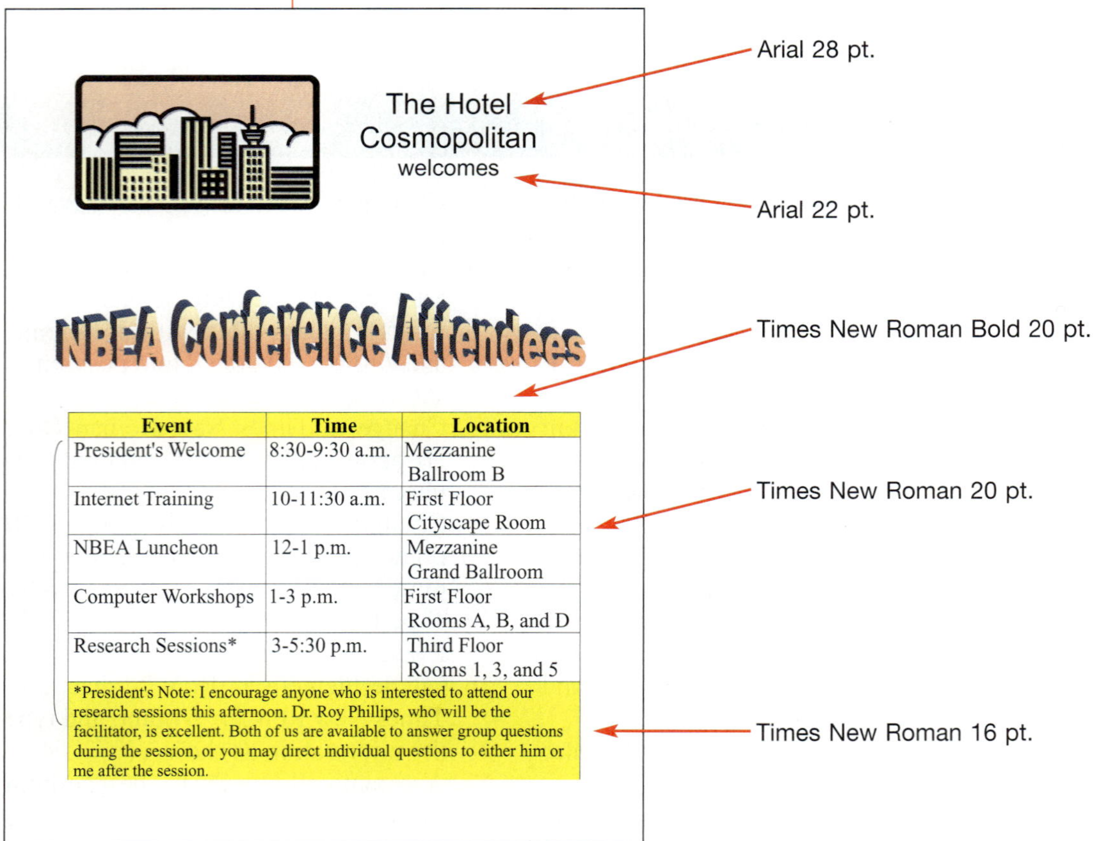

The Hotel Cosmopolitan
welcomes

NBEA Conference Attendees

Event	Time	Location
President's Welcome	8:30-9:30 a.m.	Mezzanine Ballroom B
Internet Training	10-11:30 a.m.	First Floor Cityscape Room
NBEA Luncheon	12-1 p.m.	Mezzanine Grand Ballroom
Computer Workshops	1-3 p.m.	First Floor Rooms A, B, and D
Research Sessions*	3-5:30 p.m.	Third Floor Rooms 1, 3, and 5

*President's Note: I encourage anyone who is interested to attend our research sessions this afternoon. Dr. Roy Phillips, who will be the facilitator, is excellent. Both of us are available to answer group questions during the session, or you may direct individual questions to either him or me after the session.

Report 107-80

Flyer

1. Press the SPACE BAR 2 times, and insert a picture associated with the summer season.
2. Drag and size the picture so that it looks similar to the one shown in the illustration.
3. Insert word art about the size and in the same position as the one at the top of the illustration with the words `Summerset Homes`.
4. Choose a style and color for the word art to coordinate with the picture.

(Continued on next page)

5. Create a text box about the size and in the same position as the one in the middle of the illustration to hold the message.
6. Remove the line around the text box, and change the fill to none.
7. Change to Arial 28 point; center and type `Summerset Homes proudly invites you to the grand opening of our newest group of single-family homes!` as shown in the illustration.
8. Create a text box about the size and in the same position as the one at the bottom of the illustration to hold the address information.
9. Remove the line around the text box, and add a fill using a color to coordinate with the word art and the fill.
10. Change to Arial 12 point; center and type as shown in the illustration:

```
Summerset Homes
520 SW Harbor Way
Portland, OR 97201
800-555-2649
www.Summerset.com
```

11. Insert a star-shaped symbol between each item in the address block as shown in the illustration.
12. Insert 2 spaces before and after the star-shaped symbol.
13. Insert a boxed table with 3 columns and 5 rows, and drag it into position as shown in the illustration.
14. Change to Times New Roman 22 point, and type the column entries.
15. Automatically adjust the column width for all entries, and drag the table into position again.

Shadow Pines	1,235 sq. ft.	$209,990
Ocean View	1,495 sq. ft.	223,990
Country Meadow	1,759 sq. ft.	265,990
Desert Breeze	2,042 sq. ft.	295,990
Valley Oasis	2,537 sq. ft.	322,990

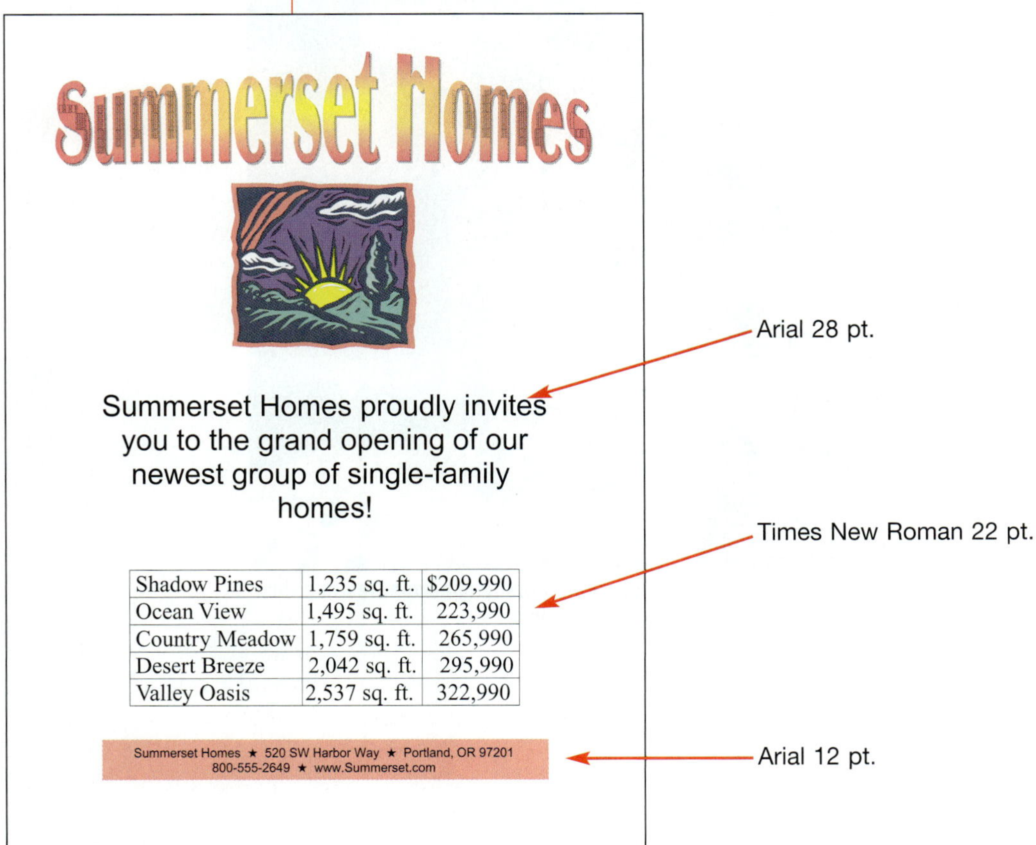

Report 107-81

Announcement or Flyer

1. Create an announcement or flyer design of your own for an upcoming event at work or on campus.
2. Press the SPACE BAR 2 times and insert at least one picture related to the topic of the announcement or flyer.
3. Insert at least one text box with a fill.
4. Insert some word art.
5. Apply color to your fonts to coordinate with the picture or word art.
6. Insert a table that contains information related to the topic of the flyer or announcement.

The demand for multimedia products has created many opportunities in sales careers, all requiring the use of keyboarding skills.

Lesson 108

Designing Newsletters: A

GOALS

- Type at least 49wpm/5′/5e
- Design newsletters

A. Type 2 times.

A. WARMUP

```
     Does Pamela know if Region 29* (*Ventura) has met the    11
sales quota? Their exact target zone is just not clear;       22
they don't have to submit their totals until 4:30 on 5/7.     33
| 1 | 2 | 3 | 4 | 5 | 6 | 7 | 8 | 9 | 10 | 11 | 12
```

SKILLBUILDING

B. PACED PRACTICE

If you are not using the GDP software, turn to page SB-14 and follow the directions for this activity.

STRATEGIES FOR Career Success

Managing Business Phone Time

The average American spends an hour a day on the phone. Phone calls can be extremely distracting from necessary tasks. Time is spent taking the call and following up after the call. You can take steps to reduce wasted time on the phone.

When you make an outgoing call, organize the topics you want to discuss. Have all the materials you need: pencils, paper, order forms, etc. When you take an incoming call, answer it promptly. Identify yourself. It is common to answer the phone with your first and last name (e.g., “Mary Smith speaking.” or “Mary Smith”).

Limit social conversation; it wastes time. Give concise answers to questions. At the end of the call, summarize the points made. End the conversation politely.

YOUR TURN Keep a log of your time on the phone for one day. What is your average conversation time? What can you do to reduce your average phone conversation time?

C. Take two 5-minute timings. Review your speed and errors.

Goal: At least 49wpm/5′/5e

C. 5-MINUTE TIMING

The personal use of computers and the Internet in the 11
workplace has contributed some new issues for employers 22
and employees. Are employees entitled to privacy in the 33
workplace? Do employers have a right to monitor workers 44
who are using company computers for personal use? Should 55
employers impose restrictions regarding Internet activity 67
and email use to protect their businesses? 75

Employers should scrutinize the Internet sites and 85
chat rooms that workers may be accessing on company time. 97
Also, employers may want to check on their workers during 109
office hours to determine if they are using their time 120
effectively on the job. Employers have a right to expect 131
high levels of productivity from their employees during 142
office hours. Employees should realize that excessively 153
using company computers for personal email messages and 164
Internet activity is not acceptable. 171

The company policy on personal computer usage should 182
be explained to all employees. Employees must understand 193
that the surveillance of their computer usage is required 205
in order to protect the business from possible lawsuits. 216
Employees should be given the opportunity to ask questions 228
to make sure they understand the penalties they may incur 240
if they violate the policy. 245

| 1 | 2 | 3 | 4 | 5 | 6 | 7 | 8 | 9 | 10 | 11 | 12

FORMATTING

D. NEWSLETTER DESIGN

Newsletters are an excellent forum for communicating information on a wide range of subjects. A well-planned newsletter will employ all the basic principles of good design. However, because newsletters usually include information on a wide variety of topics, they are generally more complex in their layout.

Most newsletters have the following elements in common: mastheads, main headings and subheadings, text arranged in flowing newspaper-column format using various column widths to add interest, text boxes to emphasize and summarize, pictures to draw readers' attention and interest to a topic, and a variety of borders and fills.

The design of a multipage newsletter must look consistent from one page to the next. This consistency provides unity to the newsletter design and is often achieved through the use of headers and footers.

DOCUMENT PROCESSING

Report 108-82

Newsletter

Reminder: You will finish the newsletter in Lessons 109 and 110.

Follow these steps to create the masthead and footer for the first page of the newsletter shown on page 421.

1. Set all margins at 0.75 inch.
2. Create an open table with 2 columns and 2 rows. Drag the middle column border to the left so the first column is about 1.75 inches wide.
3. Right-align Column B.
4. In Column B, Row 1, change to Times New Roman Bold 48 point, and type `The Traveler's Connection`.
5. Press ENTER 1 time, change to Arial Bold 14 point, and type `A Newsletter From E-Travel.com`.
6. Move to Column A, Row 2, and type `Volume 9, Issue No. 5`.
7. Move to Column B, Row 2, and type `Spring 20--`.
8. Apply borders to the top and bottom of Row 2.
9. In Column A, Row 1, insert a picture associated with world travel.
10. Drag and size the picture so that it looks similar to the one shown in the illustration.
11. Insert a footer, and center and type `Page` followed by 1 space.
12. Insert a page number field and close the footer.

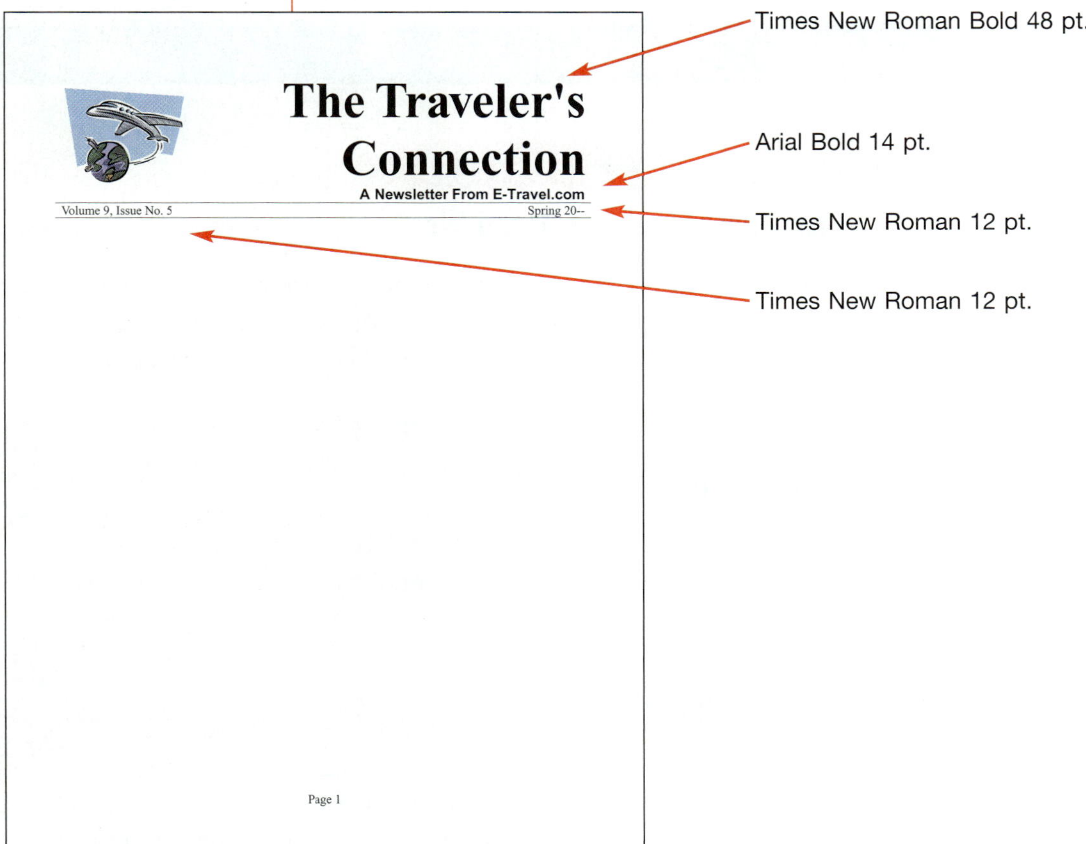

Report 108-83

Newsletter

1. Create a newsletter masthead of your own related to travel and similar to the one in Report 108-82.
2. Use any picture that enhances the purpose of your travel newsletter.

Lesson 109

Designing Newsletters: B

GOALS

- Improve speed and accuracy
- Refine language arts skills in spelling
- Design newsletters

A. Type 2 times.

A. WARMUP

Approximately 90% of the weekly budget was just used 11
to buy equipment. A very sizable amount totaling $12,654 22
was spent on "necessities" as requested by the department! 34

| 1 | 2 | 3 | 4 | 5 | 6 | 7 | 8 | 9 | 10 | 11 | 12

SKILLBUILDING

PPP

PRETEST → PRACTICE → POSTTEST

PRETEST
Take a 1-minute timing. Review your speed and errors.

B. PRETEST: Alternate- and One-Hand Words

A great auditor is eager to spend a minimum of eighty 11
hours to amend a problem. If he assessed a penalty that 22
exceeded the usual fee, I reserve the right to correct it. 34

| 1 | 2 | 3 | 4 | 5 | 6 | 7 | 8 | 9 | 10 | 11 | 12

PRACTICE
Speed Emphasis:
If you made no more than 1 error on the Pretest, type each *individual* line 2 times.
Accuracy Emphasis:
If you made 2 or more errors, type each *group* of lines (as though it were a paragraph) 2 times.

C. PRACTICE: Alternate-Hand Words

also amend maps thrown blame city problem panel formal down
snap rigid lens social visit with penalty right height half
chap usual such enrich shape dish auditor spend eighty kept

D. PRACTICE: One-Hand Words

was only great pupil regret uphill scatter homonym assessed
bed join water nylon target pompon savages minimum exceeded
age hook eager union teased limply reserve opinion attracts

POSTTEST
Repeat the Pretest timing and compare performance.

E. POSTTEST: Alternate- and One-Hand Words

F. Take a 1-minute timing on the first paragraph to establish your base speed. Then take four 1-minute timings on the remaining paragraphs. As soon as you equal or exceed your base speed on one paragraph, advance to the next, more difficult paragraph.

F. SUSTAINED PRACTICE: NUMBERS AND SYMBOLS

Shopping in the comfort and convenience of your own 11
living room has never been more popular than it is right 22
now. Shopping clubs abound on cable channels. You could 33
buy anything from exotic pets to computers by mail order. 44

Sometimes you can find discounts as high as 20% off 11
the retail price; for example, a printer that sells for 22
$565 might be discounted 20% and be sold for $452. You 33
should always investigate quality before buying anything. 44

Sometimes hidden charges are involved; for example, 11
a printer costing $475.50 that promises a discount of 12% 23
($57.06) has a net price of $418.44. However, if charges 34
for shipping range from 12% to 15%, you did not save money. 46

You must also check for errors. Several errors have 11
been noted so far: Invoice #223, #789, #273, and #904 had 23
errors totaling $21.35, $43.44, $79.23, and $91.23 for a 34
grand total of $235.25. As always, let the buyer beware. 45

LANGUAGE ARTS

G. Type these frequently misspelled words, paying special attention to any spelling problems in each word.

G. SPELLING

operations health individual considered expenditures vendor
beginning internal pursuant president union written develop
hours enclosing situation function including standard shown
engineering payable suggested participants providing orders
toward nays total without paragraph meetings different vice

Edit the sentences to correct any misspellings.

The participents in the different meetings voted for hours.
The presdent of the union is working toward a resolution.
The health of each individual must be seriously considered.
Engineering has suggested providing orders for the vendor.
One expanditure has been written off as part of oparations.
He is inclosing the accounts payible record as shown today.

DOCUMENT PROCESSING

Report 109-84

Newsletter (continued)

! Reminder: You will finish the newsletter in Lesson 110.

Open the file for Report 108-82 shown on page 433. Follow these steps to create the second page of the newsletter shown on page 421.

1. Move outside the table below Column A and press ENTER 2 times.
2. Insert File 109, and turn on automatic hyphenation.
3. Carefully place your insertion point in front of the second blank line under the masthead, and select all the newly inserted text including 1 blank line below the last line of text.
4. Create 3 columns with a line between columns.
5. Select the following headings in the newsletter, and change the font to Arial 24 point:
   `A Few Tips for the Smart Traveler`
   `Planning Your Travel Online`
   `Focus on Dallas-Fort Worth`
6. Select the following subheadings in the newsletter and bold them:
   `THE AIRPORT`
   `LOVE FIELD`
   `BETWEEN THE AIRPORT AND TOWN`
7. Place your insertion point in front of the second blank line under the masthead.
8. Insert a table with 1 column and 1 row.
9. Change to Arial 12 point, and type `In This Issue:`.
10. Change to Times New Roman Italic 12 point, and type the following lines:
    `A Few Tips for the Smart Traveler, Page 1`
    `Planning Your Travel Online, Page 1`
    `Focus on Dallas-Fort Worth, Page 2`
    `Texas Tidbits, Page 2`
    `Thistle Hill, Page 2`
11. Add a shading color to the table to coordinate with the picture in the masthead.
12. Insert a picture in the space above each of the bulleted items in the first article on the first page of the newsletter. The pictures should be associated in some way with the topic in each of the bulleted items.
13. Drag and size the pictures so that they look similar to the ones shown in the illustration.
14. Place your insertion point in the blank line above the heading "Planning Your Online Travel," and apply a top border.
15. Place your insertion point in the blank line above the heading "Focus on Dallas-Fort Worth," and apply a top border.

(Continued on next page)

The Traveler's Connection

A Newsletter From E-Travel.com

Volume 9, Issue No. 5 | Spring 20--

In This Issue:
A Few Tips for the Smart Traveler, Page 1
Planning Your Travel Online, Page 1
Focus on Dallas-Fort Worth, Page 2
Texas Tidbits, Page 2
Thistle Hill, Page 2

A Few Tips for the Smart Traveler

We all have visions of the perfect vacation. They usually include a beautiful hotel, a comfortable room, great food, and wonderful entertainment. Unfortunately, sometimes our vision doesn't exactly align itself with reality, and our dream has suddenly turned into a nightmare. You can avoid this situation if you do some smart advance planning.

Here are some smart travel tips that can turn your dream vacation into a reality:

- Do your homework. Your best bet is to find out all you can about your destination before you do anything else. Find a good travel agent, do your own research on the Internet, and buy some good travel books on your destination in your favorite bookstore.

- Carry medications and other essentials with you. To avoid a disaster, carry everything you can't function without in the event that your luggage is lost. These items would include medications, money, tickets, toiletries, visas, passports, eyeglasses, and anything else you can think of that is irreplaceable in the course of a day or two.

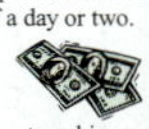

- Buy travel insurance. If you are taking an expensive vacation and are not completely sure you can make it, buying travel insurance is a wise expenditure. Many people today have children and aging parents whose needs are unpredictable.

- Confirm all reservations. Be sure that all your reservations, including hotels, cars, and entertainment, are confirmed and that you have the different confirmation numbers and phone numbers written down. Nothing can ruin a trip faster than finding out that you don't have a place to sleep or suitable transportation.

You will find that if you take these tips to heart, your vacation will be just as wonderful as you imagined!

Planning Your Travel Online

The Internet has opened up a wealth of information that used to be the domain of individual travel agencies. If you have a computer and Internet access, you can make reservations, buy tickets, book entertainment packages, and do any number of other things.

Page 1

Arial 12 pt.

Times New Roman Italic 12 pt.

Arial 24 pt.

Arial 24 pt.

Save hours of time and lots of money by using the Internet wisely when you plan your travel. You can shop for the best airline rates and even name your own price if you are flexible in your travel plans.

Several good books are available to help you use the Internet for your travel plans. Please check our Web site at www.TTC.com for suggested books.

Focus on Dallas-Fort Worth

This month's focus is on the Dallas-Fort Worth area.

THE AIRPORT

The Dallas-Fort Worth International Airport is 17 miles from the business districts of each town. The phone number is 214-555-8888.

Although this is the world's second busiest airport, it is surprisingly easy to use. However, the transportation between terminals is slow.

LOVE FIELD

Love Field is a $10 to $15 taxi ride from downtown Dallas. The phone number is 214-555-6073.

Love Field is the hub of Western Airlines, which offers service within Texas, to many cities in the surrounding states, and, with stops, to destinations as far away as Chicago.

BETWEEN THE AIRPORT AND TOWN

It costs around $30 to get to downtown Dallas by taxi from the Dallas-Fort Worth International Airport. It is about $25 to downtown Fort Worth.

Cheaper bus and van service is also available. Please check our Web site at www.TTC.com. for details.

Page 2

Arial 24 pt.

Report 109-85

Newsletter

1. Open the file for Report 108-82 with the newsletter masthead you created.
2. Follow the steps for Report 109-84, and then delete everything on the second page of the newsletter.
3. Change the information in the contents text box at the top of the first column, insert a picture at the end of the last column of the newsletter to balance the page, and move any pictures around as needed.

Planning a trip online is fun, easy, and requires the use of your keyboarding skills.

Lesson 110

Designing Newsletters: C

GOALS

- Type at least 49wpm/5′/5e
- Design newsletters

A. Type 2 times.

A. WARMUP

```
     At exactly 8:30 a.m., Quigley & Co. will host a wide       11
variety of chat room discussions; send email to chat@QC.com.    23
Organizational skills will be the topics in Rooms K5 and J6.    35
| 1 | 2 | 3 | 4 | 5 | 6 | 7 | 8 | 9 | 10 | 11 | 12
```

SKILLBUILDING

B. DIAGNOSTIC PRACTICE: NUMBERS

If you are not using the GDP software, turn to page SB-5 and follow the directions for this activity.

C. MAP

Follow the GDP software directions for this exercise in improving keystroking accuracy.

Keyboarding CONNECTION

Effective Email Management

Are you bombarded with email? Take a few simple steps to manage email more efficiently and reduce wasted time.

Create separate accounts for receiving messages that require your direct attention. Keep your mailbox clean by deleting messages you no longer use. Create folders to organize messages you need to keep (e.g., folders for separate projects).

If you receive numerous email messages, consider purchasing an email manager. Email manager programs help you manage multiple email accounts, find messages using powerful search functions, and notify you when you receive a message from a specified person.

Keep backups of important files. Be cautious of email from people you do not know. Check your email on a regular basis to avoid buildup of messages.

YOUR TURN Review the current organization of your email. List ways you can improve the management of your email.

D. Take two 5-minute timings. Review your speed and errors.

Goal: At least 49wpm/5′/5e

D. 5-MINUTE TIMING

```
     When the rate of unemployment is very low, jobs are       11
easier to find. Although you may find a job easily, what       22
can you do to make sure your job is one you will enjoy?        33
Here are some suggestions to help you.                         41
     First, be certain you receive a job description when      52
you are hired. The job description should list all of the      64
requirements of the job and the details of what you will       75
be expected to do.                                             79
     Second, you should receive some type of orientation       90
to your job and the company. During orientation, you will     102
fill out various tax forms, benefit forms, and insurance      113
papers. You may view a video that will help you learn more    125
about the company and available benefits.                     133
     Third, when you start your training, you should take     144
notes, pay attention, and ask questions. You should also      155
have your trainer check your work for a period of time to     167
be sure you are performing your duties correctly. If your     179
tasks are complex, you can break them down into smaller       190
parts so you can remember all parts of the job.               199
     Finally, when you know your job requirements, chart      210
your work each day. Concentrate on being part of the team.    222
Be zealous in striving to work beyond the expectations of     234
your supervisor. Then, you will achieve job satisfaction.     245
| 1 | 2 | 3 | 4 | 5 | 6 | 7 | 8 | 9 | 10 | 11 | 12
```

DOCUMENT PROCESSING

Report 110-86

Newsletter (continued)

Open the file for Report 109-84 shown on page 436. Follow these steps to finish creating the newsletter shown on page 441.

1. Place your insertion point directly in front of the first blank line underneath the last line of text in the newsletter.
2. Insert File 110A.
3. Insert a picture in the space to the right of the heading "Focus on Dallas-Fort Worth" on the second page of the newsletter. The pictures should be associated with the concept of focusing on a subject or associated with Texas.
4. Drag and size the picture so that it looks similar to the one shown in the illustration.
5. Insert word art, about the size and in the same position as the word art at the top of the bulleted list on the second page of the newsletter, with the words `Texas Tidbits`.
6. Choose a style and color for the word art to coordinate with the newsletter.
7. Insert a picture at the bottom of the second page in the space to the left of the information on "Thistle Hill." The

(Continued on next page)

If your printer or computer memory is limited, try previewing the document before you print, and then print only one page at a time.

picture should be associated with the information about Thistle Hill or with Texas.

8. Drag and size the picture so that it looks similar to the one shown in the illustration.
9. Create a text box about the size and in the same position as the one at the bottom of the newsletter to hold the information about Thistle Hill.
10. Insert File 110B and adjust the size of the text box as needed.
11. Add a fill color or fill effect to the text box to coordinate with the picture to the left of the text box.
12. Create a text box about the size and in the same position as the one at the bottom of the newsletter to hold the information about tours.
13. Change to Times New Roman Bold 12 point, and center and type `For tour information, call 817-555-2663.`
14. Remove the lines around the text box, and change the fill to none.
15. The first page of the newsletter should look like the illustration below.
16. The second page of the newsletter should look like the illustration on page 442.

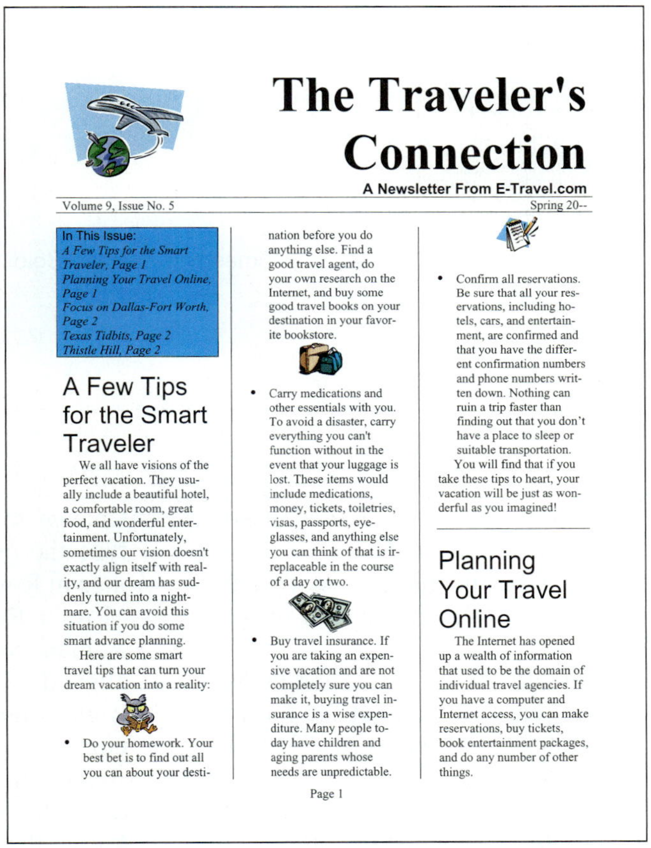

The Traveler's Connection

A Newsletter From E-Travel.com

Volume 9, Issue No. 5 Spring 20--

In This Issue:
A Few Tips for the Smart Traveler, Page 1
Planning Your Travel Online, Page 1
Focus on Dallas-Fort Worth, Page 2
Texas Tidbits, Page 2
Thistle Hill, Page 2

A Few Tips for the Smart Traveler

We all have visions of the perfect vacation. They usually include a beautiful hotel, a comfortable room, great food, and wonderful entertainment. Unfortunately, sometimes our vision doesn't exactly align itself with reality, and our dream has suddenly turned into a nightmare. You can avoid this situation if you do some smart advance planning.

Here are some smart travel tips that can turn your dream vacation into a reality:

- Do your homework. Your best bet is to find out all you can about your destination before you do anything else. Find a good travel agent, do your own research on the Internet, and buy some good travel books on your destination in your favorite bookstore.
- Carry medications and other essentials with you. To avoid a disaster, carry everything you can't function without in the event that your luggage is lost. These items would include medications, money, tickets, toiletries, visas, passports, eyeglasses, and anything else you can think of that is irreplaceable in the course of a day or two.
- Buy travel insurance. If you are taking an expensive vacation and are not completely sure you can make it, buying travel insurance is a wise expenditure. Many people today have children and aging parents whose needs are unpredictable.
- Confirm all reservations. Be sure that all your reservations, including hotels, cars, and entertainment, are confirmed and that you have the different confirmation numbers and phone numbers written down. Nothing can ruin a trip faster than finding out that you don't have a place to sleep or suitable transportation.

You will find that if you take these tips to heart, your vacation will be just as wonderful as you imagined!

Planning Your Travel Online

The Internet has opened up a wealth of information that used to be the domain of individual travel agencies. If you have a computer and Internet access, you can make reservations, buy tickets, book entertainment packages, and do any number of other things.

Page 1

(Continued on next page)

Save hours of time and lots of money by using the Internet wisely when you plan your travel. You can shop for the best airline rates and even name your own price if you are flexible in your travel plans.

Several good books are available to help you use the Internet for your travel plans. Please check our web site at www.TTC.com for suggested books.

Focus on Dallas-Fort Worth

This month's focus is on the Dallas-Fort Worth area.

THE AIRPORT

The Dallas-Fort Worth International Airport is 17 miles from the business districts of each town. The phone number is 214-555-8888.

Although this is the world's second busiest airport, it is surprisingly easy to use. However, the transportation between terminals is slow.

LOVE FIELD

Love Field is a $10 to $15 taxi ride from downtown Dallas. The phone number is 214-555-6073.

Love Field is the hub of Western Airlines, which offers service within Texas, to many cities in the surrounding states, and, with stops, to destinations as far away as Chicago.

BETWEEN THE AIRPORT AND TOWN

It costs around $30 to get to downtown Dallas by taxi from the Dallas-Fort Worth International Airport. It is about $25 to downtown Fort Worth.

Cheaper bus and van service is also available. Please check our web site at www.TTC.com. for details.

Texas Tidbits

- To receive mail while traveling in Dallas, have it sent c/o General Delivery at the city's main post office.
- Most businesses open between 8 a.m. and 10 a.m. and close around 6 p.m. Many are also open on weekends.
- Banks operate weekdays from 9 a.m. until 2 or 3 p.m., and some are also open on Saturday mornings.
- Post offices are open weekdays from 8 a.m. to 5 p.m. and Saturday mornings.
- At traffic lights, it's legal to make a right turn on a red light except when there is a sign at the intersection stating that such a turn is *not* permitted. Of course, come to a full stop first and make sure no traffic is coming.

Thistle Hill

In 1903, cattle baron William T. Waggoner built his daughter this three-story mansion as a wedding present. The house was built in a wealthy neighborhood known as Quality Hill. This Georgian Revival-style mansion has been restored to its 1912 condition and is listed in the National Register.

It is located today on Pennsylvania Avenue near the hospital district. It cost about $38,000 when the nearly 11,000-square-foot, red brick structure was built back in 1903. The house was used for lavish dinners and parties to entertain many of Fort Worth's powerful and elite. It was often referred to as the "honeymoon cottage" and was restored in the 1970s.

For tour information, call 817-555-2663

Page 2

Times New Roman Bold 12 pt.

Report 110-87

Flyer

Progress Check
Proofreading Check

Documents designated as Proofreading Checks serve as a check of your proofreading skill. Your goal is to have zero typographical errors when the GDP software first scores the document.

1. Press the SPACE BAR 2 times, and insert a picture related to a globe.
2. Drag and size the picture so that it looks similar to the one shown in the illustration.
3. Insert word art about the size and in the same position as the one at the top of the illustration, with the words `Global Savings & Loan`.
4. Choose a style and color for the word art to coordinate with the picture.
5. Create a text box with no lines and fill and about the size and in the same position as the one shown at the middle of the illustration.
6. Change to Times New Roman 48 point, and center and type `Your Guide to Online Banking` in 2 lines as shown.
7. Insert a boxed table with 4 columns and 6 rows, and drag it into position as shown in the illustration.
8. Change to Arial Bold 18 point, and type the one- and two-column headings in Row 1 aligned as shown.
9. Move to Row 2, change to Times New Roman 20 point, and type the left-aligned column entries as shown.
10. Right-align the information in Column D, and add spaces after the dollar sign to align the dollar sign just to the left of the widest entry below it.
11. Merge the cells in Row 6, change to Times New Roman 14 point, and type the information as shown.
12. Adjust the column widths manually as shown.
13. Add a shading color to the first and last row to coordinate with the word art and picture.

(Continued on next page)

↓1X Account	↓1X ATM Card	Check Writing	Monthly Fee
Regular Checking	None	Unlimited	$ 9.00
Interest Checking	Express Card	Unlimited	10.00
Basic Checking	Express Card	Unlimited	4.50
Student Checking	Express Card	Unlimited	3.00
Note: Fees may apply to telephone banking calls and the use of the ATM Express Card.			

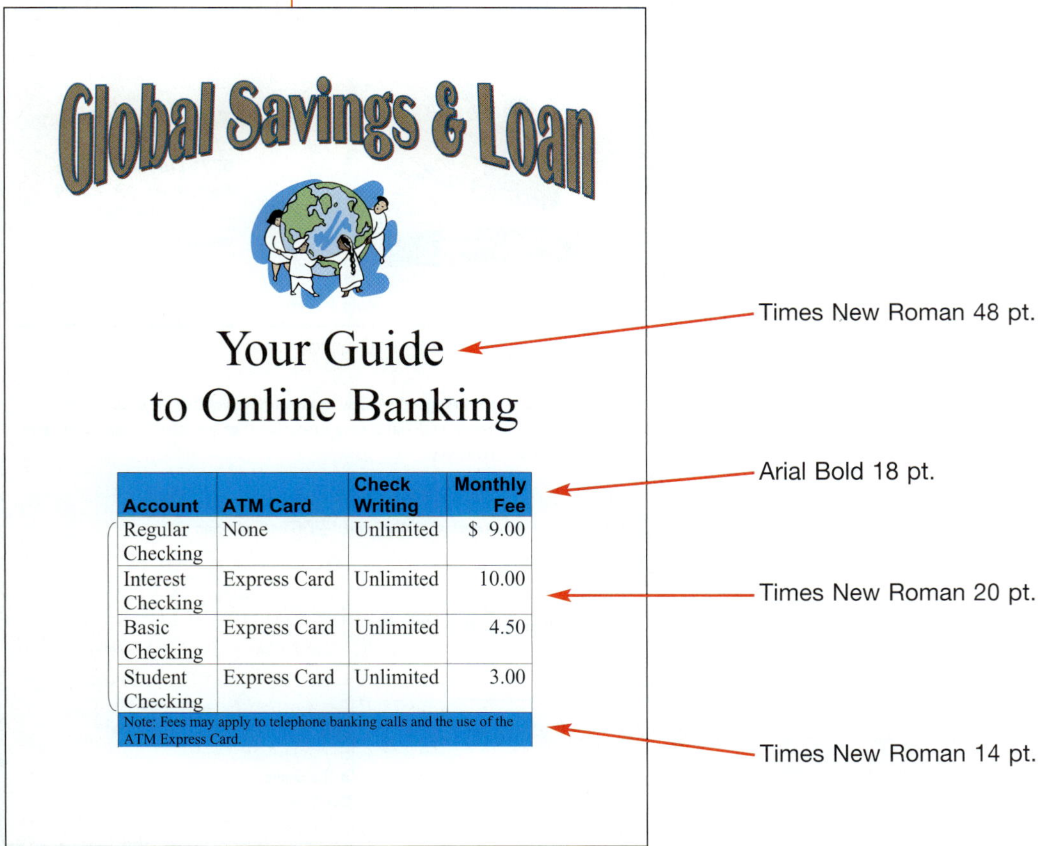

Unit 23

Designing Web Pages

LESSON 111
Creating, Saving, and Viewing Web Pages

LESSON 112
Creating Frames

LESSON 113
Creating and Saving More Web Pages

LESSON 114
Creating Web Pages With Hyperlinks

LESSON 115
Formatting Web Pages

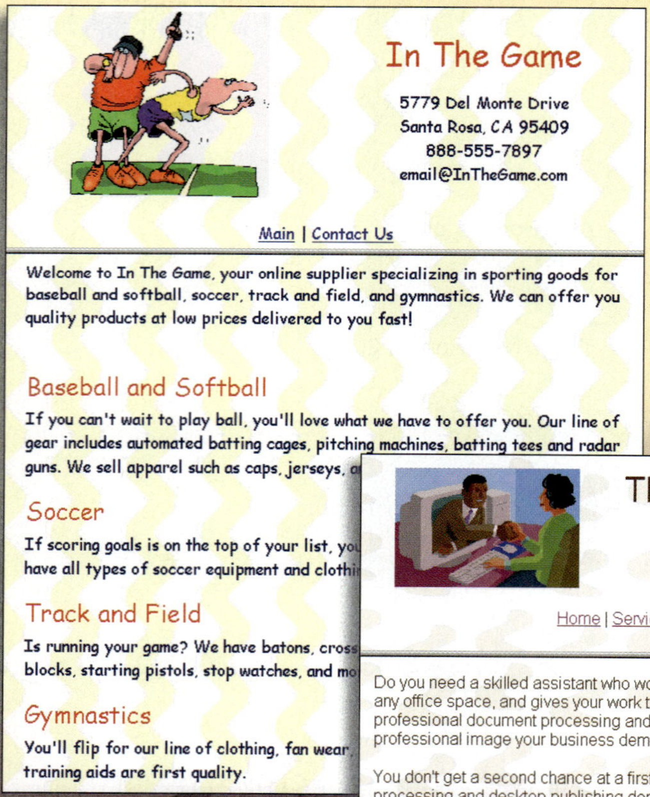

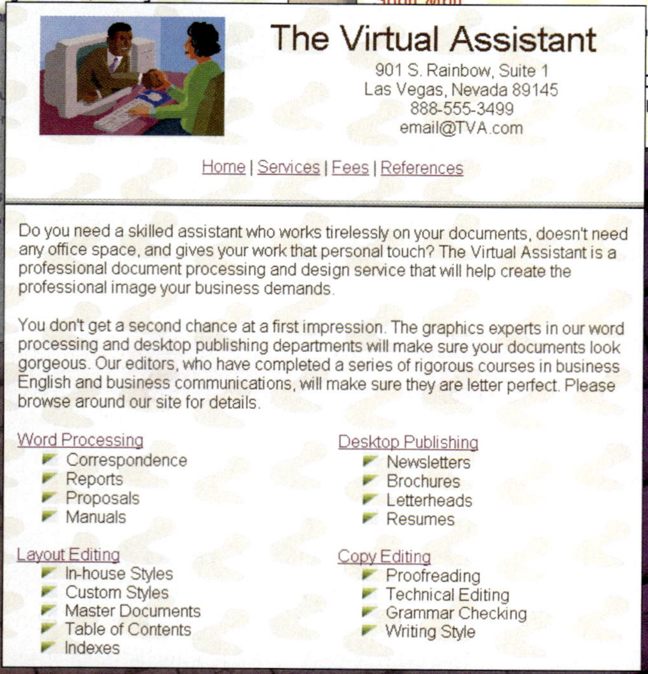

Creating, Saving, and Viewing Web Pages

GOALS

- Improve speed and accuracy
- Refine language arts skills in capitalization
- Create, save, and view web pages

A. Type 2 times.

A. WARMUP

1 The taxes* were quickly adjusted upward by 20 percent 11
2 because of the improvements to her house (built in 1901). 23
3 A proposed law will not penalize good homeowners like this. 35

| 1 | 2 | 3 | 4 | 5 | 6 | 7 | 8 | 9 | 10 | 11 | 12

SKILLBUILDING

B. Take three 12-second timings on each line. The scale below the last line shows your wpm speed for a 12-second timing.

B. 12-SECOND SPEED SPRINTS

4 Their home is on a lake that is just east of her old house.
5 He has an old boat that is in bad need of a good paint job.
6 He got so many fish that she gave some to the nice old man.
7 She was so nice that it was easy for him to help her drive.

5 10 15 20 25 30 35 40 45 50 55 60

C. PROGRESSIVE PRACTICE: ALPHABET

If you are not using the GDP software, turn to page SB-7 and follow the directions for this activity.

D. PROGRESSIVE PRACTICE: NUMBERS

If you are not using the GDP software, turn to page SB-11 and follow the directions for this activity.

LANGUAGE ARTS

E. Study the rules at the right.

E. CAPITALIZATION

RULE ≡ organization

Capitalize common organizational terms (such as *advertising department* and *finance committee*) only when they are the actual names of the units in the writer's own organization and when they are preceded by the word *the*.

The report from the Advertising Department is due today.

But: Our advertising department will submit its report today.

(Continued on next page)

RULE ≡ course

Capitalize the names of specific course titles but not the names of subjects or areas of study.

I have enrolled in Accounting 201 and will also take the marketing course.

Edit the sentences to correct any errors in capitalization.

8 Our advertising department consistently delivers quality work.
9 The Finance Committee must submit the report by noon today.
10 I think I am going to pass keyboarding 1 with flying colors.
11 The marketing department must approve the proposal first.
12 A class in Business Communications would be very helpful.
13 To take Math 102, you must have taken a beginning math course.

FORMATTING

F. BASIC PARTS OF A WEB PAGE

LAYOUT VIEW. Working view of a Web page in a word processor with certain elements, such as table gridlines, visible.

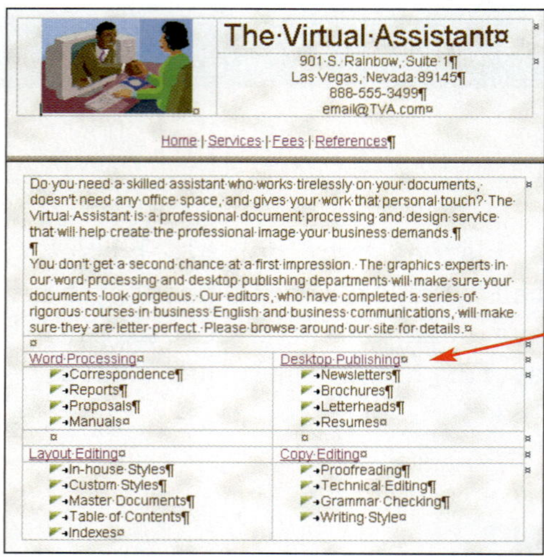

FRAMES PAGE. A Web page divided into independent sections or frames, each displaying a different Web page.

HEADER FRAME. Displays the same information at the top of every page of the Web site.

MAIN FRAME. Displays content of different Web pages each time a page hyperlink is clicked.

HYPERLINKS. Are clicked to move from one page or place on a page to another within a Web site.

BROWSER VIEW. Final view of a Web page as displayed in a browser; text and tables wrap to fit window; table gridlines are invisible. Different browser views may vary.

G. WEB SITE DESIGN GUIDELINES

Follow these guidelines to design effective Web sites:

- Plan appropriate, specific content first. Define the purpose of the site, and make a list of what visitors need to know.
- Organize the content into logical groups and subgroups similar to an outline in a report.
- Plan the main page (usually called a home page), which should identify the business and its services.
- Plan and test the site navigation. Hyperlinks help visitors jump from one spot or page to another.
- Plan the content and design details of specific pages, and use tables to position information.
- Design an appropriate, attractive visual theme with consistent design elements on each page to unify your site. Many programs come with a gallery of attractive themes with unified design elements and eye-catching color schemes.
- Use graphics to enhance your page, but use them sparingly because they increase download times.
- Use color to create a mood, attract attention, and categorize information.

Go To
Word Processing Manual

H. WEB PAGE—SAVING AND VIEWING

Study Lesson 111 in your word processing manual. Complete all of the shaded steps while at your computer. Then format the jobs that follow.

DOCUMENT PROCESSING

Report 111-88

Web Site

Computers that run the UNIX operating system generally use the html extension for the home page of a Web site. Personal computers that run Windows or Macintosh operating systems usually use the htm extension. If you are planning on publishing the Web site you create on a commercial server, you should ask your host server which extension is required.

Follow these steps to create the main page of the Web site named *main.htm*:

1. GDP will automatically open a blank document. Save it as a Web page named *main.htm*.
2. Create an open table with 2 columns and 7 rows. Note: Refer to the layout view on page 446 for the placement of information within rows.
3. Merge the cells in Row 1, and type the information in the first row as shown below.
4. Move to Row 3, and continue typing the rest of the table as shown on page 446, leaving Row 2 and Row 4 empty.
5. View the Web page in a browser (if one is available), and compare this view with the layout view in your word processor.

Do you need a skilled assistant who works tirelessly on your documents, doesn't need any office space, and gives your work that personal touch? The Virtual Assistant is a professional document processing and design service that will help create the professional image your business demands.

You don't get a second chance at a first impression. The graphics experts in our word processing and desktop publishing departments will make sure your documents look gorgeous. Our editors, who have completed a series of rigorous courses in business English and business communications, will make sure your documents are letter perfect. Please browse around our site for details.

≡ organization

≡ course

(Continued on next page)

Word Processing
Correspondence
Reports
Proposals
Manuals

Layout Editing
In-house Styles
Custom Styles
Master Documents
Table of Contents
Indexes

Desktop Publishing
Newsletters
Brochures
Letterheads
Resumes

Copy Editing
Proofreading
Technical Editing
Grammar Checking
Writing Style

Reminder: You will finish building the Web site in Lessons 112 through 115.

Report 111-89

Your Web Site

Plan and write the content for a Web site for a business of your own to include a main page and three related pages very similar to the project in this unit. You may want to look at the Web site for Report 115-100 on pages 465-466 for ideas.

1. GDP will automatically open a blank document. Save it as *my main.htm*.
2. Create an open table with 2 columns and 7 rows, and type the information for this main page inside the table similar to Report 115-100.
3. View the Web page in a browser (if one is available), and compare it with the layout view in your word processor.

STRATEGIES FOR *Career Success*

Types of Interviews

Most employers conduct two or three interviews before making a job offer. The first interview, held at the company or conducted by phone, is usually a screening interview. This determines if you are qualified for the job.

The next set of interviews is more selective. At the company, you might have a panel interview with several interviewers who ask directed, prepared questions; or you might have an open-ended interview that is relatively unstructured. Interviewing by video teleconference is another possibility.

No matter what type of interview you encounter, the outcome will be better if you have enthusiasm for the job, match your qualifications to the company's needs, ask relevant questions, and listen well.

YOUR TURN Visit career Web sites for articles on preparing for job interviews as well as information on employers, resumes, job searches, etc.

Creating Frames

GOALS

- Type at least 50wpm/5′/5e
- Create frames

A. Type 2 times.

A. WARMUP

```
1      Missy examined these items: the #426 oil painting, a      11
2  Bowes & Elkjer porcelain vase, and the 86-piece collection   23
3  of glazed antique pitchers. There were 337 people present.   35
   | 1 | 2 | 3 | 4 | 5 | 6 | 7 | 8 | 9 | 10 | 11 | 12
```

SKILLBUILDING

B. PACED PRACTICE

If you are not using the GDP software, turn to page SB-14 and follow the directions for this activity.

Keyboarding skills are essential in the retail sales and services industry.

C. Take two 5-minute timings. Review your speed and errors.

Goal: At least 50wpm/5′/5e

C. 5-MINUTE TIMING

Employers want the people who work for them to have 11
many qualities of good character. Character is defined as 23
a distinguishing feature of a person or thing. Character 34
may be what you are remembered for or why you remember 45
someone else. What are some of the traits associated with 57
good character? Respect, honesty, trustworthiness, caring, 69
leadership, responsibility, attitude, tolerance, fairness, 81
and citizenship are a few traits. 88

All people should have respect for themselves and for 99
others. If you respect people, you have a high regard for 111
the way they conduct themselves in all aspects of life. 122
However, before you can respect others, you need to have 133
respect for yourself. 137

Honesty and trustworthiness are similar traits. In 147
business dealings, people expect honesty and will admire 158
people who have this quality. They like to build business 170
relationships with companies whose employees are honest 181
and trustworthy. 184

Your attitude is reflected in the way you act toward 195
other people or in the way you speak to them. You can make 206
great strides in advancing your career by taking a look at 219
the way you interact with people. You may want to take a 230
closer look at some character traits you want to improve. 242
The improvements in life will amaze you. 250

| 1 | 2 | 3 | 4 | 5 | 6 | 7 | 8 | 9 | 10 | 11 | 12

FORMATTING

Refer to the illustration of a frames page shown on page 446.

D. WEB PAGE FRAMES

A frame is a defined section on a Web page that divides it into two or more windows. Frames organize and link the pages in a Web site and make navigation easy and seamless. A frames page is usually the opening page in a Web site.

The header frame displays the same information consistently at the top of every page. The design and content of the header frame varies but commonly includes identifying information, a related picture, and navigational hyperlinks.

The main frame displays the individual pages of the Web site when a hyperlink is clicked. The home page is usually the first page displayed in the main frame. Using a header frame in conjunction with a main frame and navigational hyperlinks helps the user change pages easily and unifies the Web site.

Go To
Word Processing Manual

E. WEB PAGE—FRAMES

Study Lesson 112 in your word processing manual. Complete all of the shaded steps while at your computer. Then format the jobs that follow.

DOCUMENT PROCESSING

Report 112-90

Web Site (continued)

Some Internet Service Providers use an extension of .htm and some use. html. You must name your Web page to conform to the requirements of your ISP.

Follow these steps to finish the main page and create a frames page for this Web site named *index.htm*:

1. Open the file for Report 111-88, named *main.htm*.
2. Horizontally center the table on this page.
3. Insert a header frame above the main page to create a frames page, and drag the bottom border of the frame to adjust the frame size if necessary.
4. Create an open table with 2 rows and 2 columns inside the header frame, and center it horizontally.
5. In Column B, Row 1, center and type `The Virtual Assistant`.
6. In Column B, Row 2, center and type these lines:
```
901 S. Rainbow, Suite 1
Las Vegas, Nevada 89145
888-555-3499
email@TVA.com
```
7. Merge the cells in Column A, and insert a picture with an office theme.
8. Resize the picture proportionately until it is about 2 inches wide, and center the picture.
9. Move the insertion point under the table in the top frame, and press ENTER 1 time.
10. Type the following line centered using the pipe symbol, with one space before and after it, as shown:
`Home | Services | Fees | References`
Note: The pipe symbol (|) is above the backslash symbol on most keyboards.
11. Resize the header frame as shown by dragging on the bottom border.
12. Save the frames page and name it *index.htm*.
13. View the Web page in a browser.

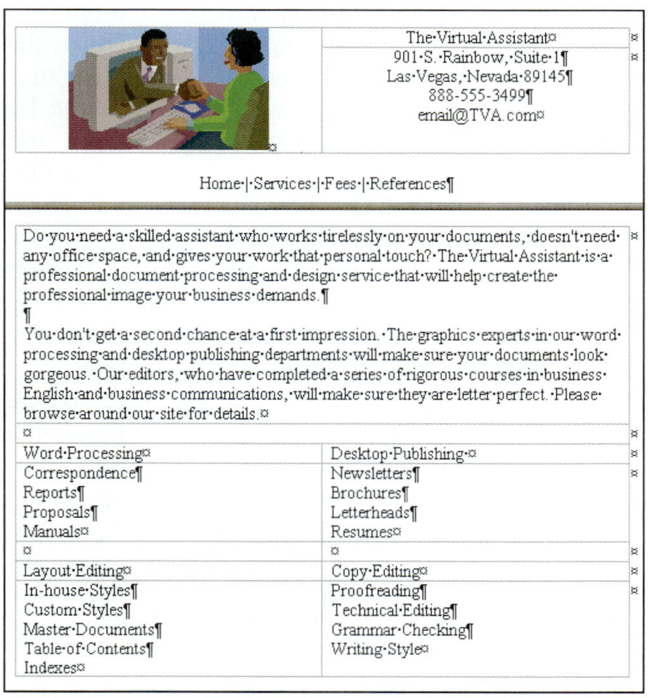

The Virtual Assistant
901 S. Rainbow, Suite 1
Las Vegas, Nevada 89145
888-555-3499
email@TVA.com

Home | Services | Fees | References

Do you need a skilled assistant who works tirelessly on your documents, doesn't need any office space, and gives your work that personal touch? The Virtual Assistant is a professional document processing and design service that will help create the professional image your business demands.

You don't get a second chance at a first impression. The graphics experts in our word processing and desktop publishing departments will make sure your documents look gorgeous. Our editors, who have completed a series of rigorous courses in business English and business communications, will make sure they are letter perfect. Please browse around our site for details.

Word Processing	Desktop Publishing
Correspondence Reports Proposals Manuals	Newsletters Brochures Letterheads Resumes
Layout Editing	Copy Editing
In-house Styles Custom Styles Master Documents Table of Contents Indexes	Proofreading Technical Editing Grammar Checking Writing Style

Layout View of Frames Page

(Continued on next page)

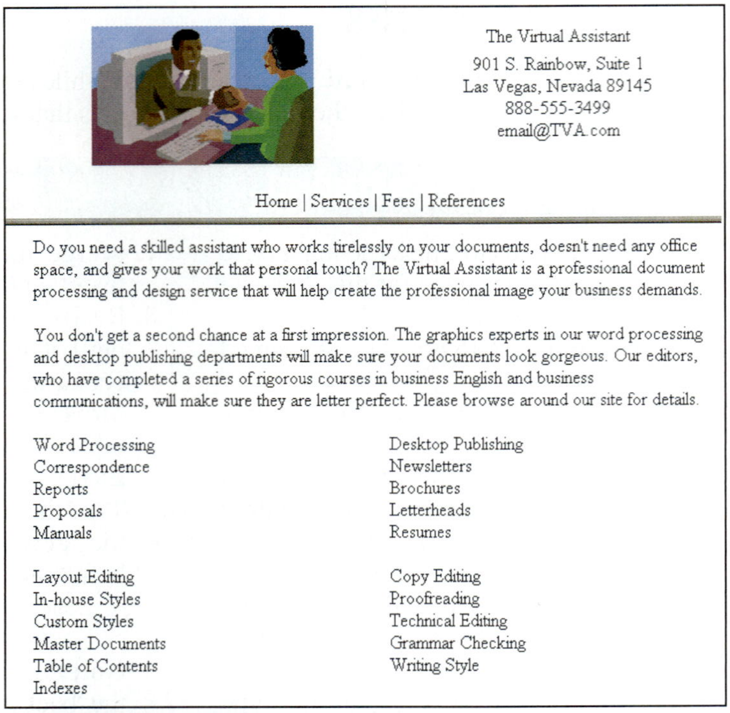

The Virtual Assistant
901 S. Rainbow, Suite 1
Las Vegas, Nevada 89145
888-555-3499
email@TVA.com

Home | Services | Fees | References

Do you need a skilled assistant who works tirelessly on your documents, doesn't need any office space, and gives your work that personal touch? The Virtual Assistant is a professional document processing and design service that will help create the professional image your business demands.

You don't get a second chance at a first impression. The graphics experts in our word processing and desktop publishing departments will make sure your documents look gorgeous. Our editors, who have completed a series of rigorous courses in business English and business communications, will make sure they are letter perfect. Please browse around our site for details.

Word Processing	Desktop Publishing
Correspondence	Newsletters
Reports	Brochures
Proposals	Letterheads
Manuals	Resumes
Layout Editing	Copy Editing
In-house Styles	Proofreading
Custom Styles	Technical Editing
Master Documents	Grammar Checking
Table of Contents	Writing Style
Indexes	

Browser View of Frames Page

Report 112-91

Your Web Site (continued)

Follow these steps to finish your main page (*my index.htm*) and create a frames page for your Web site named *index.htm*:

1. Open the file for Report 111-89, named *my main.htm*.
2. Horizontally center the table on the page.
3. Insert a header frame above the main page to create a frames page, and drag the bottom border of the frame to adjust the frame size if necessary.
4. Create an open table with 2 rows and 2 columns inside the header frame, and center it horizontally.
5. In Column B, Row 1, center and type the name of the Web site.
6. In Column B, Row 2, center and type the mailing address and email address of the Web site.
7. Merge the cells in Column A, and insert a picture related to the Web site business.
8. Resize the picture as needed, and align the picture as needed.
9. Move the insertion point under the table in the top frame, and press ENTER 1 time.
10. Type the following line centered, using the pipe symbol with one space before and after it as shown:

    Home | Services | Fees | References

    Note: The pipe symbol (|) is above the backslash symbol on most keyboards.
11. Resize the header frame as shown by dragging on the bottom border.
12. Save the frames page, and name it *my index.htm*.
13. View the Web page in a browser.

Lesson 113

Creating and Saving More Web Pages

GOALS

- Improve speed and accuracy
- Refine language arts skills in composing
- Create and save more Web pages

A. Type 2 times.

A. WARMUP

Did you hear the excellent quartet of junior cadets? 11
Everybody in the crowd (estimated at over 500) applauded 22
"with gusto." The sizable crowd filled the 3/4-acre park. 33

| 1 | 2 | 3 | 4 | 5 | 6 | 7 | 8 | 9 | 10 | 11 | 12

SKILLBUILDING

B. DIAGNOSTIC PRACTICE: ALPHABET

If you are not using the GDP software, turn to page SB-2 and follow the directions for this activity.

C. Type the columns 2 times. Press TAB to move from column to column.

C. TECHNIQUE PRACTICE: TAB KEY

T. Waters	L. Vigil	S. Zimmerly	D. Colwell	C. Foster
M. Goldbach	R. Hempker	G. Beckert	M. Kinsey	A. Lucero
C. Maclean	J. Nichols	I. Ohlsen	R. Parlee	S. Quale
J. Rondeau	G. Snowden	Y. Tokita	C. Upton	C. Vaughn

LANGUAGE ARTS

D. COMPOSING A PERSONAL-BUSINESS LETTER

Compose a two-paragraph personal-business letter that summarizes the content of the Web site design guidelines on page 447. Address the letter to your instructor; provide a suitable inside address and salutation for your letter. Also, provide a complimentary closing and sign the letter yourself.

In the letter, discuss the following:

Paragraph 1. Describe how to plan an effective Web site.

Paragraph 2. Describe how to design an effective Web site.

DOCUMENT PROCESSING

Report 113-92

Web Site (continued)

Follow these steps to create a new page for the Web site named *fees.htm*:

1. Type `Fees` centered on the first line, and press ENTER 2 times.
2. Create an open table with 1 cell, and center it horizontally.
3. Type the information as shown below inside the table.
4. View the Web page in a browser.

The Virtual Assistant strives to work within your organization's budget. We will review your individual needs and tailor the pricing to fit your project. We welcome the opportunity to provide an individual estimate. Be assured that our prices are extremely competitive. Here are some general guidelines regarding our fees:
¶
We typically charge by the hour or by the page, depending upon the job. ¶
Most fees are based on the length of the document and the amount of editing deemed necessary. ¶
We offer substantial discounts for volume work and repeat clients. ¶
A surcharge is added for rush jobs. ¶
Payment for services rendered should be made by credit card, check, or money order. ¶
¶
For a copy of our current rate guide, please send an email message to rateguide@TVA.com. ¶

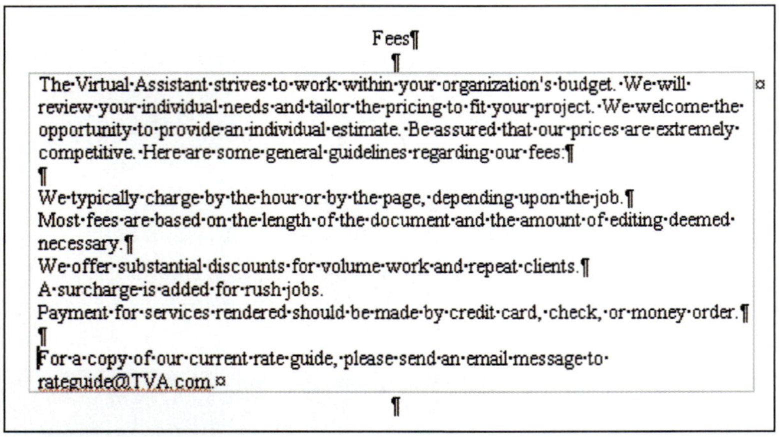

Fees¶
¶
The·Virtual·Assistant·strives·to·work·within·your·organization's·budget.·We·will·review·your·individual·needs·and·tailor·the·pricing·to·fit·your·project.·We·welcome·the·opportunity·to·provide·an·individual·estimate.·Be·assured·that·our·prices·are·extremely·competitive.·Here·are·some·general·guidelines·regarding·our·fees:¶
¶
We·typically·charge·by·the·hour·or·by·the·page,·depending·upon·the·job.¶
Most·fees·are·based·on·the·length·of·the·document·and·the·amount·of·editing·deemed·necessary.¶
We·offer·substantial·discounts·for·volume·work·and·repeat·clients.¶
A·surcharge·is·added·for·rush·jobs.
Payment·for·services·rendered·should·be·made·by·credit·card,·check,·or·money·order.¶
¶
For·a·copy·of·our·current·rate·guide,·please·send·an·email·message·to·rateguide@TVA.com.¤
¶

Layout View of Fees Page

Report 113-93

Web Site (continued)

Follow these steps to create a new page for the Web site named *references.htm*:

1. Type `References` centered on the first line, and press ENTER 2 times.
2. Create an open table with 1 cell, and center it horizontally.
3. Type the information below inside the table.
4. View the Web page in a browser.

↓2X

I've been in a highly successful business for over 10 years and attribute much of that success to the skilled professionals at The Virtual Assistant. I am always confident that my work will go out error free. They are top-notch professionals and can work for my team anytime! ↓2X

Mike Rashid
Network Engineer
Denver, Colorado ↓4X

The documents produced by The Virtual Assistant are impeccable! I can count on professional, reliable, competent, and efficient service without question. It is so easy to send documents back and forth via the Internet, and we all know that time is money. I highly recommend TVA for any of your word processing needs. ↓2X

Nancy Shipley
Attorney at Law
Chicago, Illinois ↓4X

As the president of a dynamic company with tremendous growth potential, I have to be concerned with my image in the business world and with the bottom line. I have counted on the services of The Virtual Assistant for the past five years, and I have always been thrilled with their reliability and consistency. I particularly like the discounts we enjoy as a repeat customer. ↓2X

I have worked closely with Kevin Nguyen, who now has a sixth sense about my needs. He can always anticipate my thoughts and can substitute the right meaning when it is necessary. I would be lost without Kevin and TVA. I wouldn't trust my documents or my image to anyone else!! ↓2X

Debbie Matte, President
New Millennium Designs
Orlando, Florida ↓2X

(Continued on next page)

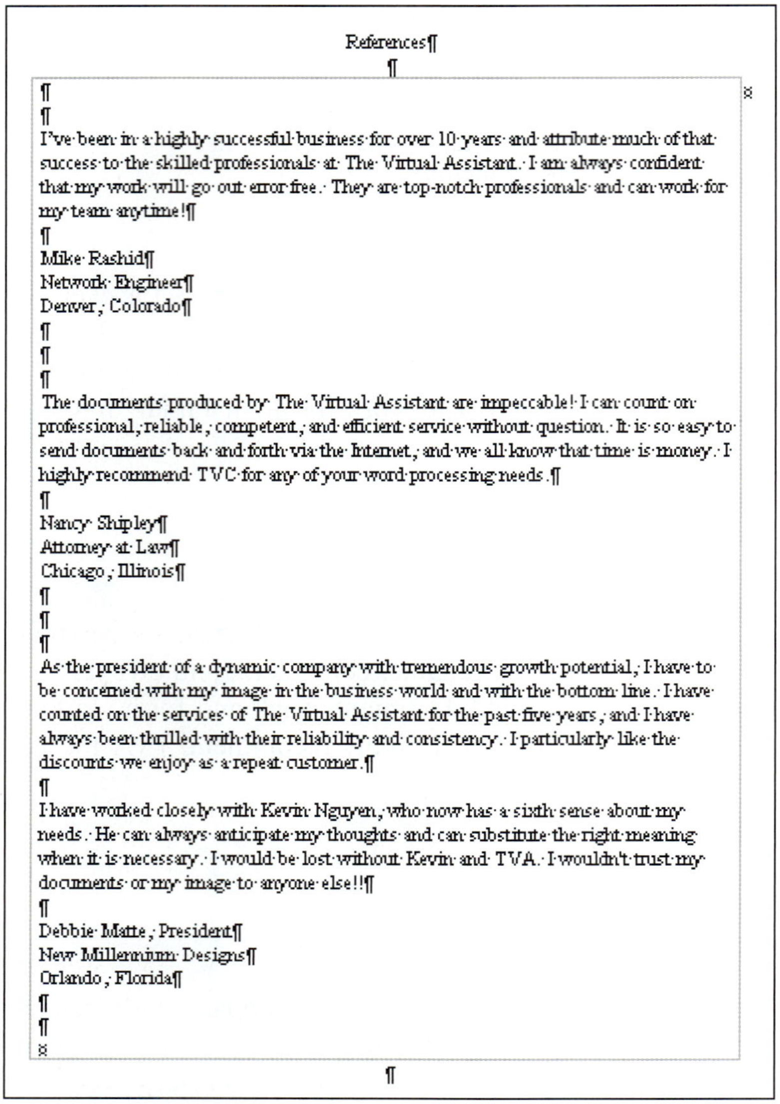

References

I've been in a highly successful business for over 10 years and attribute much of that success to the skilled professionals at The Virtual Assistant. I am always confident that my work will go out error free. They are top-notch professionals and can work for my team anytime!

Mike Rashid
Network Engineer
Denver, Colorado

The documents produced by The Virtual Assistant are impeccable! I can count on professional, reliable, competent, and efficient service without question. It is so easy to send documents back and forth via the Internet, and we all know that time is money. I highly recommend TVC for any of your word processing needs.

Nancy Shipley
Attorney at Law
Chicago, Illinois

As the president of a dynamic company with tremendous growth potential, I have to be concerned with my image in the business world and with the bottom line. I have counted on the services of The Virtual Assistant for the past five years, and I have always been thrilled with their reliability and consistency. I particularly like the discounts we enjoy as a repeat customer.

I have worked closely with Kevin Nguyen, who now has a sixth sense about my needs. He can always anticipate my thoughts and can substitute the right meaning when it is necessary. I would be lost without Kevin and TVA. I wouldn't trust my documents or my image to anyone else!!

Debbie Matte, President
New Millennium Designs
Orlando, Florida

Layout View of References Page

Report 113-94

Your Web Site (continued)

Follow these steps to create a new page for the Web site named *my fees.htm* similar to Report 113-92:

1. Type `Fees` centered on the first line, and press ENTER 2 times.
2. Create an open table with 1 cell, and center it horizontally.
3. Type content similar to Report 113-92.
4. View the Web page in a browser.

Report 113-95

Your Web Site (continued)

Follow these steps to create a new page for the Web site named *my references.htm* similar to Report 113-93:

1. Type `References` centered on the first line, and press ENTER 2 times.
2. Create an open table with 1 cell, and center it horizontally.
3. Type the information for the 3 references inside the table similar to Report 113-93.
4. View the Web page in a browser.

Lesson 114

Creating Web Pages With Hyperlinks

GOALS
- Type at least 50wpm/5′/5e
- Create hyperlinks

A. Type 2 times.

A. WARMUP

```
     This series* (*6 films, 28 minutes) by J. Zeller goes    11
beyond the "basics" of computers. Viewers keep requesting     23
an extension on the dates; this includes 3/2, 5/5, and 8/9.   35
| 1 | 2 | 3 | 4 | 5 | 6 | 7 | 8 | 9 | 10 | 11 | 12
```

SKILLBUILDING

B. MAP

Follow the GDP software directions for this exercise in improving keystroking accuracy.

Keyboarding CONNECTION

Using Hypertext

Do you know how to surf the Web? It's easy! The Web contains pages, which are blocks of text, visuals, sound, or animation. Hypertext is a technique where certain words in the text of a Web page are highlighted, underlined, or colored differently from the other words. These colored or highlighted words link to other pages on the Web.

When you point to one of these hyperlinks and click the mouse button, the page connected to that word is displayed. Therefore, one page on the Web can link to many other pages. Hypertext pages do not have to be read in any specific order.

Hypertext enables you to connect and retrieve Web pages from computer networks worldwide. With hypertext, you can point and click or surf your way all over the Web.

YOUR TURN Open a page on the Web. Surf the Web using the hyperlinks displayed on the page.

C. Take two 5-minute timings. Review your speed and errors.

Goal: At least 50wpm/5'/5e

C. 5-MINUTE TIMING

```
     Before you apply for jobs, you will want to do some          11
detective work. First, choose the company for which you           22
want to work and then use the Internet to find out about          33
the company. If you find a Web site for the organization,         45
then you can learn about the company, its hiring policies,        57
available jobs, and how to apply for a job opening.               67
     When you are researching a company, you want to learn        78
about the history of the company. You may be able to find         90
out how stock analysts expect the company stock to perform       102
in the coming months if the company is publicly held.            113
     When you find a job opening for which you wish to           123
apply, read carefully to see what type of work experience        135
and education the company requires for the job. When you         146
prepare your resume, emphasize your qualifications based         157
on the requirements listed for the job. If the person who        169
should receive job inquiries is not listed, contact the          180
company by phone or email to get a name. Personalize your        192
cover letter and resume, if possible.                            200
     The information you find in your research will be very      211
helpful during the interview with a representative of the        223
company. Ask intelligent questions and speak confidently         234
about the position. Emphasize how your skills would be           245
valuable to the company.                                         250
|  1  |  2  |  3  |  4  |  5  |  6  |  7  |  8  |  9  |  10  |  11  |  12
```

FORMATTING

D. HYPERLINKS

Hyperlinks are powerful navigational tools that are critical to the overall plan and design of a Web site. When clicked, they move a visitor from one page or one location on a page to another.

When you create a hyperlink, you must indicate the target. The hyperlink can point to the same page, to a different page, to another site, or perhaps to an email address. You can assign a hyperlink to a word, a group of words, or a picture.

The presence of a text hyperlink is usually indicated by underlined text with a different color from the rest of the words on the page. Also, the mouse pointer changes to a hand shape when hovering over a hyperlink.

Go To
Word Processing Manual

E. WEB PAGE—HYPERLINKS

Study Lesson 114 in your word processing manual. Complete all of the shaded steps while at your computer. Then format the jobs that follow.

DOCUMENT PROCESSING

Report 114-96

Web Site (continued)

Follow these steps to create a new page for the Web site named *services.htm*:

1. Type `Services` centered on the first line, and press ENTER 2 times.
2. Create an open table with 1 cell, and center it horizontally.
3. Type the information as shown below inside the table.
4. View the Web page in a browser.

Word Processing ¶
We prepare documents with a professional look for correspondence of all types as well as reports, proposals, manuals, etc. ¶
Desktop Publishing ¶
Our professional design specialists will create newsletters, brochures, letterheads, etc., that are sure to capture your imagination. ¶
Layout Editing ¶
Our layout editors will transform your documents using in-house styles or custom styles. For your longer projects, they are experts at building master documents that include a cover page, table of contents, and index. ¶
Copy Editing ¶
Our copy editors will make sure that your document content is perfect. Proofreading, grammar, and writing style will all be checked so that your ideas are expressed clearly and effectively.

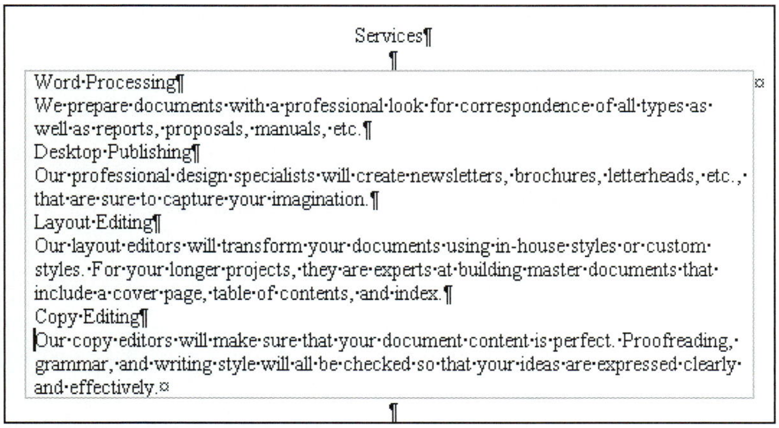
Services¶
¶
Word·Processing¶
We·prepare·documents·with·a·professional·look·for·correspondence·of·all·types·as·well·as·reports,·proposals,·manuals,·etc.¶
Desktop·Publishing¶
Our·professional·design·specialists·will·create·newsletters,·brochures,·letterheads,·etc.,·that·are·sure·to·capture·your·imagination.¶
Layout·Editing¶
Our·layout·editors·will·transform·your·documents·using·in-house·styles·or·custom·styles.·For·your·longer·projects,·they·are·experts·at·building·master·documents·that·include·a·cover·page,·table·of·contents,·and·index.¶
Copy·Editing¶
Our·copy·editors·will·make·sure·that·your·document·content·is·perfect.·Proofreading,·grammar,·and·writing·style·will·all·be·checked·so·that·your·ideas·are·expressed·clearly·and·effectively.¤
¶

Layout View of Services Page

Report 114-97

Web Site (continued)

Follow these steps to create hyperlinks for the frames page:

1. Open the file for Report 112-90 (*index.htm*), the frames page.
2. Create four text hyperlinks for each of the four words in the header frame as follows:

   Home, opens *main.htm*
   Services opens *services.htm*
   Fees opens *fees.htm*
   References opens *references.htm*

3. Create the hyperlinks so that the corresponding target document will display in the main fame below the header frame.
4. Create a hyperlink for each of the four headings on the main page (*Word Processing, Desktop Publishing*, etc.) to open *services.htm*.
5. View the Web page in a browser.

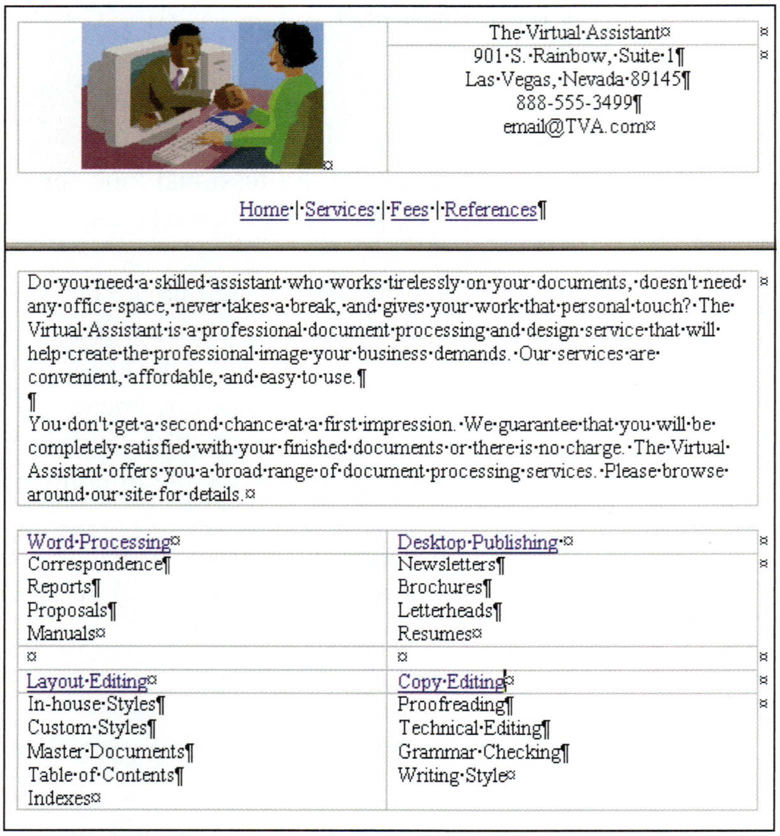

The·Virtual·Assistant¤
901·S.·Rainbow,·Suite·1¶
Las·Vegas,·Nevada·89145¶
888-555-3499¶
email@TVA.com¤

Home·|·Services·|·Fees·|·References¶

Do·you·need·a·skilled·assistant·who·works·tirelessly·on·your·documents,·doesn't·need·any·office·space,·never·takes·a·break,·and·gives·your·work·that·personal·touch?·The·Virtual·Assistant·is·a·professional·document·processing·and·design·service·that·will·help·create·the·professional·image·your·business·demands.·Our·services·are·convenient,·affordable,·and·easy·to·use.¶
¶
You·don't·get·a·second·chance·at·a·first·impression.·We·guarantee·that·you·will·be·completely·satisfied·with·your·finished·documents·or·there·is·no·charge.·The·Virtual·Assistant·offers·you·a·broad·range·of·document·processing·services.·Please·browse·around·our·site·for·details.¤

Word·Processing¤	Desktop·Publishing·¤
Correspondence¶ Reports¶ Proposals¶ Manuals¤	Newsletters¶ Brochures¶ Letterheads¶ Resumes¤
¤	¤
Layout·Editing¤	Copy·Editing¤
In-house·Styles¶ Custom·Styles¶ Master·Documents¶ Table·of·Contents¶ Indexes¤	Proofreading¶ Technical·Editing¶ Grammar·Checking¶ Writing·Style¤

Layout View of Frames Page

(Continued on next page)

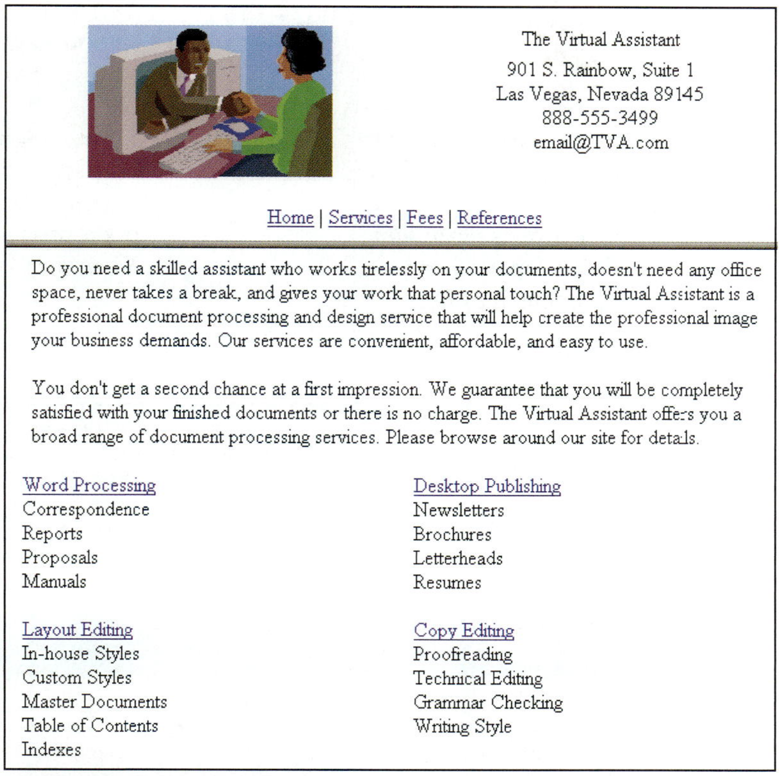

The Virtual Assistant
901 S. Rainbow, Suite 1
Las Vegas, Nevada 89145
888-555-3499
email@TVA.com

Home | Services | Fees | References

Do you need a skilled assistant who works tirelessly on your documents, doesn't need any office space, never takes a break, and gives your work that personal touch? The Virtual Assistant is a professional document processing and design service that will help create the professional image your business demands. Our services are convenient, affordable, and easy to use.

You don't get a second chance at a first impression. We guarantee that you will be completely satisfied with your finished documents or there is no charge. The Virtual Assistant offers you a broad range of document processing services. Please browse around our site for details.

Word Processing
Correspondence
Reports
Proposals
Manuals

Desktop Publishing
Newsletters
Brochures
Letterheads
Resumes

Layout Editing
In-house Styles
Custom Styles
Master Documents
Table of Contents
Indexes

Copy Editing
Proofreading
Technical Editing
Grammar Checking
Writing Style

Browser View of Frames Page

Report 114-98

Your Web Site (continued)

Follow these steps to create the final page for your Web site named *my services.htm*:

1. Type `Services` centered on the first line, and press ENTER 2 times.
2. Create an open table with 1 cell, and center it horizontally.
3. Inside the table, type four headings followed by one or two sentences each describing the services of your business.
4. View the Web page in a browser.

Report 114-99

Your Web Site (continued)

Follow these steps to finish your Web site.

1. Open the file for Report 112-91 (*my index.htm*), the frames page.
2. Create four text hyperlinks for each of the four words in the header frame as follows:
   Home, opens *my main.htm*
   Services opens *my services.htm*
   Fees opens *my fees.htm*
   References opens *my references.htm*
3. Create the hyperlinks so that the corresponding target document will display in the main fame below the header frame.
4. Create a hyperlink for each of the four headings on the main page to open *my services.htm*.
5. View the Web page in a browser.

Lesson 115

Formatting Web Pages

GOALS
- Improve speed and accuracy
- Refine language arts skills in proofreading
- Format Web pages

A. Type 2 times.

A. WARMUP

Contact bxvacuum@clean.com to order the large-sized 11
grips. They were just lowered to $160 from $240 (a 33 1/3% 23
markdown). Jay's #55 quilts were reduced to $88 from $99. 34

| 1 | 2 | 3 | 4 | 5 | 6 | 7 | 8 | 9 | 10 | 11 | 12

SKILLBUILDING

PPP

PRETEST → PRACTICE → POSTTEST

PRETEST
Take a 1-minute timing. Review your speed and errors.

B. PRETEST: Common Letter Combinations

He did mention that they are sending a lawful taping 11
of the comedy format to a performing combo. A motion to 22
commit a useful option forced a fusion of forty persons. 33

| 1 | 2 | 3 | 4 | 5 | 6 | 7 | 8 | 9 | 10 | 11 | 12

PRACTICE
Speed Emphasis:
If you made no more than 1 error on the Pretest, type each *individual* line twice.
Accuracy Emphasis:
If you made 3 or more errors, type each *group* of lines (as though it were a paragraph) 2 times.

C. PRACTICE: Word Beginnings

for forty forth format former forget forest forearm forbear
per peril perky period permit person peruse perform persist
com combo comic combat commit common combed compose complex

D. PRACTICE: Word Endings

ing doing mixing living filing taping sending biking hiding
ion onion nation lotion motion option mention fusion legion
ful awful useful joyful earful lawful helpful sinful armful

POSTTEST
Repeat the Pretest timing and compare performance.

E. POSTTEST: Common Letter Combinations

F. Take a 1-minute timing on the first paragraph to establish your base speed. Then take four 1-minute timings on the remaining paragraphs. As soon as you equal or exceed your base speed on one paragraph, advance to the next, more difficult paragraph.

F. SUSTAINED PRACTICE: CAPITALIZATION

Even though he was only about thirty years old, Jason 11
knew that it was not too soon to begin thinking about his 23
retirement. He soon found out that there were many things 35
involved in his plans for an early and long retirement. 46

Even without considering the uncertainty of social 10
security, Jason knew that he should plan his career moves 22
so that he would have a strong company retirement plan. He 34
realized that he should have an Individual Retirement Plan. 46

When he became aware that The Longman Company, the 10
firm that employed him, would match his contributions to a 22
supplemental retirement account, he began saving even more. 34
He used the Payroll Department funds from the Goplin Group. 46

He also learned that The Longman Company retirement 11
plan, his Individual Retirement Plan, and his supplemental 23
retirement account are all deferred savings. With those 34
tax-dollar savings, Jason bought New Venture Group mutuals. 46

LANGUAGE ARTS

G. Edit this paragraph to correct any typing or formatting errors.

G. PROOFREADING

The idea and practise of sharing risk originated in
antiquetry. Many years ago, Chinese merchants deviced an
injenious way of protecting themselves against the chance
of a financialy ruinous accadent in the dangerous river
along the trade routtes when they were delivring goods.

FORMATTING

H. MORE WEB SITE DESIGN GUIDELINES

Follow these guidelines to design effective Web sites:

- Experiment with the themes that come with most programs.
- If you use a theme, experiment with the embedded styles that can be applied to titles, headings, subheadings, etc., for design consistency.
- Choose a consistent look for headings and subheadings, including font size, color, and alignment, for design unity.
- Use color to establish moods: black is somber; white is clean, organized, or sterile; bright colors are energetic, but may be hard to read. Experiment and use your judgment.

Go To
Word Processing Manual

I. WEB PAGE—DESIGN THEMES

Study Lesson 115 in your word processing manual. Complete all of the shaded steps while at your computer. Then format the jobs that follow.

DOCUMENT PROCESSING

Report 115-100

Web Site (continued)

Follow these steps to format the Web site:

1. Open the file for Report 114-97 (*index.htm*), the frames page.
2. Apply a design theme to the main frame that coordinates with the picture in the frame on top.
3. Jump to *services.htm* and apply the same design theme to this page.
4. Apply a Heading 2 style to the first line, and center the line.
5. Add a bullet to each sentence under each heading beginning with the heading "Word Processing."
6. Apply a Heading 3 style to each heading beginning with the heading "Word Processing."
7. Jump to *fees.htm* and apply the same design theme to this page as used in Step 2.
8. Apply a Heading 2 style to the first line, and center the line.
9. Add a bullet to each sentence under the first paragraph except for the last sentence on the page.
10. Insert a horizontal line after the last bulleted item.
11. Jump to *references.htm* and apply the same design theme to this page as used in Step 2.
12. Apply a Heading 2 style to the first line, and center the line.
13. Place the insertion point in front of the first blank line in the table, and insert a horizontal line.
14. Place the insertion point in front of the second blank line between each reference, and insert a horizontal line.
15. Place the insertion point in front of the second blank line under the last reference, and insert a horizontal line.
16. Change any styles, fonts, or colors as desired.
17. View your finished Web site in a browser.

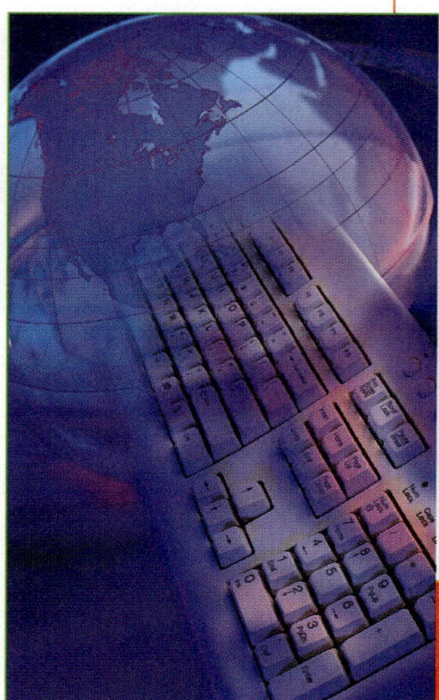

Keyboarding CONNECTION

Choosing a Different Home Page

You don't have to start at the same home page every time you use your browser. You can change the browser's home page to start at one of your favorite Web pages. Here's how to do it.

In Netscape, go to the chosen page and select Preferences from the Edit menu. Click the Navigator category in the Preferences dialog box. Click the Use Current Page button in the "Home page" area. Choose Home Page in the "Navigator starts with" area. Click OK.

In Internet Explorer, from the chosen page, select Internet Options from the Tools menu. Click the General tab, and then click the Use Current button in the "Home page" area. Click OK.

YOUR TURN Using your browser, access a favorite Web page. Make it your browser's home page.

(Continued on next page)

The Virtual Assistant

901 S. Rainbow, Suite 1
Las Vegas, Nevada 89145
888-555-3499
email@TVA.com

Home | Services | Fees | References

Do you need a skilled assistant who works tirelessly on your documents, doesn't need any office space, never takes a break, and gives your work that personal touch? The Virtual Assistant is a professional document processing and design service that will help create the professional image your business demands. Our services are convenient, affordable, and easy to use.

You don't get a second chance at a first impression. We guarantee that you will be completely satisfied with your finished documents or there is no charge. The Virtual Assistant offers you a broad range of document processing services. Please browse around our site for details.

Word Processing
- Correspondence
- Reports
- Proposals
- Manuals

Layout Editing
- In-house Styles
- Custom Styles
- Master Documents
- Table of Contents
- Indexes

Desktop Publishing
- Newsletters
- Brochures
- Letterheads
- Resumes

Copy Editing
- Proofreading
- Technical Editing
- Grammar Checking
- Writing Style

The Virtual Assistant

901 S. Rainbow, Suite 1
Las Vegas, Nevada 89145
888-555-3499
email@TVA.com

Home | Services | Fees | References

Services

Word Processing

- We prepare documents with a professional look for correspondence of all types as well as reports, proposals, manuals, etc.

Desktop Publishing

- Our professional design specialists will create newsletters, brochures, letterheads, etc., that are sure to capture your imagination.

Layout Editing

- Our layout editors will transform your documents using in-house styles or custom styles. For your longer projects, they are experts at building master documents that include a cover page, table of contents, and index.

Copy Editing

- Our copy editors will make sure that your document content is perfect. Proofreading, grammar, and writing style will all be checked so that your ideas are expressed clearly and effectively.

(Continued on next page)

The Virtual Assistant

901 S. Rainbow, Suite 1
Las Vegas, Nevada 89145
888-555-3499
email@TVA.com

Home | Services | Fees | References

Fees

The Virtual Assistant strives to work within your organization's budget. We will review your individual needs and tailor the pricing to fit your project. We welcome the opportunity to provide an individual estimate. Be assured that our prices are extremely competitive. Here are some general guidelines regarding our fees:

- We typically charge by the hour or by the page, depending upon the job.
- Most fees are based on the length of the document and the amount of editing deemed necessary.
- We offer substantial discounts for volume work and repeat clients.
- A surcharge is added for rush jobs.
- Payment for services rendered should be made by credit card, check, or money order.

For a copy of our current rate guide, please send
an email message to rateguide@TVA.com.

The Virtual Assistant

901 S. Rainbow, Suite 1
Las Vegas, Nevada 89145
888-555-3499
email@TVA.com

Home | Services | Fees | References

References

I've been in a highly successful business for over 10 years and attribute much of that success to the skilled professionals at The Virtual Assistant. I am always confident that my work will go out error free. They are top-notch professionals and can work for my team anytime!

Mike Rashid
Network Engineer
Denver, Colorado

The documents produced by The Virtual Assistant are impeccable! I can count on professional, reliable, competent, and efficient service without question. It is so easy to send documents back and forth via the Internet, and we all know that time is money. I highly recommend TVC for any of your word processing needs.

Nancy Shipley
Attorney at Law
Chicago, Illinois

Report 115-101

Web Site

Progress Check
Proofreading Check

Documents designated as Proofreading Checks serve as a check of your proofreading skill. Your goal is to have zero typographical errors when the GDP software first scores the document.

Follow these steps to create this Web site:

1. GDP will automatically open a blank document. Save it as a Web page named *main page.htm*.
2. Insert File 115A.
3. Insert a header frame above the main page to create a frames page. Save the frames page as *index page.htm*.
4. Insert File 115B.
5. Insert a picture related to sports in the open cell in Column A.
6. Resize the picture proportionately until it is about 2 inches wide, and center the picture.
7. Click outside the table when you have finished.
8. Create a text hyperlink in the header frame for the word "Main" so that the target document, *main page.htm*, will display in the main frame.
9. Create a text hyperlink in the header frame for the words "Contact Us" so that the target document, *contact us.htm*, will display in the main frame.
10. Apply a design theme to the header frame and both pages in the main frame that coordinates with the picture in the header frame.
11. Move to the header frame, apply a Heading 1 style to the business name *In The Game,* and center it.
12. Move to *main page.htm* in the main frame, and apply a Heading 2 style to each of the four headings (*Baseball and Softball, Soccer, Track and Field,* and *Gymnastics*) on the main page.
13. Move to the *contact us.htm* in the main frame.
14. Apply a Heading 2 style to the title "Contact Us" at the top of the page, and center the title if needed.
15. Apply a Heading 3 style to each of the three headings (*Email, Call Us,* and *Snail Mail*) on the page.
16. Resize the header frame as shown below by dragging the bottom border.
17. Save the frames page again.
18. View the Web page in a browser.

Unit 24

Skillbuilding and In-Basket Review

LESSON 116
In-Basket Review (Insurance)

LESSON 117
In-Basket Review (Hospitality)

LESSON 118
In-Basket Review (Retail)

LESSON 119
In-Basket Review (Government)

LESSON 120
In-Basket Review (Manufacturing)

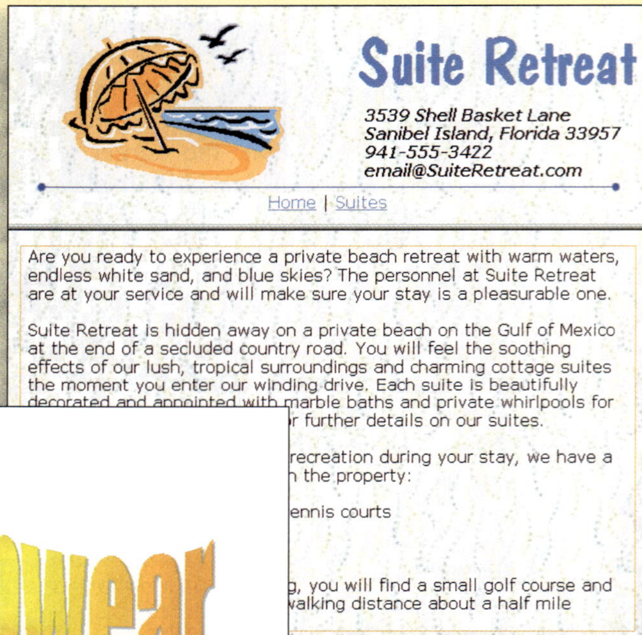
Suite Retreat
3539 Shell Basket Lane
Sanibel Island, Florida 33957
941-555-3422
email@SuiteRetreat.com
Home | Suites

Are you ready to experience a private beach retreat with warm waters, endless white sand, and blue skies? The personnel at Suite Retreat are at your service and will make sure your stay is a pleasurable one.

Suite Retreat is hidden away on a private beach on the Gulf of Mexico at the end of a secluded country road. You will feel the soothing effects of our lush, tropical surroundings and charming cottage suites the moment you enter our winding drive. Each suite is beautifully decorated and appointed with marble baths and private whirlpools for ... r further details on our suites.

... recreation during your stay, we have a ... n the property:

... ennis courts

... g, you will find a small golf course and ... walking distance about a half mile

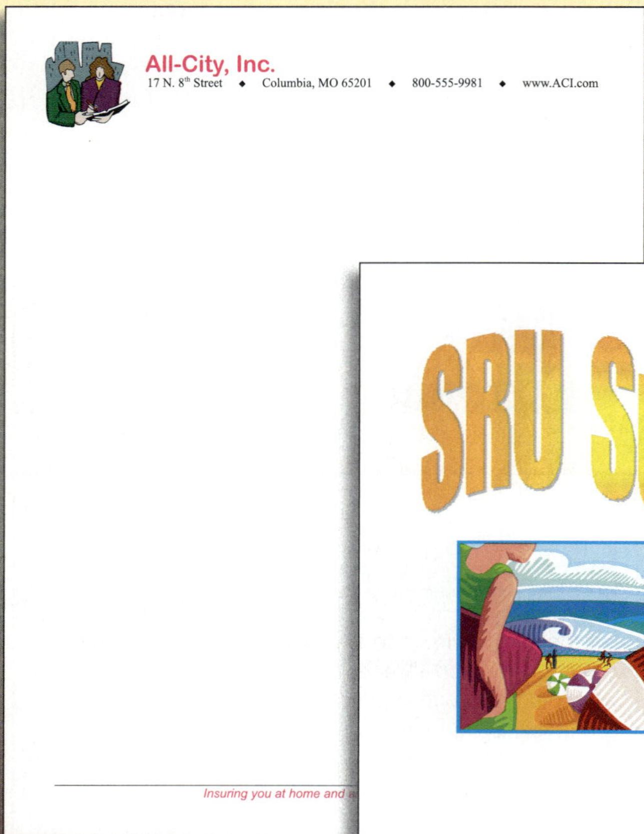
All-City, Inc.
17 N. 8th Street ◆ Columbia, MO 65201 ◆ 800-555-9981 ◆ www.ACI.com

Insuring you at home and ...

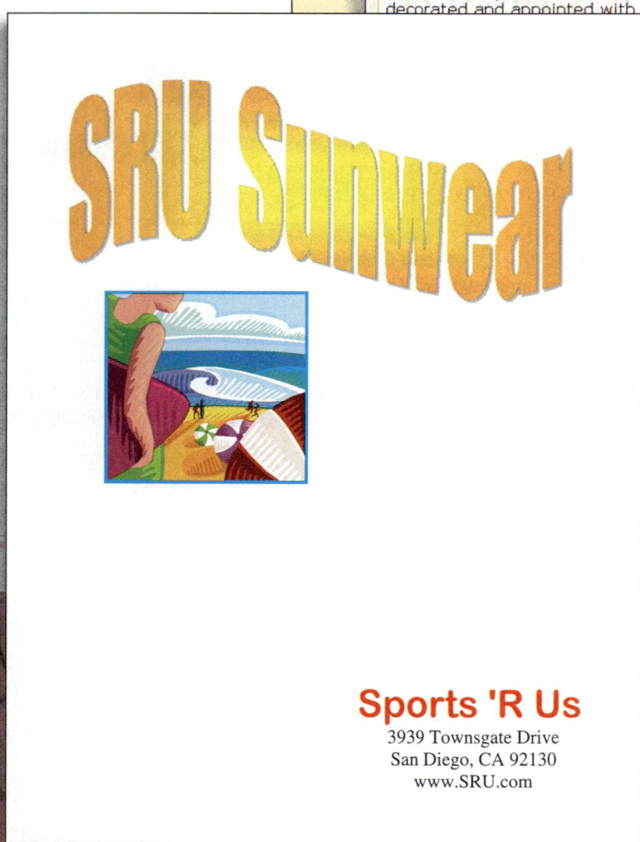
SRU Sunwear

Sports 'R Us
3939 Townsgate Drive
San Diego, CA 92130
www.SRU.com

In-Basket Review (Insurance)

GOALS
- Type at least 50wpm/5′/5e
- Format insurance documents

A. Type 2 times.

A. WARMUP

```
     He realized that exactly 10% of the budget ($62,475)    11
was questionable. Several key people reviewed it; most of    23
them wanted to reject about 1/3 of the proposed line items!  35
| 1 | 2 | 3 | 4 | 5 | 6 | 7 | 8 | 9 | 10 | 11 | 12
```

SKILLBUILDING

B. PROGRESSIVE PRACTICE: ALPHABET

If you are not using the GDP software, turn to page SB-7 and follow the directions for this activity.

STRATEGIES FOR *Career Success*

Managing Group Conflict

Not all team members have the same opinion or approach to solving a problem. Before a group can reach an agreement, conflicts must be addressed and expressed openly. Follow these steps to manage group conflict.

Take everyone's feelings and opinions seriously. Don't be afraid to disagree. Offer and accept constructive criticism. Find points of agreement. When the group makes a decision, support it fully.

Be a good listener. Take notes, maintain eye contact, restate what you hear, and listen for the emotions behind the words. Try to view the situation through the other person's eyes. Don't jump to conclusions. Ask non-threatening questions to clarify meaning, and listen without interrupting. Most group conflicts don't get resolved until everyone feels he or she has had a chance to be heard.

YOUR TURN When is the last time you had a conflict with a coworker? What did you do about it? What was the result?

C. Take two 5-minute timings. Review your speed and errors.

Goal: At least 50wpm/5'/5e

C. 5-MINUTE TIMING

```
     Several factors should be considered before you buy      11
a new printer for your computer. First, decide how you will   23
use the new printer. If you plan to use the printer for       34
composing letters or reports, you may want to shop for an     46
ink jet printer that is reasonably priced and capable of      57
doing general tasks. If you are purchasing the printer for    69
office use, you may wish to shop for a printer that prints    81
documents more quickly and of exceptional quality. Finally,   93
if you plan to use a digital camera with the printer, you    105
will want a printer that is designed to print documents of   117
photo quality.                                               120
     Resolution, speed, and paper handling are some other    131
factors you should consider when you purchase a printer.     142
Resolution refers to how sharp the image appears on the      153
paper. With printers producing a higher resolution, the      164
imaging gives a higher quality output. You will see this     175
amazing difference in imaging when you compare samples of    187
print from various types of printers.                        195
     If you expect to print long documents, then you will    206
want to look for a reliable printer with a feed tray that    218
holds large amounts of paper. The more expensive printers    230
are usually faster printers. After assessing your printer    241
needs, you are ready to make your purchase.                  250
| 1 | 2 | 3 | 4 | 5 | 6 | 7 | 8 | 9 | 10 | 11 | 12
```

DOCUMENT PROCESSING

Form 116-15

Letter Template With Enclosure Notation

Use the first letter template in your word processing software.

Situation: You are employed in the office of All-City, Inc., an insurance company in Columbia, Missouri. Their offices are located at 17 N. 8th Street, Columbia, MO 65201, and their phone number is 800-555-9981. All City, Inc., handles auto, home, and life insurance coverage. The Web site address is www.ACI.com.

Mr. Greg Scher, executive vice president, has written the letter shown on page 471 using the current date. You are to type it using a correspondence template. He prefers block-style letters with *Sincerely* as his complimentary closing and uses his title in the writer's identification. The letter should be addressed to Ms. Thelma Day, 731 Broad Street, Newark, NJ 07102, and you should use standard punctuation. This letter includes two enclosures. The company slogan is "Insuring you at home and around the world."

¶ Your recent letter was filled with excellent questions, Ms. Day, and I am more than happy to answer them for you.

¶ All City, Inc., handles auto, home, and life insurance coverage for you and your family. However, since you are primarily interested in auto insurance, I have enclosed a brochure with the details and a table with required minimum coverage for the states you mentioned.

¶ ACI's automobile policy combines both mandatory and optional coverages in one package. This policy can be tailored to meet your individual needs so that you end up with a policy that provides comprehensive protection. However, the best way for you to understand fully what we can offer you is to schedule a meeting at your convenience.

¶ Ms. Elena Ortega will be calling you in the next day or two to arrange an appointment after you have had a chance to review the enclosed materials. We also have an excellent Web site at ACI.com filled with helpful information. Again, thank you for your inquiry, Ms. Day.

Table 116-55

Three-Column Boxed Table

The boxed table below is to be enclosed with the letter when it is sent to Ms. Day.

STATE MINIMUM COVERAGE REQUIREMENTS		
Minimum Limits	**State**	**Required Coverage**
25/50/10	NY	Bodily Injury and Property Damage Liability, Personal Injury Protection, Uninsured Motorist
15/30/5	NJ	Bodily Injury and Property Damage Liability, Personal Injury Protection, Uninsured Motorist
15/30/5	PA	Bodily Injury and Property Damage Liability, Medical Payments
20/40/10	CT	Bodily Injury and Property Damage Liability, Uninsured and Underinsured Motorist

Form 116-16

Letterhead Form

Mr. Scher has sketched out a letterhead form, and he would like you to design the finished letterhead for All-City, Inc.

Insert a decorative image.

Identify our company, including our Web site.

Insert our company slogan with a border above it.

Lesson 117

In-Basket Review (Hospitality)

GOALS

- Improve speed and accuracy
- Refine language arts skills in word usage
- Format documents used in the hospitality industry

A. Type 2 times.

A. WARMUP

```
1      The executive meeting won't begin until 8:15; please    11
2  contact just the key people at zfnet@mail.com. Did Kay say  23
3  that quite a group* (*234) is expected by 9 o'clock today?  35
   | 1 | 2 | 3 | 4 | 5 | 6 | 7 | 8 | 9 | 10 | 11 | 12
```

SKILLBUILDING

B. Take three 12-second timings on each line. The scale below the last line shows your wpm speed for a 12-second timing.

B. 12-SECOND SPEED SPRINTS

```
4  Half of the space was going to be used for seven new desks.
5  She will soon know if all their goals have been met or not.
6  You must learn to focus on each one of your jobs every day.
7  The group will meet in the new suite that is down the hall.
   | | | | 5 | | | | 10 | | | | 15 | | | | 20 | | | | 25 | | | | 30 | | | | 35 | | | | 40 | | | | 45 | | | | 50 | | | | 55 | | | | 60
```

C. Type line 8. Then type lines 9-11 (as a paragraph), reading the words from right to left. Type 2 times.

C. TECHNIQUE PRACTICE: CONCENTRATION

```
8       When typing, always strive for complete concentration.
9   concentration. complete for strive always typing, When
10  errors. your on down cut may rate typing your in decrease A
11  errors. of number the reduce to rate reading your down Slow
```

D. DIAGNOSTIC PRACTICE: ALPHABET

If you are not using the GDP software, turn to page SB-2 and follow the directions for this activity.

LANGUAGE ARTS

E. Study the rules at the right.

E. WORD USAGE

RULE ▶ accept/except

***Accept* means "to agree to"; *except* means "to leave out."**

All employees except the maintenance staff should accept the agreement.

RULE ▶ affect/effect

***Affect* is most often used as a verb meaning "to influence"; *effect* is most often used as a noun meaning "result."**

The ruling will affect our domestic operations but will have no effect on Asian operations.

RULE ▶ farther/further

***Farther* refers to distance; *further* refers to extent or degree.**

The farther we drove, the further agitated he became.

RULE ▶ personal/personnel

***Personal* means "private"; *personnel* means "employees."**

All personnel agreed not to use email for personal business.

RULE ▶ principal/principle

***Principal* means "primary"; *principle* means "rule."**

The principle of fairness is our principal means of dealing with customers.

Edit the sentences to correct any errors in word usage.

```
12 The company cannot accept any collect calls, except for his.
13 The affect of the speech was dramatic; everyone was affected.
14 Further discussion by office personal was not appropriate.
15 Comments made during any meeting should never be personal.
16 If the meeting is held any further away, no one will attend.
17 The principle reason for the decision was to save money.
18 Office ethics is a basic principle that should be practiced.
19 He cannot except the fact that the job was delegated to Jack.
20 Any further effects on office personnel will be evaluated.
```

DOCUMENT PROCESSING

Situation: You are employed at the office of Suite Retreat, a group of vacation cottage-style suites in Sanibel, Florida. The office and suites are located at 3539 Shell Basket Lane, Sanibel Island, Florida 33957. The phone number is 941-555-3422, and the email address is email@SuiteRetreat.com.

Ms. Maxwell, your boss, has asked you to redesign the home page for Suite Retreat. She has written a description of Suite Retreat that she wants you to use in the main frame. The header frame should include identifying information and a picture that will capture the feeling of a carefree beach vacation spot. The theme and styles you choose for the header and main frame should reflect this same image.

Begin by creating the file for Web page 117-102 named *main suite.htm*. Create the main page first by typing the information inside a one-row, centered open table, followed by the frames page, and save the frames page as *index suite.htm*.

(Continued on next page)

Report 117-102

Web Site

personal/personnel

¶ Are you ready to experience a private beach retreat with warm waters, endless white sand, and blue skies? The personnel at Suite Retreat are at your service and will make sure your stay is a pleasurable one.

¶ Suite Retreat is hidden away on a private beach on the Gulf of Mexico at the end of a secluded country road. You will feel the soothing

affect/effect

effects of our lush, tropical surroundings and charming cottage suites the moment you enter our winding drive. Each suite is beautifully decorated and appointed with marble baths and

personal/personnel

private whirlpools for your personal use. Click

farther/further

here for further details on our suites.

¶ If you are interested in a little recreation during your stay, we have a variety of activities available on the property:

- shuffleboard courts and tennis courts
- bicycles and kayaks
- swimming and shelling

¶ If you enjoy golf and fine dining, you will find a small golf course and excellent seafood within easy walking distance about a half mile

farther/further

farther down the beach.

STRATEGIES FOR Career Success

What to Exclude From Your Resume

What items should you remove from your resume? Don't list salary demands. If the job posting requires a salary history, create a separate page listing the salaries for each position you've held. If the job posting wants your salary requirements, in the application letter state, "Salary expectation is in the range...", and provide a range (usually a $5000 range).

Exclude personal information such as race, gender, health status, age, marital status, religious preference, political preference, national origin, and physical characteristics (e.g., height, weight). Do not provide your Social Security number or your photograph.

Exceptions to listing personal information do exist. For example, if you are applying for a job at a political party's headquarters and you are a member of that party, listing your party affiliation might be important to your potential employer.

YOUR TURN Review your resume. Have you included any personal information? If yes, does it serve a purpose for being in your resume?

Report 117-103

Web Site

Ms. Maxwell has asked you to continue building the Web site by opening the frames page (index suite.htm) and adding two hyperlinks at the bottom of the header frame named "home" and "suites." These hyperlinks should point to the main page (main suite.htm) and a second page named *suites.htm*, which has already been created and includes details on the suite rates.

She also wants you to add a hyperlink on the main page on the word *here* in the last sentence of the second paragraph to link to the second page. After you create these hyperlinks, she wants you to add formatting, themes, etc., to the second page.

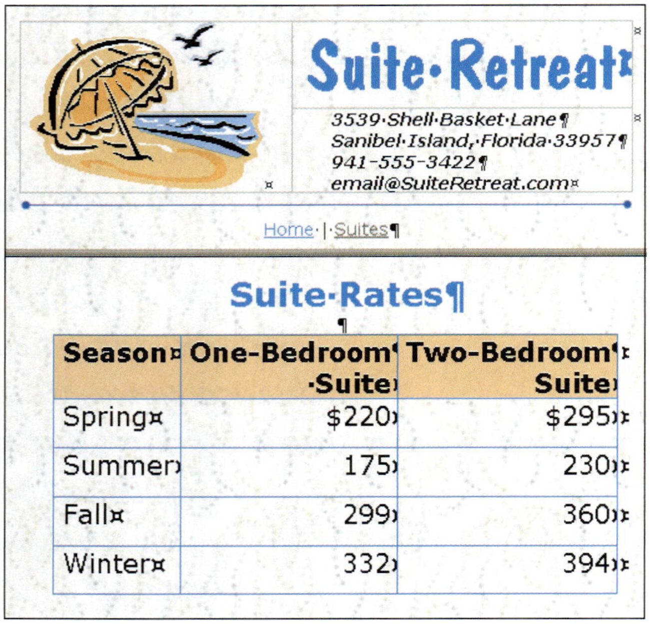

These are suggestions for a Web site design. Use your own judgment in the layout and design of the Web site.

Lesson 118

In-Basket Review (Retail)

GOALS

- Type at least 50wpm/5′/5e
- To format retail documents

A. Type 2 times.

A. WARMUP

```
     Does Pamela know if Region 29* (*Ventura) has met the    11
sales quota? Their exact target zone is just not clear;       22
they don't have to submit their totals until 4:30 on 5/7.     33
| 1 | 2 | 3 | 4 | 5 | 6 | 7 | 8 | 9 | 10 | 11 | 12
```

SKILLBUILDING

B. PACED PRACTICE

If you are not using the GDP software, turn to page SB-14 and follow the directions for this activity.

State-of-the-art technology is readily available to consumers at retail stores. Success in retail sales takes initiative, energy, self-confidence, and keyboarding skills.

C. Take two 5-minute timings. Review your speed and errors.

Goal: At least 50wpm/5'/5e

C. 5-MINUTE TIMING

Job sharing is a current concept that many employers 11
are using to keep valued workers. People are finding a 22
variety of reasons for preferring not to work full time. 33
Here are some tips on how to approach your employer if you 45
would like to try job sharing. 51

First, check your company handbook for an official 61
policy regarding this concept. If there is no policy that 73
prohibits the concept, then try to enlist a coworker who 84
would like to job share and help you in writing a proposal 96
for job sharing. 99

Next, define your needs and objectives. Develop a 109
work schedule that will meet your personal and monetary 120
needs. Be sure to include adequate time to get the work 131
done. If you want to work from home occasionally, be sure 143
to indicate your preference. You may find it quite useful 155
to maintain a journal of your job responsibilities, noting 167
how much time is devoted to each task. 175

Your plan also should include information about the 186
logistics of your proposal. Determine how you will deal 197
with unexpected and crisis situations. 205

Finally, time your presentation so there will be no 216
unnecessary interruptions. Be organized, persistent, and 227
professional in your presentation. Prepare to be successful 239
by compiling clearly defined ideas to support your plan. 250

| 1 | 2 | 3 | 4 | 5 | 6 | 7 | 8 | 9 | 10 | 11 | 12

DOCUMENT PROCESSING

Form 118-17

Memo Template

Use the first memo template in your word processing software.

Situation: Today is January 5. You are employed as an administrative assistant to Kelley O'Brian. Ms. O'Brian is Vice President of Marketing for Sports 'R Us, a retailer for sports equipment and clothing in San Diego, California at 3939 Townsgate Drive, San Diego, CA 92130. The Web site is www.SRU.com.

The company is in the midst of launching a brand new line of women's sportswear for the beach. Ms. O'Brian has written the memo below to Hitochi Morimoto, President of Sports 'R Us, with a copy to Barbara Warrick, Vice President of Sales. You are to type the memo, using a memo template. The subject of the memo is `SRU Sunwear Ad Campaign`.

(Continued on next page)

¶ I am pleased to tell you that we are in the final stages of our ad campaign to launch our newest line of women's beach sportswear named SRU Sunwear. We are just about to sign Cindy Bloom to serve as our spokesperson and featured model in our magazine ad campaign.

¶ I have scheduled a meeting for next week so that you can meet Cindy and see a representative sampling of our exciting new sportswear line. My staff members will also be ready with a presentation for our ad campaign, which will focus on the practicality and smart good looks of our newest beachwear. I have attached an agenda for your review.

¶ Our company has always been known for the value and quality of our sportswear. This line is based on a smaller emerging brand that will save our customers money while still maintaining the high quality they have come to expect. I look forward to our meeting next week.

Report 118-104

Agenda

The meeting agenda entitled SRU SUNWEAR AD CAMPAIGN shown below is to be attached to the memo when it is sent to Mr. Morimoto. The meeting will be held January 12, 20--, at 11 a.m.

Call to order
Approval of minutes of December 20 meeting
Introduction of Cindy Bloom
Progress report on the status of the ad campaign
Presentation of the ad campaign
Presentation of some samples from the new sportswear line
Announcements
Miscellaneous
Adjournment

Report 118-105

Cover Page

Ms. O'Brian has sketched out a cover page for the ad campaign report and would like you to design the finished cover page for the SRU Sunwear line of beach apparel. The report will be distributed at the meeting.

Insert some word art with the name of our sportswear line.

Insert a picture related to our new line of beach sportswear.

Identify our company and our address, including our Web site.

Lesson 119

In-Basket Review (Government)

GOALS

- Improve speed and accuracy
- Refine language arts skills in spelling
- Format government documents

A. Type 2 times.

A. WARMUP

1 Turner & Finch will charge us $10,234 to complete the 11
2 job. Do they realize that they quoted us an initial fee of 23
3 exactly $9,876? Kelly will call them very soon to verify. 34

| 1 | 2 | 3 | 4 | 5 | 6 | 7 | 8 | 9 | 10 | 11 | 12

SKILLBUILDING

PPP

PRETEST → PRACTICE → POSTTEST

PRETEST
Take a 1-minute timing. Review your speed and errors.

B. PRETEST: Close Reaches

4 Sadly, the same essay was used to oppose and deny the 11
5 phony felony charge. After the weapon was located in his 22
6 pocket, the jury was left to cast the joint ballot anyway. 34

| 1 | 2 | 3 | 4 | 5 | 6 | 7 | 8 | 9 | 10 | 11 | 12

PRACTICE
Speed Emphasis:
If you made no more than 1 error on the Pretest, type each *individual* line 2 times.
Accuracy Emphasis:
If you made 2 or more errors, type each *group* of lines (as though it were a paragraph) 2 times.

C. PRACTICE: Adjacent Keys

7 po post spot pours vapor poker powder oppose weapon pockets
8 sa sash same usage essay sadly safety dosage sample sailing
9 oi oily join point voice doing choice boiled egoist loiters

D. PRACTICE: Conscecutive Fingers

10 ft left soft often after shift gifted crafts thrift uplifts
11 ny onyx deny nylon vinyl phony anyway skinny felony canyons
12 lo loss solo loser flood color locate floral ballot loaders

POSTTEST
Repeat the Pretest timing and compare performance.

E. POSTTEST: Close Reaches

F. Take a 1-minute timing on the first paragraph to establish your base speed. Then take four 1-minute timings on the remaining paragraphs. As soon as you equal or exceed your base speed on one paragraph, advance to the next, more difficult paragraph.

F. SUSTAINED PRACTICE: PUNCTUATION

Have you ever noticed that a good laugh every now and 11
then really makes you feel better? Research has shown that 23
laughter can have a very healing effect on our bodies. It 35
is an excellent way to relieve tension and stress all over. 47

When you laugh, your heart beats faster, you breathe 11
deeper, and you exercise your lungs. When you laugh, your 23
body produces endorphins--a natural painkiller that gives 35
you a sense of euphoria that is very powerful and pleasant. 47

Someone said, "Laugh in the face of adversity." As it 11
happens, this is first-rate advice. It's a great way to 22
cope with life's trials and tribulations; it's also a good 34
way to raise other people's spirits and relieve tension. 45

Finding "humor" in any situation takes practice--try 11
to make it a full-time habit. We're all looking for ways 22
to relieve stress. Any exercise--jogging, tennis, biking, 34
swimming, or golfing--is a proven remedy for "the blues." 45

LANGUAGE ARTS

G. Type these frequently misspelled words, paying special attention to any spelling problems in each word.

G. SPELLING

practice continue regular entitled course resolution assist
weeks preparation purposes referred communication potential
environmental specifications original contractor associated
principal systems client excellent estimated administration
responsibility mentioned utilized materials criteria campus

Edit the sentences to correct any misspellings.

It is the responsability of the administration to assist.
The principle client prepared the excellent specifications.
He mentioned that the critiria for the decision were clear.
The contractor associated with the project referred them.
He estamated that the potential for resolution was great.
I was told that weeks of reguler practice were required.

DOCUMENT PROCESSING

Correspondence 119-99

Business Letter in Block Style With Postscript Notation

Situation: You work as an administrative assistant for Ruth McBride. She is Research Director for Ride Share, a free government-funded commuter service in Chicago that informs people about commuting alternatives.

Ms. McBride has left the letter below in your in-basket to be sent to Mr. Jason Davis, Executive Director for Canadian CarShare, which is located at 1233 West 3rd Ave., Vancouver, BC V6J 1K1 in Canada. When communicating with Canadian firms, use A4 metric size paper and adhere to Canadian mailing guidelines.

Ms. McBride prefers a block-style letter with standard punctuation, uses *Sincerely* as the complimentary close, and likes her business title typed below her name in a letter closing. Use the current date, and add this postscript notation at the end of the letter:

```
Any statistics you might
choose to include on the
environmental impact
associated with car sharing
in your Web site at
http://www.carshare.ca would
be very helpful.
```

Words shown in a different color are spelling words from the language arts activities.

¶ Ride Share is a government funded commuter service whose mission is to inform our citizens about commuting alternatives in the Chicago area. My responsibility is to gather as many facts as possible regarding the regular practice of car sharing in Canada.

¶ As I understand this concept, a car share client could conceivably mix and match alternative modes of transportation and also have exclusive use of a reserved car for a fixed period of time. For example, a commuter could arrive at work on a train, pick up a reserved car at a nearby parking lot to run errands at lunch, return the car an hour later, and then continue home perhaps using a van pool or bus. The commuter would pay about 20 to 40 cents a kilometer along with some monthly membership fees.

¶ If you can tell me which cities have successfully utilized car sharing in Canada since it was first introduced and why, I can begin preparation for a proposal for a car sharing pilot project as a potential commuter alternative here in the Chicago area.

Correspondence 119-100

Business Letter in Block Style With Postscript Notation

Open the file for Correspondence 119-99. Ms. McBride would like you to send the same letter to Mr. Frans Zimmerly, Executive Director of Europa CarShare at Siesmayerstrasse 23, 60323 Frankfurt, GERMANY. When communicating with German firms, use A4 metric size paper and adhere to German mailing guidelines.

Find and replace all instances of Canada with Germany. Use the current date (use day/month/year format), and add this postscript at the end of the letter:

```
Any statistics you might
choose to fax to me at
+1.217.782.5553 regarding
the environmental impact
associated with car sharing
in Germany would be very
helpful.
```

Correspondence 119-101

Email Message

Send the email message below to Ms. McBride (mcbride@commerce.state.il.us). The subject line is `Car Sharing`. Type an appropriate greeting for Ms. McBride and a closing and signature line for yourself.

¶ I sent the two letters to the executive directors of CarShare as you requested. I will follow up in a week with phone calls and email messages as follows:

¶ Mr. Jason Davis
+1.604.877.5555
jdavis@carshare.ubc.ca

¶ Mr. Frans Zimmerly
+49.30.20304-0
fzimmerly@carshare.de

¶ I found some statistics about car sharing that might be useful. Car sharing was first introduced in Quebec City in 1994 and now has about 1,200 users in six Canadian cities. About 90,000 car share commuters are located worldwide, with about half of them in Europe.

Keyboarding CONNECTION

Email Privacy

How private are your email messages? Although there has been a lot of discussion about hacking and Internet security, email may be more secure than your phone or postal mail. In fact, most new-generation email programs have some kind of encryption built in.

It is not hackers who are the most likely to read your email. It is anyone with access to your incoming mail server or your computer. If your computer and incoming server are at work, then you can assume that your supervisor can read your email. In some companies, it is a normal practice to monitor employees' email. Therefore, you should not send email from work that you wouldn't want anyone there to read.

If you are serious about email privacy, you may want to examine other encryption methods. Different products are available to ensure that your email is only read by the intended recipient(s).

YOUR TURN Perform a keyword search, using a search engine (e.g., *www.altavista.com*), for information on different products that are available to protect your email privacy.

In-Basket Review (Manufacturing)

GOALS

- Type at least 50wpm/5′/5e
- Format manufacturing documents

A. Type 2 times.

A. WARMUP

Order extra color cartridges very soon! G & K Supply 11
just announced a 15% discount on orders for the following 23
cartridges: QB728 and ZM 436* (*for the ink-jet printers). 35

| 1 | 2 | 3 | 4 | 5 | 6 | 7 | 8 | 9 | 10 | 11 | 12

SKILLBUILDING

B. DIAGNOSTIC PRACTICE: NUMBERS

If you are not using the GDP software, turn to page SB-5 and follow the directions for this activity.

C. MAP

Follow the GDP software directions for this exercise in improving keystroking accuracy.

Fast and accurate keyboarding skills are critical in providing service to people who are traveling.

D. Take two 5-minute timings. Review your speed and errors.

Goal: At least 50wpm/5′/5e

D. 5-MINUTE TIMING

With modern technology, it is possible to work at a 11
job full time and never leave your home. You can set up a 22
home office with a phone line, fax machine, and a computer 34
system. Before choosing to work at home, however, you will 46
want to examine carefully your reasons for working at home. 58

Some people think about working at home so they can 69
have more time to spend with their families. Other people 81
like to have more flexibility in their work schedule. They 93
are looking for the opportunity to enjoy a better quality 105
of life or to participate in other activities. 114

There are some factors to consider before you make 124
the decision to work at home. You will want to consider 135
the ultimate cost of benefits that you may give up if you 147
change your place of work. You will want to check with 158
your employer to see if you are entitled to paid vacation 170
days and health insurance or to make contributions to your 181
retirement plan. Another factor to consider is the limited 193
contact with peers. 197

Before making the ultimate decision to work at home, 208
develop some realistic expectations of how you will spend 220
each day. Although you can organize your work to fit your 232
schedule, you will find the real challenge is to determine 244
a routine that works for you. 250

| 1 | 2 | 3 | 4 | 5 | 6 | 7 | 8 | 9 | 10 | 11 | 12

DOCUMENT PROCESSING

Situation: You work as an administrative assistant for Melanie Stone at MedPro Manufacturing, one of the largest medical diagnostic equipment manufacturers in the world. The home office is located in Arden, North Carolina, with branch offices located worldwide.

Your boss has left a business report in your in-basket for you to format and type. The title of the report is `MedPro Manufacturing`. The subtitle of the report is `Vision, Innovation, and Partnership`. Use the current date after the subtitle.

(Continued on next page)

Report 120-106

Multipage Business Report

Introduction

¶ Med Pro Manufacturing is 1 of the largest medical diagnostic equipment manufacturers in the world. We have been in business for almost eighty 80 years and our company has a solid reputation for quality and reliability in all our manufacturing processes. We take great pride in our current state-of-the-art manufacturing facilitise because we realize that doctors' reputations and patients' lives depend on the quality and reliability of our products and medical supplies.

VISION

¶ MedPro's vision for the New Millennium is to continue the manufacturing of circuit boards, light sources, fiber optic light guides, and scanning engines.We have in place a stringent quality management process so that our customers are guaranteed a superior product at a competitive price. Because of these high standards, we have our company has attained the most current ISO Certification. We have reduced consistently our manufacturing cycles without sacrificing quality.

INNOVATION

¶ Everyone at MedPro from those on the manufacturing floor to those in the presidents office are is committed to the continuation of the research and development of innovative products and state-of-the-art high-tech manufacturing processes.

Products. Our electronic stethoscope system combined a revolutionary acoustic technology and teamed it with the power of a computer to produce extraordinary results in doctors offices. We specialize in innovative products for kids children. Our autorefractor has allowed optome-trists and ophthalmologists to perform an objective refraction on children that is faster and easier than ever before. We are committed to the continuous development of innovative products like these.

Manufacturing processes. Our fiber optic light guides and scanning engines are 2 more examples of how MedPro is committed to innovation in the manufacturing process as well. Our computercontrolled manufacturing

(Continued on next page)

and CAD/ECAD equipment helps us to control precisely the manufacturing of all our medical equipment. These same innovative processes have helped us reduce our costs and reduce our manufacturing cycle.

PARTNERSHIP

¶ One of the most effective ways to ensure success is to develop partnerships with other innovative business es that have the same commitment to high standards and are leaders in ~~there~~ their respective fields. Our team work and collaboration with our partners have helped us to establish an international presence and reputation. ¶ Our website ~~is~~ can be found at http://medpro.com, and it is filled with a wealth of ~~excellent~~ information. All details of our products services, employees, contact information, etc., can be foundthere. We look forward to your business.

Correspondence 120-102

Multipage Business Letter in Block Style With Three-Column Boxed Table

Progress Check Proofreading Check

Documents designated as Proofreading Checks serve as a check of your proofreading skill. Your goal is to have zero typographical errors when the GDP software first scores the document.

A letter that includes a table has also been left in your in-basket to be typed with the current date (use day/month/year format). The letter is to be sent to Mrs. Carmen Tamashiro, Associate Director for Medical Relief International, which is located at 3-5-1 Kanda Jinbo-cho, Chiyoda-ku Tokyo 101, Japan. The subject line is `Relief Medical Supplies`. When communicating with Japanese firms, you are to use A4 metric size paper and adhere to Japanese mailing guidelines.

Ms. Stone, Public Relations Director, prefers a block-style letter with standard punctuation and likes to use a predesigned format for tables. She prefers *Sincerely* as the complimentary close, uses the company name in the closing, and likes her business title typed below her name in the closing. She does not use a courtesy title.

¶ MedPro Manufacturing is happy to send our tenth shipment of relief medical supplies to be distributed as needed to the people of Japan who have been devastated by recent earthquakes and other natural disasters.

(Continued on next page)

¶ Our previous shipments to Japan have amounted to well over $1 million worth of medical supplies such as antibiotics, surgical supplies, catheters, packs, crutches, splints, braces, and slings. MedPro Manufacturing usually sends medical goods and equipment exclusively; however, some of the earlier shipments have also included basic survival supplies. Our employees have helped us in our efforts to gather hundreds of tents, sleeping bags, blankets, flashlights, coats, socks, gloves, and all-weather apparel.

¶ Several international branches of our company would also like to offer their help if you need it. The table below includes all the pertinent information:

Address	Email	Telephone
Marie Desaulnier 4, rue Galvani Massy, F-91745 FRANCE	medpro.com@email.fr	+33.1.64531515
Frank Liberman Mittlerer Pfad 9 D-70499 Stuttgart GERMANY	medpro.com@email.de	+49.711.8871624
Manny Yamamoto 16-13, 2-chome Hongo Tokyo 113-0033 JAPAN	medpro.com@email.jp	+81.3.38138841

¶ If I can offer you any further assistance or information, please don't hesitate to contact me at +1.704.555.8945.

Test 6

Skills Assessment on Part 6

5-Minute Timing

The potential to reach your career goals has never 10
been better. The person who will advance in a career is 21
the one who will make the bold moves to follow his or her 33
dreams. He or she will have the required attributes of 44
initiative and motivation to put forth maximum efforts 55
in order to realize a fulfilling career. 63
If you want to get ahead in the highly competitive 73
business world today, you need a personal coach or mentor 85
who is experienced in motivating people who want to reach 97
their potential. You may be afraid to go after your dream 109
career because you are afraid of failure. Your personal 120
mentor will help you to minimize any problems you incur. 131
He or she will encourage you to strive for more. 141
When you decide to work with a professional coach, 151
you are investing in yourself. You can trust your coach to 163
work with you through the entire process of expanding your 175
horizons until you reach your goal. When you think you 186
have reached your limit, your coach will make suggestions 198
for additional improvement. He or she will present the 209
strategies you can use to be successful. Your coach will 220
guide you in making the critical decisions for advancing 231
your career. The final decision to improve your skills 242
and become successful is yours, however. 250

| 1 | 2 | 3 | 4 | 5 | 6 | 7 | 8 | 9 | 10 | 11 | 12

Form Test 6-18

Memo Template With Attachment Notation

Select the first memo template listed in your word processing software.

To: Michael Lani, Human Resources Director | **CC:** Armando Lopez, President | **From:** Charlene Morimoto, Committee Chairperson | **Date:** Current Date | **Re:** Turkey Trot Fun Run Fundraiser

¶ It's time once again for our annual Turkey Trot Fun Run, in which all proceeds are donated to the Read-2-Learn literacy program for inner-city youth. Since 1980, our Read-2-Learn Committee has donated over $150,000 to this very worthy cause, and we have every intention of raising at least $8,000 in this Fun Run on Thanksgiving Day, but we need your help.

¶ As our director of human resources, you are in a unique position to help us raise funds. If you could encourage each of our employees to donate $20 to sponsor one runner in this event, we would easily meet our goals this year. Last year we had over 400 sponsored runners.

(Continued on next page)

¶ The Read-2-Learn program is specifically targeted at the inner-city elementary students in our neighborhood in their quest for basic literacy skills. Our business is located in a rich, multicultural urban neighborhood that is in desperate need of this type of program. I have attached a brochure that explains all details of this reading program and an event flyer. If you need additional copies, please let me know. Also, please visit our Web site at http://www.turkeytrot.org for further details.

¶ urs | Attachments

Report Test 6-107 ▶

Web Page

1. Save a new, unnamed document as a Web page and name it *main read.htm.*
2. Create a centered, boxed table with 2 columns and 4 rows.
3. Type this information in the open table as shown in the illustration.
4. Insert a picture related to reading and size it approximately as shown. Apply a coordinated design theme.
5. Insert horizontal lines in Rows 2 and 4. Change any styles, fonts, or colors as desired.

Read-2-Learn

A Youth Literacy Program of the Los Angeles Public Library

Our mission is to provide instructions in the basic literacy skills of reading and writing for elementary school children. Read-2-Learn offers participants free tutoring and a variety of other support services. Our volunteer tutors have been trained and will be matched with students to provide optimal conditions for learning and practicing basic reading and writing skills. The learner's interests and needs are always considered first.

This literacy program is funded by the Los Angeles Public Library; government grants; special events; and contributions from corporations, foundations and individuals. Our services include the following:

- Free individualized tutoring
- A resource library including books, tapes, games, and manuals
- Basic computer literacy instruction
- Small group or one-on-one instruction for learners
- Ongoing evaluation and instructional support with a reading specialist
- Referrals to other literacy programs

(Continued on next page)

Read-2-Learn

A Youth Literacy Program of the Los Angeles Public Library

Our mission is to provide instructions in the basic literacy skills of reading and writing for elementary school children. Read-2-Learn offers participants free tutoring and a variety of other support services. Our volunteer tutors have been trained and will be matched with students to provide optimal conditions for learning and practicing basic reading and writing skills. The learner's interests and needs are always considered first.

This literacy program is funded by the Los Angeles Public Library; government grants; special events; and contributions from corporations, foundations, and individuals. Our services include the following:

- Free individualized tutoring
- A resource library including books, tapes, games, and manuals
- Basic computer literacy instruction
- Small group or one-on-one instruction for learners
- Ongoing evaluation and instructional support with a reading specialist
- Referrals to other literacy programs

Report Test 6-108

Flyer

Press the SPACE BAR 2 times, and create the flyer as shown in the illustration.

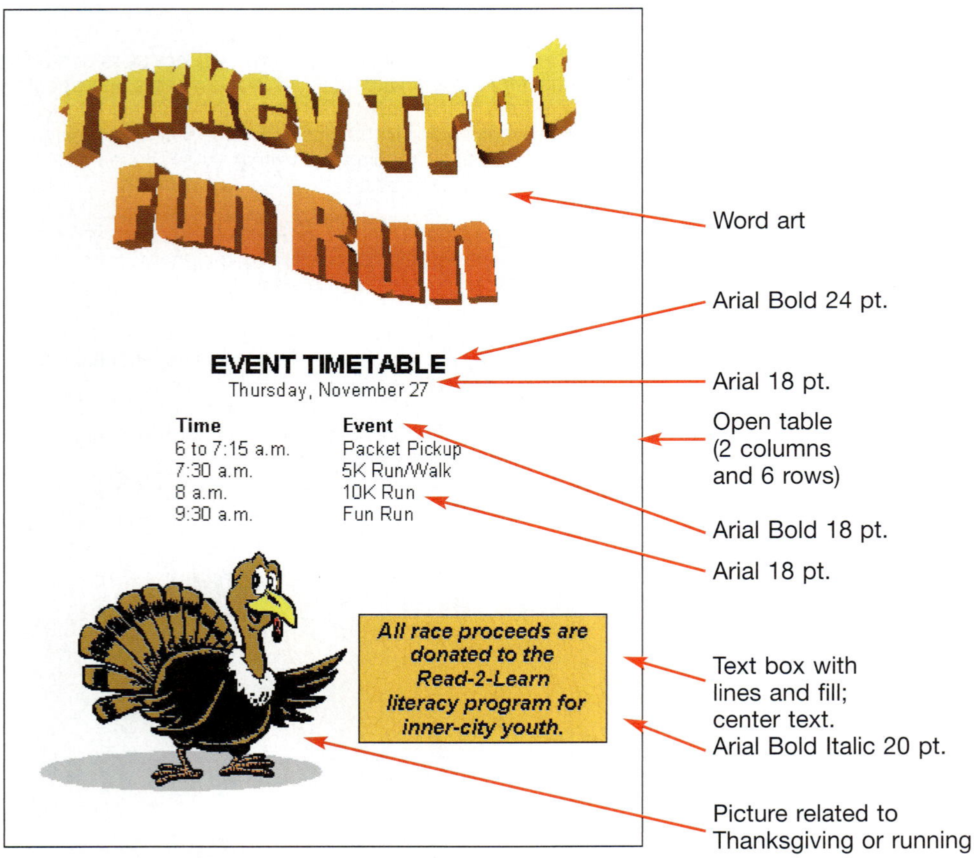

(Continued on next page)

Type this information in the open table and text box as shown in the flyer illustration.

EVENT TIMETABLE

Thursday, November 27

Time	**Event**
6 to 7:15 a.m.	Packet Pickup
7:30 a.m.	5K Run/Walk
8 a.m.	10K Run
9:30 a.m.	Fun Run

All race proceeds are donated to the Read-2-Learn literacy program for inner-city youth.

. . . Your keyboarding skills—just the beginning . . .

SKILLBUILDING

Diagnostic Practice: ALPHABET — SB-2

Diagnostic Practice: NUMBERS — SB-5

Progressive Practice: ALPHABET — SB-7

Progressive Practice: NUMBERS — SB-11

Paced Practice — SB-14

Supplementary Timings — SB-28

Diagnostic Practice: Alphabet

The Diagnostic Practice: Alphabet program is designed to diagnose and then correct your keystroking errors. You may use this program at any time throughout the course after completing Lesson 9.

Directions

1. Type one of the three Pretest/Posttest paragraphs 1 time, pushing *moderately* for speed. Review your errors.
2. Note your results—the number of errors you made on each key and your total number of errors. For example, if you typed *rhe* for *the,* you would count 1 error on the letter *t.*
3. For any letter on which you made 2 or more errors, select the corresponding drill lines and type the lines 2 times. If you made only 1 error, type the drill 1 time.
4. If you made no errors on the Pretest/Posttest paragraph, type one 3-line set of the Troublesome Pairs on page SB-4.
5. Finally, retype the same Pretest/Posttest, and compare your performance with your Pretest.

PRETEST/POSTTEST

Paragraph 1

```
     Sylvia and Julia made six quilts that were sold at the
bazaar. Several kinds of new craft projects were judged to
be quite complex and were given five kinds of prizes. Most
sizable quarterly taxes were backed by both boys and girls.
```

Paragraph 2

```
     Jacob and Zeke Koufax quietly enjoyed jazz music on my
new jukebox. The six or seven pieces of exquisite equipment
helped both create lovely music by Richard Wagner; I picked
five very quaint waltzes from Gregg Ward's jazz recordings.
```

Paragraph 3

```
     A quiet girl seized the black vase and gave it to five
judges who examined it carefully. Two quickly gave it high
marks. Forty people in the adjoining zone were quite vexed
at some lazy judges who were lax about keeping on schedule.
```

PRACTICE: Individual Reaches

Note that each letter drill provides practice in typing that letter combination with as many other letters as possible. For example, in the A drill, the first word (Isaac) practices *aa,* the second word (badge) practices *ba,* the third word (carry) practices *ca,* and so on, through *za* in Zaire.

```
aa Isaac badge carry dared eager faced gains habit dials AA
aa jaunt kayak label mamma Nancy oasis paint Qatar rapid AA
aa safer taken guard vague waves exact yacht Zaire Aaron AA

bb about ebbed ebony rugby fiber elbow amber unbar oboes BB
bb arbor cubic oxbow maybe abate abbot debit libel album BB
bb embed obeys urban tubes Sybil above lobby webby bribe BB

cc acted occur recap icing ulcer emcee uncle ocean force CC
cc scale itchy bucks excel Joyce acute yucca decal micro CC
cc mulch McCoy incur octet birch scrub latch couch cycle CC
```

```
dd admit daddy edict Magda ideal older index oddly order DD
dd outdo udder crowd Floyd adapt added Edith Idaho folds DD
dd under modem sword misdo fudge rowdy Lydia adept buddy DD

ee aegis beach cents dense eerie fence germs hence piece EE
ee jewel keyed leads media nerve poems penny reach seize EE
ee teach guest verse Wendy Xerox years zesty aerie begin EE

ff after defer offer jiffy gulfs infer often dwarf cuffs FF
ff awful afoul refer affix edify Wolfe infra aloof scarf FF
ff bluff afoot defer daffy fifty sulfa softy surfs stuff FF

gg again edges egged soggy igloo Elgin angel ogled Marge GG
gg outgo auger pygmy agape Edgar Egypt buggy light bulge GG
gg singe doggy organ bugle agree hedge began baggy Niger GG

hh ahead abhor chili Nehru ghost Elihu khaki Lhasa unhat HH
hh aloha phony myrrh shale Ethan while yahoo choir jihad HH
hh ghoul Khmer Delhi hoard photo rhino shake think while HH

ii aired bides cider dices eight fifth vigil highs radii II
ii jiffy kinds lives mired niece oiled piped rigid siren II
ii tired build visit wider exist yield aimed binds cigar II

jj major eject fjord Ouija enjoy Cajun Fijis Benjy bijou JJ
jj banjo jabot jacks jaded jails Japan jaunt jazzy jeans JJ
jj jeeps jeers jelly jerks jibed jiffy jilts joint joker JJ

kk Akron locks vodka peeks mikes sulky links okras larks KK
kk skins Yukon hawks tykes makes socks seeks hiker sulks KK
kk tanks Tokyo jerky pesky nukes gawks maker ducks cheek KK

ll alarm blame clank idled elope flame glows Chloe Iliad LL
ll ankle Lloyd inlet olive plane burly sleet atlas Tulsa LL
ll yowls axles nylon alone blunt claim idler elite flute LL

mm among adman demit pigmy times calms comma unman omits MM
mm armor smell umber axmen lymph gizmo amass admit demon MM
mm dogma imply films mommy omits armed smear bumpy adman MM

nn ankle Abner envoy gnome Johns input knife kilns hymns NN
nn Donna onion apnea angle snore undid owned cynic angle NN
nn entry gnash inset knoll nanny onset barns sneer unfit NN

oo aorta bolts coats dolls peony fouls goofs hoped iotas OO
oo jolts kooky loins moral noise poled Roger soaks total OO
oo quote voter would Saxon yo-yo zones bombs colts doles OO

pp apple epoch flips alpha ample input droop puppy sharp PP
pp spunk soups expel typed April Epsom slips helps empty PP
pp unpin optic peppy corps spite upset types apply creep PP
```

```
qq Iraqi equal pique roque squad tuque aquae equip toque QQ
qq squab squat squid squaw quail qualm quart queen quell QQ
qq query quest quick quiet quilt quirk quota quote quoth QQ

rr array bring crave drive erode freak grain three irate RR
rr kraft honor orate Barry tramp urges liver wrote lyric RR
rr rears armor broth crown drawl erect freer grade throw RR

ss ashen bombs specs binds bares leafs bangs sighs issue SS
ss necks mills teams turns solos stops stirs dress diets SS
ss usury Slavs stows abyss asked stabs cords mares beefs SS

tt attic debts pacts width Ethel often eight itchy alter TT
tt until motto optic earth stops petty couth newts extra TT
tt myths Aztec atone doubt facts veldt ether sight Italy TT

uu audio bumps cured dumps deuce fuels gulps huffy opium UU
uu junta kudos lulls mumps nudge outdo purer ruler super UU
uu tulip revue exult yucca azure auger burns curve duels UU

vv avows event ivory elves envoy overt larva mauve savvy VV
vv avant every rivet Elvis anvil coves curvy divvy avert VV
vv evict given valve ovens serve paves evade wives hover VV

ww awash bwana dwarf brews Gwenn schwa kiwis Elwin unwed WW
ww owner Irwin sweet twins byway awake dwell pewee tower WW
ww Erwin swims twirl awful dwelt Dewey owlet swamp twine WW

xx axiom exile fixed Bronx toxin Sioux Exxon pyxie axman XX
xx exert fixes foxes oxbow beaux calyx maxim exact sixth XX
xx proxy taxes excel mixed boxer axing Texas sixty epoxy XX

yy maybe bylaw cynic dying eying unify gypsy hypos Benjy YY
yy Tokyo hilly rummy Ronny loyal pygmy diary Syria types YY
yy buyer vying Wyatt epoxy crazy kayak ready cycle bawdy YY

zz azure Czech adzes bezel dizzy Franz froze Liszt ritzy ZZ
zz abuzz tizzy hazed czars maize Ginza oozes blitz fuzzy ZZ
zz jazzy mazes mezzo sized woozy Hertz fizzy Hazel Gomez ZZ
```

PRACTICE: Troublesome Pairs

```
B/V Beverly believes Bob behaved very bravely in Beaverton.
F/G Griffin goofed in figuring their gifted golfer's score.
H/J Joseph joshed with Judith when John jogged to Johnetta.

M/N Many women managed to move among the mounds of masonry.
O/P A pollster polled a population in Phoenix by telephone.
Q/A Quincy acquired one quality quartz ring at the banquet.

U/Y Buy your supply of gifts during your busy July journey.
X/C The exemptions exceed the expert's wildest expectation.
Z/A Liza gazed as four lazy zebras zigzagged near a gazebo.
```

Diagnostic Practice: Numbers

The Diagnostic Practice: Numbers program is designed to diagnose and then correct your keystroking errors. You may use this program at any time throughout the course after completing Lesson 14.

Directions

1. Type one of the three Pretest/Posttest paragraphs 1 time, pushing *moderately* for speed. Review your errors.
2. Note your results—the number of errors you made on each key and your total number of errors. For example, if you type *24* for *25,* you would count 1 error on the number *5.*
3. For any number on which you made 2 or more errors, select the corresponding drill lines and type the drills 2 times. If you made only 1 error, type the drill 1 time.
4. If you made no errors on the Pretest/Posttest paragraph, type 1 set of the drills that contain all numbers on page SB-6.
5. Finally, retype the same Pretest/Posttest, and compare your performance with your Pretest.

PRETEST/POSTTEST

Paragraph 1

```
     The statement dated May 24, 1995, listed 56 clamps; 14
batteries; 160 hammers; 358 screwdrivers; 1,208 pliers; and
2,475 files. The invoice numbered 379 showed 387 hoes, 406
rakes, 92 lawn mowers, 63 tillers, and 807 more lawn items.
```

Paragraph 2

```
     My inventory records dated May 31, 1994, revealed that
we had 458 pints; 2,069 quarts; and 8,774 gallons of paint.
We had 2,053 brushes; 568 scrapers; 12,063 wallpaper rolls;
897 knives; 5,692 mixers; 480 ladders; and 371 step stools.
```

Paragraph 3

```
     Almost 270 hot meals were delivered to the 15 shut-ins
in April, 260 in May, and 280 in June. Several workers had
volunteered 7,534 hours in 1996; 6,348 hours in 1995; 5,438
in 1994; and 6,277 in 1993. About 80 people were involved.
```

PRACTICE: Individual Reaches

```
1 aq aq1 aq1qa 111 ants 101 aunts 131 apples 171 animals a1
They got 11 answers correct for the 11 questions in BE 121.
Those 11 adults loaded the 711 animals between 1 and 2 p.m.
All 111 agreed that 21 of those 31 are worthy of the honor.

2 sw sw2 sw2ws 222 sets 242 steps 226 salads 252 saddles s2
The 272 summer tourists saw the 22 soldiers and 32 sailors.
Your September 2 date was all right for 292 of 322 persons.
The 22 surgeons said 221 of those 225 operations went well.

3 de de3 de3ed 333 dots 303 drops 313 demons 393 dollars d3
Bus 333 departed at 3 p.m. with the 43 dentists and 5 boys.
She left 33 dolls and 73 decoys at 353 West Addison Street.
The 13 doctors helped some of the 33 druggists in Room 336.
```

4 fr fr4 fr4rf 444 fans 844 farms 444 fishes 644 fiddles f4
My 44 friends bought 84 farms and sold over 144 franchises.
She sold 44 fish and 440 beef dinners for $9.40 per dinner.
The '54 Ford had only 40,434 fairly smooth miles by July 4.

5 fr fr5 fr5rf 555 furs 655 foxes 555 flares 455 fingers f5
They now own 155 restaurants, 45 food stores, and 55 farms.
They ordered 45, 55, 65, and 75 yards of that new material.
Flight 855 flew over Farmington at 5:50 p.m. on December 5.

6 jy jy6 jy6yj 666 jets 266 jeeps 666 jewels 866 jaguars j6
Purchase orders numbered 6667 and 6668 were sent yesterday.
Those 66 jazz players played for 46 juveniles in Room 6966.
The 6 judges reviewed the 66 journals on November 16 or 26.

7 ju ju7 ju7uj 777 jays 377 jokes 777 joists 577 juniors j7
The 17 jets carried 977 jocular passengers above 77 cities.
Those 277 jumping beans went to 77 junior scouts on May 17.
The 7 jockeys rode 77 jumpy horses between March 17 and 27.

8 ki ki8 ki8ik 888 keys 488 kites 888 knives 788 kittens k8
My 8 kennels housed 83 dogs, 28 kids, and 88 other animals.
The 18 kind ladies tied 88 knots in the 880 pieces of rope.
The 8 men saw 88 kelp bass, 38 kingfish, and 98 king crabs.

9 lo lo9 lo9ol 999 lads 599 larks 999 ladies 699 leaders 19
All 999 leaves fell from the 9 large oaks at 389 Largemont.
The 99 linemen put 399 large rolls of tape on for 19 games.
Those 99 lawyers put 899 legal-size sheets in the 19 limos.

0 ;p ;p0 ;p0p; 100 pens 900 pages 200 pandas 800 pencils ;0
There were 1,000 people who lived in the 300 private homes.
The 10 party stores are open from 1:00 p.m. until 9:00 p.m.
They edited 500 pages in 1 book and 1,000 pages in 2 books.

All numbers

a1a s2s d3d f4f f5f j6j j7j k8k l9l ;0; Add 6 and 8 and 29.
That 349-page script called for 10 actors and 18 actresses.
The check for $50 was sent to 705 Garfield Street, not 507.
The 14 researchers asked the 469 Californians 23 questions.

All numbers

a1a s2s d3d f4f f5f j6j j7j k8k l9l ;0; Add 3 and 4 and 70.
They built 1,200 houses on the 345-acre site by the canyon.
Her research showed that gold was at 397 in September 1994.
For $868 extra, they bought 15 new books and 62 used books.

All numbers

a1a s2s d3d f4f f5f j6j j7j k8k l9l ;0; Add 5 and 7 and 68.
A bank auditor arrived on May 26, 1994, and left on May 30.
The 4 owners open the stores from 9:30 a.m. until 6:00 p.m.
After 1,374 miles on the bus, she must then drive 185 more.

Progressive Practice: Alphabet

This skillbuilding routine contains a series of 30-second timings that range from 16wpm to 104wpm. The first time you use these timings, take a 1-minute timing on the Entry Timing paragraph. Note your speed.

Select a passage that is 2 words per minute higher than your current speed. Then take six 30-second timings on the passage.

Your goal each time is to complete the passage within 30 seconds with no errors. When you have achieved your goal, move on to the next passage and repeat the procedure.

Entry Timing

Bev was very lucky when she found extra quality in the 11
home she was buying. She quietly told the builder that she 23
was extremely satisfied with the work done on her new home. 35
The builder said she can move into her new house next week. 47

| 1 | 2 | 3 | 4 | 5 | 6 | 7 | 8 | 9 | 10 | 11 | 12

16wpm The author is the creator of a document.

18wpm Open means to access a previously saved file.

20wpm A byte represents one character to every computer.

22wpm A mouse may be used when running Windows on a computer.

24wpm Soft copy is text that is displayed on your computer screen.

26wpm Memory is the part of the word processor that stores information.

28wpm A menu is a list of choices to direct the operator through a function.

30wpm A sheet feeder is a device that will insert sheets of paper into a printer.

32wpm An icon is a small picture that illustrates a function or an object in software.

34wpm A window is a rectangular area with borders that displays the contents of open files.

36wpm To execute means to perform an action specified by an operator or by the computer program.

38wpm Output is the result of a word processing operation. It can be either printed or magnetic form.

40wpm Format refers to the physical features which affect the appearance and arrangement of your document.

42wpm	A font is a style of type of one size or kind which includes all letters, numbers, and punctuation marks.
44wpm	Ergonomics is the science of adapting working conditions or equipment to meet the physical needs of employees.
46wpm	Home position is the starting position of a document; it is typically the upper left corner of the display monitor.
48wpm	The mouse may be used to change the size of a window and to move a window to a different location on the display screen.
50wpm	An optical scanner is a device that can read text and enter it into a word processor without the need to type the data again.
52wpm	Hardware refers to the physical equipment used, such as the central processing unit, display screen, keyboard, printer, or drives.
54wpm	A peripheral device is any piece of equipment that will extend the capabilities of a computer system but is not required for operation.
56wpm	A split screen displays two or more different images at the same time; it can, for example, display two different pages of a legal document.
58wpm	When using Windows, it's possible to place several programs on a screen and to change the size of a window or to change its position on a screen.
60wpm	With the click of a mouse, one can use a Button Bar or a toolbar for fast access to features that are frequently applied when using a Windows program.
62wpm	An active window can be reduced to an icon when you use Windows, enabling you to double-click another icon to open a new window for formatting and editing.
64wpm	Turnaround time is the length of time needed for a document to be keyboarded, edited, proofread, corrected if required, printed, and returned to the originator.
66wpm	A local area network is a system that uses cable or another means to allow high-speed communication among many kinds of electronic equipment within particular areas.
68wpm	To search and replace means to direct the word processor to locate a character, word, or group of words wherever it occurs in the document and replace it with newer text.

70wpm Indexing is the ability of a word processor to accumulate a list of words that appear in a document, including page numbers, and then print a revised list in alphabetic order.

72wpm When a program needs information from you, a dialog box will appear on the desktop. Once the dialog box appears, you must identify the option you desire and then choose that option.

74wpm A facsimile is an exact copy of a document, and it is also a process by which images, such as typed letters, graphs, and signatures, are scanned, transmitted, and then printed on paper.

76wpm Compatibility refers to the ability of a computer to share information with another computer or to communicate with some other apparatus. It can be accomplished by using hardware or software.

78wpm Some operators like to personalize their desktops when they use Windows by making various changes. For example, they can change their screen colors and the pointer so that they will have more fun.

80wpm Wraparound is the ability of a word processor to move words from one line to another line and from one page to the next page as a result of inserting and deleting text or changing the size of margins.

82wpm It is possible when using Windows to evaluate the contents of different directories on the screen at the very same time. You can then choose to copy or move a particular file from one directory to another.

84wpm List processing is a capability of a word processor to keep lists of data that can be updated and sorted in alphabetic or numeric order. A list can also be added to any document that is stored in one's computer.

86wpm A computer is a wondrous device, which accepts data that are input and then processes the data and produces output. The computer performs its work by using one or more stored programs, which provide the instructions.

88wpm The configuration is the components that make up your word processing system. Mainly systems include a keyboard that is used for entering data, a central processing unit, at least one disk drive, a monitor, and a printer.

90wpm Help for Windows can be used whenever you see a Help button in a dialog box or on a menu bar. Once you finish reading about a topic that you have selected, you will see a list of some related topics from which you can choose.

92wpm When you want to look at the contents of two windows when using Windows, you will want to reduce the window size. Do this by pointing to a border or a corner of a window and dragging it until the window is the size that you want.

94wpm Scrolling means to display a large quantity of text by rolling it horizontally or vertically past the display screen. As the text disappears from the top section of the monitor, new text will appear at the bottom section of the monitor.

96wpm The Windows Print Manager is used to install and configure printers, join network printers, and monitor the printing of documents. Windows requires that a default printer be identified, but you can change the designation of it at any point.

98wpm A stop code is a command that makes a printer pause while it is printing to permit an operator to insert text, change the font style, or change the kind of paper in the printer. To resume printing, the operator must use a special key or command.

100wpm A computerized message system is a class of electronic mail that enables any operator to key a message on any computer terminal and have the message stored for later retrieval by the recipient, who can then display the message on his or her terminal.

102wpm Many different graphics software programs have been brought on the market in recent years. These programs can be very powerful in helping with a business presentation. If there is any need to share data, using one of these programs could be quite helpful.

104wpm Voice mail has become an essential service that many people in the business world use. This enables anyone who places a call to your phone to leave a message if you cannot answer it at that time. This special feature helps lots of workers to be more productive.

Progressive Practice: Numbers

This skillbuilding routine contains a series of 30-second timings that range from 16wpm to 80wpm. The first time you use these timings, take a 1-minute timing on the Entry Timing paragraph. Note your speed.

Select a passage that is 4 to 6 words per minute *lower* than your current alphabetic speed. (The reason for selecting a lower speed goal is that sentences with numbers are more difficult to type.) Take six 30-second timings on the passage.

Your goal each time is to complete the passage within 30 seconds with no errors. When you have achieved your goal, move on to the next passage and repeat the procedure.

Entry Timing

Their bags were filled with 10 sets of jars, 23 cookie 11
cutters, 4 baking pans, 6 coffee mugs, 25 plates, 9 dessert 23
plates, 7 soup bowls, 125 recipe cards, and 8 recipe boxes. 35
They delivered these 217 items to 20487 Mountain Boulevard. 47

| 1 | 2 | 3 | 4 | 5 | 6 | 7 | 8 | 9 | 10 | 11 | 12

16wpm There were now 21 children in Room 2110.

18wpm Fewer than 12 of the 121 boxes arrived today.

20wpm Maybe 12 of the 21 applicants met all 15 criteria.

22wpm There were 34 letters addressed to 434 West Cranbrooke.

24wpm Jane reported that there were 434 freshmen and 43 transfers.

26wpm The principal assigned 3 of those 4 students to Room 343 at noon.

28wpm Only 1 or 2 of the 34 latest invoices were more than 1 page in length.

30wpm They met 11 of the 12 players who received awards from 3 of the 4 trainers.

32wpm Those 5 vans carried 46 passengers on the first trip and 65 on the next 3 trips.

34wpm We first saw 3 and then 4 beautiful eagles on Route 65 at 5 a.m. on Tuesday, June 12.

36wpm The 16 companies produced 51 of the 62 records that received awards for 3 of 4 categories.

38wpm The 12 trucks hauled the 87 cows and 65 horses to the farm, which was about 21 miles northeast.

40wpm She moved from 87 Bayview Drive to 657 Cole Street and then 3 blocks south to 412 Gulbranson Avenue.

42wpm My 7 or 8 buyers ordered 7 dozen in sizes 5 and 6 after the 14 to 32 percent discounts had been bestowed.

44wpm There were 34 men and 121 women waiting in line at the gates for the 65 to 87 tickets to the Cape Cod concert.

46wpm Steve had listed 5 or 6 items on Purchase Order 241 when he saw that Purchase Requisition 87 contained 3 or 4 more.

48wpm Your items numbered 278 will sell for about 90 percent of the value of the 16 items that have code numbers shown as 435.

50wpm The managers stated that 98 of those 750 randomly selected new valves had about 264 defects, far exceeding the usual 31 norm.

52wpm Half of the 625 volunteers received over 90 percent of the charity pledges. Approximately 83 of the 147 agencies will have funds.

54wpm Merico hired 94 part-time workers to help the 378 full-time employees during the 62-day period when sales go up by 150 percent or more.

56wpm Kaye only hit 1 for 4 in the first 29 games after an 8-game streak in which she batted 3 for 4. She then hit at a .570 average for 6 games.

58wpm The mail carrier delivered 98 letters during the week to 734 Oak Street and also took 52 letters to 610 Faulkner Road as he returned on Route 58.

60wpm Pat said that about 1 in 5 of the 379 swimmers had a chance of being among the top 20. The best 6 of those 48 divers will receive the 16 best awards.

62wpm It rained from 3 to 6 inches, and 18 of those 20 farmers were fearful that 4 to 7 inches more would flood about 95 acres along 3 miles of the new Route 78.

64wpm Those 7 sacks weighed 48 pounds, more than the 30 pounds that I had thought. All 24 believe the 92-pound bag is at least 15 or 16 pounds above its true weight.

66wpm They bought 7 of the 8 options for 54 of the 63 vehicles last month. They now own over 120 dump trucks for use in 9 of the 15 new regions in the big 20-county area.

68wpm Andy was 8 or 9 years old when they moved to 632 Glendale Street away from the 1700 block of Horseshoe Lane, which is about 45 miles directly west of Boca Raton, FL 33434.

70wpm Doug had read 575 pages in the 760-page book by March 30; Darlene had read only 468 pages. Darlene has read 29 of those optional books since October 19, and Doug has read 18.

72wpm That school district has 985 elementary students, 507 middle school students, and 463 high school students; the total of 1,955 is 54, or 2.84 percent, over last year's grand total.

74wpm Attendance at last year's meeting was 10,835. The goal for this year is to have 11,764 people. This will enable us to plan for an increase of 929 participants, a rise of 8.57 percent.

76wpm John's firm has 158 stores, located in 109 cities in the West. The company employs 3,540 males and 2,624 females, a total of 6,164 employees. About 4,750 of those employees work part-time.

78wpm Memberships were as follows: 98 members in the Drama Guild, 90 members in Zeta Tau, 82 members in Theta Phi, 75 in the Bowling Club, and 136 in the Ski Club. This meant that 481 joined a group.

80wpm The association had 684 members from the South, 830 members from the North, 1,023 members from the East, and 751 from the West. The total membership was 3,288; these numbers increased by 9.8 percent.

Paced Practice

The Paced Practice skillbuilding routine builds speed and accuracy in short, easy steps by using individualized goals and immediate feedback. You may use this program at any time after completing Lesson 9.

This section contains a series of 2-minute timings for speeds ranging from 16wpm to 96wpm. The first time you use these timings, take the 1-minute Entry Timing.

Select a passage that is 2wpm higher than your current typing speed. Then use this two-stage practice pattern to achieve each speed goal: (1) concentrate on speed, and (2) work on accuracy.

Speed Goal. To determine your speed goal, take three 2-minute timings in total. Your goal each time is to complete the passage in 2 minutes without regard to errors. When you have achieved your speed goal, work on accuracy.

Accuracy Goal. To type accurately, you need to slow down—just a bit. Therefore, to reach your accuracy goal, drop back 2wpm to the previous passage. Take consecutive timings on this passage until you can complete the passage in 2 minutes with no more than 2 errors.

For example, if you achieved a speed goal of 54wpm, you should then work on an accuracy goal of 52wpm. When you have achieved 52wpm for accuracy, move up 4wpm (for example, to the 56-wpm passage) and work for speed again.

Entry Timing

If you can dream it, you can live it. Follow your 10
bliss. There are many careers, from the mundane to the 21
exotic to the sublime. Start your career planning now. 32
Prepare for the future by exploring your talents, skills, 43
and interests.

| 1 | 2 | 3 | 4 | 5 | 6 | 7 | 8 | 9 | 10 | 11 | 12

16wpm

Your future is now.[1] Seize each day. After you[2] have explored[3] your personal interests,[4] study the sixteen[5] career clusters[6] for a broad range of[7] job possibilities.[8]

18wpm

While exploring various[1] job options, think about[2] what a job means[3] to you. A job can mean[4] something you do simply[5] to earn money or something[6] you find more rewarding[7] and challenging.[8]

20wpm

If you have a job you enjoy,[1] work means more than[2] just receiving wages.[3] It means using your talents,[4] being among people[5] with like interests, making a[6] contribution, and gaining[7] a sense of satisfaction.[8]

22wpm

What is the difference between a job and a career? Think carefully. A job is work that people do for money. A career is a sequence of related jobs built on a foundation of interests, knowledge, training, and experiences.

24wpm

Learn more about the world of work by looking at the sixteen career clusters. Most jobs are included in one of the clusters that have been organized by the government. During your exploration of careers, list the clusters that interest you.

26wpm

Once you identify your career clusters of interest, look at the jobs within each cluster. Find out what skills and aptitudes are needed, what education and training are required, what the work environment is like, and what is the possibility for advancements.

28wpm

Use your career center and school or public libraries to research career choices. Search the Internet. Consult with professionals for another perspective of a specific career. As you gather information about career options, you may discover other interesting career possibilities.

30wpm

Gain insights into a career by becoming a volunteer, participating in an internship, or working a part-time or temporary job within a chosen field. You will become more familiar with a specific job while developing your skills. You'll gain valuable experience, whether you choose that career or not.

32wpm

Whichever path you choose, strive for a high level of pride in yourself and your work. Your image is affected by what you believe other people think of you as well as by how you view yourself. Evaluate your level of confidence in yourself. If you have self-doubts, begin to build up your self-confidence and self-esteem.

34wpm

Self-esteem is essential for a positive attitude, and a positive attitude is essential for success in the world of work. While you cannot control everything that happens at work, you can control how you react. Your attitude matters. Becoming more confident and cultivating positive thoughts can bring you power in your life and on the job.

36wpm

Several factors lead to success on the job. People who have studied the factors say that it is the personal traits that often determine who is promoted or who is not. One of the finest traits a person can possess is the trait of being likable. Being likable means a person is honest, courteous, loyal, thoughtful, pleasant, kind, and most assuredly, positive.

38wpm

If you are likable, probably you relate well with others. Your kindness serves you well in the workplace. Developing good interpersonal relationships with coworkers will make work more enjoyable. After all, think of all the hours you will spend together. By showing that you are willing to collaborate with your coworkers, most likely you will receive their cooperation in return.

40wpm

Cooperation begins on the first day of your new job. When you work for a company, you become part of the team. Meeting people and learning new skills can be exciting. For some people, however, any new situation can trigger anxiety. The best advice is to remain calm, do your job to the best of your ability, learn the workplace policies, be flexible, avoid being too critical, and always be positive.

42wpm

When you begin a new job, even if you have recently received your college diploma, chances are you will start at the bottom of the organizational chart. Each of us has to start somewhere. But don't despair. With hard work and determination, soon you will be climbing up the corporate ladder. If you are clever, you will embrace even the most tedious tasks, take everything in stride, and use every opportunity to learn.

44wpm

If you think learning is restricted to the confines of an academic institution, think again. You have plenty to learn on the job, even if it is a job for which you have been trained. As a new worker, you won't be expected to know everything. When necessary, do not hesitate to ask your employer questions. Learn all you can about your job and the company. Use the new information to enhance your job performance and to prepare for success.

46wpm

Begin every valuable workday by prioritizing all your tasks. Decide which tasks must be done immediately and which can wait. List the most important tasks first; then determine the order in which each task must be done. After you complete a task, triumphantly cross it off your priority list. Do not procrastinate; that is, don't put off work you should do. If a task needs to be done, do it. You will be on top of your task list if you use your time wisely.

48wpm

Prevent the telephone from controlling your time by learning to manage your business phone calls. Phone calls can be extremely distracting from necessary tasks. When making an outgoing call, organize the topics you want to discuss. Gather needed materials such as pencils, papers, and files. Set a time limit, and stick to business. Give concise answers, summarize the points discussed, and end the conversation politely. Efficient telephone usage will help you manage your time.

50wpm

As with anything, practice makes perfect, but along the way,[1] we all make mistakes. The difference between the successful people[2] and those who are less successful is not that the successful[3] people make fewer mistakes. It's that they don't give up. Instead[4] of letting mistakes bring them down, they use their mistakes[5] as opportunities to grow. If you make a mistake, be patient[6] with yourself. You might be able to fix your mistake. Look for[7] more opportunities for success to be just around the corner.[8]

52wpm

Be patient with yourself when handling problems and accepting criticism.[1] Handling criticism gracefully and maturely may be a challenge.[2] Still, it is vital in the workplace. Criticism presented in[3] a way that can help you learn and grow is constructive criticism.[4] When you see criticism as helpful, it's easier to handle. Believe[5] it or not, there are some employees who welcome criticism. It[6] teaches them better ways to succeed on the job. Strive to improve[7] how you accept constructive criticism, and embrace your growth.[8]

54wpm

People experience continuous growth during a career. Goal setting[1] is a helpful tool along any career path. Some people believe that goals[2] provide the motivation needed to get to the place they want to[3] be. Setting goals encourages greater achievements. The higher we set[4] our goals, the greater the effort we will need to reach these goals.[5] Each time we reach a target or come closer to a goal, we see an[6] increase in our confidence and our performance, leading to greater[7] accomplishments. And the cycle continues to spiral onward and upward.[8]

56wpm

One goal we should all strive for is punctuality. When employees are tardy or absent from the workplace, it costs the company money. If you are frequently tardy or absent, others have to do their own work and cover for you. If you are absent often, your peers will begin to resent you, causing everyone stress in the department. Being late and missing work can damage the relationship with your manager and have a negative effect on your career. To avoid these potential problems, develop a personal plan to assure that you arrive every day on time or early.

58wpm

Holding a job is a major part of being an adult. Some people begin their work careers as adolescents. From the beginning, various work habits are developed that are as crucial to success as the actual job skills and knowledge that a person brings to the job. What traits are expected of workers? What do employers look for when they evaluate their employees? Important personal traits include being confident, cooperative, positive and dependable. If you are organized, enthusiastic, and understanding, you have many of the qualities that employers value most in their employees.

60wpm

Being dependable is a desirable trait. When a project must be completed by a specific time, a manager will be reassured to know that reliable workers are going to meet the deadline. Workers who are dependable learn to utilize their time to achieve maximum results. Dependable workers can always be counted on, have good attendance records, are well prepared, and arrive on time ready to work. If a company wants to meet its goals, it must have a team of responsible and dependable workers. You, your coworkers, your supervisors, and your managers are all team members, working to reach common goals.

62wpm

The ability to organize is an important quality for the employee who wishes to display good work habits. The worker should have the ability to plan the work that needs to be completed and then be able to execute the plan in a timely manner. An employer requires a competent worker to be well organized. If an office worker is efficient, he or she handles requests swiftly and deals with correspondence without delay. The organized worker does not allow work to accumulate on the desk. Also, the organized office worker returns all phone calls immediately and makes lists of the activities that need to be done each day.

64wpm

Efficiency is another work habit that is desired. An efficient worker completes a task quickly and begins work on the next project eagerly. He or she thinks about ways to save steps and time. For example, an efficient worker may plan a single trip to the copier with several copying jobs rather than multiple trips to do each separate job. Being efficient also means having the required supplies to successfully complete each job. An efficient employee zips along on each project, uses time wisely, and stays focused on the present task. With careful and thorough planning, a worker who is efficient can accomplish more tasks in less time.

66wpm

Cooperation is another ideal work habit. As previously mentioned, cooperation begins on the first day on the job. Cooperation is thinking of all team members when making a decision. A person who cooperates is willing to do what is necessary for the good of the whole group. For you to be a team player, it is essential that you take extra steps to cooperate. Cooperation may mean being a good sport if you are asked to do something you would rather not do. It may mean you have to correct a mistake made by another person in the office. If every employee has the interests of the company at heart and works well as a team player, then cooperation is at work.

68wpm

Enthusiasm is still another work trait that is eagerly sought after by employers. Being enthusiastic means that a person has lots of positive energy. This is reflected in actions toward your work, coworkers, and employer. It has been noted that eagerness can be catching. If workers show they are eager to attempt any project, they will not only achieve the highest praise but will also be considered for career advancement. How much enthusiasm do you show at the workplace? Do you encourage people or complain to people? There will always be plenty of good jobs for employees who are known to have a wealth of zeal and a positive approach to the projects that they are assigned.

70wpm

Understanding is also a preferred work habit for every excellent worker. In today's world, virtually all business includes both men and women of different religions, races, cultures, work ethic, abilities, aptitudes, and attitudes. You'll interact with various types of people as customers, coworkers, and owners. Treat everyone fairly, openly, and honestly. Any type of prejudice is hurtful, offensive, and unacceptable. Prejudice cannot be tolerated in the office. Each employee must try to understand and accept everyone's differences. Because so many diverse groups of people work side by side in the workplace, it is essential that all coworkers maintain a high degree of mutual understanding.

72wpm

It can be concluded that certain work habits or traits can play a major role in determining the success of an employee. Most managers would be quick to agree on the importance of these traits. It is most probable that these habits would be evaluated on performance appraisal forms. Promotions, pay increases, new responsibilities, and your future with the company may be based on these evaluations. You should request regular job performance evaluations even if your company does not conduct them. This feedback will improve your job performance and career development by helping you grow. If you continually look for ways to improve your work habits and skills, then you will enjoy success in the workplace and beyond.

74wpm

You can be certain that no matter where you work, you will use some form of computer technology.[1] Almost every business is dependent upon computers. Companies use such devices as voice[2] mail, fax machines, cellular phones, and electronic schedules. Technology helps to accomplish[3] work quickly and efficiently. A result of this rapidly changing technology is globalization,[4] which is the establishment of worldwide communication links between people. Our world is [5]becoming a smaller, global village. We must expand our thinking beyond the office walls. We must[6] become aware of what happens in other parts of the world. Those events may directly affect[7] you and your workplace. The more you know, the more valuable you will become to the company.[8]

76wpm

Technological advancements are affecting every aspect of our lives. For example, the advent of[1] the Internet has changed how we receive and send information. It is the world's largest information[2] network. The Internet is often called the information superhighway because it is a vast [3]network of computers that connect people and resources worldwide. It is an exciting medium to help[4] you access the latest information. You can even learn about companies by visiting their Web[5] sites. Without any doubt, we are all globally connected, and information technology services [6]support those necessary connections. This industry offers many different employment opportunities.[7] Keep in mind that proficiency in keyboarding is beneficial in this field and in other fields.[8]

78wpm

It is amazing to discover the many careers in which keyboarding skill is necessary today, and the use of the computer keyboard by executive chefs is a prime example. The chefs in major restaurants must prepare parts or all of the meals served while directing the work of a staff of chefs, cooks, and other kitchen staff. The computer has become a necessary tool for a variety of tasks, including tracking inventories of food supplies. By observing which items are favorites and which items are not requested, the chef can calculate food requirements, order food, and supervise the food purchases. Additionally, the computer has proven to be a very practical tool for such tasks as planning budgets, preparing purchase orders for vendors, creating menus, and printing out reports.

80wpm

Advanced technology has opened the doors to a wider variety of amazing new products and services to sell. It seems the more complex the products, the higher the price of the products, or the greater the sales commission, the stiffer the competition. Selling these technical products requires detailed product knowledge, good verbal skills, smooth sales rapport, and proficient keyboarding skills. Business favors people with special training. For example, a pharmacy company may prefer a person with knowledge in chemistry to sell its products. Selling is for people who thrive on challenges and changes in products and services. Sales is appealing to people who enjoy using their powers of persuasion to make the sales. The potential for good earnings is very high for the well-trained salesperson.

82wpm

As you travel about in your sales job or type a report at the office or create Friday night's pasta [1] special for your five-star restaurant, always remember to put safety first. Accidents happen, but they [2] don't have to happen regularly or to have such serious consequences. Accidents cost businesses billions [3] of dollars annually in medical expenses, lost wages, and insurance claims. A part of your job is to [4] make certain you're not one of the millions of people injured on the job every year. You may believe you [5] work in a safe place, but accidents occur in all types of businesses. A few careless people cause most [6] accidents, so ensure your safety on the job. Safety doesn't just happen. Safety is the result of the [7] careful awareness of many people who plan and put into action a safety program that benefits everyone. [8]

84wpm

In today's market, you need more than the necessary skills or the personal qualities described above to [1] exceed in the workplace. Employers also expect their employees to have ethics. Ethics are the principles [2] of conduct governing an individual or a group. Employees who work ethically do not lie, cheat, or steal. [3] They are honest and fair in their dealings with others. Employees who act ethically build a good reputation [4] for themselves and their company. They are known to be dependable and trustworthy. Unethical behavior [5] can have a spiraling effect. A single act can do a lot of damage. Even if you haven't held a job yet, you [6] have had experience with ethical problems. Life is full of many opportunities to behave ethically. Do the [7] right thing when faced with a decision. The ethics you practice today will carry over to your workplace. [8]

86wpm

Now that you know what is expected of you on the job, how do you make sure you will get the job? Almost everyone has experienced the interview process for a job. For some, the interview is a traumatic event, but it doesn't have to be stressful. Preparation is the key. Research the company for which you are seeking employment. Formulate a list of questions. Your interview provides you the opportunity to interview the organization. Don't go empty-handed. Take a portfolio of items with you. Include copies of your resume with a list of three or more professional references, your academic transcript, and your certificates and licenses. Be sure to wear appropriate business attire. The outcome of the interview will be positive if you have enthusiasm for the job, match your qualifications to the company's needs, ask relevant questions, and listen clearly.

88wpm

How can you be the strongest candidate for the job? Be sure that your skills in reading, writing, mathematics, speaking, and listening are solid. These basic skills will help you listen well and communicate clearly, not only during a job interview, but also at your workplace. The exchange of information between senders and receivers is called communication. It doesn't matter which occupation you choose; you will spend most of your career using these basic skills to communicate with others. You will use the basic skills as tools to gain information, solve problems, and share ideas. You will use these skills to meet the needs of your customers. The majority of jobs available during the next century will be in the industries that will require direct customer contacts. Your success will be based upon your ability to communicate effectively with customers and coworkers.

90wpm

Writing effectively can help you gain a competitive edge in your job search and throughout your career. Most of[1] us have had occasion to write business letters whether to apply for a job, to comment on a product or service, or[2] to place an order. Often it seems easy to sit and let our thoughts flow freely. In other cases, we seem to struggle[3] to find the proper wording while trying to express our thoughts in exactly the right way. Writing skill can[4] improve with practice. Implement the following principles to develop your writing skill. Try to use language that[5] you would be comfortable using in person. Use words that are simple, direct, kind, confident, and professional[6]. When possible, use words that emphasize the positive side. Remember to proofread your work. Well-organized thoughts[7] and proper grammar, spelling, and punctuation show the reader that you care about the quality of your work.[8]

92wpm

Listening is an essential skill of the communication process. It is crucial for learning, getting along, and forming[1] relationships. Do you think you are an active or passive listener? Listening is not a passive activity. Conversely,[2] active listening is hearing what is being said and interpreting its meaning. Active listening makes you a more[3] effective communicator because you react to what you have heard. Study the following steps to increase your listening[4] skills. Do not cut people off; let them develop their ideas before you speak. If a message is vague, write down[5] your questions or comments, and wait for the entire presentation or discussion to be finished. Reduce personal and[6] environmental distractions by focusing on the message. Keep an open mind. Be attentive and maintain eye contact whenever[7] possible. By developing these basic communication skills, you will become more confident and more effective.[8]

94wpm

Speaking is also a form of communication. In the world of work, speaking is an important way in which to share information.[1] Regardless of whether you are speaking to an audience of one or one hundred, you will want to make sure that your[2] listeners get your message. Be clear about your purpose, your audience, and your subject. A purpose is the overall[3] goal or reason for speaking. An audience is anyone who receives information. The subject is the main topic or key idea.[4] Research your subject. Using specific facts and examples will give you credibility. As you speak, be brief and direct.[5] Progress logically from point to point. Speak slowly and pronounce clearly all your words. Do people understand[6] what you say or ask you to repeat what you've said? Is the sound of your voice friendly and pleasant or shrill and off-putting?[7] These factors influence how your message is received. A good idea is worthless if you can't communicate it.[8]

96wpm

Developing a career is a process. You have looked at your interests, values, skills, aptitudes, and attitudes. Your exploration[1] into the world of work has begun. The journey doesn't stop here, for the present is the perfect place to start[2] thinking about the future. It's where you begin to take steps toward your goals. It's where you can really make a difference.[3] As you set personal and career goals, remember the importance of small steps. Each step toward a personal goal or[4] career goal is a small victory. That feeling of success encourages you to take other small steps. Each step builds onto[5] the next. Continue exploring your personal world as well as the world you share with others. Expect the best as you go forward.[6] Expect a happy life. Expect loving relationships. Expect success in life. Expect fulfilling and satisfying work[7] in a job you truly love. Last but not least, expect that you have something special to offer the world, because you do.[8]

Supplementary Timings

Supplementary Timing 1

All problem solving, whether personal or academic, 10
involves decision making. You make decisions in order to 21
solve problems. On occasion, problems occur as a result of 33
decisions you have made. For example, you may decide to 44
smoke, but later in life, you face the problem of nicotine 56
addiction. You may decide not to study mathematics and 67
science because you think that they are too difficult. 78
Because of this choice, many career opportunities will be 90
closed to you. There is a consequence for every action. Do 102
you see that events in your life do not just happen, but 113
that they are the result of your choices and decisions? 124

How can you prepare your mind for problem solving? A 135
positive attitude is a great start. Indeed, your attitude 147
affects the way in which you solve a problem or make a 158
decision. Approach your studies, such as science and math 170
courses, with a positive and inquisitive attitude. Try to 182
perceive academic problems as puzzles to solve rather than 192
homework to avoid. 198

Critical thinking is a method of problem solving that 209
involves decoding, analyzing, reasoning, evaluating, and 220
processing information. It is fundamental for successful 231
problem solving. Critical thinking is a willingness to 242
explore, probe, question, and search for answers. Problems 254
may not always be solved on the first try. Don't give up. 266
Try, try again. Finding a solution takes sustained effort. 278
Use critical thinking skills to achieve success in today's 290
fast-paced and highly competitive world of business. 300

| 1 | 2 | 3 | 4 | 5 | 6 | 7 | 8 | 9 | 10 | 11 | 12

Supplementary Timing 2

For many, the Internet is an important resource in 10
their private and professional lives. The Internet provides 22
quick access to countless Web sites that contain news, 33
products, games, entertainment, and many other types of 44
information. The Web pages on these sites can be designed, 56
authored, and posted by anyone, anywhere around the world. 68
Utilize critical thinking when reviewing all Web sites. 79

Just because something is stated on the radio, printed 90
in the newspaper, or shown on television doesn't mean that 102
it's true, real, accurate, or correct. This applies to 113
information found on the Internet as well. Don't fall into 125
the trap of believing that if it's on the Net, it must be 137
true. A wise user of the Internet thinks critically about 149
data found on the Net and evaluates this material before 160
using it. 162

When evaluating a new Web site, think about who, what, 173
how, when, and where. Who refers to the author of the Web 185
site. The author may be a business, an organization, or a 197
person. What refers to the validity of the data. Can this 209
data be verified by a reputable source? How refers to the 221
viewpoint of the author. Is the data presented without 232
prejudice? When refers to the time frame of the data. Is 244
this recent data? Where refers to the source of the data. 256
Is this data from an accurate source? By answering these 267
critical questions, you will learn more about the accuracy 279
and dependability of a Web site. As you surf the Net, be 290
very cautious. Anyone can publish on the Internet. 300

| 1 | 2 | 3 | 4 | 5 | 6 | 7 | 8 | 9 | 10 | 11 | 12

Supplementary Timing 3

Office employees perform a variety of tasks during 10
their workday. These tasks vary from handling telephone 21
calls to forwarding personal messages, from sending short 33
email messages to compiling complex office reports, and 44
from writing simple letters to assembling detailed letters 56
with tables, graphics, and imported data. Office workers 67
are a fundamental part of a company's structure. 77

The office worker uses critical thinking in order to 88
accomplish a wide array of daily tasks. Some of the tasks 100
are more urgent than other tasks and should be completed 111
first. Some tasks take only a short time, while others take 123
a lot more time. Some tasks demand a quick response, while 135
others may be attended as time permits or even postponed 147
until the future. Some of the tasks require input from 158
coworkers or managers. Whether a job is simple or complex, 170
big or small, the office worker must decide what is to be 182
tackled first by determining the priority of each task. 193

When setting priorities, critical thinking skills are 204
essential. The office worker evaluates each aspect of the 216
task. It is a good idea to identify the size of the task, 228
determine its complexity, estimate its effort, judge its 239
importance, and set its deadline. Once the office worker 250
assesses each task that is to be finished within a certain 262
period of time, then the priority for completing all tasks 274
can be set. Critical thinking skills, if applied well, 285
can save the employer money or, if executed poorly, can 296
cost the employer. 300

| 1 | 2 | 3 | 4 | 5 | 6 | 7 | 8 | 9 | 10 | 11 | 12

Supplementary Timing 4

Each day business managers make choices that keep 10
businesses running smoothly, skillfully, and profitably. 21
Each decision regarding staff, finances, operations, and 32
resources often needs to be quick and precise. To develop 44
sound decisions, managers must use critical thinking. They 56
gather all the essential facts so that they can make good, 68
well-informed choices. After making a decision, skilled 79
managers review their thinking process. Over time, they 90
refine their critical thinking skills. When they encounter 102
similar problems, they use their prior experiences to help 114
them solve problems with ease and in less time. 124

What type of decisions do you think managers make that 135
involve critical thinking? Human Resources managers decide 147
who to employ, what to pay a new employee, and where to 158
place a new worker. In addition, Human Resources managers 170
should be unbiased negotiators, resolving conflict between 182
other employees. Office managers purchase copy machines, 194
computers, software, and office supplies. Finance officers 206
prepare precise, timely financial statements. Top managers 218
control business policies, appoint mid-level managers, and 230
assess the success of the business. Plant supervisors set 242
schedules, gauge work quality, and evaluate workers. Sales 254
managers study all of the new sales trends, as well as 265
provide sales training and promotion materials. 275

Most managers use critical thinking to make wise, well 286
thought-out decisions. They carefully check their facts, 297
analyze these facts, and make a final judgment based upon 309
these facts. They should also be able to clearly discern 320
fact from fiction. Through trial and error, managers learn 332
their own ways of solving problems and finding the most 343
effective and creative solutions. 350

| 1 | 2 | 3 | 4 | 5 | 6 | 7 | 8 | 9 | 10 | 11 | 12

Supplementary Timing 5

In most classes, teachers want students to analyze 10
situations, draw conclusions, and solve problems. Each 21
of these tasks requires students to use thinking skills. 32
How do students acquire these skills? What is the process 44
students follow to develop thinking skills? 53

During the early years of life, students learn words 63
and then combine these words into sentences. From there, 74
they learn to declare ideas, share thoughts, and express 85
feelings. Students learn numbers and simple math concepts. 97
They may learn to read musical notes, to keep rhythm, to 108
sing songs, and to recognize many popular and classical 119
pieces of music. Students learn colors, identify shapes, 130
and begin drawing. During the early years, students learn 142
the basic problem-solving models. 149

One way to solve problems and apply thinking skills 159
is to use the scientific approach. This approach requires 171
the student to state the problem to be solved, gather all 183
the facts about the problem, analyze the problem, and pose 195
viable solutions. Throughout this process, teachers ask 206
questions that force students to expand their thinking 217
skills. Teachers may ask questions such as these: Did you 229
clearly state the problem? Did you get all the facts? Did 241
you get the facts from the right place? Did you assume 252
anything? Did you pose other possible solutions? Did you 263
keep an open mind to all solutions? Did you let your bias 275
come into play? Did you listen to others who might have 286
insights? Did you dig deep enough? Does the solution make 298
sense to you? 301

This simple four-step process for solving problems 311
gives students a model to use for school, for work, and 322
for life. While the process may not be used to solve every 334
problem, it does provide a starting point to begin using 345
critical thinking skills. 350

| 1 | 2 | 3 | 4 | 5 | 6 | 7 | 8 | 9 | 10 | 11 | 12

Supplementary Timing 6

A major goal for nearly all educators is to teach 10
critical thinking skills to a class. Critical thinking, 21
which is the process of reasonably or logically deciding 32
what to do or believe, involves the ability to compare and 44
contrast, resolve problems, make decisions, analyze and 55
evaluate, and combine and transfer knowledge. These skills 67
benefit the student who eventually becomes a part of the 78
workforce. Whether a person is in a corporate setting, a 89
small business, or self-employed, the business environment 101
of today is highly competitive and skilled employees are in 113
great demand. 116

One factor in achieving success in the workforce is 127
having the ability to deal with the varied demands of the 139
fast-paced business world. Required skills are insightful 150
decision making, creative problem solving, and earnest 162
communication among diverse groups. These groups could be 174
employees, management, employers, investors, customers, 185
or clients. 187

In school, we learn the details of critical thinking. 198
This knowledge extends far beyond the boundaries of the 209
classroom. It lasts a lifetime. We use critical thinking 220
throughout our daily lives. We constantly analyze and 231
evaluate music, movies, conversations, fashion, magazine 242
or newspaper articles, and television programs. We all had 254
experience using critical thinking skills before we even 265
knew what they were. So keep on learning, growing, and 276
experimenting. The classroom is the perfect setting for 287
exploration. Take this opportunity to see how others solve 299
problems, give each other feedback, and try out new ideas 311
in a safe environment. 316

A person who has learned critical thinking skills is 327
equipped with the essential skills for achieving success 338
in today's workforce. There are always new goals to reach. 350

| 1 | 2 | 3 | 4 | 5 | 6 | 7 | 8 | 9 | 10 | 11 | 12

Supplementary Timing 7

Use your unique creativity when applying critical 10
thinking skills. One of the first steps in unlocking your 22
creativity is to realize that you have control over your 33
thinking; it doesn't control you. Creativity is using new 45
or different methods to solve problems. Many inventions 56
involved a breakthrough in traditional thinking, and the 67
result was an amazing experience. For example, Einstein 78
broke with tradition by trying lots of obscure formulas 89
that changed scientific thought. Your attitude can form 100
mental blocks that keep you from being creative. When you 112
free your mind, the rest will follow. 120

Do your best to unleash your mind's innate creativity. 131
Turn problems into puzzles. When you think of a task as a 143
puzzle, a challenge, or a game instead of a difficult 154
problem, you open your mind and encourage your creative 165
side to operate. Creative ideas often come when you are 176
having fun and are involved in an unrelated activity. 187
You will find that when your defenses are down, your brain 199
is relaxed and your subconscious is alive, then creative 210
thoughts can flow. 214

Habit often restricts you from trying new approaches 225
to problem solving. Remember, there is usually more than 237
one solution. Empty your mind of the idea of only one way 249
of looking at a problem and strive to see situations in a 261
fresh, new way. How many times have you told yourself that 273
you must follow the rules and perform tasks in a certain 284
way? If you want to be creative, look at things in a new 295
way, break the pattern, explore new options, and challenge 307
the rules. If you are facing a difficult problem and can't 319
seem to find a solution, take a quick walk or relax for 330
a few minutes; then go back to the problem renewed. When 341
working on homework or taking a test, always work the 352
easiest problems first. Success builds success. 362

A sense of humor is key to being creative. Silly and 373
irrelevant ideas can lead to inventive solutions. Humor 384
generates ideas, puts you in a creative state of mind, 395
and makes work exciting! 400

| 1 | 2 | 3 | 4 | 5 | 6 | 7 | 8 | 9 | 10 | 11 | 12

Supplementary Timing 8

Keyboarding is a popular business course for many 10
students. The major objectives of a keyboarding course are 22
to develop touch control of the keyboard and proper typing 34
techniques, build basic speed and accuracy, and provide 45
practice in applying those basic skills to the formatting 57
of letters, reports, tables, memos, and other kinds of 68
personal and business communications. In the early part of 80
a keyboarding course, students learn to stroke by touch 91
using specific techniques. They learn to hit the keys in a 103
quick and accurate way. After the keys are learned and 114
practiced, students move into producing documents of all 125
sizes and types for personal and vocational use. 135

When first learning keyboarding, there are certain 145
parameters, guidelines, and exercises to follow. There are 157
rules intended to help you learn and eventually master the 169
keyboard. Creating documents requires students to apply 180
critical thinking. What format or layout should be used? 191
What font and font size would be best? Are all the words 202
spelled correctly? Does the document look neat? Are the 213
figures accurate? Are punctuation and grammar correct? 224

There is a lot to learn in the world of keyboarding. 235
Be persistent, patient, and gentle with yourself. Allow 246
failure in class and on the job; that's how we learn. It's 258
okay to admit mistakes. Mistakes are stepping stones for 269
growth and creativity. Being creative has a lot to do with 281
risk-taking and courage. It takes courage to explore new 292
ways of thinking and to risk looking different, being 303
silly and impractical, and even being wrong. Your path to 315
creativity is such a vital component of your critical 326
thinking skills. Allow your creative thoughts to flow 337
freely when producing each of your keyboarding tasks. 348

Keyboarding skill and personal creativity are valuable 359
attributes for life and on the job. The worker who can see 371
situations and problems in a fresh way, reason logically, 383
explore options, and come up with inventive ideas is sure 395
to be a valuable employee. 400

| 1 | 2 | 3 | 4 | 5 | 6 | 7 | 8 | 9 | 10 | 11 | 12

Supplementary Timing 9

One of the most important decisions we all have to 10
face is choosing a career. The possibilities can appear 21
overwhelming. Fear not! Your critical thinking skills will 33
save you! Start your career planning today. Begin with 44
self-assessment. What are your interests? Do you enjoy 55
working indoors or outdoors? Do you prefer working with 66
numbers or with words? Are you the independent type or 77
would you rather work with a group? What are your favorite 89
academic studies? Think about these questions and then 100
create a list of your interests, skills, aptitudes, and 111
values. What you discover about yourself will help you in 123
finding the career that is right for you. 131

After you have explored your personal interests, look 142
at the sixteen career clusters for a wide range of job 153
prospects. Most jobs are included in one of these clusters 165
that have been organized by the government. During your 176
exploration, make a note of the clusters that interest you 188
and investigate these clusters. 194

Gather as much information as possible by using all 205
available resources. Scan the Help Wanted section in the 216
major Sunday newspapers for job descriptions and salaries. 228
Search the Net. The Internet provides electronic access to 240
worldwide job listings. If you want to know more about a 251
specific company, access its home page. Go to your college 263
placement office. Sign up for interviews with companies 274
that visit your campus. Visit your local school or county 286
library and ask the reference librarian for occupational 297
handbooks. Talk with people in your field of interest to 308
ask questions and get advice. Attend chapter meetings of 319
professional organizations to network with people working 331
in your chosen profession. Volunteer, intern, or work a 342
part-time or temporary job within your career choice for 353
valuable, first-hand insight. Taking an initiative in your 365
job search will pay off. 370

A career search requires the use of critical thinking 381
skills. These skills will help you to choose the career 392
that will match your skills and talents. 400

| 1 | 2 | 3 | 4 | 5 | 6 | 7 | 8 | 9 | 10 | 11 | 12

Appendix

Ten-Key Numeric Keypad

GOAL:
- To control the ten-key numeric keypad keys.

Some computer keyboards have a separate ten-key numeric keypad located to the right of the alphanumeric keyboard. The arrangement of the keypad enables you to type numbers more rapidly than using the top row of the alphanumeric keyboard.

To input numbers using the ten-key numeric keypad, you must activate the Num Lock (Numeric Lock) key. Usually, an indicator light signals that the Num Lock is activated.

On the keypad, 4, 5, and 6 are the home keys. Place your fingers on the keypad home row as follows:

- First finger (J finger) on 4
- Second finger (K finger) on 5
- Third finger (L finger) on 6

The keypad keys are controlled as follows:

- First finger controls 1, 4, and 7
- Second finger controls 2, 5, and 8
- Third finger controls 3, 6, 9, and decimal point
- Right thumb controls 0
- Fourth finger controls Enter

Since different computers have different arrangements of ten-key numeric keypads, study the arrangement of your keypad. The illustration shows the most common arrangement. If your keypad is arranged differently from the illustration, check with your instructor for the correct placement of your fingers on the keypad.

NEW KEYS

A. Use the first finger to control the 4 key, the second finger to control the 5 key, and the third finger to control the 6 key.

Keep your eyes on the copy.

Before beginning, check to be sure the Num Lock Key is activated.

Type first column from top to bottom. Next, type the second column; then type the third column. Press Enter after typing the final digit of each number.

A. THE 4, 5, AND 6 KEYS

444	456	454
555	654	464
666	445	546
455	446	564
466	554	654
544	556	645
566	664	666
644	665	555
655	456	444
456	654	456

B. Use the 4 finger to control the 7 key, the 5 finger to control the 8 key, and the 6 finger to control the 9 key.

Keep your eyes on the copy.

Press ENTER after typing the final digit of each number.

B. THE 7, 8, AND 9 KEYS

474	585	696
747	858	969
774	885	996
447	558	669
744	855	966
477	588	699
444	555	666
747	858	969
774	885	996
747	858	969

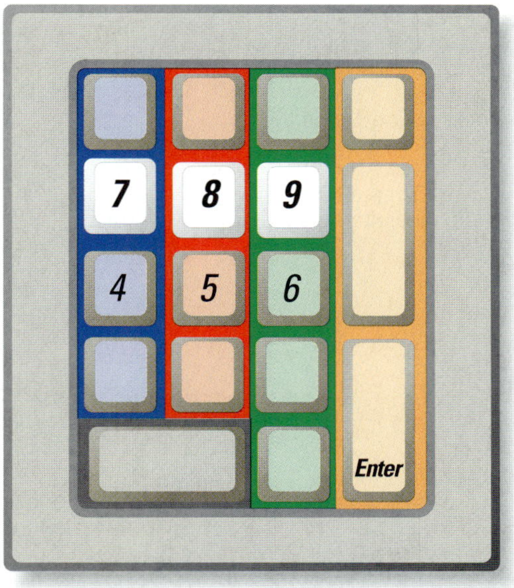

C. Use the 4 finger to control the 1 key, the 5 finger to control the 2 key, and the 6 finger to control the 3 key.

Keep your eyes on the copy.

Press ENTER after typing the final digit of each number.

C. THE 1, 2, AND 3 KEYS

444	555	666
111	222	333
144	225	336
441	552	663
144	255	366
411	522	633
444	555	666
414	525	636
141	252	363
411	525	636

D. Use the right thumb to control the 0 key.

Keep your eyes on the copy.

Press ENTER after typing the final digit of each number.

D. THE 0 KEY

404	470	502
505	580	603
606	690	140
707	410	250
808	520	360
909	630	701
101	407	802
202	508	903
303	609	405
505	401	506

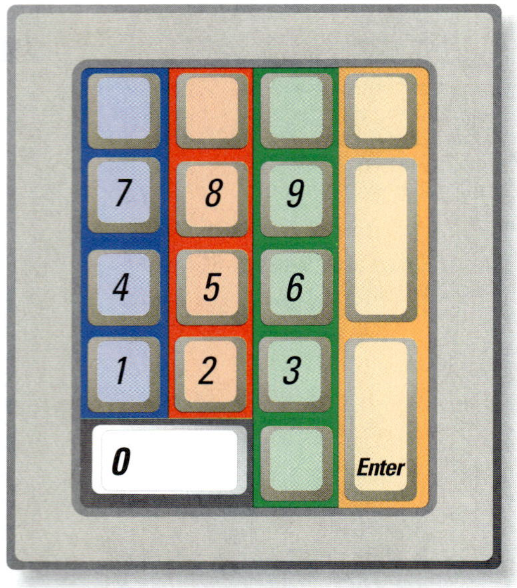

E. Use the 6 finger to control the decimal key.

Keep your eyes on the copy.

Press ENTER after typing the final digit of each number.

E. THE . KEY

4.5	7.8	1.2
6.5	9.8	3.2
4.4	7.7	1.1
4.4	7.7	1.1
5.5	8.8	2.2
5.5	8.8	2.2
6.6	9.9	3.3
6.5	9.9	3.3
4.5	7.8	1.2
6.5	8.9	1.3

Index

Abbreviations,
- rules for, R-22
  - all capitals, 330
  - in business writing, 237
  - in technical writing, 330
- U.S. Postal Service, R-14B

Academic reports, R-8B–R-8C
- in APA style, R-10A
- bibliography in, R-9B
- byline in, R-8C
- date line in, R-8C
- endnotes in, R-8D
- formatting, R-8C
- indention in, R-8D
- long quotation in, R-8D
- in MLA style, R-10C
- paragraph heading in, R-8C
- side heading in, R-8C
- spacing in, R-8C
- subtitle in, R-8C

Addresses, in letters
- inside, R-3
- international, 327

Adjectives and adverbs,
- rules for, R-20
  - comparative, 399
  - superlative, 399

A4 metric paper, 326

Agendas, R-11A, 237

Agreement,
- rules for, R-19
  - with intervening words, 306
  - with nearer noun, 400
  - with pronouns, 306
  - subjects and verbs, 236, 306, 400

Alignment,
- of guide words, R-4D
- on printed lines, R-12C
- of words in table columns, R-13

APA (American Psychological Association) style
- formatting reports in, R-10A
- References in, R-10B

Apostrophe (')
- rules for, R-17

Application letter, R-12B

Attachment
- email, R-5C
- memo, R-4D, R-7C

Author/page citations, R-10C

Author/year citations, R-10A

Bibliography,
- entry formats for,
  - annual report, R-9B
  - books, R-9B
  - email, R-9B
  - government documents, R-9B
  - journals, R-9B
  - newspaper article, R-9B
  - online database, R-9B
  - organization, R-9B
  - WWW page, R-9B
- for reports, R-9

Blind-copy (bc:) notation, R-5B, 269

Block-style letters, R-3A

Braced column headings, R-13A, 285

Business forms, R-14A

Business letters (*see* Correspondence)
- blind-copy notations in, R-5B, 269
- block-style, R-3A
- body of, R-3A
- bulleted list in, R-3C
- company name in closing line, R-5B, 268
- complimentary closing in, R-3A
- copy notations in, R-3C, R-5B
- date line in, R-3A, 336
- delivery notation in, R-4A, R-5B, 269
- enclosure notation in, R-3B, R-3C, R-5B
- envelopes for, R-6A
- folding, R-6B
- inside address in, R-3A
- international address in, R-3D, R-5A, 327, 347
- letterhead for, R-3A
- lists in, R-3B, R-3C, R-5B
- modified-block style, R-3B
- multiline list in, R-3B
- multipage, R-5A–R-5B
- on-arrival notation in, R-5A, 263
- open punctuation in, R-3B
- personal-business, R-3D
- postscript notation in, R-5B, 269
- reference initials in, R-3A, R-5B
- return address in, R-3D
- salutation in, R-3A
- single-line list, R-3C
- standard punctuation in, R-3A, R-3D
- subject line in, R-5A, 264
- table in, R-5A
- writer's identification in, R-3A

Business reports,
- bibliography in, R-9B

Business reports, (*continued*)
- byline in, R-8A
- date line in, R-8A
- footnotes in, R-8A
- left-bound, R-9A
- long quotations in, R-8A
- paragraph headings in, R-8A
- side headings in, R-8A
- single-line list in, R-8A
- table in, R-8B

Capitalization
- rules for, R-21
  - compass points, 284
  - nouns followed by a number, 282
  - organizational terms, 445
  - specific course titles, 446
- in table columns, R-13D

Career clusters
- arts, audio, video technology, and communication services, 213
- public administration/government services, 303
- wholesale/retail sales and services, 397

Citations,
- in APA style, R-10A, R-10B
- in MLA style, R-10C, R-10D
- in reports, R-9D

Clip art, 314, 315, 318, 342

Colon (:), rules for, R-18
- with explanatory material, 350

Column headings
- braced, in tables, 285
- in business forms, R-14A
- capitalization, in tables, R-13D
- in tables, R-13A

Comma (,), rules for, R-15–R-16
- adjacent adjectives, 257
- nonessential expressions, 257
- series, 215
- transitional expressions, 215

Company name, in closing lines, of letters, R-5B, 268

Complimentary closing, in letters, R-3A

Computer system
- keyboard, R-2B
- parts of, R-2A

Computing speed, viii

Continuation pages
- for letters, R-5B, 258
- for reports, R-8B, R-8D

Copy (c:) notations, R-3C, R-5B
- multiple copy notations, R-5B

Correcting errors, ix

Correspondence (*see also* Document Processing)
- business letters,
  - on A4 paper, 326
  - application, R-12A
  - blind-copy notation in, R-5A, 269
  - block-style, R-3
  - company names in closing lines of, R-5B, 268
  - delivery notation in, R-4A, R-5B, 269
  - formatted
    - on executive stationery, R-4A
    - on half-page stationery, R-4B
    - for window envelopes, R-4C
  - modified-block style, R-3B
  - multipage, R-5A–R-5B, 258
  - multiple addresses in, 263
  - on-arrival notation in, R-5A, 263
  - page numbering, 258
  - postscript notation in, R-5B, 269
  - personal-business, R-3D
  - in simplified style, R-3C
  - subject line in, R-5A, 264
- email messages,
  - in Internet Explorer, R-5C
  - in Microsoft Outlook, R-5C
  - in Netscape Navigator, R-5D
- memos, R-4D, R-7C, R-9C

Counting errors, viii

Dates
- in letters, R-3A, 336
- in memos, R-4D

Delivery notation, R-4A, R-5B, 269

Determining speed, viii

Diagnostic practice,
- alphabet, SB-2–SB-6
- numbers, SB-5–SB-6

DL Metric envelope, 326

Document processing
- academic reports,
  - on A4 paper, 342–343
  - footnotes in, 217
  - multipage, 217–218, 342–343
- agendas, 239, 254, 479
- announcement, 427–428, 430
- bibliography, 322
- business letters,
  - on A4 paper, 326, 337, 341, 345–346, 346–347, 347
  - application, 230
  - block-style, 220, 221, 230, 259, 264–265, 266, 270, 337, 341, 345–346, 346–347, 347, 350, 363, 385, 392, 483, 484, 489
  - boxed table in, 270, 489
  - copy notation in, 260, 265, 300, 328, 337, 345–346, 346–347, 372, 385, 392

Document processing, (*continued*)
enclosure notation in, 230, 258, 337, 350, 358, 372, 385
follow-up, 230
international addresses in
Canada, 328
France, 337
Germany, 341
Japan, 345–346
lists in, 385
modified-block, 221, 258-259, 260, 270-271, 300, 328, 358
multipage, 258-259, 260, 270–271, 489
on-arrival notation in, 264
open table in, 270
personal-business, 220, 266
postscript notation in, 328, 358, 483, 484
subject line in, 385
business reports,
affadavit of possession, 371–372, 391
on A4-size paper, 333
clip art in, 314, 315, 318
complaint, 388-389
footnotes in, 218, 310
formal, 306-308, 310–312, 314–315, 319, 321–322
headings in, 217–218, 277–278, 306–308, 310–312, 314–315, 319, 354–355, 359–360
judgment, 390
line numbering in, 371, 379
lists in, 354–356, 366
memo, 277, 278, 279
multipage, 217-218, 306–308, 310–312, 314, 319, 359–360, 486–488
one-page, 216–217
summons, 379, 394
tables in, 312, 333
warranty deed, 374
cover page, 423–424, 424–425, 425, 480
directory form, 418
email messages, 223, 332, 338, 341, 346, 367, 376, 484
flyers, 428–429, 430, 442, 492–493
forms, designing
directory, 418
letterhead, 409–410, 410–411, 412–413
notepad, 414, 415, 416
sign-in, 419
tables in, 351, 356
hyperlinks, 460, 461, 467
international addresses,
Canada, 328
France, 392
Japan, 347
itineraries, 234, 235
legal documents
affadavit of possession, 371–372, 391
complaint, 388–389
judgment, 390
last will and testament, 383–384
summons, 379, 394
warranty deed, 374
letterhead form, 409–410, 410–411, 412–413, 472
letter template, 401–402, 470–471
magazine articles, 248–249, 249–250, 251, 255
memo report, 299–300
boxed table in, 299–300
memos,
attachment notation in, 223, 224, 380
boxed table in, 275
copy notation in, 224, 352, 367, 380
multipage, 273, 274
open table in, 273-274, 274
memo templates, 400–401, 402, 420, 478–479, 490
minutes of meetings, 240–241, 254
newsletter, 433, 436, 440–441
notepad form, 414, 415, 416
procedures manual, 243–244, 244–245, 245
report template, 405–406, 406–407
resumes, 229
sign-in form, 419
table of contents, 321
tables,
on A4 paper, 328, 338
AutoFormat, 297, 298
boxed, 227, 275, 283, 285, 286, 288–289, 289, 290, 293–294, 297, 298, 299, 301, 312, 319, 328, 329, 347, 356, 363, 365, 375, 381, 471
braced column headings in, 285
cell shading in, 338, 351
designing forms using, 351, 356
footnotes in, 294
landscape, 288–289, 289, 290, 294, 328, 329
multipage, 293–294, 294
open, 227, 273, 274, 333, 362, 393
ruled, 227
source notes in, 283
title pages, 321
Web pages, 491–492
frames page, 452
main, 451, 452
(*see* Web site)
Web site, 447, 448, 451, 452, 454, 455, 456, 459, 460, 461, 464, 467, 474-475, 476
Drills (*see* Skillbuilding)

Employment documents
application letter, R-12B
job-application form, R-12D
resume, R-12A
Enclosure notation, R-3B, R-3C, R-5B
Endnotes, R-8D

Enumerations (*see* Lists)
Envelopes,
  folding letters for, R-6B
  formatting, R-6A
Errors,
  correcting, ix
  counting, viii

Folding letters, R-6B
Footnotes, R-8A
Formatting
  academic reports, R-8C, R-8D
  agendas, 237
  application letter, R-12B
  attachment notation, R-4D
  author/page citation, R-10C
  author/year citation, R-10A
  bibliography, R-9B
  business forms, R-13A
    designing, 409
    filling in, 400
  business letters, R-3–R-4
    multipage, R-5A–R-5B, 258
  business reports, R-8A–R-8B
    left-bound, R-9A
    headings in, 277
  day/month/year format, 336
  email messages, R-5C, R-5D
  international
    addresses, 327
    date lines, 336
    telephone access codes, 337
    URLs, 331
  itineraries, R-11C, 233
  left-bound business report, R-9A
  legal documents, R-11D, 370–371
  magazine articles, 247–248
  meeting agenda, R-11A
  memo, R-4D
  memo report, R-9C
    headings in, 277
  metric units of measure, 340
  minutes of meetings, R-11B, 238
  multipage business letters, R-5A–R-5B
  multiple addresses, 263
  newsletter design, 432
  on-arrival notations, 263
  outline, R-7A
  procedures manual, 243
  Reference list (APA), R-10B
  reports
    in APA style, R-10A
    in MLA style, R-10C
  resumes, R-12A
  subject lines, 264
  tables
    boxed, R-13A
    column headings, R-13
      braced, 285
    in documents, 268
    footnotes in, 282
    open, R-13B
    ruled, R-13C
    source notes in, 282
  telephone numbers,
    dot-style, 337
    with hyphens, 337
  title pages, R-7B
  Web pages, 446
  Web site, designing, 447, 463
  Works Cited pages (MLA), R-10D
Frames pages, 446, 451
  browser view, 452
  layout view, 451

Grammar, language arts rules for,
  adjectives and adverbs, R-20, 399
  agreement, R-19, 236, 306, 400
  pronouns, R-20, 426, 427
  word usage, R-20, 474
Guide words, in memos, R-4D

Hanging indent, R-9B, R-10D
Header frame, 446, 450
Headings
  in memos, R-4D
  in reports, R-9D, R-10, 277
  in table columns, R-13D
    braced, 285
Home page, 450
Home row, on keypad, A-1
Hyperlinks, 446, 450, 458
Hyphen (-),
  rules for, R-17
    compound adjectives, 236
  (*see also* Skillbuilding, Technique practice)

Initials (*see* Reference initials)
Inside address
  in letters, R-3A
International
  addresses,
    Canada, 327
    France, 327, 337
    Germany, 327

International, addresses, (*continued*)
- Japan, 327, 347
- Mexico, 327,
- date lines, 336
- telephone access codes, 337
- URLs, 331

Italic (or underline)
- rules for, R-18

Itineraries, R-11C, 233

Keyboard, computer, parts of
- ALTERNATE keys, R-2B
- arrow keys, R-2B
- BACKSPACE key, R-2B
- CAPS LOCK key, R-2B
- CONTROL keys, R-2B
- ENTER key, R-2B
- ESCAPE key, R-2B
- function keys, R-2B
- numeric keypad, R-2B
- SHIFT keys, R-2B
- TAB key, R-2B
- Windows keys, R-2B

Keyboarding Connections (features)
- Capturing an Image From the Internet, 369
- Choosing a Different Home Page, 464
- Coping With Spam, 381
- Effective Email Management, 439
- Email Privacy, 484
- Finding People on the Internet, 287
- Protecting Your Files With Anti-Virus Programs, 335
- Searching the Yellow Pages, 422
- Sending Email Attachments, 317
- Transferring Text From Web Pages, 402
- Using Hypertext, 457
- Virus and Spam Protection, 272

Keypad,
- ten-key numeric, A-1

Language arts activities,
- abbreviations, 237, 330
- agreement, 237, 400
- capitalization, 284, 446
- commas, 216, 258
- composing documents, 314
- composing email messages, 358
- composing memos, 408
- composing paragraphs, 223, 268
- composing personal-business letters, 453
- editing, 277
- grammar, 237, 306
- hyphens, 237
- pronouns, 427
- proofreading, 228, 277, 320, 364, 418, 463
- punctuation, 216, 237, 258, 350, 373
- semicolons, 373
- spelling, 247, 292, 340, 383, 435, 482
- word usage, 474

Language arts for business rules
- grammar,
  - adjectives and adverbs, R-20
    - comparative, 399
    - superlative, 399
  - agreement, R-19
    - with intervening words, 306
    - with nearer noun, 400
    - with pronouns, 306
    - subjects and verbs, 236, 306, 400
  - pronouns, R-20
    - nominative, 426
    - objective, 427
  - sentences, R-19
  - word usage, R-20
    - accept/except, 474
    - affect/effect, 474
    - farther/further, 474
    - personal/personnel, 474
    - principal/principle, 474
- mechanics,
  - abbreviations, R-22
    - all capitals, 330
    - in business writing, 237
    - in technical writing, 330
  - capitalization, R-21
    - compass points, 284
    - nouns followed by a number, 282
    - organizational terms, 445
    - specific course titles, 446
  - number expression, R-21–R-22
- punctuation,
  - apostrophes, R-17
  - colons, R-18
    - with explanatory material, 350
  - commas, R-15–R-16
    - adjacent adjectives, 257
    - nonessential expressions, 257
    - series, 215
    - transitional expressions, 215
  - hyphens, R-17
    - with compound adjectives, 236
  - italic (or underline), R-18
  - periods, R-18
    - with polite request, 350
  - quotation marks, R-18
- semicolons, R-16
  - with independent clauses, 373
  - series, 373

Legal cap, 370
Legal documents, R-11D
  formatting, 370–371
Letters (*see also* Correspondence, business letters)
  block-style, R-3A
  modified-block, R-3B
  personal-business, R-3D
Lists
  bulleted, R-3C
  multiline, R-3B, R-5B, R-8C
  numbered, R-3B
  single-line, R-3C, R-8A, R-9A, R-9C

Magazine articles, 247–248
Main frame, 446, 450
Margins,
  academic reports, R-10
  agendas, 237
  business reports, R-9D
  itineraries, 233
  legal documents, 370
  letters, R-3A, R-4A, R-4B
  magazine articles, 247–248
  minutes of meetings, 238
Measuring straight-copy skill, viii
  counting errors, viii
  determining speed, viii
Mechanics,
  language arts rules for,
    abbreviations, R-22, 237, 330
    capitalization, R-21, 282, 284, 445, 446
  number expression, R-21–R-22
Memos,
  attachment notation in, R-4D, R-7C
  guide words in, R-4D
  table in, R-4D, R-7C
  transmittal, R-7C
Metric-size envelope, 326
Metric-size paper, 326
Microcomputer system, parts of,
  CD/DVD drive, R-2A
  disk drive, R-2A
  display screen, R-2A
  keyboard, R-2A
  mouse, R-2A
  printer, R-2A
Minutes of a meeting, R-11B, 238
MLA (Modern Language Association) style,
  formatting reports in, R-10C
  Works Cited pages, R-10D
Modified-block letters, R-3B, R-3D
Multipage letters, R-5A–R-5B, 258
Multiple addresses, in letters, 263

Navigational tools (*see* Hyperlinks)
Newsletter
  footer, 432, 433
  masthead, 432, 433
  parts of, 432, 433
Number expression,
  rules for, R-21–R-22
Num Lock, key, A-1

On-arrival notations, in letters, R-5, 263
Open punctuation,
  in business letters, R-3B

Paced Practice, SB-14–SB-27
Page numbering, for letters, 258
Percentages in tables, R-13D
Period (.),
  rule for, R-18
    polite request, 350
Personal-business letters, R-3D
Personal data sheets (*see* Resumes)
Phrases, (*see* Skillbuilding)
Postal code regulations,
  in Japan, 347
Postscript notation, R-5B, 269
Pretest/Practice/Posttest
  (*see* Skillbuilding)
Procedures manual, 243
Progressive practice
  alphabet, SB-7–SB-10
  numbers, SB-11–SB-13
Progress/Proofreading Checks, 230, 255, 279, 298, 322, 347, 367, 391, 420, 442-443, 467, 488–489
Pronouns,
  rules for, R-20
    nominative, 426
    objective, 427
Proofreaders' marks, R-14C
Punctuation, (*see also specific mark of punctuation; for example,* comma)
  open, in letters, R-3B
  rules for, R-15–R-18, 215, 257, 350, 373
  standard, in letters, R-3A

Quotation mark ("), rules for, R-18

Reference initials, in letters, R-3A
Reference list (APA), R-10B
Reports
  academic, R-8C, R-8D
    headings in, R-8C, R-10A
    list in, R-8C

Reports, *(continued)*
- agendas, R-11A, 237
- in APA style, R-10A
- author/page citations in, R-10B
- author/year citations in, R-10A
- bibliography for, R-9B
- business, R-8A–R-8B
  - headings in, R-8A, R-9A
  - list in, R-8A
- continuation pages in, R-8B, R-8D
- endnotes in, R-8D
- footnotes references in, R-8A
- headings in, R-10A
- itineraries, R-11C, 233
- left-bound, R-9A
- long quotations in, R-8B
- magazine articles, 247–248
- memo, R-9C
- minutes of meetings, R-11B, 238
- in MLA style, R-10C
- multipage, R-8
- outlines, R-7A
- paragraph headings in, R-8A
- procedures manual, 243
- side headings in, R-8A

Resumes, R-12A

Return address
- on envelopes, R-6A
- in personal-business letters, R-3D

Reviews, In-Basket
- Government, 481–484
- Hospitality, 473–476
- Insurance, 469–472
- Manufacturing, 485–489
- Retail, 477–480

Revision marks (*see* Proofreaders' marks)

Semicolon,
- rules for, R-16
  - clauses, 373
  - series, 373

Sentences, rules for, R-19

Skill, measuring, viii

Skillbuilding (*see also* Skillbuilding, back-of-book exercises)
- Pretest/Practice/Posttest, 222, 246, 267, 291, 313, 344, 357, 386, 417, 434, 462, 481
  - adjacent keys, 344, 481
  - alternate-hand words, 291, 434
  - close reaches, 344, 481
  - common letter combinations, 313, 462
  - consecutive fingers, 344, 481
  - discrimination practice, 222, 357
  - down reaches, 267, 417
  - horizontal reaches, 246, 386
  - in reaches, 246, 386
  - left hand, 222, 357
  - one-hand words, 291, 434
  - out reaches, 246, 386
  - right hand, 222, 357
  - up reaches, 267, 417
  - vertical reaches, 267, 417
  - word beginnings, 313, 462
  - word endings, 313, 462
- sustained practice
  - alternate-hand words, 225, 349
  - capitalization, 305, 463
  - numbers and symbols, 295, 435
  - punctuation, 339, 482
  - rough draft, 252, 382
  - syllabic intensity, 276, 418
- technique practice
  - BACKSPACE key, 228, 364
  - concentration, 473
  - ENTER key, 285, 426
  - SHIFT/CAPS LOCK, 253, 377
  - SPACE BAR, 276, 408
  - TAB, 320
- timings
  - 5-minute,
    - 40wpm, 220, 226
    - 41wpm, 233, 242, 253
    - 42wpm, 262, 273
    - 43wpm, 282, 287, 296, 299
    - 44wpm, 310, 317
    - 45wpm, 325, 336, 345
    - 46wpm, 354, 362
    - 47wpm, 370, 378, 387
    - 48wpm, 404, 413
    - 49wpm, 423, 432, 440
    - 50wpm, 450, 458, 470, 478, 486
  - 12-second speed sprints, 215, 232, 257, 281, 309, 324, 353, 369, 399, 426, 445, 473

Skillbuilding (back-of-book exercises)
- Diagnostic Practice: Alphabet, SB-2–SB-4
- Diagnostic Practice: Numbers, SB-5–SB-6
- Paced Practice, SB-14–SB-27
- Progressive Practice: Alphabet, SB-7–SB-10
- Progressive Practice: Numbers, SB-11–SB-13
- Supplementary Timings: SB-28–SB-36

Spacing,
- in agendas, R-11A
- in itineraries, R-11C
- in legal documents, R-11D
- in letters, R-3–R-5
- in memos, R-4D, R-7C
- in minutes of meetings, R-11B
- in outlines, R-7A
- in reports, R-8, R-9

Spacing, *(continued)*
  in resumes, R-12A
  in table of contents, R-7D
  in tables, R-13
  in title page, R-7B
  with ZIP Code, R-15
Speed, measuring, viii
Standard punctuation,
  in business letters, R-3A, 153
Straight-copy skill, viii
  building, viii
  measuring, viii
Strategies for Career Success (features)
  Audience Analysis, 261
  Business Communication, 353
  Cellular Phone Manners Matter, 281
  Corrective Feedback, 219
  Designing the Page for Readability, 411
  Developing Confidence as a Presenter, 275
  Effective Teleconferencing for Meetings, 325
  Enhance Your Presentation With Visual Arts, 377
  Letter of Complaint, 309
  Letter of Resignation, 387
  Managing Business Phone Time, 431
  Observing Netiquette, 232
  Types of Interviews, 448
  What to Exclude From Your Resume, 475
Subject lines,
  in letters, R-5A, 264
  in memos, R-4D
  two-line, R-7C
Subtitles
  in reports, R-8A, R-9D
  in tables, R-3A, R-13B, R-13D
Supplementary timings, SB-28–SB-36
Sustained practice (*see* Skillbuilding)
Symbols, 331

Table of contents, R-7D
Tables
  boxed, R-13A
  in documents, 268
  features in, R-13D
    column capitalization, R-13D
    column headings, R-13D
      braced, 285
    dollar signs, R-13D
    footnotes in, 282
    percentages, R-13D
    title block, R-13D
    total line, R-13D
    vertical placement, R-13D
  multipage, 292
  open, R-13B
  ruled, R-13C
  source notes in, 282
Tab stops, setting, R-7A, R-7D
Technique practice (*see* Skillbuilding)
Telephone access codes, 337
Ten-key numeric keypad, A-1–A-3
  home row, A-1
  Num Lock key, A-1
Title block, in tables, R-13D
Title page, R-7B
Transmittal memo, R-7D
Typing technique, ix

Underlining, (*see* Italic)
  book and magazine titles, R-18
Uniform Resource Locators (URLs), 331
  Canada, 331
  France, 331
  Germany, 331
  Japan, 331
  Mexico, 331
U.S. Postal Service abbreviations, R-14B

Web page
  basic parts of, 446
  browser view, 452
  design guidelines, 447
  frames, 450
  layout view, 451, 454, 456
Web site
  designing, 447, 463
Window envelopes,
  folding, R-6B
  formatting, R-6A
Word usage,
  rules for, R-20
    accept/except, 474
    affect/effect, 474
    farther/further, 474
    personal/personnel, 474
    principal/principle, 474
WPM (words per minute), viii
Writer's address (*see* Return address)
Writer's name in letters, R-3A

Your Turn, 219, 232, 261, 272, 281, 287, 309, 317, 325, 335, 353, 369, 377, 381, 387, 402, 411, 422, 431, 439, 448, 457, 475, 484

ZIP Code, spacing with, R-15

Photo credits

Michael Agliolo/International Stock 334, 493; Adrian Arbib/Corbis 251; Peter Beck/Corbis Stock Market 302; Jim Cummins/FPG International LLC 252; Robert E Daemmrich/Stone 316; Davis Factor/Corbis 485; Kevin Fleming/ Corbis 212, 271; Franz-Marc Frei/Corbis 286; Walter Hodges/Stone 361, 396; Kevin Horan/Stone 262; David De Lossy/Image Bank 416; Michael Malyszko/FPG International LLC 378; Don Mason/Corbis Stock Market 449; C. Moore/Corbis 394; Michael Newman/Photo Edit 376; Charles Orrico/ SuperStock 403; Stan Pak/International Stock 380; Donata Pizzi/Image Bank 438; Andreas Pollock/Stone 352; Premium Stock/Corbis 391; Jon Riley/Stone 329; Mark Romin/Superstock v; Chuck Savage/Corbis Stock Market 412, 430; SuperStock 173, 324, 343; Telegraph Colour Graphics/FPG International LLC 298; Bill Varie/Corbis 477; Stephen Welstead/Corbis Stock Market 407